Learning and Instruction

Learning and Instruction

Theory into Practice

Margaret E. Bell-Gredler
University of South Carolina

Macmillan Publishing Company
New York

Collier Macmillan Publishers
London

Macmillan Publishing Company
866 Third Avenue, New York, New York 10022

Collier Macmillan Canada, Inc.

Library of Congress Cataloging-in-Publication Data

Bell-Gredler, Margaret E.
    Learning and instruction.

    Includes index.
    1. Learning. 2. Cognition in children. 3. Teaching.
I. Title.
LB1060.B45   1986   370.15′23   85–24137
ISBN   0–02–307930–4

Printing: 1 2 3 4 5 6 7 8   Year: 6 7 8 9 0 1 2 3 4 5

Figure 7-2 on p. 130 from PRINCIPLES OF INSTRUCTIONAL DESIGN by
Robert M. Gagné and Leslie J. Briggs. Copyright © 1974 by Holt, Rinehart and
Winston, Inc. Reprinted by permission of Holt, Rinehart and Winston, CBS Col-
lege Publishing.

ISBN   0-02-307930-4

In memory of my beloved daughter,
Margaret Lynn,
and for her sister,
Elizabeth Lee

Preface

Early in the twentieth century, Edward Thorndike chided his fellow psychologists for not becoming involved in the problems of school learning. Maintaining that the appropriate psychological laboratory is the classroom and the proper subject of study is the student, Thorndike applied his theory, connectionism, to the analysis of several school subjects.

Today, partly as a result of the curriculum reforms of the 1960s, the problems of school learning are addressed in more depth by current theories. Each contemporary theory of learning provides important information about some facet of the learning process that may be implemented in the classroom. Therefore, the primary goal of this text is to present each theory's contribution to our understanding of human learning and the implications for the practitioner.

I am deeply indebted in the preparation of this manuscript to Albert Bandura, Robert Gagné, Bernard Weiner, and particularly B. F. Skinner. Each of these theorists took the time to personally review my interpretation of his work. Their comments and suggestions enhanced the discussions of their theories. I would also like to thank Frances O'Tuel, for her review of Jean Piaget's theory, and Joan Gallini, Ellen Potter, Donald Felker, and R. Stewart Jones, for their helpful suggestions in the later stages of manuscript preparation.

The search for a complete understanding of human learning has occupied philosophers, psychologists, and educators for centuries. The search itself is a rich and compelling enterprise that has yet to discover the ultimate capacity for human accomplishment.

Margaret E. Bell-Gredler

Contents

Chapter 6.   B. F. Skinner's Operant Conditioning   76

Chapter 7.   Robert Gagné's Conditions of Learning   116

Chapter 8.   Information-Processing Theories   151

Chapter 11. Bernard Weiner's Attribution Theory 274

Chapter 12. Summary 314

Index 325

Learning
and
Instruction

CHAPTER 1 _____

The Role of Theory
in Learning and Instruction

Man's power to change himself, that is, to
learn, is perhaps the most impressive thing
about him.
Thorndike, 1931, p. 3

WHY IS THE STUDY OF LEARNING IMPORTANT?

Learning is the process by which human beings acquire a vast variety
of competencies, skills, and attitudes. Learning begins in infancy with
the baby's acquisition of a few simple skills, such as holding its own bottle
and recognizing its mother. During childhood and adolescence, a number
of attitudes, values, and social interaction skills are acquired as well as
competencies in various subject areas. In adulthood, the individual is
expected to have mastered specific job tasks and other functional skills.
Included are driving a car, balancing a checkbook, and getting along with
others.

The human capacity for learning is an important characteristic that sets
the species apart from all others. It provides benefits for both the individual and society. For the individual in our culture, the capacity for
continued learning contributes to the development of highly diverse life-
styles. Sewing, basic home repair, water skiing, playing Scrabble, and
mountain climbing are only a few of the leisure-time activities acquired
through learning. In our society, we are not surprised to find engineers
who are gourmet cooks and college professors who grow prize-winning
roses.

For society, learning plays a key role in transmitting the culture's

1

accumulated knowledge to new generations. It makes possible new discoveries and inventions that build on past developments. Our grandparents, for example, marveled at the changes in daily life brought by electricity. They were also intrigued with the new invention of the day, the telephone. Our children, in contrast, are growing up with electricity, the telephone, and television transmitted by satellite. They, in turn, are intrigued with that new invention, the microcomputer.

Both the individual and society have a vested interest in the successful management of learning. Individuals who have become skilled at self-directed learning are able to acquire a variety of new leisure-time and job skills. They also have developed the capacity to endow their lives with life-long creativity.

Society, on the other hand, cannot risk leaving the acquisition of learning to chance. Some system is needed for transmitting the cultural heritage and for training the young to take on productive adult roles in the society. In primitive societies, the collective wisdom and folklore often are acquired by each member, usually by word of mouth. In technological societies, the available knowledge and information is so vast that no one can begin to learn all of it. Instead, the members acquire some common knowledge and skills and then acquire expertise within a particular area. This process requires several years and often includes the learning of particular prerequisite knowledge, such as chemistry for pharmacists and music theory for symphony conductors.

The importance of learning to society is illustrated in an example by Edward Thorndike (1931). He hypothesized the outcome of the situation in which each new generation would only be able to learn those things that are half as difficult as the things currently learned. Thorndike noted that in such an event, most of the accomplishments of human civilization would be unusable in one generation and civilization itself would soon disappear from the face of the earth.

WHAT ARE THE SOURCES OF KNOWLEDGE ABOUT LEARNING?

Several sources of information about learning may be identified. Included are folklore or traditional wisdom, philosophy, empirical research, and learning theory.

Traditional Wisdom

Included in traditional wisdom are proverbs or maxims that often are derived from extensive experience. An example of a maxim is "Spare the rod and spoil the child." One problem with maxims, however, is that the conditions of effective implementation are unclear. The example above implies that discipline is essential for child rearing; however, the extent, degree, and exact nature of the discipline are not identified.

Hilgard (1964, p. 404) notes that some individuals argue that teaching is an art. Therefore, more can be learned from good teachers than from either research or psychology. In other words, good teaching practice constitutes a "traditional wisdom" that can serve to teach others. Of course, much can be learned from skilled teachers. However, ignoring the possibility of improving instruction through well-designed research is like "returning medical practice to the prescientific physician because we still value the bedside manner" (Hilgard, 1964, p. 404).

Philosophy

Unlike folklore or traditional wisdom, which tend to be loosely organized, philosophers have developed systematic conceptions of learning. Some early examples and their particular limitations are discussed in Chapter 2.

Empirical Research

A quite different source of information about learning is that of empirical research. It includes experiments on objects and events in the physical world. Galileo, often referred to as the father of the scientific method, initiated experimentation with real objects. In one experiment, he timed the descent of falling objects from the top of a tower and found that a pound of feathers falls to earth at the same speed as a pound of lead. His experiments disproved the intuitive belief that a pound of lead will fall faster than a bag of feathers of the same weight.

The difficulty with the use of empirical research as the sole source of knowledge is that the studies conducted do not automatically advance our knowledge about important phenomena. For example, Suppes (1974) describes the period in educational research referred to as "the golden age of empiricism." This period, the decade of the 1920s, was characterized by questionnaires, surveys, and studies on almost every aspect of school life. The extensive data collection, however, did not contribute to an understanding of the basic processes of learning and instruction.

Theory

A fourth source of knowledge is theory. Briefly defined, a theory is a set of organized principles about particular events in the real world. One important characteristic of theory is that it "rescues the individual research finding from the momentary circumstance of time and place to give it a place in a broader world" (McKeachie, 1976, p. 829).

Specifically, theories provide two advantages over the other knowledge sources. One is that principles, unlike maxims, are testable. Experiments may be conducted to determine whether the principle is verified by actual events. An example is the statement "Practice with corrective feedback on performance facilitates the learning of motor skills." One way of testing this principle is to compare the performance of learners that have been given practice and feedback with the performance of learners taught other ways.

The second advantage of theories is that unlike isolated observations, they include generalizations about events and thus are applicable to several situations. The statement above about the relationship between the learning of motor skills and practice with feedback is a generalization that applies to simple skills, such as balancing on a beam, and to complex skills, such as playing tennis or fencing.

WHAT ARE THE FUNCTIONS OF LEARNING THEORY?

Four general functions of theory have been identified by Patrick Suppes (1974). These functions also apply to learning theory. Two functions, already mentioned, are that theories (1) serve as a framework for conducting research, and (2) provide an organizing framework for specific items of information. Also, they often (3) reveal the complexity of apparently simple events, and (4) reorganize prior experience (Suppes, 1974).

A Framework for Research

The importance of serving as a framework for research is to prevent the practice of data collection that does not contribute to an understanding of events. Bare empiricism, Suppes (1974, p. 6) notes, is a mental form of streaking, and nudity of body is much more appealing than nudity of thought.

Organization of Knowledge

The second function of theory is that it provides an organizing framework for specific items of information. All the contemporary learning theories, of course, fulfill this function. One example, however, is the set of learning conditions developed by Robert Gagné (1970). Prior research into the elements of learning had indicated that some tasks are learned when the individual has established an association between a presented stimulus and a particular response. Other studies, however, indicated that learning occurs when the learner first reorganizes the stimulus situation and then applies a particular strategy appropriate for the situation. The theoretical position formulated by Gagné provides a synthesis of these discrepant findings. He proposes that more than one type of learning exists. That is, learning the letters of the alphabet is one type that requires the establishment of an association between each of the letters and the learner's mental or verbal response. In contrast, learning to solve algebraic equations is another type. Learning to solve problems requires that the learner reorganize the situation presented and apply several operations correctly and in the right sequence. The former type of learning is referred to as verbal information, whereas the latter is an intellectual skill (Gagné, 1970).

Identification of Complex Events

The third general function is that theory often reveals the complexity and subtlety of apparently simple events. A specific example is the nature and variety of factors that influence learning from models (Bandura, 1971). For the most part, early explanations were confined to the mimicry aspects of modeling. That is, the learner imitates the model and is rewarded for the behavior. However, Bandura's social learning theory (1) identifies the situation in which the observer performs the modeled behavior days or weeks later, and (2) identifies the learning conditions for this phenomenon. A relatively simple event, imitation, was found to be complex and to have important implications for learning and instruction.

More generally, an examination of contemporary theories indicates the variety of factors that influences what was once thought to be a relatively simple process (i.e., learning). In the classroom, the developmental level of the learner; the nature of the task; the models observed by the learner; the learner's capacity to receive, encode, and store the learning in memory; and the learner's perceptions of his or her work in terms of success or failure are all important influences.

Reorganization of Prior Experience

A fourth and related function of theory is that it reorganizes prior experience (Suppes, 1974). An example in physics that reorganized intuitive beliefs is the law of inertia: a body continues in its direction of motion until some external force acts on it. The commonly accepted belief that had originated with Aristotle, however, was the opposite. His analysis described a body as being in motion only if it is acted on by force. Thus the discovery of the law of inertia required a reorganization of the commonsense belief (Suppes, 1974, p. 5).

The function of reorganizing prior beliefs is particularly important with regard to classroom learning. Such learning occurs in a social context. Sometimes variables that were of little consequence a few decades ago may become important factors in the management of learning. In the early twentieth century, for example, many students did not continue their education beyond the elementary grades. The effects of students' perceptions of their academic successes and failures were not of vital concern to the educational system. At that time a large segment of the potential student population self-selected out of the system for the world of work. Today, however, students are expected to pursue the study of academic subjects in a formal structured setting for 10 to 12 of their formative years. The effects of the students' beliefs about their successes and failures influence their learning. This issue is addressed by Bernard Weiner's theory of motivation, referred to as attribution theory.

Theories as Working Models

An unrealistic expectation for a theory is that it should explain events for all time. During the 1930s and 1940s, psychologists had hoped to develop the one "grand theory" that would explain all learning. The model was classical physics (also known as Newtonian mechanics). This theory explained the actions of physical forces in the universe.

Psychologists, however, were not successful in developing eternal principles of learning. The training problems posed by the country's involvement in World War II and the development of high-speed computers raised new questions about human learning and thinking (see Chapter 5).

A reasonable expectation for theories, however, is that they serve as working models for particular phenomena until new theories are needed. As new information is discovered and new questions are raised, early theories give way to redefined relationships and new generalizations. Therefore, at one point in time, a generalization may adequately describe a particular system, but at a later point in time, it may be valid only as history (Cronbach, 1975).

The redirection or replacement of theories is not unique to psychology. The example mentioned above, classical physics, was insufficient to describe *precisely* the actions of physical forces in the entire universe. In classical physics, time is treated as a constant. With Einstein's discovery of the theory of relativity in which time is a relative variable, classical physics became a special case of that theory. Classical physics is sufficiently accurate for activities on our planet and it was sufficient for a civilization undertaking the industrial revolution. Interplanetary travel, however, requires a more precise theory of time and motion.

Similarly, Edward Thorndike's learning theory was sufficient to explain school learning when memorization and recitation occupied a major portion of the school day. In today's society, however, much learning occurs outside the school setting through the media of television and film. Albert Bandura's social learning theory addresses the psychological mechanisms underlying this particular learning phenomenon.

WHY A TEXT ON LEARNING THEORY?

Since theories cannot be expected to stand for all time, what is the purpose of a text on learning theory? Why not, instead, simply develop a few classroom prescriptions from each theory and learn the prescriptions? Isolated prescriptions out of context, however, like the maxims of traditional wisdom, are of limited use. Further, many of the failures of experiments to improve educational practice have been the result of the application of distorted prescriptions derived from theory. Some of the token economy programs developed in the 1960s, for example, failed to demonstrate success for the use of tokens in altering classroom behaviors. Among other problems, program developers ignored B. F. Skinner's statements that (1) the teacher cannot possibly provide all the needed reinforcements for a classroom of students, and (2) in the classroom, reinforcement is a two-way street between students and teacher.

An understanding of the principles of learning theory can serve as a knowledge base in two ways. They are (1) the analysis of the mechanisms operating in the classroom, and (2) the critique of research conducted on classroom processes.

Analysis of Psychological Mechanisms

The classroom is a complex, interactive, and dynamic setting. Learning theory can contribute to an understanding of that setting. An example is the situation in which young children are busily engaged in trying to topple a plastic dummy using a ball on a string suspended from the ceiling. A few of the children will be able to observe the arc that is made by the ball, modify their pitches, and successfully strike the dummy. Others, however, will tend to verbalize contradictory and often illogical explanations for the ball's actions. Examples include: "The string is too short," "The string is too long," "The ball isn't heavy enough," and so on.

The tendency of the typical adult is to attempt to correct the child's illogical statements. Jean Piaget's (1963) extensive analyses of children's thinking, however, have revealed that these "illogical" statements are a natural and essential stage of a child's development. Repeated interaction and experimentation with concrete objects by the child will contribute to the subsequent development of more logical modes of thinking.

Another classroom example is that of reprimanding a disruptive student in front of the entire class. On the surface, the reprimand appears to be punishment. However, getting the teacher's attention and bringing the class to a standstill are events that can provide students with increased status in the eyes of some of their peers. In such a situation, the disruptive behavior is likely to occur more often. B. F. Skinner's analysis (1969) of reinforcement in the classroom setting refers to this situation. The attention-getter and the show-off are receiving reinforcement for inappropriate behavior and the behavior is likely to be repeated.

Analysis of Research on Classroom Processes

A vast number of research studies are reported monthly in the educational and psychological journals. Aside from weaknesses in experimental design or statistical analyses, how are we to determine if a particular study "disproves" a theory? For example, one study implemented models for children's prosocial behavior and posttested the children at the end of the experimental sessions. The children's lack of model imitation was taken as evidence by the researcher that Bandura's social learning theory does not always apply to social situations. However, according to the theory, observers do not enact everything they learn. An accurate assessment of learning from models must include incentives for performance of the observed behaviors, a factor omitted in the particular study. Understanding the principles of learning theory can provide a framework for differentiating inappropriate research from the studies of substance.

HOW DOES THIS TEXT PRESENT KNOWLEDGE ABOUT LEARNING?

The primary purpose of this text is to reflect the current state of the art in theory development related to classroom learning. Toward this end, six contemporary theories have been selected for presentation. They are

B. F. Skinner's operant conditioning, Robert Gagné's conditions of learning, information-processing theories, Jean Piaget's cognitive-development theory, Albert Bandura's social learning theory, and Bernard Weiner's theory of motivation (known as attribution theory).

These theories were selected because they each describe particular psychological mechanisms of importance to classroom learning. B. F. Skinner details the role of reinforcement in behavioral change, Robert Gagné describes the internal processes and environmental conditions essential for different kinds of learning outcomes, and Albert Bandura describes the ways in which human beings learn from observing the behaviors of others.

The other three theories in the text technically are not categorized as learning theories. Nevertheless, they have important implications for classroom practice. Information-processing theories focus primarily on the ways that individuals perceive, organize, and then store information in long-term memory. Jean Piaget, in contrast, describes the development of logical thinking processes from infancy to adulthood. Bernard Weiner, on the other hand, presents the ways in which individuals identify the causes of success and failure outcomes. Each of these theories has been applied to particular issues in the design and implementation of instruction.

A second purpose of this text is to set the stage for understanding contemporary developments. For example, psychological advances are sometimes compared with those in the natural sciences and found wanting. However, research in the physical sciences has a 300 year lead on psychological research. Why did this happen, and what were some of the early problems in conducting psychological research? These questions are answered in Chapters 2 and 3.

Organization of the Text

Chapters 2 through 5 trace the major events and trends in the development of knowledge about learning. The information is organized in each of these short chapters in a particular way. First, each chapter discusses a particular period, for example, 1900–1930 (see Table 1-1).

Second, each chapter is divided into two sections. The first section of each chapter describes the major events of the particullar period and the second section discusses the developments produced during the period. For example, the first section of Chapter 3 describes the rise of behaviorism and the beginnings of Gestalt psychology in the years from 1900 to 1930. The second section describes the three learning theories developed during these years. In addition, each section of each chapter concludes with a summary chart.

Table 1-1. Developments in Learning and Organization of Chapters 2–5

Sequence of Events and Developments	Textbook Chapter	Chapter Organization
400 B.C.–A.D. 1874 Dominance of philosophy	Chapter 2	The Beginning of Psychology
1874 Birth of psychological research		
1890–1900 A functional psychology and new research directions		The Intellectual Foundations of American Psychology
1900–1930 Rise of behaviorism and Gestalt psychology	Chapter 3	Two Competitors: Behaviorism and Gestalt Psychology
Developments: connectionism, classical conditioning, Gestalt theory		Three Learning Theories
1930–1950 The era of comprehensive theory construction	Chapter 4	The Retreat to the Laboratory
Developments: theories developed by Hull, Guthrie, Tolman, and Lewin		Two Perspectives Refined
1950–present Dominance of Skinner's theory, return to instructionally relevant research, the rise of the "new cognition"	Chapter 5	The Classroom and the "New Cognition"
Developments—six selected theories: Skinner, Gagné, information processing, Piaget, Bandura, and Weiner		Introduction to Selected Contemporary Theories

This organization permits the information to be used in a variety of ways. Both the events (the first section) and the developments (the second section) in each chapter may be read in detail or simply to provide an overview. However, either the events or developments in a particular period or an entire chapter that is not of particular interest may be omitted.

Chapters 6 through 11 present the six selected contemporary theories. A common framework is used for this discussion to facilitate comparisons across the theories (see Table 1-2). The framework is also designed so that discussion proceeds from the theoretical to the practical. The basic principles of each theory are presented in the first section of each chapter, entitled "Principles of Learning." Then the instructional principles for classroom implementation (implied or explicit) are discussed in the section section, "Principles of Instruction." Finally, application of the theory to major educational issues and a classroom example are presented and discussed in the third section, "Educational Applications."

The text concludes with a discussion of the ways in which the theories may be selected for use in the psychological reality of the classroom (Chapter 12). Six major instructional needs present in the classroom are described, and the applicability of each of the theories to these needs is reviewed briefly.

Table 1-2. Framework for Chapters 6–12

Chapter 6	B. F. Skinner's operant conditioning	
Chapter 7	Robert Gagné's conditions of learning	Principles of Learning Principles of Instruction Educational Applications
Chapter 8	Information-processing theories	
Chapter 9	Jean Piaget's cognitive-development theory	Principles of Cognitive Development Principles of Instruction Educational Applications
Chapter 10	Albert Bandura's social learning theory	Principles of Learning Principles of Instruction Educational Applications
Chapter 11	Bernard Weiner's attribution theory	Principles of Motivation Principles of Instruction Educational Applications
Chapter 12	Brief discussion of the theories in the broad classroom context	

REFERENCES

Bandura, A. (1971). *Social learning theory*. Englewood Cliffs, NJ: Prentice-Hall.

Cronbach, L. J. (1975). Beyond the two disciplines of scientific psychology. *American Psychologist, 30,* 116–127.

Gagné, R. M. (1970). *The conditions of learning*. New York: Holt, Rinehart and Winston.

Hilgard, E. R. (1964). A perspective on the relationship between learning theory and educational practices. In E. R. Hilgard (Ed.), *Theories of learning and instruction. The sixty-third yearbook of the National Society for the Study of Education, Part I* (pp. 402–415). Chicago: University of Chicago Press.

McKeachie, W. J. (1976). Psychology in America's bicentennial year. *American Psychologist, 31,* 819–833.

Piaget, J. (1963). *The origins of intelligence in children*. New York: W. W. Norton.

Skinner, B. F. (1968). *The technology of teaching*. New York: Appleton-Century-Crofts.

Suppes, P. (1974). The place of theory in educational research. *Educational Researcher, 3*(6), 3–10.

Thorndike, E. L. (1931). *Human learning*, New York: Century.

CHAPTER 2

The Antecedents
of a Psychology of Learning

The special task of the social scientist in
each generation is to pin down the contemporary facts. Beyond that, he shares
with the humanistic scholar and the artist
in the effort to gain insight into contemporary relationships, and to realign the
culture's view of man with the present
realities. To know man as he is is no mean
aspiration.
Cronbach, 1975, p. 127

Each generation seeks an explanation of the contemporary reality to
which it belongs. Early societies sought to explain the mysterious forces
of nature that influenced their daily lives. Included were thunder, lightning, the seasons, and the movements of the sun and moon. Twentieth-
century cultures, on the other hand, are attempting to understand the
effects on everyday events of sophisticated computers and other communications technologies.

The search for understanding by any generation is restricted somewhat
by the methods available at the time. Early societies lacked a systematic
means for analyzing events. They relied instead on myths and superstitions as a major source of knowledge. The early Greeks, for example,
believed that ocean storms were caused by Poseidon the sea god and
lightning bolts were Zeus' arrows unleashed in punishment. In human
affairs, the goddess Aphrodite was believed to influence love relationships, and wisdom was the gift of Athena.

THE BEGINNING OF PSYCHOLOGY

The early myths and superstitions were gradually replaced by organized belief systems referred to as philosophies. For over 2000 years, from approximately 400 B.C. to the mid-nineteenth century, philosophy served as the chief source of information about learning. Although experimental methods were introduced in the natural sciences in the sixteenth century, they were not applied to the study of mental functions until 300 years later. The introduction of laboratory research to the study of the mind's operations signaled the birth of a new discipline, psychology.

The Philosophical Perspective

Philosophies are organized belief systems based on reasoned judgment and logic. A philosophy provides a consistent explanation of the nature of reality, truth, virtue, and beauty. Thus a philosophy is a coherent set of values that provides a framework for understanding the relationship between the human race and the universe.

In addition, some philosophies developed information about the human role in society, the function of the mind, and the nature of knowledge. Some of the questions addressed by philosophers are: What is knowledge? What is the origin of knowledge? What does it mean "to know"? The answers to these questions were the first systematic source of information about learning.

Idealism and Realism.   One of the early views on learning was developed by the Greek philosopher Plato (ca. 427–327 B.C.). His philosophy, idealism, describes mind or spirit as basic to everything that exists. Reality, according to idealism, includes only the pure ideas that are in the mind. Therefore, human knowledge is derived from the ideas present in the mind since birth. Consistent with this view, learning is described as the development of these innate ideas by the mind. This is accomplished through the "mind's eye," by turning one's thoughts inward. Plato recommended the study of mathematics and the classics to develop the mind. This belief later was referred to as the "mental discipline" concept.

In Plato's view, knowledge is innate or inborn. A contrasting perspective, however, was developed by Aristotle, Plato's pupil. Aristotle believed that reality exists in the physical world, not in the mind's conception of it. Universal laws or ideas are not innate ideas. Instead, they are relationships observed in nature. The source of human knowledge, therefore, is the physical environment and learning occurs through contact with that environment. The role of the mind, according to Aristotle, is to organize and to structure the sensory experience received from the outside world.

Table 2-1 illustrates these two perspectives on learning. Both Plato and Aristotle believed that the mind plays an important role in learning. They differed on the issue of the basic component on which the mind operates: innate ideas or sensory experience.

Rationalism and Empiricism.   Two later philosophers refined the concepts introduced by Plato and Aristotle. René Descartes, a seventeenth-century mathematician and philosopher, further developed the concept of innate knowledge. Descartes maintained that individuals develop knowledge through the process of deductive reasoning from a few basic ideas. His model for the acquisition of knowledge was mathematics, which is an entire system deduced from a few basic axioms. This reliance on rational thought processes in Descartes' model led to the name rationalism.

In contrast, Aristotle's ideas became the basis for the British philosophy referred to as empiricism. Introduced by Thomas Hobbes in the seventeenth century, empiricism was formally developed by the later philosopher, John Locke. According to Locke, the mind at birth is a *tabula rasa* or blank tablet. Ideas, which he referred to as the building blocks of the mind, are developed through two types of experience. One is sensation, defined as the acquisition of information through the senses. The other is reflection, described as the process of combining simple ideas into complex ones. The immediate appeal of empiricism was that it accounted for "higher" mental processes while relying on experience as the basis of knowledge (Boring, 1950).

The Philosophical Dilemma.   The views developed by Descartes and the British empiricists extended the ideas originally proposed by Plato and Aristotle. However, like idealism and realism, they each produced a truncated conception of learning (see Table 2-2). That is, learning can

Table 2-1. Comparison of Idealism and Realism

	Idealism	**Realism**
Nature of reality	Pure ideas of the mind	Physical world
Source of knowledge	Innate ideas	Sensory experience
Learning	Development of ideas already in the mind	Contact with the physical environment

Table 2-2. Descriptions of Learning Derived from Two Opposing Views of Reality

Innate Ideas		Knowledge from the Physical World	
Idealism	**Rationalism**	**Realism**	**Empiricism**
Study of the ideal forms of mathematics improves the mind	Knowledge is formed through deductive reasoning from a few innate ideas; included are knowledge of God, self, and mathematical concepts	Knowledge is acquired through the senses; the role of the mind is to structure and to organize sensory experience	Ideas are developed through two types of sensory experience: sensation and reflection

occur by means other than the study of classical subjects (idealism) or sensory experience, such as watching a sunrise (realism).

Furthermore, the philosophical issue of the source of human knowledge influenced discussions of human intelligence later undertaken by psychologists. Referred to as the nature/nurture controversy, the issue revolved around the factor responsible for intelligence. That is, is intelligence an inborn trait or does it develop through experience with the environment? The debate eventually subsided in the 1950s with the consensus that both heredity and the environment are important.

The Separation of Psychology from Philosophy

From 400 b.c. to the late nineteenth century, philosophy served as the primary source of information about the human mind. Meanwhile, since the sixteenth century, the scientific method had been used to investigate the physical world. This method, based on the observation of natural events, greatly expanded knowledge about the physical environment. Mystical beliefs and untested maxims gradually were replaced by reliable laws and principles. The science of chemistry supplanted the practice of alchemy, and the methods of astrology were replaced by the science of astronomy.

For almost 300 years, however, the use of experimentation was confined to the natural sciences. Why was the scientific method not applied also to the study of learning? First, the mind, like the soul, was viewed as the gift of God. The mind was considered to be a given: it was an absolute. To conduct research on the mind would be to call into question the gift of God. Second, the primary function of the mind was to become attuned to ultimate reality. Therefore, descriptions of reality developed by philosophers were sufficient to account for the primary role of the mind's activities.

A Rationale for Psychological Research. Two events set the stage for the scientific investigations of mental functions. One was the publication of Darwin's theory of evolution in 1859 as *Origin of Species*. The other event was the introduction of the concept *scientific empiricism*.

The Concept of Evolution. According to Darwin's theory, the biological species present on earth are not a preestablished set or group. Instead, species survive, perish, or develop new variations as a result of their ability to adapt biologically to changing conditions.

What was the impact of this theory? First, it upset the accepted order of the universe, and second, it focused attention on the processes of change. In other words, it defined a new reality, one in which change rather than some static order predominates. One result was that formerly accepted views about the mind were altered. That is, if the human mind is part of the evolutionary process, then defining the static relationship between the human mind and the mind of God is no longer a major issue.

The influence of evolution on psychology was later analyzed by John Dewey in 1910. He described it as the introduction of responsibility into intellectual life. As long as human beings rationalized the universe, they were confessing an inability to master the course of human events. Responsibility for events is shifted to God. Evolution, however, with the emphasis on survival as adaptation to the environment, places the responsibility for meaningful change on the human race.

Scientific Empiricism. Accepting an altered view of the human intellect was one thing; conducting research on the human mind, however, was quite a different matter. The arguments that legitimized such research were provided by Hermann von Helmholtz, a medical doctor, scientist, and philosopher. Von Helmholtz refuted Descartes' arguments that knowledge is innate (Boring, 1950). Even mathematical concepts are the product of experience. For example, the axiom that parallel lines do not meet is the result of the type of space inhabited by the human race. The axiom would be false if human beings lived inside a sphere. Therefore, since ideas are products of human experience, they are subject to human observation and analysis.

Von Helmholtz introduced the term "scientific empiricism" to describe the accumulation of facts through carefully designed experiments, or "controlled experience." The usefulness of scientific empiricism in developing new knowledge was demonstrated by his own research. Among other developments are his textbook on the eye's functions and his invention of the opthalmoscope for observing the operations of the eye.

The First Psychological Research.   From research on the senses, which are living tissue, to research on the mind was only one short step. That step was taken by Wilhelm Wundt, often referred to as the father of experimental psychology. Like von Helmholtz, he was both a philosopher and a scientist.

The new field was born in 1874 with the publication of Wundt's text summarizing the research on sensory functions. He named the research "physiological psychology" to signal the inspiration provided by physiological methods to the launching of his new experimental psychology (Watson, 1977, p. 311). (See Table 2-3.)

Five years later (1879), Wundt established the first formal laboratory for the study of psychology at the University of Leipzig. Studies included research on reaction times, sensation, auditory perception, and attention.

The goal of psychology, according to Wundt, was to identify the elements or "structure" of the mind. His model was chemistry, which had identified atoms and molecules as the basic elements of matter. This approach to psychology was later to be named *structuralism*. It was soon to compete with other views on the scope and direction of the new science.

Late in the nineteenth century, another German psychologist, Hermann Ebbinghaus, added a new dimension to the research. He invented the nonsense syllable and measured the amount learned, the time involved in learning, and the effects of different word lists on learning. The importance of the research is that it involved responses other than sensory reactions. Since the research was not immediately translated into English, its impact on American psychology did not come until later.

The Architects of American Psychology.   Unlike the direction pursued by Wilhelm Wundt, American psychology developed rapidly into a diverse discipline with a variety of interests and research directions. By 1895, twenty-four laboratories were in existence, three journals (*Psychologial Monographs, Psychological Review,* and *American Journal of Psychology*), and several textbooks. A growing scientific society had also been founded, the American Psychological Association, of which many members were full-time psychologists (Watson, 1963, p. 367).

What were the circumstances of this development, and who were its chief architects? First, psychology was introduced to higher education in the United States just prior to the reform of that institution (Watson, 1963). Thus a favorable climate existed for its expansion. Briefly summarized, graduate schools in 1880 were one-curriculum schools and, unlike European universities, research was excluded. The drain of graduate students to Europe to complete their studies prompted the revamping of the American system. New topics and departments were initiated, including politics, economics, and psychology; furthermore, research became a primary goal.

Psychology fared well in these reorganizations because it involved experimentation and was, therefore, "modern" and "up to date." Also, unlike European universities, psychology tended to be installed as a separate department rather than attached to schools of philosophy. This gave the discipline both greater latitude in scope of study and an "acceptable" research methodology.

The two early architects of American psychology were William James

Table 2-3. Major Events in the Separation of Psychology from Philosophy

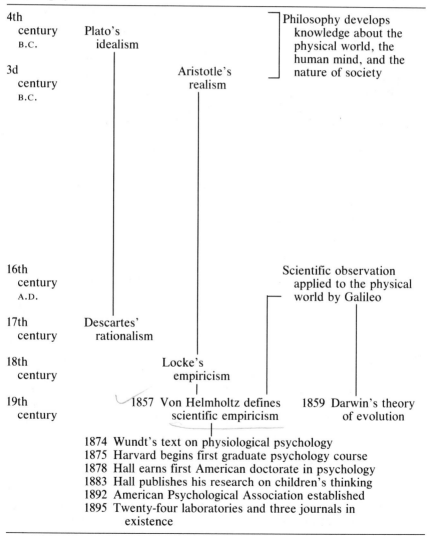

4th century B.C.	Plato's idealism		Philosophy develops knowledge about the physical world, the human mind, and the nature of society
3d century B.C.		Aristotle's realism	
16th century A.D.			Scientific observation applied to the physical world by Galileo
17th century	Descartes' rationalism		
18th century		Locke's empiricism	
19th century	1857 Von Helmholtz defines scientific empiricism		1859 Darwin's theory of evolution

1874 Wundt's text on physiological psychology
1875 Harvard begins first graduate psychology course
1878 Hall earns first American doctorate in psychology
1883 Hall publishes his research on children's thinking
1892 American Psychological Association established
1895 Twenty-four laboratories and three journals in
    existence

and G. Stanley Hall. They were soon joined by John Dewey, James Cattell, and Edward Thorndike. Each left his unique stamp on the new discipline. James established the first graduate course and an informal laboratory at Harvard in 1875 and he was the chief scholar of the new discipline (see the following section).

Hall was a student of William James and he earned the first American doctorate in psychology in 1878. Unlike James, he was an innovator and administrator. He initiated one project after another, often leaving the tidying up of the details to others (Watson, 1963). He founded the first laboratory at Johns Hopkins, a psychological journal, and the American Psychological Association in 1892 with 26 charter members. He also conducted the first research on children's thinking, using the method newly developed in Germany, the questionnaire. Published in 1883 as *The Contents of Children's Minds,* this publication and his work as president of Clark University initiated the child-study movement and the child-centered school.

Hall, however, was no theorist. Strongly influenced by evolution, and referred to as "the Darwin of the mind" (Cremin, 1961), Hall maintained that child development mirrored the development of humankind. However, his view that the child progresses from savagery to civilization in the manner of human progress was later refuted.

Some events in the development of psychology are summarized in Table 2-3. The rapid growth of American psychology in the few short years from 1874 to 1895 is illustrated by these events.

THE INTELLECTUAL FOUNDATIONS OF AMERICAN PSYCHOLOGY (1890–1900)

The decade from 1890 to 1900 was a unique 10-year period in American psychology. The scholarship of William James, John Dewey, James Cattell, and Edward Thorndike during those 10 years established new frontiers for psychology and education. Included are animal psychology, educational psychology, functional psychology, and the experiential curriculum. All trace their roots to this period.

The Basis for a Functional Psychology

The scholarship and writings of William James and John Dewey gave psychology a broad and diverse role. Both men were philosophers as well as leaders in psychology and they contributed to both disciplines.

Topics in Psychology. With careful scholarship and breadth, James summarized the existing topics in psychology in his two-volume text *Principles of Psychology.* Twelve years in preparation, this 1890 text gave psychologists a subject matter of both scope and substance. Included were discussions of hypnosis with mental patients, the role of emotion, free will, habit formation, and others.

The breadth of the work may be the result in part of the unorganized nature of James' schooling. He studied painting for six months, then took up engineering, which he dropped for biology. Finding classification boring, James then entered medical school and earned a degree in medicine. These various changes prompted McKeachie (1976) to comment, humorously, on the need for psychological tests and career counseling in psychology in the nineteenth century.

In the text on psychology, James (1890) also criticized Wundt's structural approach, referring to it as a "microscopic psychology." He pointed out that to learn whether feeling is a part of the element "sensation" or is an element in its own right is to learn nothing new. James also contended that the analysis of the mind into elements would lead to a distorted picture of mental functioning. Psychologists, he predicted, would read into experience what they believed should be there. James also stated that psychology should study the adjustment of the organism to the environment and all that such study implies.

John Dewey's Functionalism. Perhaps best remembered as the chosen leader of the reform movement in public education, John Dewey also was the architect of an applied psychology. Dewey (1896) referred to Wundt's structural analyses as psychology's "classification period." Dewey compared it to biology's classification period in which living organisms were placed in taxonomic categories. However, psychology, like biology, he noted, should move beyond classification to the more important issue, the study of process.

He also emphasized the artificiality of Wundt's analyses. For example, "stimulus/response" or "sensation/movement" designations are not based on reality (Dewey, 1896). Any distinction between "stimulus" or "response" represents only the different roles that each plays in the individual's total action. Instead of studying these artificial distinctions, psychologists should study the total act or process, for example, "seeing-reaching-touching."

The arguments later used by the Gestalt psychologists against both Wundt's approach and behaviorism were very similar to the case made by Dewey. According to the Gestalt theorists, to study stimulus-response elements is like trying to understand a song by studying the individual notes (Murphy, 1949).

Dewey's position (1896) formally initiated the school of thought referred to as functionalism. The movement derived from no particular doctrine and it included any research that studied the relationships between biological creatures and the environment. Functionalism, like the structural approach, was to compete in the early twentieth century with two other perspectives in defining the appropriate role for psychology.

Applications to Educational Practice

The work of James and Dewey established the definition and scope of functionalism. They both also illustrated the importance of a practical psychology through their involvement in education. In *Talks to Teachers*, James described the teacher's role as that of developing good habits and productive thinking in the student. This text for several years was the model of educational practice derived from psychology.

Dewey, on the other hand, called for the transformation of education. He viewed the school as the agent of social change that must ease society's transition into the industrial age. In *The School and Society*, he described education as "one-sided" and "dominated by medieval conceptions of learning." That is, the school emphasized the accumulation of facts and the memorization of large quantities of information.

Dewey's solution was to change the school into an embryonic community that would include study of the occupations as well as art, history, and science. More importantly, the child would learn intellectual responsibility by selecting and implementing a plan of work and receiving guidance when errors were made (Dewey, 1899). The changes suggested by Dewey led to the development of the experiential curriculum in the public school.

Research on Individual Differences and Learning

Test development and the development of learning theory are both accepted research areas in contemporary psychology. Each was introduced during the early period of the development of psychology. The measurement of individual differences was initiated by James M. Cattell, and learning theory began with Edward L. Thorndike.

The Study of Individual Differences. Wilhelm Wundt initiated psychological measurements in order to quantify the common characteristics of the human mind. His goal was to study the mind's unchanging elements, such as reaction time. One of Wundt's American students, however, was interested instead in the study of the variability of human mental characteristics. That student, James M. Cattell, was influenced by Sir Francis

Galton's research on inherited individual differences. Galton had identified several British families that, for several generations, had produced outstanding leaders and scholars and he surmised that differences in intellectual capacity might be inherited.

Why was Cattell's research interest in individual differences of such importance to American psychology? Cattell's independence in going against the prevailing measurement trend established by Wundt legitimized the classification of individuals on the basis of differential performance on psychological tests. Cattell developed over 50 tests of sensory and motor reactions, coined the term "mental test" in an 1890 paper, and applied Sir Francis Galton's statistics to the analysis of individual differences. Thus he paved the way for the use of tests of individual differences, such as the Binet scale and Army Alpha.

Cattell later was to lose his academic position at Princeton because of his pacifist beliefs in World War I. He then founded The Psychological Corporation, which today continues to publish and market psychological tests.

The First Learning Theory. Edward Thorndike's dissertation, *An Experimental Study of the Associative Process in Animals* (1898), was a landmark experiment. First, it initiated the laboratory study of animal subjects. Investigations of learning prior to Thorndike included only the rote-memorization experiments developed by Ebbinghaus and the psychomotor skills acquired in learning telegraphy (Boring, 1950). The major purpose for studying the animal mind, according to Thorndike (1911, p. 22), was to discover the development of mental life in different species, and particularly, the origin of human intelligence.

Second, Thorndike's research was the first experimental analysis of the sequence of stimulus situations, behaviors, and consequences.

Third, the theory established both major and minor laws that govern learning in both animals and human beings. It therefore demonstrated the feasibility of behavioral research in generating laws about mental events. (See Chapter 3 for a description of the theory.)

In summary, American psychology developed rapidly during the first 25 years of its existence. From 1875 to the turn of the century, psychology had progressed from one graduate course in physiological psychology to a viable discipline with several research directions. Included were the child-study movement, the measurement of individual differences, laboratory research on animal learning, and the involvement of psychologists in education (see Table 2-4). To Wilhelm Wundt, who wished to develop a science removed from the problems of daily living, the diverse American developments must have resembled the actions of an undisciplined country cousin.

Table 2-4. Early Developments in American Psychology

Date	Event	Contribution
1883	Hall's research on children's thinking	Initiated the child-study movement
1890	James' *Principles of Psychology*	Summarizd psychological knowledge; established basis for functional psychology
1890	Cattel coins the term *mental test*	Introduced testing to American psychology
1892	Cattell's monograph on testing	
1896	Dewey's essay on artificial distinctions	Formally initiated functionalism
1898	Thorndike's dissertation on animal learning	First learning theory; initiated laboratory research on animals
1899	James' *Talks to Teachers*	Initiated the involvement of psychologists in educational practice
1899	Dewey's *The School and Society*	

SUMMARY

Over 400 years before the birth of Christ, philosophers began their deliberations on the nature of thinking and learning. Using the only method available at the time, logical analysis, they developed explanations of the ways in which human beings acquire knowledge. Plato's philosophy, idealism, identified knowledge as inborn, whereas Aristotle's view, realism, described knowledge as formed from sensory experience. These views were further refined by later philosophers. The extension of Plato's basic position developed by Descartes became known as rationalism. Similarly, Aristotle's position was developed further by Locke in the philosophy known as empiricism.

The doctrine of empiricism took on new meaning with the work of Hermann von Helmholtz, a philosopher and scientist. He refuted the concept of innate ideas and demonstrated the importance of acquiring facts through controlled observation. This method, referred to as scientific empiricism, led to the discovery of new information about the sensory functions of sight and hearing.

The separation of psychology from philosophy was initiated by Wilhelm Wundt in his 1874 test on physiological psychology. Following that publication, events progressed rapidly. Graduate courses were established at Harvard in 1875 and Wundt established the first laboratory at the University of Leipzig in 1879.

In the 1890s William James and John Dewey rejected Wundt's structural approach to psychology. Influenced by the theory of evolution, they formally initiated the functionalist movement. The dimensions of study established by American psychologists by the turn of the century included (1) the child-study focus begun by Hall, (2) the study of individual differences and testing begun by Cattell, and (3) the learning-theory research initiated by Thorndike.

DISCUSSION QUESTIONS

1. What is the major difference in the methods of study used by philosophy and the new psychology?
2. How did the prespective established by James and Dewey differ from Wundt's view of psychology?
3. According to Dewey, in what ways did the theory of evolution influence human thought?
4. What new perspective on psychological research was provided by Thorndike's dissertation?

REFERENCES

Boring, E. G. (1950). *A history of experimental psychology* (2nd ed.). New York: Appleton-Century-Crofts.

Cremin, L. A. (1961). *The transformation of the school: Progressivism in American education.* New York: Vintage Books.

Cronbach, L. J. (1975). Beyond the two disciplines of scientific psychology. *American Psychologist, 30*(2), 116–127.

Dewey, J. (1896). The reflex-arc concept in psychology. *Psychological Review, 3,* 357–370.

Dewey, J. (1899). *The school and society.* Chicago: University of Chicago Press.

Dewey, J. (1900). Psychology and social practice. *Psychological Review, 7,* 105–124.

Dewey, J. (1910). "Consciousness" and experience. In *The influence of Darwin on philosophy* (pp. 242–270). New York: Peter Smith.

James, W. (1890). *The principles of psychology* (Vols. I and II). New York: Henry Holt.

McKeachie, W. J. (1976). Psychology in America's bicentennial year. *American Psychologist, 31,* 819–833.

Murphy, G. (1949). *Historical introduction to modern psychology.* New York: Harcourt Brace & World.

Thorndike, E. L. (1898). Animal intelligence: An experimental study of the associative processes in animals. *The Psychological Review Monograph Supplements, 2,* 4–160.
Thorndike, E. L. (1911). *Animal intelligence.* New York: Macmillan.
Watson, R. I. (1963). *The great psychologists* (4th ed.). New York: J. B. Lippincott.
Watson, R. I. (1977). The individual, social-educational, economic, and political conditions for the original practices of detection and utilization of individual aptitude differences. In J. Brozek & R. B. Evans (Eds.), *R. I. Watson's selected papers on the history of psychology* (pp. 309–324) Hanover, NH: University of New Hampshire.

CHAPTER 3

Approaches to Psychology and Learning

At any one time, a science is simply what its researches yield, and the researches are nothing more than those problems for which effective methods have been found and for which the times are ready. Each step in scientific progress depends on the previous one, and the process is not much hurried by wishing.
Boring, 1950, p. 343

At the beginning of the century, the discipline of psychology was firmly established in the United States. Research on testing, the study of individual differences, and research on learning were among the developments already under way.

The early years of the twentieth century, from 1900 to approximately 1930, were a period of transition. The new discipline had yet to identify a major purpose, the scope of the subject matter, and an acceptable research methodology.

TWO COMPETITORS: BEHAVIORISM AND GESTALT PSYCHOLOGY

The two dominant perspectives on the role of psychology at the turn of the century were Wundt's structuralism and Dewey's functional psychology. The limitations of these two views became evident with the rise of behaviorism and its chief competitor, Gestalt psychology. Although these four perspectives have been referred to as schools, they are described more accurately as approaches to problems rather than schools of thought (Mueller, 1979).

Each of the four perspectives proposed a different role for psychology. However, only behaviorism and Gestalt psychology survived the decade of the 1920s. During these efforts to define the appropriate subject matter for psychology, the study of learning began to acquire a central position in psychological research. By 1930, three learning theories had been developed. They were Edward Thorndike's connectionism, classical conditioning, and Gestalt theory.

The Rise of Behaviorism

The limitations of both structuralism and functionalism contributed to the rise of other movements that described different roles for psychology.

Limitations of the Early Perspectives. The problems with structuralism were related to the basic purpose of the movement. In their efforts to develop a "pure" science that described the generalized human mind, animal research was excluded. Instead, the structuralists relied on introspection, which is the self-report of one's own thought processes. The inconsistent results and the failure of psychologists to agree on the meanings of such terms as sensation, imagery, and feeling, led to a dead end for the research.

A more serious problem, however, was that structuralism remained aloof from the mainstream of psychology. Rejecting the concept of evolution, structuralism also ignored the applied direction taken by most psychologists. Consequently, the movement formally ended in 1927 with the death of the leader, Edward Titchener.

The narrowness of structuralism led to the death of the movement. In contrast, the broad, diffuse role proposed by functionalism was responsible for the end of that movement. The functionalists maintained that psychology should include studies of behavior, the function of mental processes, and the mind-body relationship (Angell, 1907). Although this tolerance for diversity prevented the development of a sterile discipline, it lacked organization and focus.

A Rationale for Behaviorism. The inability of structuralism and functionalism to establish well-defined research methods and a clearly defined subject matter established the climate for change. In that context, John B. Watson launched the movement to study behavior rather than mental processes or states.

In the article "Psychology as the Behaviorist Views It," published in 1913, Watson made a case for the study of behavior. In some 50-odd years, said Watson, psychology had failed to establish itself as a natural science. The focus on consciousness and mental processes had led psychology into a dead end where the topics are "threadbare from much handling" (Watson, 1913, p. 174). Furthermore, when human consciousness is the reference point for research, the behaviorist is forced to ignore all data that do not relate to human mental processes. Other sciences, such as physics and chemistry, Watson noted, do not so restrict their definitions of the subject matter to the extent that information must be discarded.

The starting point for psychology, therefore, should be the fact that all organisms adjust to the environment through responses (Watson, 1913). Since certain responses follow certain stimuli, psychologists should be able to predict the response from the stimulus, and vice versa. When this goal is achieved, according to Watson, psychology would then become an objective, experimental science. In addition, the discipline would also provide useful knowledge for the educator, physician, business leader, and others.

A Methodology for Behaviorism. After the appeal to study behavior, Watson became acquainted with the motor-reflex research of V. M. Bekheterev, a Russian physiologist. His work clearly demonstrated the feasibility of behavioral research. Reflexes such as finger retraction were elicited by a variety of sights and sounds associated with an electric-shock stimulus (Murphy, 1949). Bekheterev also theorized that complex habits were composed of similar associations of reflexes.

The procedure by which new stimuli gradually acquire the power to elicit reflex responses became known as *classical conditioning.* The best known studies are those conducted by Ivan Pavlov, for which he received the 1904 Nobel Prize. Pavlov noted that animal salivation often was triggered by approaching footsteps prior to the presentation of meat powder to the experimental animal. He began to study the role of different stimuli in eliciting animal reflexes (Murphy, 1949).

Classical conditioning was tailor-made for the concepts of behaviorism. The method eliminated all references to mental states and it was easily executed. Also, unlike Thorndike's trial-and-error laboratory method, conditioning demonstrated that behavioral responses could be manipulated in the laboratory. That is, new stimuli could be made to elicit particular reflexes. Therein lay the promise that a science of behavior could be developed in the psychologist's laboratory.

In a now-famous experiment, Watson successfully conditioned the fear reaction of an 11-month-old child, Albert, to a white rat and other furry objects (see the next section). He concluded that behaviorism was the mechanism that could provide a foundation for living. In his usual persuasive style, Watson (1925) made the following claims for conditioning:

Give me a dozen healthy infants, well formed, and my own specified world to bring them up in, and I'll guarantee to take any one at random and train him to become any type of specialist I might select—doctor, lawyer, artist, merchant-chief—regardless of his talents, penchants, tendencies, abilities, vocations, and race of his ancestors. (p. 65)

Needless to say, behaviorism became immediately popular. The simplicity of the method for conditioning responses and the novelty of the procedure led to a multitude of applications and experiments. In the 1920s, almost every psychologist seemed to be a behaviorist and none appeared to agree with any other (Boring, 1950). The term "behaviorism" became attached to several developments, including a particular research method, objective data in general, a materialistic view of psychology, and others.

Watson also believed that behaviorism would place psychology in the ranks of the "true" sciences, along with zoology, physiology, physical chemistry, and others. These same views on the potential of behaviorism were to be reiterated in the 1950s by B. F. Skinner.

The Beginning of Gestalt Psychology

The rise of behaviorism was not completely unchallenged, however. The movement was soon to be opposed by Gestalt psychology. Like the functionalists, Gestalt psychologists reacted against the analysis of experience into its separate elements. Unlike the functionalists, however, the Gestalt psychologists provided research data on the differences between elements and the individual's total experience.

Gestalt psychology began quite by accident when Max Wertheimer was on his way by train from Vienna to Germany for a vacation (Watson, 1963). Leaving the train at Frankfurt to follow up a sudden hunch, he bought a toy stroboscope. A stroboscope is an instrument that presents pictures at such a rapid rate that the illusion of motion is created; it was popular before the invention of motion pictures. As a result of this preliminary investigation, Wertheimer canceled his vacation plans and took his research to the laboratory.

What was this research that launched a new movement in psychology? Named the *phi phenomenon* in the 1912 publication of the research, it describes the perception of motion from separate, stationary stimuli. In the laboratory experiments, Wertheimer found that two stationary projections of light are sometimes perceived as light in motion. In other words, if light is first projected through a vertical slit and then through

Table 3-1. Summary of Some Major Events in Learning Theory from 1900 to 1930

1900 Center for structuralism functioning at Cornell

1927 Titchener's death ends structuralism

1900 Cattell, Thorndike represent the Columbia school of functionalism

1901 Thorndike and Woodworth's transfer of training experiments

1907 Angell emphasizes importance of mental processes in functionalism

1911 Thorndike's *Animal Intelligence*

Thorndike applies his theory to the analyses of school subjects

Functional research is absorbed into behaviorism

1904 Pavlov's classical conditioning model developed

1907 Bekheterev's *Objective Psychology*

1913 Watson launches behaviorism

1920 Watson applies classical conditioning to human infants

"Behaviorism" adopted as a method and a philosophy of science by many psychologists

---

1912 Wertheimer's light perception experiments initiate Gestalt psychology

1913–1915 Köhler's experiments with apes

1922 Koffka introduces Gestalt psychology in the United States

1929 Koffka publishes *Gestalt Psychology*

a slit inclined to the right, the light appears to fall from the first to the second position. Similarly, the exposure of two lines in quick succession, if carefully placed, are perceived as movement. In both cases, two stationary stimuli are presented, but they are not perceived as such.

The importance of these experiments is that the perception of the whole (motion) cannot be obtained from the specific elements (two stimuli). In other words, the "whole" possesses emergent properties that differ from those of its separate elements. For example, water has a different set of properties from that of its elements, oxygen and hydrogen. Therefore, in the Gestalt view, the behaviorists' analysis into separate elements results in a distortion of the very phenomenon under study.

Gestalt psychology was introduced in the United States 10 years after its inception (see Table 3-1). The three leaders, Max Wertheimer, Kurt Koffka, and Wolfgang Köhler, left Germany in the 1930s to continue their writing and teaching in the United States. They investigated more than 100 laws that govern perception and conducted experiments on learning with animal subjects and human beings.

The Gestalt perspective, however, was viewed by American psychologists as an interesting, yet minor, development. The dominant movement in American psychology for the next few decades was behaviorism. Gestalt theory, however, was the beginning of a cognitive psychology, and it kept alive the interest in mental events.

THREE LEARNING THEORIES

The rise of behaviorism as the dominant voice for psychology was one transition that occurred in the years from 1900 to 1930. The other transition was the increased focus on the processes of learning. The three views of learning developed during this period were Edward Thorndike's connectionism, classical conditioning, and Gestalt theory.

Edward Thorndike's Connectionism

Developing the first learning theory was only one of the many contributions made by Edward Thorndike to psychology. His more than 500 articles and several texts included test statistics, educational practice, classroom research, test development, and specific tests in handwriting, arithmetic, reading, and others.

The foundations of Thorndike's theory were established initially in experiments with animals. The research was designed to determine whether animals "solved" a problem through reasoning or by a more basic process. Research was needed, according to Thorndike, because objective data were lacking. "Dogs get lost hundreds of times and no one ever notices it or sends an account of it to a scientific magazine. But let one find his way from Brooklyn to Yonkers and the fact immediately becomes a circulating anecdote" (Thorndike, 1911, p. 24).

Experimental Procedure.   Thorndike experimented with baby chicks, dogs, fish, cats, and monkeys. However, while he was a student at Harvard, his landlady forbid him to continue hatching chicks in his room. William James offered the basement of his home for Thorndike's research, to the dismay of Mrs. James and the excitement of the children.

The typical experimental procedure required each animal to escape from a confined space in order to reach food. A puzzle box was used that required the tripping of a latch or some other mechanism in order to effect escape (see Figure 3-1).

When confined, the animal often engaged in a variety of behaviors, including scratching, biting, clawing, and rubbing against the sides of the box. Sooner or later the animal tripped the latch and escaped to the food. Repeated confinements were characterized by a decrease in the behaviors unrelated to escape and, of course, a shorter escape time. The most dramatic change was observed with monkeys. In one experiment, a box containing a banana was placed inside the cage. Thirty-six minutes was

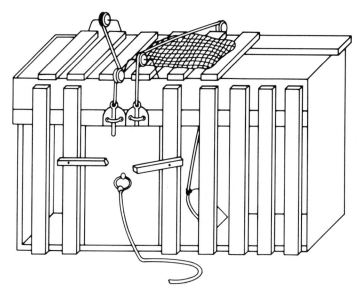

Figure 3-1. Puzzle cage used in some of Thorndike's experiments.

required for the monkey to pull out the nail that held the wire fastener closed. On the second trial, only 2 minutes 20 seconds was required (Thorndike, 1911).

Thorndike concluded from his research that the escape response gradually became associated with the stimulus situation in trial-and-error learning. The correct response was gradually "stamped in" or strengthened over repeated trials. Incorrect responses were weakened or "stamped out." This phenomenon is referred to as *response substitution*. The theory is also known as *instrumental conditioning* because the selection of a particular response is instrumental in obtaining the reward.

The Laws of Learning.   Three major laws of learning were derived from the results of the research. They are the law of effect, the law of exercise, and the law of readiness. The *law of effect* states that a satisfying state of affairs following the response strengthens the connection between the stimulus and the behavior, whereas an annoying state weakens the connection. Thorndike later revised the law so that punishment was not equal to reward in its influence on learning.

The *law of exercise* describes the conditions implied in the adage "Practice makes perfect." Repetition of the experience, in other words, increases the probability of a correct response. However, repetition in the absence of a satisfying state of affairs does not enhance learning (Thorndike, 1913b, p. 20).

The *law of readiness* describes the conditions that govern the states referred to as "satisfying" or "annoying" (Thorndike, 1913a). Briefly summarized, the execution of an action in response to a strong impulse is satisfying, whereas the blocking of that action or forcing it under other conditions is annoying.

Applications to School Learning.   In the laboratory, Thorndike researched the relationship between physical stimuli and physical actions, and his interpretations of learning were based on these behavioral studies. However, his theory also includes references to mental events. Thus it occupied a middle ground between the concerns of functionalism and the "pure" behaviorism of other researchers.

Thorndike described human mental life as composed of both mental states and movements with connections between each type (Thorndike, 1905, p. 12). In his view, connections between ideas accounted for the major portion of "knowledge" in its popular sense (Thorndike, 1913b, p. 19). Included are numerical problems and their answers, such as $9 \times 5 = 45$; events and dates, such as Columbus and 1492; and persons and characteristics, such as John and blue eyes.

Of particular interest to the educator is Thorndike's description of his five minor laws in relation to school learning. They are the first efforts to account for the complexity of human learning. These subsidiary laws and their applications are summarized in Table 3-2. These laws were believed to interact with the laws of effect and exercise to account for human learning.

Of major importance to education is Thorndike's research on the effects of particular kinds of learning activities on subsequent learning. First, a series of studies conducted by Thorndike and Woodworth (1901) found that training in particular tasks facilitated the later learning only of similar

Table 3-2. Application of Thorndike's Minor Laws to Education

Law	Description	Examples
1. Multiple response or varied reaction	A variety of responses often occurs initially to a stimulus	Pronunciation of a foreign language Skill in tennis Coherence in English composition
2. Attitudes, dispositions, or states	Condition of the learner that influences the learning; includes stable attitudes and temporary factors of the situation	Individual competing to throw a ball the longest distance or throw a player out in a baseball game Instructions for the problem $\frac{7}{6}$ to add or to subtract
3. Partial or piecemeal activity of a situation	The tendency to respond to particular elements or features of a stimulus situation (also referred to as analytic learning)	Responses to the qualities of shape, color, number, use, intent, and others Responses to relations of space, time, causation, and others
4. Assimilation of response by analogy	The tendency of situation B to arouse in part the same response as situation A	The foreigner pronouncing English
5. Associative shifting	Successively altering the stimulus until the response is bound by a new stimulus	*abcde* is altered to *abcdef* to *abcfg* and so on

Source: Thorndike (1913b, chap. 3, pp. 19–31)

tasks, not dissimilar ones. This relationship is known as *transfer of training*.

Second, Thorndike (1924) investigated the popular "mental discipline" concept originally described by Plato. According to the mental discipline advocates, the study of certain curricula, particularly mathematics and the classics, enhanced intellectual functioning. That is, such school subjects were believed to discipline the mind. Thorndike (1924) tested this concept by comparing the postcourse achievement of high school students enrolled in classical and vocational curricula and found no significant differences. In succeeding years, Thorndike's research was named as a major influence in turning curriculum designers away from the mental discipline concept and toward the practice of designing curriculum for social utility (Cushman and Fox, 1938; Gates, 1938).

Reflex or Classical Conditioning

Thorndike's research demonstrated that particular responses can become associated with certain stimulus situations through trial-and-error learning. The reflex conditioning methodology developed by the Russian physiologists used a different experimental procedure. In classical conditioning, an arbitrary stimulus is repeatedly paired with the stimulus that naturally elicits a particular reflex. An example is the pairing of a light signal with the mild electric shock that elicits finger retraction. After repeated pairings, the light signal alone elicits the finger retraction.

Perhaps the best known example is Pavlov's research, in which the sound of a tuning fork is presented immediately prior to the presentation of meat powder to a dog. After several repetitions, the sound alone elicits salivation in the animal.

In the classical conditioning methodology, the naturally occurring stimulus and reflex response are unconditioned. That is, they occur without training and are referred to as *unconditioned stimulus,* or UCS, and *unconditioned response,* or UCR. After training, the new stimulus that elicits the response, such as the light signal, is a *conditioned stimulus* (CS). The reflex, formerly unconditioned, is conditioned to the new stimulus (light signal) and is referred to after training as a *conditioned response* (CR). Table 3-3 presents several examples of this type of conditioning.

The development of classical conditioning introduced a number of variables and new relationships that could be researched and precisely measured in the laboratory setting. Included are the amount or strength of the response (referred to as amplitude), the length of time between the stimulus and the response (latency), and the tendency of similar stimuli to elicit the reflex (stimulus generalization). For example, studies indi-

Table 3-3. Examples of Classical Conditioning

Preexperimental ("Natural") Relationship		Experimental Trials		Postexperimental (Conditioned) Relationship	
Unconditional (Eliciting) Stimulus (UCS)	Associated Reflex Response (UCR)	Paired Stimuli	Reflex Responses	Conditioned Stimulus (CS)	Conditioned Reflex (CR)
Meat powder	Salivation	Meat powder Tuning fork	Salivation	Tuning fork	Salivation
Air puff	Eye blink	Air puff Bright light	Eye blink	Bright light	Eye blink
Electric shock	Finger retraction	Electric shock Buzzer	Finger retraction	Buzzer	Finger retraction

cated that a reflex conditioned to a sound pitch of 256 is also conditioned to sound pitches of 255 and 257 (Murphy, 1949).

Two other relationships introduced in classical conditioning include resistance to extinction and inhibition. *Resistance to extinction* is the tendency of a response to persist after the supporting conditions are withdrawn; *inhibition* refers to the reduction in the response caused by the introduction of extraneous stimuli.

Classical conditioning represented a new approach to the study of behavior. It became the cornerstone of Watson's descriptions of learning and it established a new research direction in psychology.

John Watson's Behaviorism. Watson's contribution to psychology is that he organized the findings of current research into a new perspective and persuaded other psychologists of the importance of his views. Behaviorism, as Watson viewed it, should apply the techniques of animal research, conditioning, to the study of human beings. He therefore redefined mental concepts (which he considered to be unnecessary) as behavioral responses. Thinking, for example, was identified as subvocal speech, and feeling was defined as a glandular reaction (Watson, 1925).

Watson also believed that the human personality developed through the conditioning of various reflexes. He maintained that the human infant at birth possesses only three emotional responses (Watson, 1928). They are fear, rage, and love. The fear response, for example, begins with the jumping or starting of the body and an interruption in breathing. Then, depending on the infant's age, crying, falling, and crawling or running away follow. The fear response was observed in the natural environment after a loud noise or loss of support for the infant. According to Watson (1928), an adult's complex emotional life is the result of the conditioning of the three basic responses to a variety of situations.

Conditioning Experiments with Infants. Watson applied reflex conditioning to the emotional responses of infants. His subjects were infants who were hospitalized until approximately 2 years of age. In Watson's well-known experiment with Albert, the 11-month-old child's fear reaction was conditioned to several furry objects.

The reaction was conditioned first to the sight of a white rat. For several trials, the rat's appearance was paired with the sound of a hammer striking a steel bar. On the first trial (pairing of stimuli), the infant jumped violently, and on the second trial it began to cry. On the eighth trial, the white rat alone elicited crying and crawling away (Watson & Raynor, 1920). Five days later, the fear reaction also appeared in response to a white rabbit. Nonfurry objects, such as the child's blocks, did not elicit the fear response; however, mild fear reactions occurred in response to a dog and a sealskin fur coat. The child's emotional response had transferred to furry animals and objects, and it persisted for longer than a month.

Watson also experimented with the retraining or "unconditioning" of fear responses. Verbal discussions with the child or disuse (extended removal of the stimulus) were insufficient for eliminating the fear reaction. Instead, acceptance of the stimulus by other children and a planned program of accommodation were successful. Included, for example, was the gradual presentation of the stimulus during a favorite or enjoyable activity, such as eating (Watson, 1925).

Gestalt Theory

Unlike Thorndike's connectionism and Watson's behaviorism, Gestalt theory emphasized the importance of mental processes. The basis for Gestalt theory is that subjects react to "unitary meaningful wholes" (Koffka, 1935, p. 141). The Gestalt position is derived from the concept *Gestalt qualitat* or *form quality* described by Christian von Ehrenfels in 1890. The term refers to the particular quality possessed by a sonnet or painting that is not in the separate notes, colors, or words (Murphy, 1949). In other words, a melody played in another key (different individual notes) is perceived as the same melody.

The Gestalt position is reflected in the color-perception research of Wolfgang Köhler (1928, 1929). In these experiments, hens were presented equal amounts of grain on two papers of different shades of gray, but they were permitted to eat only from the darker shade. Following training, the hens were again presented with two papers of different shades. However, one was the original dark gray from the prior training and the other was a darker shade. In 59 of the 85 trials, the hens responded to the new dark shade. The hens had not learned an absolute response to a particular color, according to Köhler. Instead, they learned to respond to "relative brightness," referred to later as the *law of transformation.*

Laws of Perceptual Organization. In the Gestalt view, describing perceptual organization is the key to understanding learning. Four primary laws that govern the individual's perceptual organization of a stimulus situation were identified by Wertheimer (1938). Each law describes a characteristic of a visual field that influences perception. These characteristics are *proximity, similarity, open direction,* and *simplicity.* That is, the nearness of elements to each other (proximity), shared features such as color (similarity), the tendency of elements to complete a pattern (open direction), and the contributions of stimulus elements to a total simple structure (simplicity) are factors that govern the perception of groups from separate elements (see Figure 3-2).

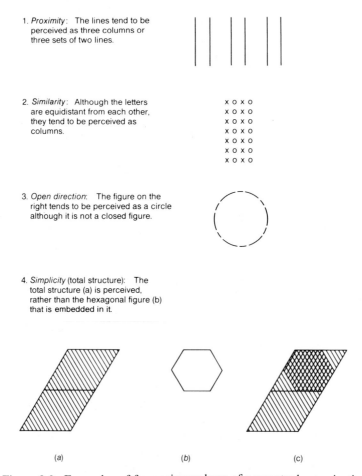

1. *Proximity*: The lines tend to be perceived as three columns or three sets of two lines.

2. *Similarity*: Although the letters are equidistant from each other, they tend to be perceived as columns.

```
x o x o
x o x o
x o x o
x o x o
x o x o
x o x o
x o x o
```

3. *Open direction*: The figure on the right tends to be perceived as a circle although it is not a closed figure.

4. *Simplicity* (total structure): The total structure (a) is perceived, rather than the hexagonal figure (b) that is embedded in it.

(a)   (b)   (c)

Figure 3-2. Examples of four primary laws of perceptual organization.

The laws of perceptual organization operate in conjunction with the general law of *Prägnanz*. That is, psychological events tend to be meaningful and complete and the foregoing laws influence the completeness.

Research on Learning. According to Gestalt theory, a change in the perceptual process is the basis for learning. This concept is illustrated by Wolfgang Köhler's experiments with anthropoid apes. Assigned by the Prussian Academy to the Canary Islands in World War I, Köhler conducted a variety of studies on learning.

The basic experimental situation included two components: food placed out of the animal's reach and a type of mechanism placed nearby. If properly utilized, the mechanism would help the animal obtain the food.

In the simplest experiment, food was hung from the roof near a scaffold. In other experiments food was placed outside the cage with a stick or dead branch nearby. In one complex situation, reaching the food required the fitting together of two separate sticks.

Köhler noted that when the stick, branch, or other mechanism was perceived by the animal as a tool, the problem was solved. This process is referred to in Gestalt psychology as *insight*. Köhler therefore maintained that the learning formula of "stimulus-response" should be replaced. Instead, he recommended that the learning formula should be "constellation of stimuli-organization-reaction to the results of the organization" (Köhler, 1929, p. 108).

Max Wertheimer's posthumous book *Productive Thinking* (1945) describes the application of Gestalt concepts to problem solving by human subjects. In one example, a group of children were asked to find the area of a parallelogram. Their only similar experience is that of finding the areas of rectangles. After some false starts, some children cut off the "triangle" at one end of the parallelogram and placed it on the other end, thereby forming a rectangle (see Figure 3-3). They then proceeded to solve for the area of the rectangle that they had just constructed. Others, however, perceived the rectangle formation in a different way. They cut the figure in half, inverted one of the halves, and placed the diagonal ends together to form a rectangle.

Each of the foregoing problems was solved by the subject's reorganization of the field and reorientation toward the field. Thus the phenomenon of insight is primarily one of perception. When the chimpanzees in Köhler's experiments "saw" that sticks or boxes could be used to obtain out-of-reach food, they had acquired insight.

The Gestalt psychologists also believed that perceptions were retained in memory in the form of "traces." That is, the neural processes active

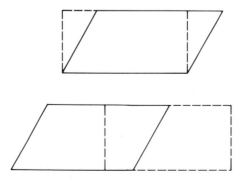

Figure 3-3. Children's solutions to the parallelogram problem.

during perception left traces in the brain tissues and the process of recall simply reactivated a particular trace. This concept of memory and recall is consistent with the Gestalt efforts to link perceptual processes to neurological events.

A Comparison of Thorndike's Connectionism, Classical Conditioning, and Gestalt Psychology

Each of the three learning theories developed in the early twentieth century differed from philosophical views of learning in three ways. First, the learning theories were developed from experimental observations of behavior. Second, they established, even if in rudimentary form, laws and principles that were testable. Third, they applied the principles to real-world situations. Thorndike applied his habit-formation theory to the analysis of school subjects, Watson conditioned fear reactions in infants, and Wertheimer extended Gestalt theory to children's problem solving.

Each of the three descriptions of learning was derived from a particular set of assumptions and a particular experimental procedure (see Table 3-4). Classical conditioning used stimulus substitution. Existing responses became associated with new stimuli by procedures that substituted one stimulus for another. In contrast, the conditions established in Thorndike's experiments favored the selection of one response over the others in repeated trials. The Gestalt theorists, on the other hand, presented the subjects with elements that could be rearranged or manipulated in various ways. Learning was therefore described as the result of perceptual reorganization.

Thorndike and the Gestalt psychologists differed primarily in their descriptions of the basic processes that occur during learning. Thorndike maintained that a connection was formed between the stimulus and the response, whereas the Gestalt theorists identified learning as insight.

Table 3-4 includes examples of each of the three learning theories. Note that the classical conditioning example illustrates the conditioning of the fear reaction. In contrast, a positive example of classical conditioning is the nostalgic reaction (response) to a song (conditioned stimulus) that was a hit during a former love affair. The song has acquired the power to elicit some of the same feelings originally associated with the person in the former relationship.

"Pure" examples of classical conditioning to aversive stimuli are difficult to find in the natural setting because individuals are not "trapped" by emotion-producing stimuli. Like Thorndike's cats, they may engage in escape behaviors that are then rewarded by a satisfying state of affairs. For example, Albert's fear responses of crying and whining (conditioned response) to the furry object (conditioned stimulus) was followed by

Table 3-4. Comparison of Three Perspectives on Learning

Characteristic	Thorndike's Connectionism	Behaviorism	Gestalt Psychology
Basic premise	Learning is the formation of connections between stimuli (thoughts, feelings, or movements) and responses (thoughts, feelings, or movements).	*Watson:* All organisms adjust to the environment; therefore, psychology should study behavior, not mental states.	Individuals react to unitary, meaningful wholes; therefore, learning involves a perceptual reorganization. The whole posesses emergent properties that differ from and of the elements.
Learning formula	Stimulus-response-reward situation.	Stimulus 1 ⎤—Response. Stimulus 2 ⎦	Constellation of stimuli-organization reaction.
Synonyms	Instrumental conditioning; trial-and-error learning.	Classical conditioning; stimulus substitution.	Insightful learning.
Experimental studies	Chicks, cats, and other animals escaped from confinement to obtain food reward.	*Pavlov's classical conditioning:* conditioned reflexes to arbitrary stimuli. *Watson:* conditioned emotional responses to arbitrary stimuli.	Chimpanzees, children, and college students were given problems to solve that required perceptual reorganization.
Example	Connections established between verbal stimuli and verbal responses; "9 + 5" (stimulus); "14" (response).	A spider is thrust in a child's face at the same time her friends scream and shout "Boo!" The next night, her friends scare her just when she turns down the bedcovers and finds a spider.	Task is to entwine the ends of two strings that are suspended from the ceiling. Only the end of one string can be reached by standing on a chair. Solution depends on perceiving the only piece of equipment, a pair of pliers, as a weight to make a pendulum of one string. The string is then swung to catch the other one.

43

crawling away (escape behavior). In the natural setting, the baby's mother would likely pick him up and comfort him, perhaps even rock him a few minutes. Thus, a selected response, the escape behavior of crawling away, is rewarded by receiving the mother's attention and comfort.

Classical conditioning, Thorndike's connectionism, and Gestalt psychology each raised new questions about the process of learning and each provided a basis for future developments. The laboratory conditioning of fear reactions and avoidance behaviors developed from the classical conditioning model, whereas Thorndike's instrumental-response model became the nucleus for B. F. Skinner's operant conditioning. Gestalt psychology kept alive the research on mental activities and contributed to the later development of cognitive psychology.

SUMMARY

At the beginning of the twentieth century, psychology was a new discipline faced with the problem of defining a mission, a scope of study, and a methodology for research. Two perspectives, structuralism and functionalism, proposed competing roles for the new science. Both the goal of identifying the elements of the mind (structuralism) and the goal of investigating the organism's adaptation to the environment (functionalism) were replaced by other views.

Structuralism gained few advocates, because its perspective was so narrow. Functionalism, however, was broad, diverse, and undisciplined. The dominant movement that emerged from the 1920s was behaviorism. Launched by John Watson in 1913, the movement demonstrated an easily understood methodology and held out the promise of developing a science of behavior. The major opponent to behaviorism, Gestalt psychology, emphasized the learner's mental activity in the perception and solution of difficult problems. Gestalt psychologists, through their emphasis on insight, established the beginnings of a cognitive psychology.

During the efforts to define the role and scope of psychology, learning came to be the primary research focus. Psychology emerged from the decade of the 1920s, quite without design, with three experimentally derived theories of learning: classical conditioning, Thorndike's connectionism, and Gestalt psychology. Classical conditioning linked responses to new stimuli, whereas Thorndike's connectionism (instrumental conditioning) linked new responses to a particular stimulus situation. In contrast, Gestalt psychologists recorded subjects' reactions to complex unstructured problems. The structuralists' method of introspection had been discarded, and new methods of laboratory research for the new science had been developed.

DISCUSSION QUESTIONS

1. Discussions of the origin of psychology have included the observation that psychology's founder did not use a "true" experimental method. What does this observation mean?
2. Why was functionalism supplanted by behaviorism?
3. What were Watson's telling points about behaviorism as a science that led to its popularity?
4. According to Gestalt psychology, what were the deficiencies of behaviorism?
5. What were the major differences between Thorndike's connectionism and classical conditioning?

REFERENCES

Angell, J. R. (1907). The province of functional psychology. *Psychological Review, 14,* 61–91.
Boring, E. G. (1950). *A history of experimental psychology* (2nd ed.). New York: Appleton-Century-Crofts.
Cushman, C. L., & Fox, G. (1938). Research and the public school curriculum. In G. Whipple (Ed.), *The scientific movement in education. The thirty-seventh yearbook of the National Society for the Study of Education, Part II,* (pp. 67–78). Chicago: University of Chicago Press.
Gates, A. (1938). Contributions of research on the general methods of education. In G. Whipple (Ed.), *The scientific movement in education. The thirty-seventh yearbook of the National Society for the Study of Education, Part II,* (pp. 79–80). Chicago: University of Chicago Press.
Koffka, K. (1922). Perception: An introduction to the Gestalt-theorie. *Psychological Bulletin, 19,* 531–585.
Koffka, K. (1935). *Principles of Gestalt psychology.* New York: Harcourt Brace.
Köhler, W. (1928). Chapter VII. Intelligence in apes. Chapter VIII. An aspect of Gestalt psychology. In C. Murchison (Ed.), *Psychologies of 1925* (pp. 145–195). Worcester, MA: Clark University Press.
Köhler, W. (1929). *Gestalt psychology.* New York: Horace Liveright.
Mueller, C. G. (1979). Some origins of psychology as a science. *Annual Review of Psychology, 30,* 9–39.

Murphy, G. (1949). *Historical introduction to modern psychology.* New York: Harcourt Brace & World.

Thorndike, E. L. (1905). *The elements of psychology.* New York: A. G. Seiler.

Thorndike, E. L. (1911). *Animal intelligence.* New York: Macmillan.

Thorndike, E. L. (1913a). *Educational psychology: Vol. I. The original nature of man.* New York: Teacher's College Press.

Thorndike, E. L. (1913b). *Educational psychology: Vol. II. The psychology of learning.* New York: Teacher's College Press.

Thorndike, E. L. (1924). Mental discipline in high school studies. *Journal of Educational Psychology, 15,* 1–22, 83–98.

Thorndike, E. L. (1965). *Animal intelligence: Experimental studies* (facsimile of 1911 edition). New York: Hafner.

Thorndike, E. L., & Woodworth, R. S. (1901). The influence of improvement in one mental function upon the efficiency of other functions: I, II, & III. *Psychological Review, 8,* 247–261, 384–395, 553–564.

Watson, J. B. (1913). Psychology as the behaviorist views it. *Psychological Bulletin, 20,* 158–177.

Watson, J. B. (1925). *Behaviorism.* New York: W. W. Norton.

Watson, J. B. (1928). Chapter I. What the nursery has to say about instincts. Chapter II. Experimental studies on the growth of emotions. In C. Murchison (Ed.), *Psychologies of 1925* (pp. 1–37). Worcester, MA: Clark University Press.

Watson, J. B., & Raynor, R. (1920). Conditioned emotional reactions. *Journal of Experimental Psychology, 3,* 1–14.

Watson, R. I. (1963). *The great psychologists* (4th ed.). Philadelphia: J. B. Lippincott.

Wertheimer, M. (1938). Laws of organization in perceptual forms. In. W. Ellis (Ed.), *A source book of Gestalt psychology* (pp. 71–88). New York: Harcourt Brace.

Wertheimer, M. (1945). *Productive thinking.* New York: Harper & Brothers.

CHAPTER 4

Theory Development
and the Dynamics of Learning

Man is powerless without structure and
unable to conceive without imposing some
order, no matter how poor it is in capturing
the qualities of the world.
Posner, 1973, p. 169

The development of connectionism, classical conditioning, and Gestalt
theory in the early twentieth century presented psychologists and educators with competing explanations of learning. The next two decades,
from 1930 to approximately 1950, were dominated by further laboratory
research by proponents of each perspective. The goal was to develop the
one comprehensive theory that would explain all learning. These efforts
have been described as psychology's period of self-consciousness and
concern about the nature of the science (Mueller, 1979). This period has
also been described as a change in focus from the issue of coverage in
the 1920s to that of consistency in the 1930s (Boring, 1963b).

THE RETREAT TO THE LABORATORY (1930–1950)

Early in the twentieth century, Edward Thorndike cautioned his fellow
psychologists that the proper laboratory for research was the classroom
and the appropriate experimental subject was the student (Shulman,
1970). For the most part, however, the learning theorists of this period
ignored Thorndike's advice. Research was conducted instead on animals
and human beings in artificially contrived situations: Rats ran mazes, rats

escaped from boxes, and human subjects were given puzzles to solve. This period was characterized for the most part by refinements in the basic behaviorist and Gestalt concepts.

The Refinement of Behaviorism

The dominant movement in the 1930s and 1940s continued to be behaviorism. However, it was by no means a unitary theory, nor was it the only approach to behavioral analysis. Some psychologists, influenced by Sigmund Freud's psychoanalytic theory, were searching for deeper meanings in behavior beyond observed relationships between events and responses. Included were Robert Woodworth's "dynamic psychology" and William McDougall's "hormic psychology." McDougall described "drives" as behavioral activators. For example, the "thirst drive" activates the go-to-water mechanism (Boring, 1963a, p. 723). In contrast, McDougall developed an extensive list of instincts that he identified as goal directed. Included were flight, fear, reproduction, and others.

Clark Hull (1935, p. 491), a Yale psychologist, reviewed the status of theory in psychology in the early 1930s. He noted that

We find earnestly defending themselves against a world of enemies, a hormic psychology, an act psychology, a functional psychology, a structural psychology, a Gestalt psychology, a reflexology psychology, a behavioristic psychology, a dynamic psychology, a factor psychology, a psychoanalytic psychology, and a psychology of dialectical materialism—at least a dozen.

Concerned about the number of competing positions, Hull proposed a rigorous method of theory development. Referred to as the *hypothetico-deductive method* (Hull, 1935, 1937), it was applied by Hull in the development of his behavioral system (see the later discussion of Hull's system). Others, however, continued to develop theory in a less rigorous manner. B. F. Skinner, in fact, disregarded theory development completely because he regarded it as counterproductive to scientific progress in psychology.

Three theories emerged from the 1930s and 1940s. They are Clark Hull's behavior system, Edwin Guthrie's contiguity theory, and B. F. Skinner's operant conditioning. They are referred to as *S-R theories* because they define learning as an associative link between a particular stimulus and a particular response. They differ, however, in the identification of the specific factors believed to be of primary importance in learning. Hull's theory emphasized processes within the organism, specifically, intervening variables. Edwin Guthrie, however, maintained that the temporal relationship between the stimulus and the response was the critical factor in learning. B. F. Skinner, on the other hand, began with Edward Thorndike's law of effect, redefined "reward" as reinforcement, and described behavioral change as a function of response consequences. These three theorists also are referred to as "neobehaviorists," to distinguish their work from that of Edward Thorndike and John Watson.

The dominant theory into the 1940s was Clark Hull's system. It was later refined by Kenneth Spence (1956) and some of the concepts were applied to the analysis of maladaptive behavior by John Dollard and Neal Miller (1950). Hull's theory, however, was eclipsed by B. F. Skinner's principles (discussed in Chapter 6). The complexity of Hull's system was one factor. In the final version, the theory included 16 postulates and 133 theorems! In addition, Skinner applied his principles to the world of classroom learning, whereas Hull's theory was limited to the laboratory.

The Gestalt Influence

The major opposition to behaviorism continued to be Gestalt psychology. Although Jean Piaget's cognitive-development theory was introduced in the 1930s, it did not gain widespread acceptance.

The Gestalt influence, however, was more indirect than direct. The Gestalt psychologists tended to view the variables operating in a situation as interdependent and they concentrated on describing the ongoing processes. This perspective fit poorly with a psychology intent on scientific progress through the manipulation of independent and dependent variables in order to identify cause-effect relationships.

Stated somewhat differently, the search for deeper meanings in otherwise surface phenomena was not viewed as an important goal by most psychologists. Some charged that "more progress would be made if the Gestaltists spent a smaller proportion of their time asking, 'What do these facts mean?' and a larger proportion of their time trying to answer the question, 'What are the facts?'" (Leeper, 1943, p. 27).

A second reason for the diffused impact was the lack of a systematic set of learning principles. Hilgard (1964a) notes that the book *Productive Thinking* is rich with descriptive detail. However, the critical analysis and follow-up essential for a complete theory were not forthcoming.

The Gestalt theorists, however, continued with research on problem solving (see the next section) and two theories were also influenced by Gestalt concepts. One is Edward Tolman's purposive behaviorism. The other is Kurt Lewin's field theory, which is a theory of personality development and motivation. Although not accepted in the "inner circle" of Gestalt psychologists, Lewin's work initiated group dynamics and furthered the study of social psychology.

Table 4-1 summarizes the major events of this period. During the 1940s, the major threat to Hull's theory came from Edward Tolman. Both were overshadowed, however, by B. F. Skinner in the late 1950s.

Table 4-1. Summary of Some Major Events in Learning Theory
(1930–1950)

	1930 Tolman and Honzik's experiment on learning and performance
	1932 Edward Tolman's "purposive behaviorism" is published
1935 Clark Hull's discussion of the importance of rigorous theory	
1935 Guthrie introduces contiguity theory	
	1936 Kurt Lewin's principles of field theory published
1937 Clark Hull's hypothetico-deductive method proposed	
1938 Skinner publishes principles of operant conditioning	
1942 Guthrie describes contiguity theory for educators	1942 Lewin's field theory described for educators
	1942 Luchins' problem-solving research using water-jar problems
1943 Hull's behavior system published	
	1945 Karl Duncker's research on insight
1946 Guthrie's puzzle-box experiments with cats	1946 Tolman's research into spatial learning of rats
1948 Skinner publishes *Walden Two*	
	1949 Tolman's identification of several types of learning

TWO PERSPECTIVES REFINED

The theories developed during this period polarized the original differences between behaviorism and Gestalt psychology. No theory succeeded in describing adequately all aspects of the learning experience.

Two S-R Theories

Clark Hull's behavioral system and Edwin Guthrie's contiguity theory are in sharp contrast to each other. Hull's theory is rigorous, abstract, and complex; whereas Guthrie's theory, on the other hand, is informal and loosely organized. Practical advice for parents and teachers was also included in Guthrie's work.

Clark Hull's Behavior System. Hull's theory is an example of the rigorous method that he recommended for theory development, the hypothetico-deductive method. Application of this procedure was intended to lead to the identification of the primary laws of psychology (Hull, 1935).

The Hypothetico-deductive Method. The starting point for a theory, according to Hull (1935) is a set of explicitly stated assumptions or postulates and operational definitions of basic terms. Then propositions (hypotheses) are deduced from the postulates with careful rigor, documenting the process of deduction. The propositions, however, do not become a part of the theory until they pass the test of controlled experimentation. In Hull's view (1937, p. 8), "whenever a theorem fails to check with the relevant facts, the postulates which give rise to it must be ruthlessly revised until agreement is reached. If agreement cannot be attained, the system must be abandoned."

Hull (1937) also reminded his colleagues of the advantages of theoretical systems over philosophical systems. Both are derived from basic assumptions and both include hypothetical statements. However, only theories can be verified through scientific investigation. Therefore, only theories can contribute to the development of empirical knowledge.

Major Concepts. Influenced by the concept of evolution, Hull (1943) maintained that behavior functions to ensure the organism's survival. Therefore, the central concepts in his theory revolve around biological needs and need satisfaction, which is essential for survival. Needs were conceptualized by Hull (1943, 1952) as "drives," such as hunger, thirst, sleep, relief from pain, and others. Stimuli, referred to as *drive stimuli* (S^D), are associated with primary drives and therefore "motivate" behavior. For example, stimuli associated with pain, such as the sounds of a dentist's drill, can also arouse fear, and the fear motivates behavior.

Reinforcement was also incorporated into the theory; however, reinforcement is a biological condition. Satisfaction of the biological need, referred to as *drive reduction*, strengthens the link between the drive stimulus and the response.

The strength of an S-R link or habit can be measured on a 100-point scale. Since learning is incremental, according to Hull (1943), habit strength increases to a maximum of 1.00.

Also included in the system are concepts such as incentive, generalized habit strength, the power of a stimulus to elicit a particular response, and others. However, the efforts to develop one verified system using laboratory-derived variables resulted in a complex theory that did not generalize to the learning setting beyond the laboratory.

Edwin Guthrie's Contiguity Theory. A refreshing contrast to the other theories of this period is provided by contiguity theory. The one major learning principle is the *law of contiguity*; that is, a combination of stimuli accompanied by a movement will tend to be followed by the same movement on its recurrence (Guthrie, 1952, p. 23).

Guthrie also differentiated between movements and acts. Movements are muscle contractions and acts are combinations of movements. Examples of acts are drawing a picture, reading a book, and so on. Acts also are the components of skills, such as playing golf or typewriting. Although a single movement may be acquired in one learning trial, time and practice are required to learn all the associations in a skill.

Reinforcement, however, is not an essential factor in learning. Instead, learning occurs because the last movement that is made changes the stimulus situation and no other response can occur. For example, in solving a puzzle, the last action changes the stimulus (i.e., completes the puzzle). Therefore, in the same situation again, the same response will be repeated. Reinforcement simply protects the new learning from unlearning by preventing the acquisition of new responses (Guthrie, 1942, 1952).

Breaking Habits. A habit is defined in the theory as a response that is associated with several different stimuli (Guthrie, 1952). The greater the number of associations, the stronger the habit because the response is "cued" on many different occasions. Smoking is an example of a strong habit because so many different cues trigger lighting up a cigarette. Included are finishing a meal, taking a coffee break, sitting down with the evening paper, and so on.

Breaking habits requires breaking the associations between the cues (eliciting stimuli) and the response. The three methods suggested by Guthrie (1938) are the threshold method, the fatigue method, and the incompatible response method.

These three methods are summarized in Table 4-2. They are equivalent, according to Guthrie (1938, p. 62) because they all involve presenting the cues that elicit a particular response while preventing the performance of the response.

Uses of Punishment. An important role for punishment in altering

Table 4-2. Summary of Three Methods for Breaking Habits

Method	Characteristics	Example
Threshold method	1. Introduce the eliciting stimulus at weak strength 2. Gradually increase the stimulus strength, always keeping it below the response "threshold" (i.e., strength that will elicit the response)	*Breaking a horse to the saddle:* Begin with a light blanket, then heavier blankets, and finally, a light saddle
Fatigue method	"Exhaust" the response in the presence of the eliciting stimulus	*Breaking a horse:* Throw the saddle on the horse and ride him until he quits kicking, backing, and trying to throw the rider; the saddle and rider become the stimulus for walking and trotting calmly
Incompatible response method	Pair the eliciting stimulus (S^1) for the inappropriate behavior with a stimulus (S^2) that elicits appropriate responses; the appropriate behavior associated with S^2 becomes linked to S^1	Overcome fear and avoidance by pairing the frightening object such as a large toy tiger, with a stimulus that elicits warm feelings, such as mother

behavior is identified by Guthrie (1952). Punishment, if delivered appropriately in the presence of a stimulus that elicits inappropriate behavior, can cause the subject to do something different. Guthrie (1935) describes the example of the girl who came home repeatedly from school each day and threw her hat and coat on the floor. The girl's mother made her put her hat and coat back on, go back outside, come in again, and hang up her wraps. After a few occasions, the response of hanging up the coat and hat became associated with the stimulus of entering the house.

Suggestions for Educators. Associating stimuli and responses appropriately is the core of Guthrie's advice to teachers. The student must be led to perform what is to be learned. Students, in other words, learn only what the stimuli in lectures or books cause them to do (Guthrie, 1942, p. 55). Therefore, if students use notes or textbooks simply to memorize quantities of information, books will be the stimuli that cue rote learning.

In managing the classroom, the teacher is cautioned not to give a directive that is permitted to be disobeyed. A request for silence, if followed by a disturbance, will become the cue for disruptive behavior.

Contributions Derived from Gestalt Concepts

The research on problem solving by Gestalt theorists yielded two new phenomena in relation to problem-solving abilities. In addition, Edward Tolman's purposive behaviorism and Kurt Lewin's field theory are examples of the Gestalt "holistic" view of behavior.

Functional Fixedness and Problem Set. The phenomenon of *functional fixedness*, researched by Karl Duncker (1945), refers to the inability of the problem solver to perceive elements of a situation in a new relationship or a new way. In the problem described in Table 3-2, for example, a student is asked to tie together two strings suspended from the ceiling. The solution depends on the student's perception of the pliers as a weight in the creation of a pendulum. Failure to "see" the new use for the pliers is the phenomenon described as functional fixedness.

A related concept is *problem set* or *Einstellung*, which was identified by Abraham Luchins (1942). He devised the well-known water jar problems in which individuals are given two or three jars of different capacities. The learners are next asked to measure a particular amount of water. The solution requires pouring certain amounts of water from one jar to another (see Table 4-3).

Luchins demonstrated that in a series of such problems, already learned strategies typically produced rigidity in the selection of problem solutions. Table 4-3 illustrates a typical situation. After solving problems 2 through 6, students from kindergarten to college age used the same solution for problems 7 and 8. However, a simpler strategy solves both problems (Wertheimer, 1980).

Edward Tolman's Purposive Behaviorism. Referring to his theory as "a subvariety of Gestalt psychology," Tolman (1932, p. 330) believed that behavior is goal directed. Learning is not the acquisition of S-R connections. Instead, the subject learns the critical events that lead to some goal, referred to as a "sign-gestalt-expectation." For example, Pavlov's dogs learned that "waiting-in-the-presence-of-sound" leads to food. According to Tolman, learning occurs because the subjects bring certain expectancies to the learning situation. Confirmed expectancies are the ones that survive.

Latent Learning. Tolman and his associates designed several ingenious experiments that challenged the concepts in S-R theory. In one experiment, three different groups of rats ran a maze on 10 successive days. One group received food at the end of each run and another group received no food. The third group, however, received no food for the first 10 days, but were fed from the goalbox on the 11th day. For the

Table 4-3. Series of Water Jar Problems on Problem Set

Problem	Solution
1. *Task:* Measure 20 units of water *Given:* Jug A = 29 units; B = 3 units	Fill Jar A and pour off into B three times: $29 - (3 \times 3) = 20$ $A - 3B$
2. *Task:* Measure 100 units *Given:* Jug A = 21 units, B = 127, C = 3	Fill Jar B, pour off into A, and then fill C twice from jar A $B - A - 2C$ or $127 - 21 - 6 = 100$
3. *Task:* Measure 99 units *Given:* A = 14 units, B = 163, C = 25	Same as above: $B - A - 2C$
4. *Task:* Measure 5 units *Given:* A = 18, B = 43, C = 10	$B - A - 2C$
5. *Task:* Measure 21 units *Given:* A = 9, B = 42, C = 6	$B - A - 2C$
6. *Task:* Measure 31 units *Given:* A = 20, B = 59, C = 4	$B - A - 2C$
7. *Task:* Measure 20 units *Given:* A = 23, B = 49, C = 3	$A - C$
8. *Task:* Measure 18 units *Given:* A = 15, B = 39, C = 3	$A + C$

Source: Summarized from Wertheimer (1980, p. 239).

remaining 6 days of the experiment, the error rate of this group fell dramatically and was not significantly different from that of the group rewarded daily with food (Tolman & Honzik, 1930).

This experiment demonstrated that the subjects "learned" from being fed from the goalbox. That is, running the maze and receiving the food reward for the maze-running performance was not essential for learning. In other words, learning and performance are not synonymous. This phenomenon is referred to as *latent learning*.

Cognitive Learning. Tolman (1932) maintained that subjects learn "cognitive maps" of the environment. One study compared the perform-ance of two groups of rats, referred to as the "response learners" and the "place learners." The food reward for the response learners was located in different places on different days; however, they always had to turn in only one direction (right or left) to find the food. In contrast, the food reward for the place learners was always in the same place. However, they were started through the maze at different points; there-fore, to find the reward they had to take different routes (see Figure 4-

1). The performance of the place learners was superior, supporting the hypothesis that learners acquire cognitive maps of the environment (Tolman, Ritchie, & Kalish, 1946).

The use of rats to demonstrate cognitive learning was defended by Tolman. Rats "do not go on binges the night before one has planned an experiment; they do not kill each other off in wars; . . . they avoid politics, economics, and papers on psychology. They are marvelous, pure, and delightful" (Tolman, 1949, p. 166).

Kurt Lewin's Field Theory. Unlike the other theorists of this period, Kurt Lewin was interested primarily in motivation. The focus of his theory is the interpretation of the changes that result from psychological forces. Theoretical analysis begins with the situation, referred to as the individual's *life space,* and proceeds to identify the interacting psychological forces that influence behavior.

The basic concept in Lewin's theory is that "to understand or predict the psychological behavior (B) one has to determine for every kind of psychological event (actions, emotions, expressions, etc.), the momentary whole situation, that is, the momentary structure and state of the person (P) and of the psychological environment (E). $B = f(P, E)$"

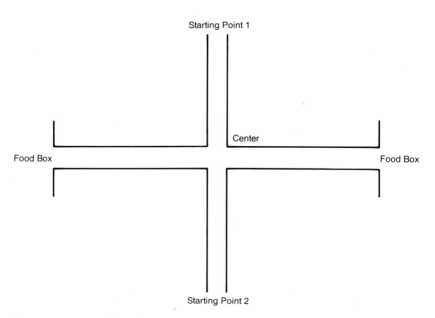

Figure 4-1. Maze with different starting points used in Tolman's latent learning experiments.

(Lewin, 1933, p. 598). In other words, behavior is a function of the person and the psychological environment.

Important terms for concepts in the theory were taken from the physical sciences. The intent was to portray psychological forces in much the same way as physical forces are described. Psychological forces include (1) tendencies to move toward or away from some object or event, and (2) restraining forces which are obstacles. The need to be liked by adults, for example, results in a psychological force that directs a shy child's responsiveness to the teacher. Similarly, for an adolescent, the need for peer approval may block a student's positive interaction with the teacher.

Vectors (→) were used by Lewin to indicate moving psychological forces within a life space. Further, regions in the life space may be of positive or negative valence. That is, they may either attract (+, or positive, valence) or repel (−, or negative, valence) the individual. A rattle held before a 6-month-old infant, for example, typically has a positive valence. It attracts the baby's attention, indicated by eye movements as well as active leg and arm movements (Lewin, 1933).

Conflict Situations. The concepts of positive and negative valence are illustrated in Lewin's classification of the three basic conflict situations. Hilgard (1964a) noted that the three types of conflict became so commonly accepted that secondary sources occasionally were credited for the idea.

The three types are (1) approach-approach, (2) approach-avoidance, and (3) avoidance-avoidance. They are illustrated in Figure 4-2. Lewin (1933) notes that if the punishment in situation 3 is to be effective, it must restrict the child's movement so that only the disagreeable task can be performed.

Motivational Learning. Lewin distinguished between learning information and motivational learning. Saying that "the spastic child has to learn to relax" is quite different from "learning French vocabulary," which also has little in common with "learning to like spinach." Therefore, we should not expect identical laws to hold for these different processes (Lewin, 1936, p. 220). Lewin also coined the term *cognitive structure* to differentiate knowledge learning from motivational learning. The term was then used by Tolman and later was adopted by cognitive psychology (see Chapter 8).

A Comparison of the S-R and Cognitive Theories

The four theories developed during the 1930s and 1940s are summarized in Table 4-4. Although the goal was to develop the one comprehensive theory that would explain all learning, these efforts were unsuccessful.

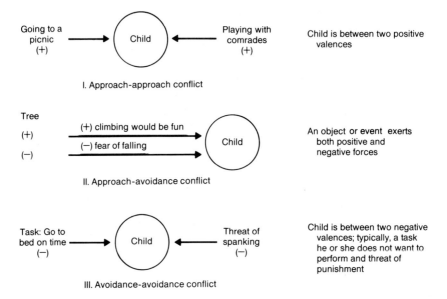

Figure 4-2. Examples of Lewin's three types of conflict situations.

Rather than consensus on the critical factors involved in learning, a greater diversity resulted.

As early as the 1940s, the conflict between the S-R and Gestalt positions was criticized for its nonproductivity. Two practices contributed to this problem (McConnell, 1942). First, the terms used by each of the theories magnified the differences among them. For example, the terms "insight" and "connection" represent extreme descriptions of the learning process. McConnell noted that the difficulty of the task set before the learner may be a major factor in the learning process that is ultimately described by the theorist. That is, if the task is so difficult that the learner cannot establish relationships within the situation, the subject must resort to trial and error. On the other hand, presenting fairly easy tasks similar to past experience may be reacted to quickly and accurately by the learner. Therefore, what may be described as flashes of insight by the Gestalt theorists also can be included under transfer through identical elements (McConnell, 1942, p. 246).

Second, differences in descriptions of the learning process arise, in part, from differences in the experimental context. Learning tasks can be arranged on a continuum according to the amount of discovery of the correct response that is required. At one end is rote learning, represented by the simple conditioning experiments. At the other end are complicated unstructured situations that require the learner's reorganization of past

Table 4-4. Comparison of the S-R and Cognitive Theories

Characteristic	Hall's Behavioral System	Guthrie's Contiguity Theory	Tolman's Purposive Behaviorism	Lewin's Field Theory
Basic premise	Behavior may be explained in terms of biological needs and need reduction	The temporal relationship between stimulus and response is the critical factor	Learning is essentially the acquisition of "cognitive maps" which direct behavior	Psychological forces in the individual's life space are activators of behavior
Learning formula	Drive stimuli (S^D) are associated with particular responses through need satisfaction (drive reduction)	Provide repeated associations of appropriate stimuli with desired responses	Organism brings various hypotheses to the learning situation; confirmed hypotheses (those that lead to goal attainment) survive	$B = f(P, E)$
Role of reinforcement	Drive reduction functions as reinforcement; habit strength increases through reinforcement	Reinforcement is not essential for learning; the last movement alters the situation and no other responses can occur; reinforcement simply protects the prior learning for unlearning	Not discussed in S-R sense; confirmation of expectancies leads to "beliefs" that certain "signs" (stimuli) will be followed by certain other signs (stimuli)	Not applicable; positive and negative forces interacting with the individual's needs and abilities are initiators of behavior

experience and the discovery of the appropriate behavior pattern (McConnell, 1942).

The most serious problem for educational practice, however, was that the theory development of this period did not clarify guidelines for instruction. The one exception is Guthrie's methods for breaking habits. The variables discussed by the other theorists, however, were not easily identifiable in the classroom context. Important classroom variables include ways to motivate student interest, methods of maintaining student attention, sequencing instruction, and others. Drive reduction, response latency, goal valence, and other similar variables are only remotely related to the planning and implementation of effective instruction.

As the decade of the 1950s approached, interest in the development of all-encompassing theory declined. An awareness that perhaps learning was more than a single process was being expressed. One example is Tolman's analysis in 1945 of six different kinds of learning. Hilgard (1964b) in his review of the end of this period of theory development, commented that the "great debate" among comprehensive theories was now over.

SUMMARY

The period from 1930 to World War II was a period in which laboratory research was dominant. The dichotomy between behaviorism and Gestalt psychology continued, and each group attempted to explain the whole of learning within one theory. The behaviorist theories of this period are identified as S-R theories because they described learning as a link between a stimulus and a response. Included are Clark Hull's hypothetico-deductive system, Edwin Guthrie's contiguity learning, and B. F. Skinner's operant conditioning. These theorists are also referred to as neobehaviorists, to distinguish their work from that of Thorndike, Pavlov, and Watson. Although Hull's system was dominant during the 1940s, it was eclipsed by Skinner's principles in the 1950s.

In contrast to the S-R theorists, the Gestalt psychologists failed to develop a systematic set of learning principles. Research continued into the phenomenon of insight; included were Max Wertheimer's investigations of children's problem solving, Karl Duncker's identification of functional fixedness, and Abraham Luchins' investigations of problem set.

The Gestalt perspective also influenced the work of two other theorists: Edward Tolman and Kurt Lewin. Tolman described the study of behavior within a Gestalt framework and added the terms *latent learning* and *cognitive structure* to psychology. Lewin developed a dynamic theory of motivation that described psychological forces as the key to understanding behavior.

Few guidelines for instruction were generated by this work, however. With the exception of Lewin's theory, which initiated research on group dynamics, the other theories were bypassed in the next few years by other developments.

REFERENCES

Boring, E. G. (1963a). *A history of experimental psychology* (2nd ed.). New York: Appleton-Century-Crofts.

Boring, E. G. (1963b). *History psychology, and science: Selected papers.* New York: Wiley.

Dollard, J., & Miller, N. E. (1950). *Personality and psychotherapy.* New York: McGraw-Hill.

Duncker, K. (1945). On problem solving. *Psychological Monographs, 58* (Whole No. 270).

Guthrie, E. R. (1935). *The psychology of learning.* New York: Harper & Brothers.

Guthrie, E. R. (1938). *The psychology of human conflict.* New York: Harper & Brothers.

Guthrie, E. R. (1942). Conditioning: A theory of learning in terms of stimulus, response, and association. In N. B. Henry (Ed.), *The psychology of learning. The forty-first yearbook of the National Society for the Study of Education, Part II,* (pp. 17–60). Chicago: University of Chicago Press.

Guthrie, E. R. (1952). *The psychology of learning.* New York: Harper & Row.

Hilgard, E. R. (1964a). The place of Gestalt psychology and field theories in contemporary learning theory. In E. R. Hilgard (Ed.), *Theories of learning and instruction. The sixty-third yearbook of the National Society for the Study of Education* (pp. 45–77). Chicago: University of Chicago Press.

Hilgard, E. R. (1964b). Postscript: Twenty years of learning theory in relation to education. In E. R. Hilgard (Ed.), *Theories of learning and instruction. The sixty-third yearbook of the National Society for the Study of Education* (pp. 416–418). Chicago: University of Chicago Press.

Hull, C. L. (1935). Conflicting psychologies of learning: A way out. *Psychological Review, 42,* 491–516.

Hull, C. L. (1937). Mind, mechanism, and adaptive behavior. *Psychological Review, 44,* 1–32.

Hull, C. L. (1943). *The principles of behavior.* New York: Appleton-Century-Crofts.

Hull, C. L. (1952). *A behavior system.* New Haven, CT: Yale University Press.

Leeper, R. W. (1943). *Lewin's topological and vector psychology: A digest and a critique.* Eugene, OR: University of Oregon Press.

Lewin, K. (1933). Environmental influences. In C. Murchison (Ed.), *A handbook of child psychology* (2nd ed., pp. 590–625). Worchester, MA: Clark University Press.

Lewin, K. (1936). *Principles of topological psychology.* New York: McGraw-Hill.

Lewin, K. (1942). Field theory of learning. In N. B. Henry (Ed.), *The psychology of learning. The forty-first yearbook of the National Society for the Study of Education, Part II* (pp. 215–242). Chicago: University of Chicago Press.

Luchins, A. S. (1942). Mechanization in problem solving: The effect of Einstellung. *Psychological Monographs, 54* (Whole No. 248).

McConnell, T. R. (1942). Reconciliation of learning theories. In N. B. Henry (Ed.), *The psychology of learning. The forty-first yearbook of the National Society for the Study of Education* (pp. 371–401). Chicago: University of Chicago Press.

Mueller, C. G. (1979). Some origins of psychology as a science. *Annual Review of Psychology, 30,* 9–39.

Posner, M. I. (1973). Cognition: Natural and artificial. In R. L. Solso (Ed.), *Contemporary issues in cognitive psychology* (pp. 167–174). Washington, D.C.: Winston.

Shulman, L. (1970). Reconstruction of educational research. *Review of Educational Research, 40,* 371–396.

Spence, K. W. (1956). *Behavior therapy and conditioning.* New Haven, CT: Yale University Press.

Tolman, E. C. (1932). *Purposive behavior in animals and men.* New York; Appleton-Century-Crofts.

Tolman, E. C. (1949). There is more than one kind of learning. *Psychological Review, 56,* 144–155.

Tolman, E. C., & Honzik, C. H. (1930). Introduction and removal of reward, and maze performance in rats. *University of California Publications in Psychology, 4,* 257–275.

Tolman, E. C., Ritchie, B. F., & Kalish, D. (1946). Studies in spatial learning, II. *Journal of Experimental Psychology, 36,* 221–229.

Wertheimer, M. (1980). Gestalt theory of learning. In G. M. Gazda & R. J. Corsini (Eds.), *Theories of learning* (pp. 208–251). Itasca, IL.: F. E. Peacock.

Learning and Instruction

Theories are nets to catch what we call
"the world;" to rationalize, to explain,
and to master it. We endeavor to make the
mesh ever finer and finer.
Popper, 1968, p. 59

Efforts in the 1940s to build a "pure" comprehensive theory were reaching a dead end when the need to solve other educational problems became a national priority. Designing effective instruction for military training needs became a priority in World War II. This event, followed by the curriculum redesign efforts after the Soviet Union's launch of *Sputnik*, redirected attention to the classroom.

B. F. Skinner's behaviorism, developed in the 1930s, was the only neobehaviorist theory to make the transition from the laboratory to classroom practice. Although dominant in the late 1950s and 1960s, Skinner's principles were gradually overtaken by cognitive issues in the 1970s. In the 1980s, instructional psychology is primarily cognitive (Resnick, 1981) and experimental psychology is almost synonymous with cognitive psychology (Hilgard, 1980a).

THE CLASSROOM AND THE "NEW COGNITION"

The years from 1950 to the present may be roughly divided into two periods. The first is the shift from laboratory research to instructionally relevant research, from 1950 to approximately 1975. The second, from 1975 to the present, may be described as the "new cognition."

The Shift from the Laboratory to the Classroom (1950–1975)

The two major trends in this period are (1) the emergence of instructional psychology, and (2) the influence of B. F. Skinner's behaviorism.

The Beginning of Instructional Psychology. The military training problems of World War II included the operation of sophisticated equipment. Such complex training tasks challenged existing concepts of learning developed in the laboratory. Examples include training for aircraft gunners, radio operators, and trouble shooters (Gagné, 1962a). Specifically, the recommended learning principles of reinforcement, distribution of practice, and response familiarity did not lead to successful instruction (Gagné, 1962a). Instead, efforts to design effective instruction indicated that topic sequencing and providing instruction on component tasks enhanced learning (Gagné, 1962a). These concepts were later developed by Robert Gagné into hierarchies of skills, the basis for his theory of conditions of learning (see Chapter 7).

Although initiated by military training needs, instructional research did not become a major priority until the late 1950s. The precipitating event was the successful launch of the space capsule *Sputnik* by the Soviet Union in 1957. This technological feat by a Cold War opponent was viewed by the American public as a failure of the country's educational system. The intensity of the international power struggle had magnified the role of education as the guardian of a free society's scholarship and technological achievement.

Curriculum Redesign. The launch of *Sputnik* sparked a massively funded curriculum reform in the United States. In general, the new curricula were to produce disciplined thinkers through discovery learning and student involvement. The learning of isolated facts was to be discarded. Mathematics, science, and foreign languages, subjects identified as essential to national security, were targeted first for development.

Subsequent legislation extended the role of the federal government in education. Included were the Elementary and Secondary Education Act (ESEA) and the Economic Opportunity Act. Funds were provided for special programs for disadvantaged children, the development of innovative programs, 10 university research and development centers, and 19 regional laboratories (ESEA). The preschool compensatory program, Head Start, was funded by the Economic Opportunity Act. Later, Follow Through projects for disadvantaged children in the elementary grades were also established.

The new emphasis on curriculum development attracted subject matter experts, psychologists, social scientists, and educators. Research on classroom learning, formerly regarded as less prestigious than "pure" laboratory research, became legitimate.

The Need for Instructional Theory. Faced with the problem of curriculum redesign for thinking skills, researchers expressed the need for an instructional technology. Such a technology would translate learning theory into educational practice (see Bruner, 1964; Hilgard, 1980b). Learning theory was described as no more capable of dictating instructional activities than the science of thermodynamics can predict whether a particular airplane will be jet propelled or propeller driven (Hilgard, 1980b). That is, answers to the question "How does learning occur?" do not answer the question "How does instruction facilitate learning?"

Jerome Bruner (1960) called for an instructional theory that would describe principles for the design of effective classroom instruction. In Bruner's view (1964), a theory of learning is descriptive, whereas a theory of instruction is prescriptive. For example, learning theory may describe the optimum age at which addition is learned, whereas instructional theory prescribes the ways to teach addition.

The impact of the curriculum redesign effort was less than originally expected. However, the new focus on instructional research led to the identification of a new area in psychology. Introduced in 1969 as instructional psychology (see Gagné & Rohwer, 1969), the area includes the interests of educators, curriculum design teams, psychologists, sociologists, and others.

Four theoretical perspectives applicable to the classroom gained prominence in this period. One is B. F. Skinner's operant conditioning (see Chapter 6). The others are (1) Jean Piaget's cognitive-development theory (see Chapter 9), (2) Robert Gagné's conditions of learning (Chapter 7), and (3) Jerome Bruner's cognitive approach to curriculum development.

Jerome Bruner's Curriculum-Development Model. Director of the Harvard Center for Cognitive Studies in the 1960s, Jerome Bruner (1962b, 1964) recommended the cognitive-development approach to curriculum design. Like John Dewey, Bruner described the knowledgeable person as one who is a problem solver; that is, one who interacts with the environment in testing hypotheses and developing generalizations. The goal of education, therefore, should be intellectual development. Further, the curriculum should foster the development of problem-solving skills through the processes of inquiry and discovery.

Degree of cognitive development is described by Bruner in three levels or stages. The first stage, *enactive,* is the representation of knowledge in actions. An example is that of a child operating a balance beam by adjusting his or her position, although the child may be unable to describe the procedure. The second stage, *iconic,* is that of the visual summarization of images. The child at this stage can represent the balance beam in a drawing or diagram. The third and most advanced stage is that of *symbolic representation*. It is the use of words and other symbols to describe experience. The learner at this stage can explain the operation of the balance beam, using the concepts fulcrum, length of the beam, and weights to be balanced.

The subject matter, therefore, should be represented in terms of the child's way of viewing the world—enactive, iconic, or symbolic. The curriculum should be designed so that the mastery of skills leads to the mastery of still more powerful ones (Bruner, 1966, p. 35). Therefore, the fundamental structure of the subject matter, referred to as "organizing concepts," should be identified and used as the basis for curriculum development. Such a practice, according to Bruner (1964, p. 33) permits the teaching of any subject effectively in an intellectually honest form to any learner at any stage of development. Referred to as a "spiral curriculum", this organization is represented in the social studies curriculum developed by Bruner, "Man: A Course of Study."

The Influence of Skinner's Behaviorism. Unlike other psychologists, B. F. Skinner is well known outside the profession of psychology. The "controlled-environment" crib used with one of his daughters was featured in the popular magazines of the 1940s and three of his books were written for the educated public. *Walden Two* describes life in a utopian society, *Beyond Freedom and Dignity* applies his behavioral management techniques to social engineering, and *Beyond Behaviorism* both responds to his critics and relates his concepts to everyday life.

Skinner is the only post–World War II psychologist to be featured on the cover of *Time* magazine, and a survey of American college students in 1975 indicated that he is the best known American scientist (Gilgen, 1982, p. 97). A survey of psychologists in the late 1970s also indicated that Skinner's behavioral management techniques were considered one of the major developments in psychology.

By the late 1950s, Skinner's principles had surpassed Hull's theory in influence within psychology (Guttman, 1977). The initiation of two journals, *The Experimental Analysis of Behavior* and *The Journal of Applied Behavioral Analysis,* widened that influence.

Programmed Instruction. At about the same time that the curriculum reform was getting under way, B. F. Skinner developed the teaching machine for classroom use. The teaching machine and the accompanying materials, programmed instruction, became a part of the "new technology" recommended for the classroom. The programmed instruction movement lasted less than 10 years, from approximately 1957 to 1965.

Poorly designed materials and the clumsiness of the early machines contributed to the decline.

Behavorial Management. The term *behavior modification* first appeared in *Psychological Abstracts* in 1967 (Gilgen, 1982). The term refers primarily to behavioral management based on operant conditioning principles, specifically the manipulation of reinforcers for appropriate behaviors.

During the 1960s and 1970s, programs for behavioral change were implemented in a variety of clinical, institutional, and educational settings. Included were schools, businesses, hospitals, clinics, prisons, and governmental settings. The programs have been referred to as *applied behavioral analysis, behavioral modification,* and *contingency management.* Some programs used tokens to reinforce appropriate behaviors that later were exchanged for privileges and are known as *token economies.*

The Dominance of Cognitive Psychology (1975–Present)

During the period that behavioral management was enjoying a wide popularity, other events were setting the stage for a renewed interest in cognitive processes. In addition to the curriculum design efforts for thinking skills, these events included communications research and the development of high-speed computers.

The "New" Cognitive Perspective. Both the military training efforts and the communications research of the 1940s indicated that the learner is a complex information-processing system. Training problems related to the sophisticated equipment included the perception, judgment, and decision-making processes of the operators. The new research area focused on the problems of integrating human skills with complex equipment functions.

These events coupled with the advent of high-speed computers provided the foundation for the information-processing theories (see Chapter 8). The capabilities of the computer in symbol manipulation, transformation and storage of information, and problem solving provided an analogy for the operations undertaken by human intelligence.

An important early development conceptualized human memory as a multistage "bin" processor. Proposed in 1958 by Donald Broadbent, this concept of memory included (1) sensory registers, (2) a short-term memory, and (3) a long-term memory. This concept was supported by Miller's (1956) description of the processing limits of short-term memory.

The application of computer operations to human problem-solving activities initiated by Newell and Simon (1961), further supported the concept of complex mental functions. This work accelerated research into the use of computers to simulate problem-solving skills (referred to as *artificial intelligence research*).

Less than 10 years later, in 1967, the study of cognitive processes as a research area was legitimized with the publication of Ulric Neisser's text *Cognitive Psychology*. New journals established between 1970 and 1973 include *Cognitive Psychology, Cognition,* and *Memory and Cognition*.

The Role of Cognitive Processes. The dominant cognitive model at present is the information-processing model of cognition. This model has "replaced the stimulus-response psychology with an input-output psychology, with due attention to transformations taking place between input and output" (Hilgard, 1980b, p. 115). In addition to the information-processing model, cognitive processes have acquired importance in other areas of psychological research, such as developmental psychology and research on motivation.

What are some of the factors that contributed to the increased emphasis on cognitive processes? One factor is the limited explanations of human activity offered by behaviorism. In one reaction to this, Bandura (1969) introduced the use of models in behavior-modification practices and then described the informational role of reinforcement and the role of the learner's internal processes in learning (Bandura, 1971).

A second and related factor is the acceptance of the view of individuals as "active, curious, social, human learners" (McKeachie, 1976, p. 230). Bernard Weiner's theory of motivation reflects this view. The earlier concept that a unidimensional factor labeled "achievement motivation" is responsible for achievement-related behavior is recast into a broader framework. Weiner's theory (1972) identifies the search for the causes of success and failure outcomes in the social setting as the key to understanding achievement-related behavior.

A third factor is the proposed view that behavioral change is the result of the interaction of persons and situations. McKeachie (1976) notes that this view, described by Bandura, is an important perspective in understanding the complexity of human behavior. "Our typical unidirectional view of behavior simply as a dependent variable misses the real dynamics of the interaction in which behavior is a determinant as well as an outcome" (Mckeachie, 1976, p. 829).

The major events in the development of learning theory from 1950 to 1980 are summarized in Table 5-1. From the dominance of behaviorism in the 1940s, psychological research in the 1980s is characterized by the dominance of research on cognitive processes.

Table 5-1. Some Major Events in Learning Theory from 1950 to 1980

	Influence of World War II research and advent of high-speed computers
1950	
	1956 Broadbent's model of human memory
1957 Soviet Union launches *Sputnik*	
1958 NDEA legislation	1958 Newell and Simon's artificial intelligence
1960	
1960–1969 Curriculum redesign	
1960 Bruner calls for a theory of instruction	
1960–1963 Piagetian concepts introduced to American education	1962 Gagné described importance of task sequencing
1961 Skinner described importance of teaching machines	
1965 Gagné's conditions of learning	
	1967 Neisser's *Cognitive Psychology*
1968 Skinner's technology of teaching	
1969 The term "instructional psychology" is coined	
1970	
1970 Piaget summarizes major concepts for psychologists	
1970–1975 Various models of human memory proposed	
1971 Bandura's social learning theory introduced	
1972 Weiner introduces attribution theory	
1974 Barbel Inhelder and colleagues publish current Genevan research	
1977 Gagné expands his theory to include information processing	
1980 Dominance of research on cognitive processes	

INTRODUCTION TO SIX CONTEMPORARY THEORIES

Research on psychological processes initiated in the late nineteenth century introduced three different models of psychological reality: the behaviorist model, the cognitive model, and the interactionist model. The behaviorist model describes the relationship between measurable stimuli and behavioral responses. Several theories have been developed from this perspective (see Figure 5-1).

The cognitive model, in contrast, focuses on the mind and the mind's operations. In this model, behavior and the role of the environment are incidental to the understanding of cognitive processes. Structuralism is the earliest example of this perspective, and theories of information processing are the most recent.

The interactionist perspective, in contrast, assumes that behavior, mental processes, and the environment are interrelated. This view was first expressed in the functionalist movement. Current perspectives that hold an interactionist view of the role of environmental influences and the individual include Robert Gagné's conditions of learning, Jean Piaget's cognitive-development theory, and Albert Bandura's social learning theory.

No one single theory is obliged to represent at once all the forces operating in psychological experience (Hilgard, 1980b). However, to the

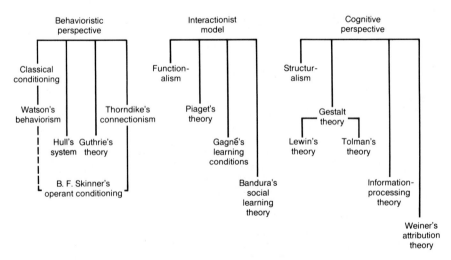

Figure 5-1. Psychological models of reality related to learning.

extent that a particular model and the theories associated with it emphasize particular aspects of experience, some components are subordinated and the description of psychological reality is not complete (Hilgard, 1980b, p. 116). Therefore, an understanding of psychological reality depends, to a certain extent, on understanding more than one theory.

Overview of Six Theories

The six theories selected for discussion in this text have influenced both psychology and education since the mid-twentieth century. These theories are B. F. Skinner's operant conditioning, Robert Gagné's conditions of learning, information-processing theory, Jean Piaget's cognitive-development theory, Albert Bandura's social learning theory, and Bernard Weiner's attribution theory.

Table 5-2 provides an orientation to the current perspective of each of these theories and illustrates their order of presentation in this text. B. F. Skinner's principles of operant conditioning describe the role of the environment in behavioral change. In contrast, Robert Gagné's theory

Table 5-2. Comparison of Six Contemporary Learning Theories

Theory	Type	Focus
Skinner's operant conditioning	Contingency theory	The arrangement of consequences for learner behavior
Gagné's conditions of learning	Task-cognition theory	The relationship of the phases of information processing to type of learning task and instruction
Information-processing theories	Cognition theories	The processes of acquiring information, remembering, and problem solving
Piaget's developmental epistemology	Cognitive-development theory	The growth of intelligence from infancy to adulthood
Bandura's social learning theory	Social-context theory	The observation of and internal processing of modeled behavior
Weiner's attribution theory	Social-context theory	The influence of learner beliefs about success and failure on achievement-related behavior

integrates the learner's cognitive processes and stimulation from the environment in the acquisition of different kinds of learning.

A radical departure from these perspectives is represented in the work of Jean Piaget. Instead of describing the acquisition of specific behaviors or skills, he describes the development of intelligence that occurs through the individual's continued interaction with the environment. The changes in the individual's thought processes from birth to adulthood are described.

Both social learning theory and attribution theory may be described as social-context theories. Both theories describe different kinds of information abstracted from the social context that influence behavior. According to Bandura's social learning theory (1971), individuals acquire patterns of behavior through the observation of others. Both prosocial and aggressive behaviors are acquired through contact with live and filmed or televised models.

Weiner's attribution theory (1972), on the other hand, is a theory of achievement motivation. Specifically, it focuses on the individual's reactions to success and failure outcomes and the effects of these beliefs on subsequent behavior.

The Analysis of Learning Theory

In this text, the discussion of each theory proceeds from the theoretical to the practical. Basic principles of learning are discussed first, then principles of instruction, followed by a discussion of the theory's relationship to classroom issues and the presentation of a classroom example (see the section "Educational Applications"). Table 5-3 illustrates the questions that are answered in each section.

The sections "Principles of Learning" and "Principles of Instruction" are parallel discussions. The fundamentals of each learning theory are explained in the former, and the ways in which these fundamentals are applied to classroom instruction are discussed in "Principles of Instruction." The purpose of this arrangement is to develop a clear understanding of each theory. Discussing the interpretation of a theory at the same time as the basic principles are being explained risks misunderstanding and confusion for the reader.

The basic assumptions of each theory are presented as an introduction to the principles of learning and instruction. No set of principles about learning is developed in a vacuum. Instead, each theory is derived from basic beliefs about the nature of learning. Such beliefs establish the emphasis and focus of the theory. For example, a theory that defines learning as behavioral change will focus on factors that influence behavior. Mental

Table 5-3. Topic Outline*ᵃ* for the Analysis of Learning Theory

Topic	Focus
Principles of learning	
Basic assumptions	What assumptions about learning are made by the theorist? How is learning defined? Is learning viewed as behavioral change, a change in cognitive structure, or as some internal process?
Components of learning	What are the essential elements that must be present in each act of learning? What are the interrelationships?
The nature of complex learning	How are the components of learning (described in the preceding section) arranged to account for complex learning, such as how to solve problems?
Principles of instruction	
Basic assumptions	What are the theorist's assumptions about school learning?
Components of instruction	How do the components of learning relate to classroom instruction?
Designing instruction for complex skills	How is instruction to be developed for skills such as learning to play tennis and learning to solve problems?
Educational applications	
Classroom issues	How does the theory explain individual differences, cognitive processes, and the social context for learning?
Designing a classroom strategy	What are the specific steps in the development of instruction?
Classroom example	

ᵃ Minor wording changes made in Piaget's cognitive-development theory and Weiner's attribution theory.

states or cognitive structures will be the emphasis of other theories that define learning in terms of qualitative processes.

The purpose of the two sections "Components of Learning" and "The Nature of Complex Learning" is twofold. One is to present and to describe the fundamental elements that must be present in every act of learning separate from any other discussion. The components of learning are the core of each theory. In B. F. Skinner's operant conditioning, for example, the components of each learning act are (1) a discriminative stimulus, (2) a learner response, and (3) a consequence. Understanding the components of learning and the relationships among them is essential to the analysis of instructional applications of the theory.

The ways in which the basic learning components are arranged in order to acquire complex skills, such as learning to solve algebra problems, are often not intuitively obvious. Therefore, the section "The Nature of Complex Learning" is included to illustrate these situations. In operant conditioning, for example, complex sequences of skills are acquired through the implementation of various patterns of subtle reinforcement contingencies.

The final section of each chapter, "Educational Applications," first relates the theory to classroom issues. Included are the theory's position on individual differences, cognitive processes, and the social context for learning. The specific steps required to develop an instructional strategy according to the theory are presented next, followed by a classroom example in a particular subject area.

Chapter 12 discusses the factors to be considered in the selection of particular theories for use in the educational setting. Application of the theories to the development of predesigned instruction is also reviewed.

DISCUSSION QUESTIONS

1. How did the priorities of World War II and the later Cold War with the Soviet Union influence perceptions about classroom instruction?
2. What were some of the reasons given in the 1960s for the prior lack of applicability of learning theory? How do these reasons compare with John Dewey's earlier call for a "linking science" between psychology and education?

REFERENCES

Bandura, A. (1969). *Principles of behavior modification*. New York: Holt, Rinehart and Winston.
Bandura, A. (1971). *Social learning theory*. Englewood Cliffs, NJ: Prentice-Hall.
Broadbent, D. E. (1958). *Perception and communication*. London: Pergamon Press.
Bruner, J. S. (1960). *The process of education*. Cambridge, MA: Harvard University Press.
Bruner, J. S. (1964). Some theorems on instruction illustrated with reference to mathematics. In E. R. Hilgard (Ed.), *Theories of learning and instruction*. The

sixty-third yearbook of the National Society for the Study of Education, Part I (pp. 306–335). Chicago: University of Chicago Press.

Bruner, J. S. (1966). *Toward a theory of instruction.* Cambridge, MA: Harvard University Press.

Gagné, R. M. (1962a). The acquisition of knowledge. *Psychological Review, 69,* 355–365.

Gagné, R. M. (1962b). Military training and principles of learning. *American Psychologist, 17,* 83–91.

Gagné, R. M. (1977). *The conditions of learning* (3rd ed.). New York: Holt, Rinehart and Winston.

Gagné, R. M., & Rohwer, W. (1969). Instructional psychology. *Annual Review of Psychology, 20,* 381–418.

Gilgen, A. R. (1982). *American psychology since World War II.* Westport, CT: Greenwood Press.

Guttman, N. (1977). On Skinner and Hull: A reminiscence and projection. *American Psychologist, 32,* 321–328.

Hilgard, E. R. (1964). A perspective on the relationship between learning theory and instructional practice. In E. R. Hilgard (Ed.), *Theories of learning and instruction. The sixty-third yearbook of the National Society for the Study of Education, Part I,* (pp. 402–415). Chicago, University of Chicago Press.

Hilgard, E. R. (1980b). The trilogy of mind: Cognition, affection, and conation. *Journal of the History of the Behavioral Sciences, 16,* 107–117.

Inhelder, B., Sinclair, H., & Bovet, S. (1974). *Learning and the process of cognition.* Cambridge, MA: Harvard University Press.

McKeachie, W. J. (1976). Psychology in America's bicentennial year. *American Psychologist, 31,* 819–833.

Miller, G. A. (1956). The magical number seven plus or minus two: Some limits on our capacity for processing information. *Psychological Review, 63,* 81–97.

Neisser, U. (1967). *Cognitive psychology.* New York: Appleton-Century-Crofts.

Newell, A., & Simon, H. (1961). *Human problem solving.* Santa Monica, CA: Rand Corporation.

Piaget, J. (1970). Piaget's theory. In P. H. Mussen (Ed.), *Carmichael's Manual of Psychology* (3rd ed., chap. 9, pp. 703–732). New York: Wiley.

Popper, K. (1968). *The logic of discovery.* New York: Harper & Row.

Resnick, L. (1981). Instructional psychology. *Annual Review of Psychology, 32,* 660–704.

Skinner, B. F. (1961, Fall). Why we need teaching machines. *Harvard Educational Review, 41*(4), 377–398.

Skinner, B. F. (1968). *The technology of teaching.* New York; Appleton-Century-Crofts.

Weiner, B. (1972). *Theories of motivation from mechanism to cognition.* Chicago: Markham.

CHAPTER 6

B. F. Skinner's Operant Conditioning

Human behavior is distinguished by the
fact that it is affected by small consequences. Describing something with the
right word is often reinforcing. So is the
clarification of a temporary puzzlement,
or the solution of a complex problem, or
simply the opportunity to move forward
after completing one stage of an activity.
Skinner, 1961, p. 380

B. F. Skinner's principles of operant conditioning were initiated in the
1930s, during the period of the S-R theories. At that time, Pavlov's model
of classical conditioning had exerted a strong influence on research.
Terms such as "cues," "purposive behavior," and "drive stimuli" were
proposed to account for the power of a stimulus to elicit or trigger a
particular response.

Skinner disagreed with the S-R position and the conditioned-reflex
description in which "the stimulus retains the character of an inexorable
force" (Skinner, 1966b, p. 214). The S-R accounting of behavioral change,
according to Skinner (1938), is an incomplete account of the organism's
interaction with the environment. Instead, many behaviors produce some
change or consequence in the environment that affects the organism and
thereby alters the likelihood of future responding. In the laboratory, for
example, key pecking or lever pressing typically "produces" the consequence of food. In the classroom, solving a problem leads to confirmation of one's skill. Therefore, the key to understanding the majority
of executed behaviors lies in an understanding of the interrelationships

between a stimulus situation, the organism's response, and the response consequences.

B. F. Skinner's principles of operant conditioning redirected the study and analysis of behavior. His work began with an analysis of the differences between reflexes and other behaviors (Skinner, 1935), and his principles of operant conditioning soon followed (Skinner, 1938). Application of the principles to a variety of settings was discussed in his *Science and Human Behavior* in 1953. He then turned his attention to the school setting with the development of the teaching machine (Skinner, 1961) and a technology of classroom teaching (Skinner, 1968a, 1968b, 1973). His recent comments include practical advice for educators on microcomputer instruction.

No one really cares whether PacMan gobbles up all those little spots on the screen. Indeed, as soon as the screen is cleared, the player covers it again with more little spots to be gobbled up. What is reinforcing is successful play, and in a well-designed instructional program students gobble up their assignments. (Skinner, 1984, p. 24)

PRINCIPLES OF LEARNING

B. F. Skinner agrees with the position taken earlier by John Watson. That is, psychology can become a science only through the study of behavior. Learning, therefore, is defined by Skinner as the process of behavioral change.

Basic Assumptions

Like Clark Hull, B. F. Skinner established rigorous procedures for the study of behavior. Unlike Hull, however, he does not believe in the use of theory as a research framework. Instead, the cornerstone of Skinner's principles of operant conditioning is his beliefs about the nature of a behavioral science and the characteristics of learned behavior.

The Nature of a Behavioral Science. The goal of any science, according to Skinner (1953), is to discover the lawful relationships among natural events in the environment. Therefore, a science of behavior must discover the lawful or "functional" relationships among physical conditions or events in the environment and behavior. The challenge is to determine which changes in independent variables (conditions or events) lead to changes in the dependent variable, behavior. For example, what are the conditions or events responsible for one student's attending to academic tasks and another's avoidance of homework? To refer to the one student as "motivated" and the other as "unmotivated" does not, in Skinner's view, answer the question.

The development of a science of behavior is by no means an easy task, cautions Skinner (1953). Behavior is both complex and varied. Further, the difficulty in studying behavior is compounded by the fact that it is a temporal, fluid, and changing process (Skinner, 1953, p. 15). However, the monumental task for the scientist, according to Skinner, is to discover its order and uniformity.

Skinner (1950, 1966b) cautions that neither theories nor discussions of inner states should be the basis for behavioral research. The problem with theories is that they explain one statement by means of another, thereby creating an artificial world of order and lawfulness. Theories, however, obscure the lawful relationships yet to be discovered. In addition, they may stifle the scientist's sense of curiosity, thereby terminating the search for clarification (Skinner, 1950).

Problems with Internal States. A typical research practice is to describe behavior as "caused" by some mental state. However, such a practice fails to complete the explanation of behavioral change. Whenever behavior is "explained" by mental or neural activities, these events must themselves also be explained (Skinner, 1963a). For example, if anxiety is proposed as an explanation for a particular behavior, then anxiety in turn remains to be explained.

The second problem is that behavior is treated as "a second-class variable." That is, behavior is regarded merely as an indicator or "symptom" of an inner mental or physiological activity (Skinner, 1966b, p. 213). It is considered important because it indicates a process (e.g., learning or maturation), identifies a state (such as alertness), or indicates a drive, emotion, or available psychic energy. An example is an emphasis on a child's sharing of personal toys only as an indicator of emerging maturity.

The preoccupation with mental states has diverted attention from the identification of the sources of problems and the actions that might solve them. For example, consumer "lack of confidence" in the economy has been described as a "problem" in the restoration of economic growth. However, Skinner (1978, p. 87) notes that people plan to buy less when their money does not go very far, and such actions are accompanied only by a lack of confidence. Thus governmental actions to "restore confidence" are, in reality, actions taken to restore consumer buying.

Another term often used in the social sciences is "alienation" (Skinner, 1978). Production-line workers are described as unhappy or apathetic, and absenteeism and strikes are described as the result of alienation. Of interest, however, is the adoption in some American industries of practices followed in Japan. Workers participate actively in decision making, and management no longer takes sole credit for cost saving, innovative ideas and other advances. Should we say that the worker is no longer alienated? Or, instead, should the conclusion be that the worker's behaviors have an effect? The worker's actions alter the environment and produce outcomes that, in turn, influence the workers and the likelihood of similar behaviors in the future.

Treating behavior as a surrogate for other variables discourages the careful specification of behavior. More importantly, the practice of viewing behavior as merely a measure of other more important variables has not been helpful in understanding behavioral change (Skinner, 1966b).

Experimental Analysis. The only legitimate source of information is behavioral change observed under carefully controlled conditions (Skinner, 1966b). Such a process requires the development of a rigorous methodology; specifically, the experimental analysis of behavior (Skinner, 1953, 1966b). This approach (1) identifies behavior as a dependent variable and (2) proceeds to account for behavior in terms of physical conditions that are both observable and manipulable. The experimenter "manipulates not hunger, but the intake of food; not fear as an acquired drive, but aversive stimuli; not anxiety, but preaversive stimuli. He administers a drug, not the physiological effects of a drug" (Skinner, 1966b, p. 215).

Experimental analysis, however, is not an instant solution to human problems. Successful application depends on rigorous definitions, attention to detail, and hard work. "We cannot deal effectively with human behavior by applying a few general principles (say of reward and punishment) any more than we can build a bridge by applying the principles of stress and strain" (Skinner, 1953, p. 27).

Experimental analysis also requires the study of individual subjects, rather than groups (Skinner, 1950). To average the results from a group of subjects is to present a distorted picture of the behavior. That is, reporting an average often involves reporting a performance that no one achieved. For example, the average score 68.33 provides little information about the set of three scores from which it was obtained; 55, 60, and 90.

Laboratory Methods. The parameters established for research by Skinner initially restricted experimentation to the laboratory. To control environmental conditions, Skinner designed an experimental space that was free of distractions. A soundproofed darkened box was used that included one or more response devices (e.g., levers, keys, or discs). Mechanisms to provide reinforcers such as food and water were also included. Sometimes other stimuli were used, such as lights, loudspeakers, or mechanisms for the delivery of mild electric shock. The chamber was automated so that reinforcers were delivered immediately after an appropriate response; written records of the responding were obtained by automatic devices.

The organisms typically used were first, rats, and later, pigeons. The information collected on these subjects also reveals information about the interactions between all organisms and the environment. "The schedule of reinforcement which makes the pigeon a pathological gambler is to be found at the racetrack and the roulette table, where it has a comparable effect" (Skinner, 1969, p. 84). Thus the research on these processes in the laboratory is considered to be applicable to human behavior.

A Definition of Learning. In Skinner's view, learning is behavior. As the subject learns, responses increase and when unlearning occurs, the rate of responding falls (Skinner, 1950). Learning is therefore formally defined as a change in the likelihood or probability of a response.

Learning and Response Rate. Probability or likelihood of responding is difficult to measure. Therefore, Skinner suggests that learning should be measured by the rate or frequency of responding. Although not precisely the same as probability of future performance, it is an initial step in the analysis of behavioral change (Skinner, 1963b).

Rate of responding provides three advantages over other learning measures, according to Skinner (1950). First, it provides an orderly and continuous record of behavioral change that is free of arbitrary criteria. Typical learning measures, for example, include number of trials, ratio of right to wrong responses, elapsed time, and reaction time. "Quickness" of response, like the other examples, is also an arbitrary measure of learning (Skinner, 1950, 1969).

The second important characteristic of response rate is that behavioral change is clearly specified. In contrast, such terms as "adjustment," "improvement," and "problem solving" leave unanswered the basic question of what is learned.

Third, response rate may be applied to a variety of behaviors, from student responses in the classroom to the behavior of pigeons in the laboratory. Furthermore, minor modifications in the rate brought about by different combinations of stimuli are easily studied.

In summary, six assumptions form the foundation of operant conditioning. They are as follows:

1. Learning is behavior.
2. Behavioral change (learning) is functionally related to changes in environmental events or conditions.
3. The lawful relationships between behavior and the environment can be determined only if behavioral properties and experimental condi-

tions are defined in physical terms and observed under carefully controlled conditions.

4. Data from the experimental study of behavior are the only acceptable sources of information about the causes of behavior.
5. The behavior of the individual organism is the appropriate data source.
6. The dynamics of an organism's interaction with the environment is the same for all species.

The Components of Learning

Development of Skinner's principles of operant conditioning began with his analysis of Pavlov's classical conditioning. According to Skinner (1938), Pavlov's model is appropriate for responses that are already associated with a particular stimulus. Examples are the leg jerk that follows the hammer tap to the knee and the eye blink that follows the insertion of a foreign object in the eye. Skinner referred to these reflexes as *elicited responses* or respondent behavior. Because the method of conditioning these responses depends on stimulus substitution, Skinner designated Pavlov's model as *Type S conditioning* (see Table 6-1).

The problem with Type S conditioning is that it accounts for a limited range of behavior. The associated stimuli for complex behaviors, such as painting a picture or singing a song, could not be found (Skinner, 1935). Because such behaviors were not elicited by particular stimuli, they were named *emitted responses*. These responses also act on the environment to produce consequences. Singing a song, for example, may produce the consequences of praise, applause, or money, among others. Such responses operate on the environment and were named *operants* (Skinner, 1935).

The key to understanding operant behaviors, in Skinner's view (1953,

Table 6-1. Comparison of Elicited Responses and Operant Behavior

Elicited Responses (Reflexes)	Emitted Responses or Operants
An observed correlation exists between stimulus and response; elicited responses exist primarily to maintain the well-being of the organism	A response acting on the environment that produces a consequence affecting the organism, and thereby altering future behavior; not correlated with preceding stimulus
Conditioned by stimulus substitution; Type S conditioning	Conditioned through response consequences that increase the likelihood of responding; Type R conditioning

1963b) was Edward Thorndike's law of effect. Thorndike's experiments were characterized by the almost simultaneous occurrence of a response and certain environmental events generated by the subject that also changed the subject. The likelihood of the recurrence of the behavior was thereby increased. Specifically, an animal's escape behavior resulted in food, and under similar confinement conditions, the escape response was repeated.

However, Skinner noted (1963b) that Thorndike's law of effect includes some terms that do not describe behavioral properties, leading to misunderstandings about behavioral change. (These terms are discussed later in this section.) Nevertheless, the law of effect identified the three components necessary in the interaction between the organism and the environment (Skinner, 1953). They are (1) the occasion on which the response occurs, (2) the subject's response, and (3) the reinforcing consequences. These three components of learning are described by Skinner (1953) as the discriminative stimulus (S^D), the response (R), and the reinforcing stimulus (S^{reinf}). The sequence of learning events is (S^D)—(R)—(S^{reinf}).

The Discriminative Stimulus.   A discriminative stimulus is any stimulus that is consistently present when a response is reinforced. For example, a pigeon may receive reinforcement only for pecking a red key. The red key in this situation is the discriminative stimulus.

The continued reinforcement for behavior in the presence of a particular stimulus property conveys a measure of behavioral control to that property. For example, food pellets received by a pigeon for pecking only the red key will increase pecking in the presence of that stimulus. If, after repeated reinforcement, the color is changed to green, pecking will not occur (Skinner, 1963b). The red key through reinforcement has gained control over the pigeon's pecking response and is referred to as the *discriminative stimulus* (S^D).

Operant conditioning can, of course, be explained without reference to the stimulus that precedes the subject's response (Skinner, 1953). An example is neck-stretching behavior in the pigeon, which typically occurs without an S^D. Like other behaviors, neck stretching will increase in rate as a result of continued reinforcement. However, if neck-stretching behavior is reinforced only when a signal light is on, then eventually the behavior will occur only in the presence of the light (Skinner, 1953, p. 107).

The Role of Discriminative Stimuli.   The probability that a response will be repeated is maximized by the presence of discriminative stimuli. Examples that exercise control over behavior in everyday life include red and green traffic lights, stop signs, and other signals (Skinner, 1953). Also included are countless verbal commands, such as "take out your pencils" and "please pass the salt." However, signals, verbals commands, and other discriminative stimuli do not elicit operant behaviors. Rather, they acquire behavioral control as a result of prior reinforcements for particular responses in their presence.

Discriminative stimuli for human behavior are not restricted to environmental events to which the individual responds. In many situations, human beings construct discriminative stimuli to which they can respond. People construct such stimuli when they make resolutions, announce expectations or intentions, and develop plans (Skinner, 1963b, p. 513). To be most effective in controlling behavior, these self-generated stimuli must be visible in some durable form, such as drafting a written plan or posting the resolutions on a bulletin board (Skinner, 1963b).

The continued reinforcement of a response in the presence of one stimulus property and nonreinforcement in the presence of other properties is the process often referred to as *discrimination*. In fact, however, a sensitive and powerful behavioral control is demonstrated (Skinner, 1963b).

Two or more different stimuli that share a common feature may also acquire control over a particular response. A pigeon's pecking response to both a lighted bar and a lighted disc and a child's verbal identification of "p," "P," and "p" are examples. This event is referred to by Skinner as *induction* (commonly referred to as *stimulus generalization*).

Operant Reinforcement. Skinner's analysis of reinforcing stimuli was derived from Edward Thorndike's law of effect. The importance of Thorndike's research, according to Skinner (1963b), is that it included the effects of the subject's action among the causes of behavior. Therefore, concepts such as purpose, intention, expectancy, and others were not needed to explain future behavior (Skinner, 1963b, p. 503).

A Definition of Reinforcement. Thorndike's law of effect, however, emphasized the terms "rewarding," "satisfying," and "trial-and-error learning," and these terms do not describe behavioral properties. Furthermore, the use of the term "reward" suggests some form of compensation for behaving in a particular way. It also carries the connotation of a contractual arrangement (Skinner, 1963b, p. 505).

The terms "reinforcing consequence" and "reinforcement" were substituted for the term "reward." The term *reinforcement* is defined as any behavioral consequence that strengthens behavior.

The reinforcing consequence increases the likelihood of the recurrence of a particular type of response. If a pigeon receives food for key pecking, then key-pecking responses will increase in frequency. The particular response that occurs immediately prior to the reinforcement has passed into history and cannot be changed. "What is changed is the future probability of a response in the same class" (Skinner, 1953, p. 87).

The Dynamics of Reinforcement. To determine whether or not a particular event is reinforcing, a direct test is needed (Skinner, 1953, p. 73). The frequency of a selected response is first observed and then a particular event is made contingent on the response. The rate of responding with the added consequence is observed next. If the response frequency increases, the selected event is therefore reinforcing in the given condition.

To be effective in altering behavior in a particular way, reinforcement must be made contingent on the execution of appropriate responses. The use of accidental contingencies leads to the development of superstitious behavior (Skinner, 1953, p. 85). Behavior that is accidentally reinforced will be strengthened. It will increase in frequency and very likely receive accidental reinforcement again. Superstitious behavior in the laboratory was demonstrated by providing food to a pigeon every 15 seconds. Behaviors that were strengthened were those behaviors that were occurring when the food was delivered. Included are strutting, wing flapping, bowing and scraping, and others (Skinner, 1948).

Reinforcement increases rate of responding; however, elimination of the reinforcing consequence decreases the rate. This decreased rate in the absence of a reinforcing consequence is referred to as *extinction* (Skinner, 1938, 1963b). If reinforcement is withdrawn completely, behavior will gradually cease. Thus, an important function of reinforcement in everyday life is to prevent the extinction of behavior.

Primary and Secondary (Conditioned) Reinforcers. The two general classes are *primary* and *secondary*. Primary reinforcers are so designated because they increase response rate without the necessity of training. Given the appropriate state of deprivation, primary reinforcers will alter the probability of responding. Food, for example, is reinforcing for a food-deprived pigeon. Liquids, sleep, and sexual contact are also examples of primary reinforcers.

In addition to primary reinforcers, behavior may be altered by secondary or conditioned reinforcers. This group, however, influences behavior through training (conditioning). Specifically, by association with a primary reinforcer, an event may acquire reinforcing power of its own. A typical example in the laboratory is the sound of the food magazine that occurs just prior to the delivery of food. Through repeated associations with food (the primary reinforcer), the click of the mechanism acquires reinforcing power.

Generalized Reinforcers. In the example above, the sound of the equipment is associated with only one primary reinforcer, food. Therefore, the sound is reinforcing only in similar situations with a food-deprived pigeon. Some conditioned reinforcers, however, can function under more than one set of circumstances through association with more than one primary reinforcer. Money is an example of such a conditioned reinforcer. It is a token that has been associated with the primary reinforcers of food, drink, and shelter.

Reinforcers such as money that function in a variety of situations are *generalized reinforcers*. Other examples include the reinforcements that are provided by other individuals (Skinner, 1953). Attention, approval, and affection are generalized reinforcers. Smiles, commendations, and the agreement of peers are all expressions of approval that function as reinforcers in numerous social situations.

One generalized reinforcer that is often overlooked is the reinforcement provided by successful manipulation of the physical environment. Our tendency to participate in activities that depend on skill, such as crafts, artistic creations, and skill sports such as bowling and tennis, may be a function of this generalized reinforcer (Skinner, 1953, p. 79).

Positive and Negative Reinforcers. The prior examples of reinforcing stimuli strengthen behavior by being added to the situation. Food, money, approval, and other reinforcers follow certain responses and the appearance of these stimuli increases response frequency. Any reinforcing stimulus that strengthens behavior in this way is referred to as a positive reinforcer (Skinner, 1953).

Some reinforcers, however, strengthen behavior by tneir removal. That is, termination of the reinforcing stimulus increases response frequency. Examples include stimuli such as electric shock, nagging, and extreme cold or heat. They function as reinforcers because the organism engages in escape behavior in order to terminate the stimulus. For example, a teenager may complete his or her chores promptly so that the parent's nagging will terminate. The initial stimulus is the nagging, which is followed by the teenager's work. If, when the nagging stops (withdrawal of the stimulus), the teenager's work habits continue, then the nagging has functioned as a response strengthener or reinforcement. The nagging has strengthened the behavior, however, by being withdrawn from the situation.

Other examples of negative reinforcers are whipping a horse so that the animal will run faster and giving "pop" quizzes in school to precipitate student study. If the horse's increased speed (response) and student diligence (response) are followed by the termination of (or escape from) the whipping and the surprise quizzes, negative reinforcement has occurred. Both the reinforcers are aversive stimuli from which the subject seeks escape or avoidance.

The similarities and differences between positive and negative reinforcement are illustrated in Table 6-2. Note that in negative reinforcement, termination of the discriminative stimulus is the key to behavioral change. In contrast, in positive reinforcement, a new stimulus enters the situation after the subject's response.

Emotional By-products.   The use of negative reinforcers to regulate behavior introduces undesirable emotional by-products that accompany the subject's escape or avoidance behavior (Skinner, 1953). The emotion commonly referred to as "anxiety" and sometimes the emotion of "fear" occurs when the subject seeks to escape aversive stimuli. The set of responses called "anxiety," for example, may include conditioned reflexes of the smooth muscles, such as gastric changes, a sudden loss of blood from the face, and possibly, increased blood pressure. Operant responses that may be included in anxiety are (1) a discontinuance of ongoing activity (described as "losing interest") and (2) changes in body musculature, such as turning away or leaving the scene (Skinner, 1953).

The set of responses described above as well as others accompany the escape response from the aversive stimulus. As a result, emotional responses become conditioned to situational characteristics that accompany the aversive stimulus. A horse that has been whipped by a rider, for example, will roll its eyes, become restive, and possibly rear up at the sight of a riding crop. On a more subtle level, the child who has been scolded for not completing his or her chores may become agitated on the parent's arrival home.

Interactive Examples.   In many situations, both positive and negative reinforcers function to strengthen the same behaviors. For example, the scientist's long hours of work in the laboratory may be positively reinforced by the conditioned reinforcers of manipulating the experimental situation and eventually, by solving a difficult problem. In addition, perhaps social "small talk" with other people is mildly aversive. If the scientist leaves a party to go to work in the laboratory, the party is functioning as a negative reinforcer that increases the escape behavior of working.

In interactions between two or more people, a careful analysis is required to determine discriminative stimuli, responses, and reinforcers. For example, a child may begin to cry whenever the parents entertain guests. The parents may turn their attention momentarily to the disruptive child so that they can continue to enjoy the visit. In that situation, the child's interruption is the aversive stimulus for the parent's attention (see Figure 6-1). Their attention terminates the interruption (withdrawal of the aversive stimulus). The child's interruption serves as a negative reinforcer for the parents. However, the attention of the adults, particularly if prolonged, serves as positive reinforcement for the child's crying and whining.

Table 6-2. Examples of Positive and Negative Reinforcement

Discriminative Stimulus	Response	Consequence	Type of Consequence	Type of Reinforcement[a]
Coffee machine	Subject puts change in machine and pushes button	Subject receives a cup of coffee	Subject's behavior "produces" new stimulus	Positive
Parent nags teenager to clean up room	Subject straightens up his room every day for two weeks	Nagging stops	Subject's behavior has been followed by the withdrawal of a stimulus	Negative

[a] The assumption here is that the response increases in frequency; therefore, the described consequence is functioning as reinforcement.

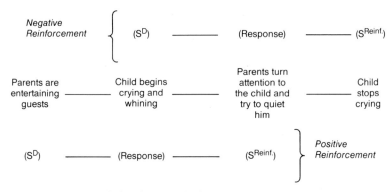

Figure 6-1. Behavioral analysis of parent-child interaction.

In the analysis of behavior, the terms "pleasant" and "unpleasant" should not be used as a basis for differentiating positive and negative reinforcers. Such a practice fails to identify common behavioral properties of positive and negative reinforcers. In addition, it can lead to errors in behavioral analysis. For example, praise, typically considered to be pleasant or satisfying, is often treated as a positive reinforcer. Consider, however, the situation of a teenage male in the classroom who is seeking status in the eyes of his peers. Special attention by the teacher and teacher praise are aversive stimuli that he seeks to escape. They therefore may serve as negative reinforcers for any of a variety of behaviors from apathy to disruptive activities.

Inappropriate uses of reinforcement are not confined to specific classroom situations. Skinner (1966a) notes that a major problem in society is the poor use of reinforcement contingencies. Wage systems, for example, are basically aversive. They primarily establish a standard that can be lost by being discharged from a job. In both affluent and welfare societies, reinforcement is not contingent on particular kinds of behavior (Skinner, 1966a, p. 166). One result is that people who are not reinforced for doing anything will indeed do nothing.

Punishment.   Reinforcers are the consequences of particular responses that strengthen behavior. Positive reinforcers are stimuli that are added to the situation, whereas negative reinforcers strengthen responses by their withdrawal from the situation.

Punishment, in contrast, involves either the *withdrawal* of a positive reinforcer or the *addition* of a negative reinforcer. Two examples are removing the privilege of watching television (withdrawal of a positive reinforcer) and confining a child to his room (addition of a negative reinforcer).

In terms of effect, Skinner (1953) maintains that punishment is not the opposite of reinforcement. According to Skinner (1953), the use of punishment leads to three undesirable side effects. First, punishment only temporarily suppresses behavior. Punished responses may cease temporarily but are likely to reappear later. Second, emotional predispositions, commonly referred to as guilt or shame, may be conditioned through the use of punishment. Third, any behavior that reduces the aversive stimulation accompanying the punishment will be reinforced. For example, a child may pretend to be ill to avoid going to school to take a test. Successful avoidance of the test (aversive stimulus) reinforces the behavior of lying in order to stay home.

The major shortcoming of punishment, however, is that the contingencies in punishment are defective. That is, punishment does not generate positive behaviors. Interest in schoolwork does not result from the punishment of indifference (Skinner, 1968b, p. 149). Therefore, reinforcement for appropriate behavior rather than punishment for inappropriate behavior is recommended.

The Nature of Complex Learning

According to Skinner (1953, 1963b), the law of effect specifies the temporal relationship between a response and a consequence. The development of new and complex patterns or "topographies" of behavior, however, results from complex and subtle contingencies of reinforcement. A child learns to pull himself up, to stand, to walk, and to move about through the reinforcement of slightly exceptional instances of behavior (Skinner, 1953). Later, the same process is responsible for his or her learning to sing, to dance, and to play games, as well as all the other behaviors found in the normal adult repertoire (Skinner, 1953, p. 93).

Reinforcement is often contingent on particular properties of response topography. The improvement of skills, for example, requires the differential reinforcement of responses with particular properties. Types of skills that depend on differential reinforcement for maximum development include sports activities, artistic performances, and certain games and other activities that require timing (Skinner, 1953).

Often, the differential reinforcement is provided by the natural events in the environment subsequent to a response. For example, a ball thrown with the appropriate force and at the correct angle will cover a greater distance than others (Skinner, 1953, p. 95), and these consequences reinforce the musculature involved in the response execution.

Shaping Behavior. The acquisition of complex behaviors—such as pigeons playing ping pong and human beings solving problems— is the result of the process referred to as *shaping* (Skinner, 1954, 1963b). This process involves a carefully designed program of discriminative stimuli and reinforcements for changing topographies of behavior. An example is that of teaching a pigeon to bowl (Skinner, 1958). The desired terminal behavior is that of swiping a wooden ball with a sideways movement of the beak so that the ball is sent down a miniature alley toward a set of toy pins.

The shaping process begins by first providing reinforcement for responses that indicate approaches to the ball. Reinforcement is then withheld until the pigeon's beak makes contact with the ball. After initial reinforcements for contact with the ball, reinforcement is again withheld until further refinement in the behavior occurs, and the pigeon sideswipes the ball. The procedure of first reinforcing responses that only remotely resemble the desired response and then reinforcing only refinements in the response is referred to as *reinforcing successive approximations* (Skinner, 1953, 1968b). The procedure is effective because it recognizes (1) the continuous nature of a complex act, and (2) the utility of constructing complex behavior by a continual process of differential reinforcement (Skinner, 1953).

The importance of shaping is that it can generate complex behaviors that have an almost zero probability of occurring naturally in the final form (Skinner, 1963a). A complex behavior is shaped by a series of changing contingencies, referred to as a *program* (Skinner, 1963b, p. 506). Each stage of the program evokes a response and also serves to prepare the organism to respond at a later point.

The process of shaping differs from the modification of behavior that occurs with puzzle boxes, mazes, and memory drums. In those situations, the organism is thrown into a problem situation and behaviors occur that eventually lead to the solution. The rat makes several turns in the maze and the subject guesses the next nonsense word to be presented (Skinner, 1963b). However, performance of the appropriate response has been left to chance; therefore, random, incorrect responses also occur. The subject has been placed in a set of terminal contingencies, and the adequate behavior for those contingencies can only be developed through trial and error.

Contingencies of Reinforcement.   Behavior that acts on the immediate physical environment, in general, is reinforced consistently (Skinner, 1953, p. 99). Standing and walking are examples. However, like the foregoing laboratory examples, a large part of behavior generates only intermittent reinforcement. Sometimes a given consequence depends on a series of events that are difficult to predict with precision. Winning at cards and roulette are examples (Skinner, 1953).

In the laboratory, intermittent reinforcement may be delivered precisely according to different schedules or combinations of schedules (see Ferster

& Skinner, 1957). The schedule may be either (1) arranged by a system outside the organism, or (2) controlled by the behavior itself (Skinner, 1953, p. 100). The former may be determined by the clock and is referred to as *interval reinforcement.* The latter, which is determined by the number of responses emitted by the organism, is referred to as *ratio reinforcement* (see Table 6-3).

When fixed schedules are used, ratio or interval, the timing of reinforcement is certain. Typically, responding slows down immediately after reinforcement and then gradually increases in rate. The "slowdown" in response rate can be avoided through the use of a variable schedule. The delivery of reinforcement is uncertain, and the rate of responding is more nearly constant.

Intermittent reinforcement for a particular response can sustain behavior for long periods of time. Reinforcement may be frequent at first, but then is gradually reduced. For example, a television program may become less reinforcing as jokes or story lines become less interesting. Someone who has followed the program from the beginning, however, may continue to watch the program for a long time (Skinner, 1966a, p. 164). The initial high frequency of reinforcement, followed by gradually decreasing reinforcements, is referred to as *stretching the ratio.*

Table 6-3. Comparison of Ratio and Interval Schedules of Reinforcement

Ratio Reinforcement	Interval Reinforcement
Reinforcement delivery is based on number of responses emitted	Reinforcement delivery is based on elapsed time *Examples:* Reading books, going to the theatre, watching television (Skinner, 1966a)
Fixed: A constant number of responses generates reinforcement (e.g., every fifth response) *Examples:* Selling on commission; pay for piecework in industry	*Fixed:* Reinforcement for a correct response at a constant time interval (e.g., every 15 seconds)
Variable: Reinforcement delivered after a varying number of correct responses (e.g., every fifth, eighth, third, etc.) *Examples:* Payoffs from slot machines, roulette, horse races, and other games of "chance"	*Variable:* Reinforcement delivered for an appropriate response at varying time intervals (e.g., every 10 seconds, 4 seconds, 7 seconds, etc.)

Rule-Governed Behavior. The process referred to as shaping exposes the subject to changing contingencies of reinforcement for the performance of progressively more accurate behaviors. This method of developing complex behaviors is referred to as contingency-governed behavior (Skinner, 1969). However, for the human learner, not all behaviors are acquired through direct exposure to response consequences. "Few people drive a car at a moderate speed and keep their seat belts fastened because they have actually avoided or escaped from serious accidents by doing so" (Skinner, 1953, p. 168). Instead, rules for behavior have been derived from the contingencies and these descriptions of contingencies are often transmitted verbally to the individual. Rules of grammar and spelling are an example (Skinner, 1969). Also, many proverbs and maxims are crude examples of social reinforcement by the culture (Skinner, 1969, p. 123). The legal, ethical, and religious practices of a society are compiled into laws and other codified procedures so that the individual may emit appropriate behavior without direct exposure to response contingencies.

The behavior emitted in the contingency-governed condition differs from the emitted behavior in the rule-governed condition (Skinner, 1953, p. 151). For example, an actor's behavior begins with a memorized script and prescribed actions. However, the behavior is influenced by the reactions of other cast members during emission so that it becomes shaped in subtly different ways. This phenomenon often is referred to as "living the part" (Skinner, 20, p. 151).

Rule-governed behavior differs from contingency-governed behavior in another way. The consequences of a response alter the probability of future occurrence of the response; however, the rule does not. The topography of a response may be controlled by a maxim, rule, or other verbal statement of contingencies; however, the probability of response execution remains undetermined (Skinner, 1953, p. 147). The rule functions as a discriminative stimulus, and may or may not be followed by the appropriate behavior.

PRINCIPLES OF INSTRUCTION

The principles of operant conditioning were developed in the experimental laboratory in the late 1930s. Then in the early 1950s, Skinner turned his attention to classroom application of the methodology. He recommended the application of the principles of operant conditioning to the design of programs to develop students' verbal responses in school subjects. These programs were to be implemented in mechanical devices referred to as teaching machines (Skinner, 1954). He also recommended the development of a technology of teaching for classroom use derived from operant conditioning (Skinner, 1958, 1968b).

Basic Assumptions

Assumptions about the nature of learning and the nature of science established the parameters within which the principles of operant conditioning were developed in the laboratory. Similarly, B. F. Skinner's beliefs about the nature of schooling and classroom learning established the parameters for his technology of teaching.

The Nature of Education.   The educational system is extremely important because the welfare of any culture depends on it. A culture is no stronger than its capacity to transmit its skills, beliefs, and practices to the next generation, and this responsibility belongs to education (Skinner, 1953).

Contemporary education, however, faces two major problems in fulfilling this mission. One is that education takes place in an artificial setting, since it must establish behaviors useful to the individual in the future rather than in the present (Skinner, 1953). For example, upon saying correctly in French to a Frenchman, "Please pass the salt," one is reinforced by receiving the salt. In the classroom, however, the behavior receives a good mark (Skinner, 1953).

A second problem for education is that increased access has reduced some of its special status. In modern society, fewer economic and social advantages are dependent on education and the system therefore has lost some of its control (Skinner, 1953).

Faced with these two problems, the school has resorted to the use of aversive control. Students complete their work primarily to avoid aversive stimuli such as teacher criticism, classroom ridicule, a trip to the principal's office, and loss of recess (Skinner, 1968b). Furthermore, the by-products of aversive control add to the problem. These by-products include apathy, forgetting, inattention, truancy, and vandalism (Skinner, 1958).

Among the solutions proposed for improving education are (1) finding better teachers, (2) emulating model schools, (3) raising standards, and (4) reorganizing the content of the curriculum. However, these solutions are deficient according to Skinner (1958) because they do not attack the basic problem. That is, none of the recommendations specifically addresses the basic process for which education is responsible: learning. Instead, the suggestions discuss only events that may or may not affect the learning process. In Skinner's view, no institution can realize progress and improvement until it analyzes the basic processes for which it is responsible.

Learning in the Classroom Setting. The classroom teacher according to Skinner (1968b) is primarily responsible for developing in the learner those verbal behaviors that represent subject-matter skills and knowledges. Specifically, the two assignments to be accomplished are (1) constructing the verbal and nonverbal behavioral repertoires that represent learning, and (2) generating a high probability of those behaviors referred to as "interest," "enthusiasm," or "motivation for learning" (Skinner, 1958, p. 379). Given these assignments, the function of teaching is to expedite the acquisition of the necessary verbal and nonverbal behaviors required by the culture (Skinner, 1968a).

However, traditional discussions of classroom learning are not based on precise analyses of the learning process (Skinner, 1968b). Instead, they are maxims or "rules of thumb." Briefly summarized, these maxims are (1) the student learns by doing, (2) the student learns from experience, and (3) the student learns by trial and error. However, simply performing some behavior does not guarantee that the behavior will be repeated. Similarly, simply bringing the student into contact with the environment does not guarantee learning. Finally, although trial-and-error learning refers to the consequences of behavior, it implies that learning occurs only when mistakes are made.

A Technology of Teaching. The specific characteristics of the educational setting differ from those of the laboratory. Nevertheless, the dynamics of behavioral change are the same (Skinner, 1968b). In the laboratory, internal states such as "hunger" were redefined in terms of observable conditions or events. In the classroom, internal states can also be defined in observable terms. "Readiness," for example, is the set of behaviors already in the student's behavioral repertoire.

Behavioral change in the laboratory setting is a function of physical conditions and observable events in the environment. Similarly, behaviors learned in the classroom are also a function of manipulable, observable factors. Skinner (1954) noted that the typical classroom is characterized by (1) the infrequency of positive reinforcement, (2) the excessive lengths of time between behavior and reinforcement, and (3) the lack of programs that lead the child through a series of successive approximations to the final behavior.

According to Skinner (1958, 1968b), the development of a technology of teaching would yield programs of carefully selected stimuli and reinforcers needed to teach verbal behaviors. In basic arithmetic alone, Skinner (1968b) estimated that approximately 50,000 reinforcements for each student would be needed to ensure that the skills are acquired. Since the teacher cannot provide the needed reinforcements, a mechanical device is needed according to Skinner. The machine presents material one step at a time, the student responds, and the machine provides feedback to the student on the correctness of the answer. If correct, the student moves forward. Both knowledge of right answers and the opportunity to operate the machine were considered to be reinforcing for appropriate responses.

In summary, three assumptions support Skinner's approach to a technology of teaching. First, the experimental analysis of behavior applied in the laboratory also applies to the classroom. Second, behavioral repertoires in the classroom may be shaped in the same manner as other behaviors. Third, teaching machines are needed to provide the large number of reinforcements for behavioral responses in the subject area.

The Components of Instruction

The design of effective instruction requires careful attention to two important issues: the selection of discriminative stimuli and the use of reinforcement.

Selecting the Stimulus. In classroom instruction, selection of stimuli for learning includes two major concerns. One is that stimulus discrimination and stimulus generalization are important prerequisites for the learning of more complex verbal behaviors. In discrimination, for example, the student must learn to respond verbally "p" to the "p," but not to "r," "d," or "b." Then the response must be reinforced in the presence of different forms of the letter, such as "P," "p," and "p."

The other important consideration is stimulus control. In many situations, the student's responses must come under the control of the student's verbal repertoire. For example, in learning to recite a poem, the student first must frequently look at the text for assistance. Eventually, however, the student is able to recite the poem without prompting. Stimulus control has been transferred from the textual material to verbal stimuli generated by the student (Skinner, 1958).

Similarly, when pictures are first associated with words to assist the student in saying the correct word, the picture is the stimulus that controls the student's response. A picture of a flag, for example, induces the student to respond "flag" to the four-letter word. Inducing a response through prompting is not learning, however (Skinner, 1968b). The picture of the flag gradually must be withdrawn so that the word alone has control over the student's verbal response.

In the social environment of the classroom, a variety of verbal and nonverbal events may serve as discriminative stimuli. Verbal examples, such as "Take out your pencils," "Look at this picture", and many others are used daily in instruction.

Planning for good management in the classroom can include nonverbal stimuli and thus reduce the need for verbal directions. In one classroom, for example, the teacher used colored name tags for the children. A particular color indicated the work or study group to which the child was to report on a particular day. This technique permitted the teacher to rotate group membership easily on a daily basis without confusion. In addition, a child who needed help with seatwork set up a little red tent provided in each work folder. The tent served as a discriminative stimulus for the teacher's behavior and it eliminated hand and arm waving (Becker, 1973).

Providing Reinforcement.   To be effective, reinforcement must be immediately contingent on the emission of the correct response. In the school setting, the conditioned reinforcers of marks, grades, and diplomas are intended to bring the ultimate consequences of graduation closer to day-by-day activities (Skinner, 1958). Such reinforcers signal progress through the system; however, the relationship between these reinforcers and particular forms of behavior is not well specified. Additional reinforcers are needed.

Natural Reinforcers.   An important consideration in using reinforcement effectively is to identify the reinforcers already available in the classroom (Skinner, 1968b). Examples include playing with mechanical toys, painting, and cutting with scissors (Skinner, 29). These examples and others are natural reinforcers. That is, they feed back nonaversive changes in the environment. Other examples of natural reinforcers are: (1) finding the right word to describe something, (2) resolving a temporary confusion, and (3) the opportunity to advance to the next stage of an activity (Skinner, 1958, p. 380). Further, a child learning to read is reinforced when his or her vocal responses to a text compose verbal stimuli known to the child (i.e., the material "makes sense"). In addition, the research conducted by David Premack (1959) indicates that children's preferred activities will reinforce their less preferred activities. For the child who prefers playing with mechanical toys to painting, time with the toys may be used to reinforce participation in art activities.

Contrived Reinforcers.   Education, however, takes place in an artificial setting and is only a small part of a student's world. To rely entirely on natural reinforcers is not possible. Instead, contrived or "arranged" reinforcers must be used to bridge the gap between the early stages of learning and the setting in which natural reinforcers can function. Contrived reinforcers include verbal comments, gold stars, early dismissal, and free time. They must be used judiciously, however, with careful attention both to effectiveness and to the transfer of stimulus control.

The Timing of Reinforcement. Particularly important in the effectiveness of reinforcement is timing the delivery of reinforcing stimuli. "A fatal principle is 'letting well enough alone'—giving no attention to a student so long as he behaves well and turning to him only when he begins to cause trouble" (Skinner, 1968b, p. 180). Since the attention of the teacher is often reinforcing in the classroom, the careless teacher unintentionally will reinforce the attention-getter and the show-off.

Another example is that of dismissing the class early. If the class is dismissed when the students are loud or disruptive, the early dismissal reinforces inappropriate behavior. Instead, the teacher must time the dismissal to occur when the class is quiet and orderly.

The mistiming of reinforcement also occurs with brightly colored and attractive learning materials. Bright colors, animated sequences, and other innovations have a temporary effect—they induce the student to look at the materials (Skinner, 1968b, p. 105). However, they reinforce the student only for looking at the materials and not for having worked through them. Thus the student is not taught to look and listen. In effective instruction, the student should attend to the situation because previous encounters were reinforcing. Similarly, an attractive school buiding reinforces the behavior of coming in view of it and a colorful classroom reinforces only the behavior of entering it (Skinner, 29, p. 105). Although attending is indeed important, good instruction reinforces the student *after* he or she has read the page, listened to the explanation, solved the problem, and so on.

The Use of Aversive Control. Classroom control often includes both the application of aversive stimuli and the withdrawal of positive reinforcement. Aversive stimuli include ridicule, criticism, detention, trips to the principal's office, and others (Skinner, 1968b). Aversive stimuli present in the normal school routine also influence behavior. For example, students may engage in study to avoid performing poorly on a test (the consequences of not studying). Furthermore, class projects may be completed, not for the positive reinforcement of solving a problem, but to avoid the consequence of not completing the project.

Problems with Aversive Control. Two problems are associated with aversive control. One is the escape behaviors and emotional responses that are by-products of the method. They include forgetting, inattention, truancy, and vandalism, as well as subtle forms of behavior, such as looking at the teacher while not paying attention (Skinner, 1968b, p. 97). The emotional side effects of such escape behaviors include apathy, anxiety, anger, and resentment, all of which inhibit learning.

The second problem associated with the use of aversive control is that punishment does not generate positive behaviors. "We do not strengthen good pronunciation by punishing bad, or skillful movements by punishing awkward" (Skinner, 1968b, p. 149).

Admonitions can be used effectively, according to Skinner, only if they are appropriately applied. Reprimands should be in the form of "gentle admonitions" for small units of behavior (Skinner, 1968b, p. 101). Slight reprimands to the child who is learning to tie a shoelace for holding the lace wrong or moving it in the wrong direction are acceptable. Such admonitions provide the opportunity for generating the correct movements. By admonishing small units of behaviors, the learner can select the correct response from a small number of possibilities and new behavior is generated.

Unfortunately, punishing contingencies are inherent in many traditional classroom practices, such as the practice of "assign and test" (Skinner, 1968b). For example, a student may be faced with an assignment to write a term paper, which is a set of terminal contingencies. The student must sink or swim in this situation. Unless the student has been taken through a carefully planned sequence of behaviors (constructing simple and complex sentences, writing topic sentences, writing paragraphs, etc.), the exercise of writing the paper constitutes escape behavior undertaken to avoid the punishment of a low grade. When the paper is returned a few days or weeks later, the errors in grammer, punctuation, and organization have been marked and the grade assigned. Furthermore, the corrections on the term paper are punishments for wrong behavior.

Designing Instruction for Complex Skills

The classroom behaviors that are the major responsibility of the educational system, according to Skinner (1954, 1958, 1968a), are verbal behaviors. In discussing the applications of operant conditioning to the classroom, Skinner originally focused on subject-matter skills. He pointed out that the teacher's role is not that of imparting information to the student; instead, "information" and "knowledge" can be defined in terms of the behavior from which knowledge is inferred and then the behavior can be taught directly (Skinner, 1958). Instead of teaching an ability to read, behavioral repertoires that differentiate children who can read from those who cannot need to be identified (Skinner, 1958).

Shaping Verbal Behaviors. Complex verbal repertoires may be established in human learners in much the same manner as behavioral repertoires are established in the animal laboratory. First, the important verbal responses that represent knowledge in the subject area are identified. Then verbal sequences composed of a stimulus, a response by the student, and confirmation of the response are designed for each term. These verbal sequences, referred to as *frames*, are arranged to lead the student from a state of no knowledge to skill in the subject matter. In other words, the process of becoming competent in a field is divided into a series of discrete steps with reinforcement for the accomplishment of each step. In this way, complex behavioral repertoires may be developed (Skinner, 1954, p. 94).

In a typical Skinnerian program, the instruction shapes the student's behavior through (1) the withdrawal of verbal cues or prompts (referred to as "vanishing"), and (2) the transfer of stimulus control. An example is the use of labeled charts to learn medical school anatomy (Skinner, 1958). The labels are covered up, one by one, until the student can respond to the particular body part with the correct medical name. Stimulus control has passed from the printed label to the body part.

The transfer of stimulus control is also illustrated by the program that teaches color names to children, developed by Taber and Glaser (1962). In the first stages of the program, wide bands of color are paired with the color names and the bands serve as prompts. Gradually, the color bands are narrowed and finally withdrawn so that the children are responding only to printed letters. Stimulus control has passed from the color to the printed word.

Successful discrimination programs have been implemented in a number of subjects. One example is a program developed to teach lisping children to discriminate the "s" sounds in words (Anderson & Faust, 1973). The initial set of frames paired the "s" sound with very unlike sounds, such as "p" and "d," with the "s" sound intensified. After correct responses to these paired stimuli, the student was presented the "s" sound paired with the similar sounds of "z" and "th."

The next set of frames required the identification of the "s" sound as the initial consonant in words. Again, the early discriminations were simple, such as "sip" and "dip," with the identifications becoming progressively more difficult. Finally, the sequence included stimuli of two- and three-syllable words. The learner identified the sound in both the medial and final word positions. The terminal skill in the program was that of identifying "s" in words that also contain the sound "th," such as the word "thistle."

Teaching Machines. The completed instruction, referred to as a program or programmed instruction, should be implemented by a mechanical device that controls the student's progress through the material. In this way, reinforcement is assured only for correct responses. When programs are implemented in a book format, students may look ahead, skip frames, or lose their places.

Early mechanical teaching machines provided contingent reinforcement for right answers in the form of (1) confirmation for correct answers, (2) the opportunity to move forward to new material, and (3) the opportunity to operate the equipment. Current versions of the teaching machine include desktop models that are equipped with earphones and voice feedback. In addition, the microcomputer, when used with drill-and-practice programs for discrimination skills, is a current example of the Skinnerian concept of programming instruction.

In the classroom, Skinner (1954, 1961) envisioned the teaching machine in the role of patient tutor. The machine would provide individualization of instruction and also develop mastery of a variety of subject-related skills. The early machines, however, were limited in the types of reinforcement that could be delivered and in the flexibility of the delivery system. The microcomputer, however, expands the range of potential reinforcers and can be programmed to provide appropriate feedback for a variety of responses. Included in the potential reinforcers are the opportunity to play simple games and the opportunity to develop one's own programs.

In summary, designing instruction for verbal behaviors requires that the stimulus-response-feedback frames build from simple to complex. Guiding the learning process occurs through the reinforcement of progressively more difficult responses, and the transfer of stimulus control passes from the text to stimuli within the learner or to new textual stimuli.

EDUCATIONAL APPLICATIONS

Like Watson's behaviorism in the 1920s, Skinner's methodology has enjoyed a wide popularity. Unfortunately, the rapid popularization of the concepts led to misapplications in the classroom setting. Many of the individualized materials copied the stimulus-response-feedback format of programmed instruction, but not the substance. Textbook materials subdivided into sentences with blanks do not shape verbal behaviors. The disillusionment of educators with these poorly developed programs and the clumsiness of the original teaching machines contributed to the rapid decline of the programmed instruction movement. Also, the token economy programs developed for behavioral management in the classroom often focused on trivial behaviors, contributing to the view that the methodology has only limited applications.

Classroom Issues

B. F. Skinner's approach to learning is in terms of the factors responsible for behavioral change. Therefore, the issues of importance to education are discussed either as behaviors or as stimuli that lead to behavioral change.

Learner Characteristics. In the Skinnerian framework, learner characteristics are particular behaviors that students bring to the learning situation, and they may influence the acquisition of new behaviors.

Individual Differences. According to Skinner (1953), individual differences in student behaviors are the result of (1) the organism's genetic endowment, and (2) a particular history of reinforcement. The behavior of mentally retarded individuals, for example, is primarily the product of a defective genetic endowment. However, planned programs can develop new skills (Skinner, 1968b).

In Skinner's view (1968b), defective reinforcement contingencies in the individual's experience result in the failure to acquire a variety of skilled behaviors. An example is "rhythm" (Skinner, 1958). Some individuals, such as skilled typists and musicians, are under the influence of reinforcers that generate subtle timing. However, the development of this and other skills that influence career choices, artistic interests, and participation in sports, typically is unplanned. Yet, important skills that presently contribute to such individual differences can be taught. A simple machine can teach a child first to tap in unison and then to echo more and more subtle rhythmic patterns that constitute "a sense of rhythm."

The potential of mechanical devices that present instruction (1968b) is (1) to provide the necessary individual reinforcement and (2) to correct the problems caused by multitrack systems and ungraded classes. In these situations, large groups of students move forward at the same speed and are required to meet the same criteria, usually those of the mediocre or average student. In contrast, teaching machines can accommodate different entry skills and are also self-paced.

Readiness for Learning. In the operant conditioning framework, "readiness" is the behavioral repertoire that the student brings to the learning situation. Deficiencies in particular entry skills may be corrected through the use of carefully designed programs.

The concept of readiness interpreted as age or maturational level is unacceptable in the Skinnerian concept of designing instruction. Chronological age is of little help in determining the presence or absence of important skills (Skinner, 1953, p. 156). Also, developmental studies may indicate the amount usually learned by a child of a given age; however, such studies do not indicate the extent of a child's intellectual development under an appropriate schedule of events (Homme, deBaca, Cottingham, & Homme, 1968). For example, once a child can discriminatively respond to objects, planned contingency management can advance the child's reading levels in a systematic way independent of age.

Motivation. Behaviors that illustrate interest, enthusiasm, appreciation, or "dedication" are included in descriptions of motivation. The diligent and eager student, the individual who enjoys "reading good books," and the scientist who works long hours in the laboratory are all said to be motivated (Skinner, 1968b).

Such sustained activity in the absence of observable reinforcement is the result of a particular history of reinforcement. It is not the result of natural contingencies. No child really learns to plant seed because he or she is reinforced by the resulting harvest, nor do we learn to read because we enjoy interesting books (Skinner, 1968b, p. 154). Such long-range natural contingencies are insufficient to develop and maintain "dedicated" behavior. Instead, dedication is the result of exposure to a gradually increasing variable-ratio schedule of reinforcements. The individual first receives an immediate "payoff" for engaging in the activity (Skinner, 1968b). Then the reinforcements are gradually extended, referred to as stretching the ratio, until the activity itself acquires secondary reinforcing power. Ironically, the same reinforcement schedule produces both the compulsive gambler and the dedicated scientist (i.e., a variable-ratio schedule). However, only the scientist is referred to by society as "dedicated" (Skinner, 1963b).

Cognitive Processes and Instruction.   Internal or mental events are included in the operant conditioning paradigm only as identified behaviors. Therefore, transfer of learning is excluded from Skinner's formulations, but learning-how-to-learn skills and problem solving, defined behaviorally, are included.

Transfer of Learning.   Thorndike and Woodworth's (1901) experiments explained students' performance on learning tasks as caused in part by the degree of similarity between those tasks and prior learning tasks. Therefore, training in particular skills, such as playing the piano, is said to improve performance in playing other instruments. According to Skinner (1953), however, transfer merely appears to strengthen behavior without reinforcing it directly. Many responses, in fact, possess common elements, such as the use of the same musculature. Skill in manipulating tools and instruments, for example, may be a part of a number of different responses. "Transfer," then, is simply the reinforcement of "common elements wherever they occur" (Skinner, 1953, p. 94).

Learning "How-to-Learn" Skills.   According to Skinner (1953, 1968b), the process commonly referred to as thinking often means behaving in a particular way with regard to certain stimuli. When a child responds to certain stimulus properties, the child's response has come under the control of those stimuli. An example is a child's identification of a closed three-sided plane figure as a triangle. The child's identification is under the control of the figure. Little is gained in such situations by describing the learning as that of "forming an abstraction."

Certain activities typically identified with thinking, however, should be analyzed and taught (Skinner, 1968b). Such behaviors are referred to as *precurrent responses* because they either change the environment or change the learner so that an effective response becomes possible. Thus precurrent responses are defined as "behavior which affects behavior" (Skinner, 1966b, p. 216). Precurrent responses are covert; that is, they are private events that are not observable.

Also, they are the self-management behaviors that increase the probability of an effective response to a stimulus. Included are (1) reviewing the characteristics of a particular problem or calculating a mathematical answer by speaking silently to oneself, and (2) visualizing a problem or situation in the "mind's eye" (i.e., covert seeing) (Skinner, 1968b).

Other self-management behaviors that are precurrent responses include (1) attending to stimuli, (2) underlining important ideas in textual material, (3) using mnemonic devices or other cues to remember important ideas, and (4) rearranging the elements in a problem situation so that a solution is more likely.

Teaching Problem Solving. In the true "problem situation," the subject has no response immediately available that will reduce the deprivation or remove the aversive stimulus (Skinner, 1953, p. 246). If the room is too warm, for example, a problem exists if we cannot open the window (Skinner, 1968b). The problem is solved when we change the situation so that either (1) the available response can occur, or (2) the deprivation or aversive stimulation is reduced in some other way. Either we find some way to get the window open or some other means to cool the room (Skinner, 1968b).

Formally defined, problem solving is "any behavior which, through the manipulation of variables, makes the appearance of a solution more probable" (Skinner, 1953, p. 247). The "difficulty" of a problem depends on the availability of a response in the subject's repertoire that solves the problem. If no response is immediately available, the problem is difficult. To maximize the likelihood of a response (solution), the individual must change the situation so that he or she can respond appropriately. Steps that may be taken include (1) reviewing the problem carefully and clarifying the problem, (2) rearranging or regrouping the components of the problem, and (3) searching for similiarities between the problem and others that have been solved. In anagrams, for example, the player maximizes the chances of forming a word from the set of letters by regrouping the letters in logical sequences (i.e., vowels separated by consonants).

Individuals learn to solve problems effectively by manipulating stimuli and receiving reinforcement for the behavior. Reinforcement for the effective manipulation of the problem situation will reduce the occurrence of haphazard or trial-and-error responses to problems.

The Social Context for Learning. Reinforcers that require the mediation of another person are referred to as social reinforcers. This group includes the positive reinforcers of attention, approval, and affection. Negative reinforcers include disapproval, insult, contempt, and ridicule.

Social reinforcers, both positive and negative, have been used in group settings for the modification and maintenance of behavior. However, the relationships between stimuli, responses, and reinforcers in a social setting are both dynamic and reciprocal. For example, two children alone in a room with few toys provide an ideal situation for the shaping of selfish behavior (Skinner, 1958).

Behavior in the classroom is also a product of ongoing and complex contingencies that include teacher and students reinforcing each other both positively and negatively (Skinner, 1968a, p. 252). If a student is not punished by his or her peers for answering the teacher's questions and is reinforced by the teacher, he or she will answer as often as possible. If the teacher calls only on students whose hands are raised, the student will raise his or her hand. Similarly, teachers who are reinforced by right answers will call on students whose hands are raised. However, teachers who are reinforced by wrong answers are exercising aversive control, and they typically call on students who do not raise their hands (Skinner, 1968a).

Therefore, designing a classroom environment to modify behavior must take into account the reciprocal reinforcement characteristics of a social setting. Brigham (1978, p. 266) describes one study in which special education children were taught to reinforce the positive comments of other children and teachers. As their behavior changed, so did the environment and they became skillful at manipulating the environment. Furthermore, the children's behaviors changed the teacher's environment as well because the children became the source of social reinforcement for their teachers.

Developing a Classroom Strategy

The classroom teacher can make use of Skinner's technology in two ways. One is the appropriate use of reinforcement in classroom interactions, and the other is in the development of individualized instructional materials.

Developing a Positive Classroom Climate. An important application of Skinner's technology is that of developing a positive classroom climate. This goal differs from that of implementing an extensive behavior modification program. Skinner (1973) notes that an obvious approach, such as a token economy, may indeed be necessary in a totally disruptive classroom. However, a teacher can make the transition from punishment to positive reinforcement with one simple change—merely by responding to student successes rather than to student failures (Skinner, 1973, p. 15). Instead of pointing out what students are doing wrong, point out what they are doing right. The result in Skinner's view will be an improved classroom atmosphere and more efficient instruction.

Applying the technology developed by Skinner in the classroom can make use of the following steps.

STEP 1.   Analyze the current classroom environment.

1.1 What are the positive student behaviors currently receiving reinforcement in the classroom? The undesirable behaviors that are receiving reinforcement? For example, withholding help so that the child has an opportunity to demonstrate his or her knowledge and then providing help when the child shows discouragement may be reinforcing behavior which indicates discouragement (Skinner, 1968b, p. 252).

1.2 For which behaviors is punishment currently dispensed in the classroom? (Recall Skinner's definition of punishment: removal of a positive reinforcer or introduction of an aversive stimulus from which the individual seeks escape.)

1.3 What is the frequency of punishment? Have the punished behaviors been suppressed, but other, related behaviors appeared?

STEP 2.   Develop a list of potential positive reinforcers.

2.1 What are the students' preferred activities? (Students can rank their preferences on a list; young children can identify pictures.)

2.2 Which of the punished behaviors identified in step 1.2 may be used as reinforcers? For example, if talking with peers currently is punished, consider incorporating it occasionally as a reinforcer for less preferred activities, such as completing seatwork assignments quietly.

2.3 Which activities that you have observed in the natural setting may serve as positive reinforcers for other behaviors? One reading teacher, for example, expressed difficulty in keeping children "on task" because they constantly interrupted to discuss the progress of their favorite TV shows that aired the previous evening. Discussing the TV programs for 10–15 minutes is a potential reinforcer in that setting.

STEP 3.   Select the behavioral sequences to be initially implemented in the classroom. Include discriminative stimuli and reinforcers.

3.1 Which of the punished behaviors identified in step 1.2 may be restructured in the form of positive behaviors? For example, use positive reinforcement for promptness instead of punishment for tardiness. Becker (1973) suggests that instead of punishment for fighting, a student may earn 1 minute of recess for no fighting.

3.2 Which of the positive student behaviors from the list in step 1.1 are occurring infrequently? Examples may include demonstrating independence in learning by getting and putting away needed materials on time, attending to relevant characteristics of stimuli during instruction, and so on.

3.3 What are the initial discriminative stimuli to be used? To which stimuli is the transfer of behavioral control to be made? For example, the verbal statement "Time to begin," may be replaced by a signal, such as a bell, and then by the students' observation of the clock time.

STEP 4.   Implement the behavioral sequences, maintaining anecdotal records and making changes when necessary.

4.1 Are the rules for classroom behavior clear and consistent?

4.2 Is the method for earning reinforcement clear, and is reinforcement provided for improved behavior?

4.3 Does every child have the opportunity to earn reinforcement for behavioral change? If reinforcement is provided only for one or two behaviors that must meet a high standard, some children have no means of earning reinforcement in the classroom. They are likely to seek attention in disruptive ways (Resnick, 1971).

4.4 Following initial behavioral change, are reinforcements provided after longer intervals (stretching the ratio), and are other reinforcers also implemented?

Programming Instruction.   Programs to develop verbal behaviors should be designed to lead the student from a state of no knowledge to proficiency in one or more skills. The following steps are recommended in the development of a Skinnerian or constructed response program.

STEP 1.   Identify the terminal skill to be acquired and analyze the subject matter to be learned.

1.1 What is the nature of the terminal behavior? Is it a discrimination skill, such as learning color names, or is it the application of a rule, such as carrying in addition?

1.2 What terms or definitions must be learned in order to acquire the skill?

1.3 What types of examples should the student respond to during learning (e.g., color bands, simple and complex addition problems)?

STEP 2. Develop the initial sequence of frames and response confirmations.

2.1 What information should be placed in the first frame (referred to as a "copying frame")?

2.2 What is a logical sequence of responses (behaviors) that can be expected of the student?

2.3 What sequence of discriminative stimuli that progress from simple to complex can provide for the transfer of stimulus control?

STEP 3. Review the sequence of frames, reordering if necessary.

3.1 Does the sequence progress from simple to complex?

3.2 Are the prompts gradually vanished in the sequence?

3.3 Does the student respond to meaningful rather than trivial content?

STEP 4. Implement the instruction with a few students and revise if necessary.

4.1 Do the students experience difficulty with any of the frames? Such frames may need to be rewritten.

4.2 Do the students race through any of the frames, getting the right answer by only reading part of the frame? The frame may be superfluous or it may be asking trivial information.

4.3 Does the program lead to mastery performance on the criterion posttest?

Classroom Example

The following frames were developed to teach the concept "morpheme" to advanced high school students or college freshmen. The terminal skills are: (1) the student can define the term "morpheme," and

(2) the student can identify examples of free morphemes and bound morphemes.

Notice that each frame in the sequence builds on the preceding one. Also, each frame asks the student to supply an important term or terms and the information in the frame is essential to the answer.

Discussion of Classroom Example. A partial program for teaching the student to discriminate morphemes is illustrated by the frames on the following pages. This style of programming is also described as "constructed response" programming because the student writes or constructs the required answers.

The first frame is referred to as a "copying frame" since essentially it involves the student's copying or repeating basic information in the stimulus. Each frame includes one item of information to which the student responds. A cardboard marker that covers the answer is then removed; the student checks his or her answer and continues to the next frame. The cues or "prompts" for the correct answers are gradually withdrawn so that stimuli within the learner or other textual stimuli are generating appropriate responses (see frame 15).

Care should be taken in the design of programmed instruction to lead the student from no knowledge to skill proficiency. Notice the examples given in the unit on morphemes shown in Table 6-4. Frames 2 and 3 present the definition, later followed by the definition of bound and free morphemes.

The advantage of several short units of programmed instruction on specific skills is twofold. Remediation is provided that is targeted to specific deficiencies. Often students are unable to participate in ongoing instruction because they lack a particular skill. Continuation of the deficiency, however, only compounds the problem. In this example, students will be unable to analyze complex word meanings unless they first are able to differentiate commonly used morphemes.

The second advantage is that such materials can assist the teacher in individualizing instruction. Students who enter a grade lacking some essential skills or students who experience difficulty with the initial instruction for a topic may be given the materials while the teacher works with other students on other problems.

Review of the Theory

B. F. Skinner's principles of operant conditioning continued the tradition established by John Watson. That is, for psychology to become a science, the study of behavior must become the focus of psychological research. Unlike the other S-R theorists, Skinner avoided the contradiction posed by Pavlov's classical conditioning model and Thorndike's in-

Table 6-4. Introductory Frames on Morphemes

1. One aspect of linguistics is the analysis of words into the smallest units that carry meaning. The study of such word parts is an areas of study in l _ _ _ _ _ _ _ _ _ .

linguistics

2. The smallest word parts that carry meaning are *morphemes*. In the word "unhappy," the part "un-" means "not." Therefore, "un-" is a m _ _ _ _ _ _ _ .

morpheme

3. Some words are composed of only one morpheme or unit of meaning. An example is *cat*. In this case, the morpheme making up the word is _ _ _ .

cat

4. Sometimes morphemes may be added to existing words, for example, the letter "s". When added to some words, "s" means "more than one." In such a situation, the "s" is a _____ .

morpheme

5. Of course, some letters do not carry any meaning in words, such as the "s" in "slide." In this case, "s" is _ _ _ a morpheme.

not

6. Some words are composed of two or more morphemes. An example is "biology" which includes "bio_" (life) and "_logy" (study of). Biology, therefore, is composed of _____ _____ .

two
morphemes

7. The word "morpheme" itself may be analyzed as follows: "Morph_" = unit or form and "_eme" = "small." The complete word is composed of _____ _____ .

two
morphemes

8. Prefixes and suffixes are word parts that frequently function as units of meaning. An example is "pre_" (before or prior) as in "preview." In this example, the prefix is also a _____ .

morpheme

9. In the earlier example, "un_" in "unhappy" was identified as a morpheme. This prefix is a morpheme because it is a u _ _ _ _ _ _ _ _ _ _ _ _ _ .

unit of
meaning

10. Language includes two kinds of morphemes, one of which is "free morphemes." they are the smallest unit of meaning that can stand alone. For example, in the word "cats," the word part "cat" is a _ _ _ _ _ _ _ _ _ _ _ _ .

free
morpheme

11. Some words are composed only of free morphemes. The word "cowboy" is composed of two free morphemes. They are _ _ _ and _ _ _ .

cow and
boy

12. The other type of morpheme is a "bound morpheme." It is a unit of meaning that cannot stand alone. For example, the morpheme "s" in the word "cats" is a _ _ _ _ _ _ _ _ _ _ _ _ _ .

(*continued*)

Table 6-4, *Continued*

bound morpheme	13. The letter "s" in the word "cats" is a bound morpheme because it is a unit of meaning that can/cannot stand alone.
cannot	14. Some words may be composed of only bound morphemes. An example is the word "biology," composed of "bio_" and "_logy." This word includes two _____ _____ .
bound morphemes	15. Still other words, like "cats," may be composed of both bound and free morphemes. Another example is the word "unhappy," which includes _____free morpheme and _____ bound morpheme.
one one	16. The study of morphemes can be a means for building vocabulary. We have learned, for example, that "_logy" means "study of." Further, "psycho_" is a morpheme that means mind or mental life. Therefore, "psychology" means "study of the mind or mental life," based on the two _ _ _ _ _ _ _ _ _ _ _ _ _ _.
bound morphemes	

Source: Terry L. Norton, Winthrop College

strumental conditioning. He proposed a paradigm that includes both types of responses and proceeded to analyze the conditions responsible for emitted responses or operant behavior. (See Table 6-5.)

Skinner's analyses yielded a parsimonious system that was applied to the dynamics of behavioral change in both the laboratory and the classroom. Learning, represented by increased response rate, was described as a function of the three-component sequence (S^D)——(R)——$S^{Reinf.}$. Skinner described the typical practice of placing experimental animals in puzzle boxes and mazes as that of placing the subject in a "terminal contingency." That is, the animal must either sink or swim in the search for escape or food. Instead, the appropriate procedure is to shape the animal's behavior through carefully established stimulus-response-reinforcement sequences. Approximations to appropriate responses are reinforced on intermittent schedules until the behavioral repetoire is acquired, such as pigeons playing ping-pong.

In the classroom, Skinner described the practice of "assign-and-test" as one example of placing the human learner in a terminal contingency. Instead, Skinner recommends the practice of reinforcing the component behaviors, such as attending to stimuli and executing appropriate study behaviors. Punishment should be avoided because it produces unwanted emotional side effects and does not generate the desired positive behaviors.

Included in Skinner's analyses are the role of conditioned and natural reinforcers, positive and negative reinforcers, and generalized reinforcers. Also included is the development of programmed learning for verbal behaviors. Individual differences in entry skills and rates of learning may be accommodated by such materials.

Disadvantages. Two major problems in the application of Skinner's recommendations may be identified. One is that the technology for the experimental analysis of complex human behaviors is incomplete. Some students respond well in highly structured situations in which objectives and the steps to be taken are clearly specified. Others, however, are

Table 6-5. Summary of Skinner's Technology

Basic Elements	Definition
Assumptions	Behavioral change is a function of environmental conditions and events
Learning	A change in behavior represented by increased response frequency
Learning outcomes	New responses (behaviors)
Components of learning	(S^D) —— (R) —— $(S^{Reinf.})$
Designing instruction for complex learning	Design sequences of stimuli-responses-reinforcements to develop sets of complex responses
Major issues in designing instruction	Transfer of stimulus control, timing of reinforcement; avoidance of punishment

Analysis of the Technology	
Disadvantages	1. Technology for complex situations is incomplete; successful analysis depends on the skill of the technologist 2. Response frequency is difficult to apply to complex behaviors as a measure of probability
Applications to classroom practice	1. Analysis of states such as "readiness" and "motivation" 2. Analysis of aversive classroom practices and interactive classroom situations 3. Individualized learning materials; teaching machines

reinforced by the opportunity to explore on their own and to relate ideas without external directives. The procedures for identifying these and other differences in the variety of potential reinforcements is yet to be developed.

Second, in the classroom, response frequency as a measure of learning may be applied to simple behaviors, such as naming colors or adding two-digit numbers. Complex behaviors, however, such as diagnosing an illness or calculating one's taxes, are not conducive to response frequency as a measure of response probability.

Contributions to Classroom Practice. Three major contributions to educational practice are illustrated in Table 6-5. First, the search for conditions and behaviors that represent states such as "unmotivated" is an important step in the identification of an appropriate course of action. Second, observation of contemporary classrooms reveals many inconsistent and noncontingent uses of reinforcement that contribute to classroom discipline problems. An analysis of these interactive situations in terms of discriminative stimuli, responses, and reinforcements is an important step in correcting the problems. Third, programmed learning materials, if properly designed, can provide for individual differences in the classroom.

DISCUSSION QUESTIONS

1. How did Skinner redefine Thorndike's concept of "reward"?
2. A teacher gives his class free time after hearing that the group behaved well for a substitute teacher the day before. The good behavior, however, does not continue and the teacher complains that reinforcement theory does not work. What are the errors in the teacher's conclusion?
3. Skinner notes that students are often thrown into terminal contingencies when they are given assignments such as term papers. The students must then "sink or swim." What are the implications of that observation for teaching?

GLOSSARY

applied behavioral analysis The application of Skinner's experimental analysis of behavior to real-world settings such as classrooms and hospitals (also referred to as contingency management).

aversive stimuli   Those stimuli from which an individual seeks avoidance or escape.

contingency-governed behavior   The acquisition of behavior through direct exposure to response consequences.

differential reinforcement   The reinforcement of particular responses to the exclusion of others.

discriminative stimulus(S^D)   The stimulus that gains control over a subject's behavior by its continued presence when responses are reinforced. Examples include red and green traffic lights and verbal stimuli such as "Please pass the salt."

elicited responses   Skinner's term for reflexes; a class of behaviors that are correlated with particular stimuli, for example, an eye blink following dirt in the eye.

emitted responses   Behaviors for which no known correlative stimulus can be identified; operants.

experimental or functional analysis   The methodology used to identify the variables of which behavior is a function; accounts for behavior in terms of physical conditions that are both observable and manipulable.

extinction   The weakening and eventual disappearance of emitted responses through nonreinforcement.

learning   A change in the likelihood or probability of a response.

operant   Any response that acts on or operates on the environment to produce some consequence or change.

operant conditioning   The process of modifying a subject's behavior through the reinforcement of appropriate responses in the presence of the appropriate stimuli.

Premack principle   The rule that describes the relative power of certain reinforcers. Specifically, preferred activities may be used to reinforce less preferred activities.

precurrent responses   Activities often referred to by others as "thinking"; behaviors that make other behaviors more probable (e.g., reviewing a problem).

program   A series of changing contingencies that shapes behavior until the identified terminal behavior is generated.

punishment   The withdrawal of a positive reinforcer or the addition of a negative reinforcer to a behavioral situation.

reinforcement   Any consequence of a response that increases the probability of the behavior's recurrence.

　contrived reinforcers   Artificial reinforcers that are not normally provided by the environment (e.g., tokens and gold stars).

　generalized reinforcers   Reinforcers that function in a variety of situations.

Examples include attention, approval, affection, the agreement of peers, money, and others.

natural reinforcers   Activities that the individual likes to engage in, (e.g., completing a puzzle).

negative reinforcers   Aversive stimuli that strengthen behavior by being withdrawn from the situation.

positive reinforcers   Strengthen behavior by being added to the situation.

primary reinforcers   Increase response rate without training given the appropriate state of deprivation. Examples include food, drink, sleep, shelter, and sexual contact.

secondary reinforcers (also referred to as conditioned reinforcers)   Influence behavior through association with primary reinforcers.

respondent conditioning   The use of stimulus substitution so that responses are elicited by new stimuli (Pavlov's conditioning paradigm, Type S).

rule-governed behavior   The performance of a behavior for which a maxim or principle serves as the discriminative stimulus; not shaped through response consequences and therefore the rule cannot predict performance.

schedules of reinforcement   Different patterns of reinforcement used in the laboratory primarily to modify behavior. Examples include fixed, variable, ratio and interval schedules.

shaping   The gradual modification of behavior by initially reinforcing approximations of the appropriate response and then reinforcing only more accurate reproductions of the desired behavior.

superstitious behavior   Behavior that is reinforced accidentally and therefore increases in frequency.

REFERENCES

Anderson, R. C., & Faust, G. W. (1973). *Educational psychology: The science of instruction and learning.* New York: Dodd, Mead.

Becker, W. D. (1973). Application of behavior principles in typical classrooms. In C. E. Thoresen (Ed.), *Behavior modification in education. The seventy-second yearbook of the National Society for the Study of Education, Part I* (pp. 77–106). Chicago: University of Chicago Press.

Brigham, T. A. (1978). Self-control: Part II. In A. C. Catania & T. A. Brigham (Eds.), *Handbook of applied behavioral analysis.* (pp. 259–274). New York: Irvington.

Ferster, C. B., & Skinner, B. F. (1957). *Schedules of reinforcement.* New York: Appleton-Century-Crofts.

Homme, L. E., deBaca, R., Cottingham, L., & Homme, A. (1968). What behavioral engineering is. *The Psychological Record, 18,* 424–434.

Premack, D. (1959). Toward empirical behavior laws. I. Positive reinforcement. *Psychological Review, 66*(4), 219–233.

Resnick, L. (1971). Applying applied reinforcement. In R. Glaser (Ed.), *The nature of reinforcement,* (pp. 326–333). New York: Academic Press.

Skinner, B. F. (1935). Two types of conditioned reflex and a pseudotype. *Journal of General Psychology, 12,* 66–77.

Skinner, B. F. (1938). *The behavior of organisms.* New York: Appleton-Century-Crofts.

Skinner, B. F. (1948). "Superstition" in the pigeon. *Journal of Experimental Psychology, 38,* 168–172.

Skinner, B. F. (1950). Are theories of learning necessary? *Psychological Review, 57,* 193–216.

Skinner, B. F. (1953). *Science and human behavior.* New York: Macmillan.

Skinner, B. F. (1954). The science of learning and the art of teaching. *Harvard Educational Review, 24*(2), 86–97.

Skinner, B. F. (1958). Reinforcement today. *American Psychologist, 13,* 94–99.

Skinner, B. F. (1961). Why we need teaching machines. *Harvard Educational Review, 31*(4), 377–398.

Skinner, B. F. (1963a). Behaviorism at fifty. *Science, 140,* 951–958.

Skinner, B. F. (1963b). Operant behavior. *American Psychologist, 18,* 503–515.

Skinner, B. F. (1966a). Contingencies of reinforcement for designing a culture. *Behavioral Science, 11,* 159–166.

Skinner, B. F. (1966b). What is the experimental analysis of behavior? *Journal of the Experimental Analysis of Behavior, 9*(3), 213–218.

Skinner, B. F. (1968a). Teaching science in high school—What is wrong? *Science, 159,* 704–710.

Skinner, B. F. (1968b). *The technology of teaching.* New York: Appleton-Century-Crofts.

Skinner, B. F. (1969). *Contingencies of reinforcement.* New York: Appleton-Century-Crofts.

Skinner, B. F. (1973). The free and happy student. *Phi Delta Kappan, 55,* 13–16.

Skinner, B. F., (1978). *Reflections on behaviorism and society.* Englewood Cliffs, NJ: Prentice-Hall.

Skinner, B. F. (1984, February). In J. O. Green, Skinner's technology of teaching. *Classroom Computer Learning,* pp. 23–29.

Taber, J. I., & Glaser, R. (1962). An exploratory evaluation of discriminative transfer learning in a program using literal prompts. *Journal of Educational Research, 55,* 508–512.

Thorndike, E. L., & Woodworth, R. S. (1901). The influence of improvement in one mental function upon the efficiency of other functions: I, II, and III. *Psychological Review, 8,* 247–261, 384–395, 553–564.

Ware, B. (1978). What rewards do students really want? *Phi Delta Kappan, 59,* 355–356.

Watson, J. B. (1913). Psychology as the behaviorist sees it. *Psychological Bulletin, 20,* 158–177.

CHAPTER 7

Robert Gagné's Conditions of Learning

> . . . human skills, appreciations, and rea-
> sonings in all their great variety, as well
> as human hopes, aspirations, attitudes,
> and values, are generally recognized to de-
> pend for their development largely on the
> events called learning.
> *Gagné, 1977a, p. 2*

Robert Gagné's learning principles are the result of his search for the factors that account for the complex nature of human learning. His investigations began in the 1960s, during the period of disillusionment with the "grand learning theories." Research on military training problems indicated that reinforcement, distribution of practice, and response familiarity were inadequate for the design of instruction. Instead, three principles that contributed to successful instruction were identified by Gagné. They are (1) providing instruction on the set of component tasks that build toward the final task, (2) ensuring that each component task is mastered, and (3) sequencing the component tasks to ensure optimal transfer to the final task (Gagné, 1962a).

These investigations initiated Gagné's work into the psychological foundations of effective instruction. Other theorists during the 1960s maintained that an instructional technology or theory could be developed from the elements in learning theory. In contrast, Gagné (1977a) believes that the basis for instructional theory should be those factors that instruction can do something about.

Gagné's analyses began with the identification of the concept of learning hierarchies, that is, the particular skills that contribute to the learning of more complex skills (Gagné, 1968a, 1968b). He then identified five unique categories of learning (Gagné, 1972) and described both the environmental events and the stages of information processing required for each learning category (Gagné, 1977a, 1980).

PRINCIPLES OF LEARNING

The key to the development of a comprehensive learning theory, according to Gagné (1974, 1977a), is to identify the factors that account for the complex nature of human learning. Other theorists typically begin with a particular explanation of the learning process and then attempt to fit that process to human learning. Gagné, in contrast, began with the analysis of the variety of performances and skills executed by human beings and then provided an explanation for this variety.

Basic Assumptions

The assumptions on which Gagné bases his work are derived from the general nature of human learning and the particular characteristics of the learning process.

The Nature of Human Learning. Several elements are included in Gagné's conception of learning. Key factors are the relationship of learning to development and the diversity of human learning.

Learning and Human Development. Gagné's view of the role of learning in development differs from both the growth-readiness model and the Piagetian cognitive-development model. According to the growth-readiness model, certain growth patterns must occur before learning can be beneficial. Some followers of this model, for example, recommend that reading should not be taught to the child until a particular age is reached, such as 6 or 7.

In contrast, the Piagetian model describes intellectual development as the internalization of progressively more complex forms of logical thinking. In this model, learning contributes to the cognitive adaptation required for the development of logical thought processes.

The model described by Gagné, however, assigns a primary role to learning. In his view, learning is an important causal factor in the individual's development (Gagné, 1968a). Within the broad parameters established by growth, *"behavioral development results from the cumulative effects of learning"* (Gagné, 1968a, p. 178).

Two characteristics of learning account for its importance in development. One is that much of human learning generalizes to a variety of situations. Addition is one example. The situations to which this skill applies include computing wages and deductions, constructing a family budget, calculating taxes, and many others.

The Cumulative Learning Model.   The other important contribution of learning to development is that learning is cumulative. That is, many skills that are learned contribute to the learning of even more complex ones. Again, addition serves as an example. The skill of adding numbers contributes to the learning of long division. The child does not need to learn to add all over again when learning to divide. Instead, addition is incorporated into the new skill.

The importance of the cumulative model is demonstrated by applying it to the analysis of Piagetian conservation tasks. Typically, experiments have used training on one or two prior tasks, with the result that children have not attained conservation. The task "conservation of liquid," for example, may first be defined as a complex rule. The rule is "judging equalities and inequalities of volumes of liquids in rectangular containers" (Gagné, 1968a, p. 184). Analysis of this skill reveals several prerequisite skills that contribute to the final learning. Included are comparing sizes of rectangles by taking length and width into account, demonstrating increases in volume by changes in height when length and width are held constant, and so on.

The cumulative learning model, in other words, provides several sequentially ordered skills that provide concrete knowledge of containers, volumes, areas, lengths, widths, heights, and liquids. Performance on these prerequisites makes possible the learning of the complex rule, or conservation task.

In summary, intellectual development "may be conceived as the building of increasingly complex and interesting structures of learned capabilities" (Gagné, 1968a, p. 190). These learned capabilities contribute to the learning of more complex skills and they also generalize to other situations. The result is that an ever-increasing intellectual competence is generated.

The Diversity of Human Learning.   In Gagné's view, prior theories presented limited views of the nature of human learning. One group includes the theories derived from laboratory studies of learning; included are the theories of Pavlov, Thorndike, Hull, and Skinner. These models do not account for the human capacity to learn complex skills and abilities, according to Gagné (1977a). Some of them do describe subcomponents of human learning; however, these subskills are not the major objectives of learning. Examples are signal learning (Pavlov's model), S-R associations, and chainlike skills (see Table 7-1).

Table 7-1. Subcomponents of Human Learning

Type	Examples[a]
Pavlov's model: signal learning	Feelings of well-being generated earlier in life by a favorite stuffed toy or later by a favorite melody
S-R associations	Infant, after several associations, can correctly position its hands on the nursing bottle for feeding
Chainlike skills	Buttoning, fastening, printing, and writing
	Verbal: memorizing the pledge of allegiance or the lines of a poem

[a] *Source:* Gagné (1977a).

Although the S-R model has been used to characterize human learning, Gagné (1977a) observes that "pure" examples of S-R learning are difficult to find. Such learnings are rapidly incorporated into longer sequences. Letters of the alphabet, for example, rapidly become a part of decoding words.

Another type of learning has been referred to also as the representation of the "true" nature of learning. It is the "insight" experience identified by Gestalt psychologists. Two problems are associated with that perspective, however. First, although Gestalt theorists maintained that learning occurs when a subject "sees" a new relationship, the process of insight is not a spontaneous occurrence (Gagné, 1977a). Instead, it is influenced by transfer from prior learnings to new situations. In the school setting, children may display insight when they are led to understand relationships. An example is the relationship between weight and the pull of gravity (Gagné, 1977a, p. 14). The major problem with the Gestalt explanation, however, is that it, too, does not explain all learning. For example, learning to speak a foreign language and learning to read are not the result of insight.

The above analysis indicates that learning is not a single process (Gagné, 1970, 1972). Neither the learning of associations nor the problem solving described by the Gestalt theorists can be reduced one to the other. The learning of associations cannot be explained by insight nor can problem-solving behavior be explained by the pairing of stimulus elements (Gagné, 1977a). Therefore, no one set of characteristics can be applied to all learning.

A Definition of Learning. The human capacity for learning makes possible an almost infinite variety of behavioral patterns (Gagné, 1977a). Given this diversity, no one set of characteristics can account for such varied activities as learning to define a word, to write an essay, or to lace a shoe (Gagné, 1972, p. 2). Therefore, the task for learning theory is to identify the principles that account for the complex nature of human learning in all its variety.

If human learning is indeed a complex, multifaceted process, how is it to be defined? First, learning is the mechanism by which an individual becomes a competently functioning member of society (Gagné, 1977a). The importance of learning is that it is responsible for all the skills, knowledges, attitudes, and values that are acquired by human beings. Learning, therefore, results in a variety of different kinds of behaviors, referred to by Gagné (1972, 1977a) as *capabilities*. They are the outcomes of learning.

Second, these capabilities are acquired by human beings from (1) the stimulation from the environment, and (2) the cognitive processing undertaken by the learner. Formally defined, learning is the set of cognitive processes that transforms the stimulation from the environment into the several phases of information processing required for acquiring a new capability (Gagné & Briggs, 1979, p. 43).

The Components of Learning

Gagné's analysis of human learning identified five categories or varieties of learning. They are verbal information, intellectual skills, motor skills, attitudes, and cognitive strategies. These varieties represent different capabilities and performances. They are also learned in different ways. Learning the definition of the term ''butterfly stroke,'' for example, requires that the learner (1) attend to and process important elements in the definition, and (2) develop cues for the later recall and retrieval. Learning is tested by asking the student to restate the definition.

In contrast, learning to execute the butterfly stroke is quite a different matter. Knowledge of the specific steps in the sequence is required as well as the executive routine for performing the activity. Practice with feedback on learner performance is essential so that the individual may develop the internal kinesthetic cues that signal correct execution. Learning is demonstrated by the student's correct execution of the butterfly stroke in the water.

Each of the five varieties of learning is acquired in different ways. That is, each requires a different set of prerequisite skills and a different set of cognitive-processing steps. These requirements are referred to by Gagné (1977a) as the *internal conditions of learning*.

Gagné (1977a) also describes the types of environmental stimuli that are required to support the learner's cognitive processes during learning.

These particular stimuli are referred to as the *external conditions of learning*. However, they are also referred to as the events of instruction and their role is to support learning (see Figure 7-1). They are discussed in the section "Principles of Instruction." Discussed here are the components of learning: (1) the five varieties of learning, (2) the prerequisite skills for each variety, and (3) the cognitive processes required for learning each type of skill.

The Varieties of Learning. In the 1960s, efforts to identify instructional objectives led to an awareness that different classes of behaviors are acquired through learning. Efforts began in the identification of behavioral categories that consistently would indicate particular requirements for instruction (Gagné, 1965a, 1965b). However, accounting for the diversity of human learning in a systematic and comprehensive way is a difficult task. Some approaches attempted to reconcile laboratory learning descriptions and the behaviors taught in the classroom (Melton, 1964). For school subjects, Gagné (1972) noted that categories such as "cognitive learning," "rote learning," "discovery learning," and "concrete versus symbolic learning" were often used. The difficulty, however, is that these learning categories do not generalize to different settings. Examples may be classified as rote learning in one context and as conceptual in another (Gagné, 1972).

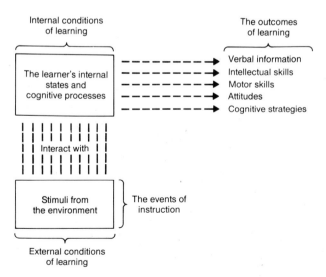

Figure 7-1. Essential components of learning and instruction.

A useful designation of different kinds of learning must be generalizable across subject areas, classrooms, and grade levels (Gagné, 1972). In addition, such categories must differ from each other in instructional requirements (Gagné, 1974, 1977a).

The five categories identified by Gagné meet the foregoing criteria. They are verbal information, intellectual skills, motor skills, attitudes, and cognitive strategies (Gagné, 1972, 1977a). Like the S-R associations and the insight experiences, none of these categories may be reduced to any other. Further, unlike associations and insight, they represent the range of human learning.

The varieties of learning are summarized in Table 7-2. They are referred to as capabilities because they make possible the prediction of many instances of performance by the learner (Gagné & Briggs, 1979, p. 51). An individual who has acquired an intellectual skill, for example, can interact with the environment using symbols. Composing sentences, adding two-digit numbers, and identifying colors are all intellectual skills. In contrast, the student who has learned verbal information can restate or paraphrase definitions and major points in bodies of knowledge. Examples include stating the formula for salt and defining the term "fulcrum." The capability of stating information, however, does not in itself imply the capability of applying information, such as identifying or using a fulcrum.

Verbal Information.   The capability represented by this category is that of acquiring labels, facts, and organized bodies of knowledge. In learning labels, a consistent verbal response or "name" is applied to an object or an object class, such as "rose" or "tiger." In learning facts, the relationships between two or more objects or events can be stated orally or in writing. "Columbus discovered America in 1492" and "rectangles have four sides" are examples. Larger bodies of knowledge that are learned as information include the Biblical story of the Creation and the contents of a local ordinance on littering.[1] The performance is that of stating, paraphrasing, or reporting a summary of learned information. This capability, however, involves only the restatement of information.

Intellectual Skills.   These capabilities are the skills that make human beings competently functioning members of society. The range of capabilities includes everyday skills such as balancing a checkbook and analyzing the evening news. Also included are the use of language concepts and almost all of mathematics. Intellectual skills may be described as including "the basic and at the same time the most pervasive structures of formal education" (Gagné & Briggs, 1974, p. 24).

Unlike factual information, however, intellectual skills cannot be learned by simply hearing them or looking them up (Gagné, 1977a, p. 11).

---

[1] Personal communication from Robert Gagné, April 7, 1983.

Table 7-2. Overview of the Five Varieties of Learning

Category of Learning	Capability	Performance	Examples
Verbal information	Retrieval of stored information (facts, labels, discourse)	Stating or communicating the information in some way	Paraphrasing a definition of patriotism
Intellectual skills	Mental operations that permit individuals to respond to conceptualizations of the environment	Interacting with the environment using symbols	Discriminating between red and blue; calculating the area of a triangle
Cognitive strategies	An executive control process that governs the learner's thinking and learning	Efficiently managing one's remembering, thinking, and learning	Developing a set of note cards for writing a term paper
Motor skills	Capability and "executive plan" for performing a sequence of physical movements	Demonstrating a physical sequence or action	Tying a shoelace; demonstrating the butterfly stroke
Attitude	Predisposition for positive or negative actions toward persons, objects, and events	Choosing personal actions toward or away from objects, events, or people	Electing to visit art museums; avoiding rock concerts

Source: Summarized from Gagné (1977a).

The major difference between information and intellectual skills is the difference between knowing *that* and knowing *how* (Gagné, 1974, p. 55). The student learns how to add integers, how to make the verbs and subjects of sentences agree, and countless other skills (Gagné, 1974). Each skill is that of interacting with the environment using a variety of symbols. Included are numbers, letters, words, and pictorial diagrams.

Unlike the other varieties of learning, intellectual skills include four discrete skills. From simple to complex, they are discrimination learning, learning of concrete and defined concepts, rule learning, and higher-order rule learning (problem solving). These skills are discussed in the section "Learning Hierarchies" and are summarized in Table 7-5.

Motor Skills. The capabilities that underlie the smooth execution of bodily performances are motor skills. Included are simple skills learned early in life, such as fastening clothing and executing communicable speech sounds (Gagné, 1977a). In the early years of schooling, important motor skills include printing and writing letters and symbols, skipping rope, balancing on a beam, and others. Later, motor skills include learning the separate skills involved in playing tennis, basketball, and other sports.

The common characteristic of all these skills is the requirement to develop smoothness of action, precision, and timing (Gagné, 1977a). The performances executed by the novice and the expert differ in these qualities.

The distinguishing feature of motor skills is that they improve through practice. Repetition of the basic movements with feedback from the environment is a requirement. It leads to the identification of the kinesthetic cues that signal the differences between inaccurate and error-free performance (Gagné, 1977a, p. 19).

Attitudes. Capabilities that influence an individual's choices about the kinds of actions to take are attitudes. An important characteristic, however, is that attitudes do not determine specific acts. Rather, they only make classes of individual actions more or less likely to be engaged in (Gagné, 1977a, p. 231). For example, the student develops attitudes toward reading books or constructing art objects (Gagné & Briggs, 1979, p. 86).

Learning attitudes is based on information about possible actions and their consequences. Gagné (1977a) concurs with Bandura (1977) that prosocial behaviors may be learned from human models.

Cognitive Strategies. Capabilities that control the learner's management of learning, remembering, and thinking are cognitive strategies; they are the learner's executive control processes. Cognitive strategies influence the learner's attending to stimuli, the encoding schemes undertaken by the learner, and the size of the "chunks" of information stored in memory. They also influence the learner's search and retrieval strategies and the organization of the learner's responses. Gagné (1977a) notes that cognitive strategies are similar to Skinner's (1968) self-management behaviors and Rothkopf's mathemagenic behaviors (1970).

An example of a cognitive strategy is the process of inference or induction (Gagné & Briggs, 1974, p. 52). Experiences with objects or events in which the individual attempts to explain a particular phenomenon lead to induction. For example, after observing the force exerted by a magnet for a nail, the student may observe this attraction with other objects, such as iron filings. When the observations lead to the inference of "magnetic force," the student has implemented the strategy referred to as induction. Once implemented, it becomes a new capability that is available for application as a strategy to other situations.

Unlike verbal information and intellectual skills, which are directly content related, the object of cognitive strategies is the learner's own thought processes. Another important characteristic of cognitive strategies is that, unlike intellectual skills, they are not critically influenced by minute-by-minute instruction. Instead, they develop over relatively long periods of time (Gagné & Briggs, 1979). To the extent that such skills can be improved by formal education, the individual becomes a self-learner and an independent thinker (Gagné, 1974, p. 64).

Essential and Supportive Prerequisites. One of the important ways that the varieties of learning differ from each other is in the internal states required for learning. These internal states are previously learned capabilities necessary for successful learning. The two types are *essential prerequisites* and *supportive prerequisites* (Gagné & Briggs, 1979). Supportive prerequisites are those capabilities that facilitate the process of learning. An attitude of confidence in the learning is an example.

Essential prerequisites, on the other hand, are particular capabilities that become an integral part of the new learning (Gagné & Briggs, 1979, p. 106). Essential prerequisites are "folded into" the more complex skill at the time of the new learning.

Prerequisites for each of the five varieties of learning are identified in Table 7-3. Essential prerequisites may be learned prior to or at the same time as the more complex capability.

The Cognitive Processes in Learning. The five varieties of learning identify the capabilities that are the outcomes of learning. They are important because different capabilities are learned in different ways and require different sets of prerequisites.

The Gestalt psychologists, like the S-R theorists, maintained that all learning was the same. Unlike the S-R theorists, however, they attempted to describe the process of learning. In their view, learning occurred when

Table 7-3. Essential and Supportive Prerequisites

Variety of Learning	Supportive Prerequisites	Essential Prerequisites
All varieties	An attitude of confidence in the learning; the learner's cognitive strategies	
Verbal information	A context of meaningful knowledge, sometimes referred to as cognitive structures	
Intellectual skills		Each specific skill is essential to the next higher skill
Attitudes	Acceptance of the model in learning through observation	Information about the situation and selected intellectual skills
Motor skills		Knowledge of how to execute the steps in sequence
Cognitive strategies		Selected intellectual skills

the subject perceptually reorganized the elements of a stimulus situation. They named this process *insight.*

Since the investigations of the Gestalt theorists, however, cognitive psychologists have identified several ways in which the learner's cognitive processes interact with the environment. Included in their discussions are the individual's perception of stimuli in the environment, the transformation of stimuli into codes to be remembered, and the later recall of stored information. They have also identified the concepts "long-term memory" and "working memory." The memory system in which all our memories and learning are stored is *long-term memory.* In contrast, *working memory* is responsible for processing stimuli from the environment. It is also referred to as *short-term memory* because it has a limited capacity for holding information.

Robert Gagné (1977a) has applied the cognitive processing concepts to his analysis of learning. He has identified nine stages of processing that are essential to learning and which must be executed in sequential order. The nine stages are referred to as *phases of learning.*[2] For the purpose of clearly understanding the functions of the nine phases, they are categorized in this text as (1) preparation for learning, (2) acquisition and performance, and (3) transfer of learning. The importance of the phases is that they are present in every act of learning and are enacted in different ways for different varieties of learning.

---

[2] Personal communication from Robert Gagné, April 7, 1983.

The nine phases are summarized in Table 7-4. Preparation for learning initiates the individual to the learning task, and these steps typically require only a few minutes. In contrast, acquisition and performance represent the learning of the new capability. Depending on the complexity of the skill to be learned, these phases may require from one to several sessions. Finally, transfer of learning may take place a few days after acquisition of the new skill.

Preparation for Learning. The initial phases of learning are attending, expectancy, and retrieval of relevant information and/or skills from long-term memory. These activities set the stage for learning. The learner first "takes in" or apprehends the relevant stimulus and an expectancy for learning is established. The stimulus may be verbal communications (oral or written), still visuals, filmed or televised visuals, or human models. (Selection of stimuli to support learning is discussed later in the section "Selecting Instructional Events.")

The importance of the learner's expectancy is that it orients the student

Table 7-4. Summary of the Nine Phases of Learning

Description	Phases	Function
Preparation for learning	1. Attending	Alerts the learner to the stimulus
	2. Expectancy	Orients the learner to the learning goal
	3. Retrieval (of relevant information and/or skills) to working memory	Provides recall of prerequisite capabilities
Acquisition and performance	4. Selective perception of stimulus features	Permits temporary storage of important stimulus features in working memory
	5. Semantic encoding	Transfers stimulus features and related information to long-term memory
	6. Retrieval and responding	Returns stored information to the individual's response generator and activates response
	7. Reinforcement	Confirms learner's expectancy about learning goal
Transfer of learning	8. Cueing retrieval	Provides additional cues for later recall of the capability
	9. Generalizability	Enhances transfer of learning to new situations

to the learning goal. For example, the student determines that he or she is to acquire a motor skill, a new definition, or learn to solve a problem. The orientation established at this point permits the student to select appropriate output at each subsequent phase in the processing of information (Gagné, 1977a, p. 61).

Expectancy is followed by the retrieval from long-term memory of previously learned capabilities essential to the new learning. In learning the concept "triangle," for example, the child must first recall that three-sided figures differ from other geometric shapes (discrimination learning).

Acquisition and Performance. The four phases known as selective perception, semantic encoding, retrieval and responding, and reinforcement are here referred to as the *core phases* of learning. Selective perception transforms physical stimuli into recognizable features and permits the brief retention of those features in working memory so that encoding may occur.

Encoding is the learning phase in which the stimulus features are given a conceptual or meaningful framework and stored in long-term memory. This process is the central and critical stage in learning (Gagné, 1977a, p. 66). Without it, learning has not occurred.

The stored code may be a concept, proposition, or some other meaningful organization (see Gagné & White, 1978). In learning the concept "triangle," the child encodes typical examples of triangles. For motor skills, however, the learner encodes a visual image of the skill and the executive routine required to enact the component performances.

The core events of learning conclude with confirmation of the new learning. The learner retrieves the newly stored code from long-term memory and executes a response. If the child is learning the concept "triangle," he or she identifies examples of triangles. For a motor skill, the student demonstrates accurate physical performance.

Feedback is provided to the learner, informing him or her about the achievement of the learning goal. The feedback may be provided by the environment or it may result from the learner's observation of his or her performance (Gagné, 1977a). Referred to as reinforcement, it is important because it confirms the acquisition of the new capability.

Transfer of Learning. An important factor in the new learning is that it should be applicable in a variety of settings. The learner should be able to generalize the capability to new examples or new situations. Learning transfer is accomplished when the learner applies the skill to new contexts. In this way, the learner acquires additional cues that later can be used in searching long-term memory for the appropriate capability.

Acquiring additional cues for retrieval and generalizing to new examples may not immediately follow the other phases of learning. Short delays of a day or two may intervene between the initial learning and opportunities to generalize (Gagné, 1974).

In summary, the internal conditions of learning include two factors. They are the learner's internal states and the cognitive processes required for learning. Internal states include both essential and supportive prerequisites, and they differ for each of the five learning varieties. The cognitive processes required for learning include nine phases that transfer physical stimuli from the environment into new capabilities. The set of nine learning phases is executed in different ways for each learning variety.

The Nature of Complex Learning

An important contribution of Gagné's work is his description of the cumulative nature of human learning. His early work (Gagné, 1962b) describes organizations of intellectual skills that build from simple to complex. Referred to as *hierarchies*, these sets of capabilities provide a mechanism for designing instruction in school subjects. (See Table 7-5.)

At the present time, Gagné's analysis includes two organizations of capabilities that progress from simple to complex. The two organizations are learning hierarchies and procedures.

Table 7-5. Summary of Intellectual Skills from Simple to Complex

Type of Skill	Description
Discrimination learning	Child responds differentially to characteristics that distinguish objects, such as shape, size, color
Concept learning Concrete concepts	Child identifies object or event as a member of a concept class; learned through direct encounters with concrete example, such as triangles
Defined concepts	Cannot be learned through concrete examples; acquired by learning a classifying rule, such as "liberty," "patriotism"
Rule learning	Student can respond to a class of situations with a class of performances that represents a relationship; for example, student responds to 5 + 2, 6 + 1, and 9 + 4 by adding each set of integers
Higher-order rule learning (problem solving)	Student combines subordinate rules in order to solve a problem; most effective learning strategy is guided discovery

Procedures. Examples of procedures are writing a check, balancing a checkbook, parking a car, and changing a tire. Procedures are sequential organizations of skills that include both motor and intellectual skills.

The motor skills in parallel parking, for example, include positioning the vehicle appropriately, backing at low speed in a certain direction, and

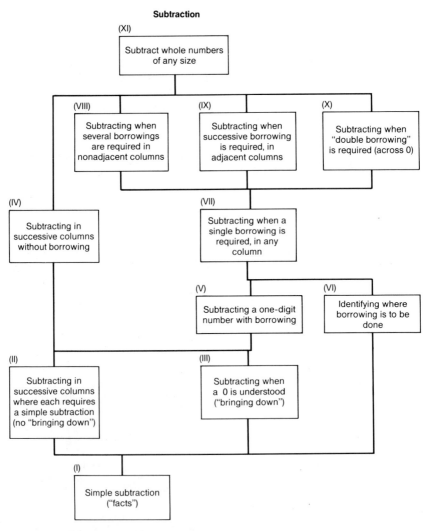

Figure 7-2. A learning hierarchy for subtracting whole numbers. (From R. M. Gagné & L. J. Briggs, 1974, p. 114.)

turning the wheels straight from the turn (Gagné, 1977a, p. 215). The intellectual skills include identifying angle of approach, identifying alignment with the other car, and so on. Learning the procedure involves learning to perform the discrete motor skills as well as the essential concepts and rules.

Some procedures, such as parking a car or changing a tire, require learning the step-by-step actions that constitute the total sequence. Others, however, require decisions about alternative steps at certain points in the procedure. This type is sometimes referred to as a conditional procedure. In such a procedure, the outcome of one step provides clues to the choice to be made in the next step (Gagné, 1977a, p. 271). When balancing a checkbook, for example, an individual must first determine if the checks are in numerical order. If not, the next step is to arrange the checks in sequence by date of issue.

Learning Hierarchies.   Procedures are organizations of motor and intellectual skills. Learning hierarchies, in contrast, are organized sets of intellectual skills only. Each capability in a hierarchy is an essential prerequisite to the next most complex skill. A hierarchy, in other words, is a *psychological organization of skills.* It is neither a logical ordering of information, concepts, and rules, nor is it a set of skills that simply supports learning (Gagné, 1977a). Instead, a connection exists between two skills if the higher element cannot be learned without first learning the lower element. This characteristic is illustrated in Figure 7-2.

Within intellectual skills, four kinds of discrete skills are organized from simple to complex into a hierarchy. They are discrimination learning, the learning of concepts, rule learning, and higher-order rule learning (problem solving). Each of these skills is an essential prerequisite to the next higher order skill. These skills are summarized in Table 7-5.

PRINCIPLES OF INSTRUCTION

Robert Gagné framed his analysis of the conditions that affect human learning from the perspective of the question: "What factors really can make a difference in instruction?" (Gagné, 1977a, p. iv). This view derives from the realization that children's experiences play a major role in their development. The situations in which learners are placed may encourage the development of great artists and scientists or they may inhibit the development of the human intellect (Gagné, 1977a, p. iv).

As a result, the transition from the principles of learning to the principles of instruction requires no translation. The five varieties of learning as outlined in Table 7-2 are capabilities that are the outcomes of school learning. Similarly, the essential internal states for each of the five varieties are important prerequisites for school learning. Finally, each of the nine phases of learning is supported by a particular type of event during classroom instruction.

Basic Assumptions

The importance of instruction is a major consideration in Gagné's discussions of learning. His assumptions about classroom learning therefore include the nature of instruction and the nature of instructional design.

The Nature of Instruction and Instructional Design. In general, instruction is described as "a human undertaking whose purpose is to help people learn" (Gagné & Briggs, 1979, p. 3). Instruction rather than simply teaching is defined because the focus is on all the events that may directly influence an individual's learning (Gagné & Briggs, 1979). In addition to teaching, instruction may be delivered by print materials, pictures, television, computers, and other media.

Five assumptions support Gagné's recommendations for designing instruction (Gagné & Briggs, 1979). First, instruction should be planned to facilitate the learning of an individual student. Although students are often grouped together for instruction, learning takes place within the individual. Therefore, the needs of the learner are placed in the planning sequence prior to grouping.

Second, both immediate and long-range phases are included in the design of instruction. The teacher or instructional designer plans daily lessons, but they occur within the larger segments of units and courses, which must also be planned. Third, instructional planning should not be haphazard nor provide merely a nurturing environment. Such a course of action can lead to the development of individuals who are not competent. In other words, to influence human development as much as possible, instruction should be systematically designed (Gagné & Briggs, 1979, p. 5).

The fourth assumption is that instruction should be designed using the systems approach. The design process should begin with the analysis of needs, continue with the development of goal statements, and then proceed step by step to develop the instruction. Empirical evidence is then obtained about the effectiveness of the instruction in order to revise the materials. Tryout and revision continue until the standards established for the instruction are met. The fifth and final assumption is that instruction should be developed from knowledge about how human beings learn (Gagné & Briggs, 1979, p. 5).

The Components of Instruction

Gagné (1977a, 1977b) defines instruction as a set of external events designed to support the several processes of learning, which are internal. For each of the nine learning phases described in the first section of this chapter, a parallel instructional event has been identified (Gagné & Briggs, 1979, p. 157; Gagné, Wager, & Rojas, 1981). For example, attending to relevant stimuli is the first learning phase. The associated instructional event is to gain the learner's attention through an unusual event, question, or change of stimulus.

The set of nine learning phases, and therefore the accompanying instructional events, occur in different ways for the different varieties of learning. A key factor in the identification of appropriate instructional events is the identification of the type of capability to be learned.

An important aspect of the varieties of learning is that they cut across school subjects. Decoding words, finding the main idea, and calculating the area of a triangle are all intellectual skills. Similarly, learning the definition of patriotism and the formula for carbon dioxide are both information skills. Identification of the capability to be learned therefore assists in the identification of portions of different subject areas for which similar instructional treatments are needed (Gagné, 1972).

Defining the outcomes of instruction is the first step in designing instruction. Gagné and Briggs (1979) suggest the development of instructional outcomes in the form of performance objectives. The essential components of instruction, therefore, are (1) designing performance objectives and (2) identifying appropriate instructional events for the selected objectives.

Designing Performance Objectives. All five varieties of learning reflect important outcomes for school learning. Motor skills are found in physical education and dance and also are subcomponents of other school subjects. Examples include the physical skills in printing and writing. In contrast, cognitive strategies and attitudes include hoped-for outcomes. Specifically, they are developing the learner's management strategies and developing positive attitudes toward learning and self-confidence in learning.

The content of the curriculum is for the most part represented by the learning of information and the acquisition of intellectual skills. All subject areas include the acquisition of basic information and interacting with the environment using symbols. Each subject will therefore include performance objectives for these two varieties of learning.

The function of performance objectives for instruction is that they are

Table 7-6. Suggested Verbs for the Varieties of Learning

Capability	Verbs
Information	States, defines, paraphrases
Motor skill	Executes, performs, enacts, pronounces
Attitudes	Chooses to . . . , freely elects to . . . selects (a preferred activity)
Cognitive strategy	Originates (a strategy)
Intellectual skills	
Discriminate	Selects (same and different)
Concept	Identifies (examples), classifies (into categories)
Rule	Demonstrates, predicts, derives
Higher-order rule	Generates (a problem solution), solves

Source: Adapted from Gagné and Briggs (1979, p. 125).

unambiguous statements of the capabilities to be learned. Terms such as "understand," "comprehend," and "appreciate" should be replaced with more precise terms that clearly communicate the skill or attitude to be acquired. An example of a performance objective is "The student can generate a solution to quadratic equations in one unknown." See Table 7-6 for a listing of sample verbs.

The importance of identifying capabilities to be learned in the form of performance objectives fulfills two functions in the school setting. First, the needs of instruction are identified, and second, the method of testing is determined. That is, different capabilities are both taught for and tested in different ways. Specifically, verbal information may be tested by asking the student to define or state the particular item of information. The testing of intellectual skills, however, requires that the student (1) interact with stimulus situations using symbols, and (2) respond to a new set of situations in addition to those used in instruction.

Selecting Instructional Events.   The function of instruction is to support the learner's internal processing referred to as learning. Each of the nine phases of learning is, to a great extent, activated internally. These processes, however, are also influenced by particular arrangements of environmental stimuli (Gagné & Briggs, 1979). Encoding, for example, may be influenced by the particular semantic framework that accompanies the new capability to be learned. The instructional events for each of the nine learning phases are illustrated in Table 7-7.

Preparation for Learning.   The three instructional events, gaining attention, informing the learner of the objective, and stimulating the recall of prior learning, are events that set the stage for new learning. Gaining the learner's attention may be accomplished by asking a provoking question, depicting an unusual event, or appealing to a child's particular interests. An example is asking if anyone knows how to figure a baseball player's batting average (for a unit on percentages) (Gagné & Briggs, 1979).

The answer to the initial question (or the response to the unusual event) provides closure and informs the learner of the new objective (event two). The teacher may say, "Today we are going to learn . . .

why leaves change colors and fall from the trees."
to figure baseball players' averages."
why the liquid changes colors when certain drops are added."

Next, in order to prepare the learner for a new level of learning, the instruction should stimulate the recall of important prerequisites (event three). Relevant information, concepts, and rules, such as how plants make food, may be needed. Recall is stimulated through the use of questions such as "Do you remember . . .?" or "What did we do yesterday that might help us answer this question?"

Materials and objects also may stimulate recall. In a unit on linear measurement, children were given sticks of different lengths. They were then asked to think about using the sticks to measure the height of a box (Gagné & Briggs, 1979, p. 167). Recall of the skill of counting numbers was initiated as each of the children used a particular length of stick to determine height.

Acquisition and Performance. The core phases of learning are selec-

Table 7-7. Relationships Between Learning Phases and Instructional Events

Description	Learning Phase	Instructional Event
Preparation for learning	1. Attending	Gain learner's attention through unusual event, question, or change of stimulus
	2. Expectancy	Inform the learner of the objective
	3. Retrieval (of relevant information and/or skills) to working memory	Stimulate recall of prior learning
Acquisition and performance	4. Selective perception of stimulus features	Present distinctive stimulus features
	5. Semantic encoding	Provide learning guidance
	6. Retrieval and responding	Elicit performance
	7. Reinforcement	Provide informative feedback
Retrieval and transfer	8. Cueing retrieval	Assess performance
	9. Generalizing	

tive perception, semantic encoding, retrieval and responding, and reinforcement. These four phases are each supported by a particular instructional event. Specifically, the four events are presenting distinctive stimulus features, providing learning guidance, eliciting performance, and providing feedback.

The stimulus characteristics or situations with which the learner is to interact during instruction are presented first. Next, specific situations accompanied by hints or prompts as needed are presented to the learner. This activity is that of providing learning guidance. The communications to the learner should stimulate a particular direction of thought and therefore prevent the learner from getting off the track (Gagné & Briggs, 1974, p. 129).

The learner is then asked to respond to particular questions that either (1) confirm the learning, or (2) indicate needed corrective feedback. If errors have been made, additional learning guidance is provided.

Providing learning guidance is a critical event in instruction (Gagné, 1980). First, it helps the learner transform the new capability into a code for later recall. Second, it "makes the difference between learning that is facile and learning that is hard; and also between learning that is relatively effective and learning that is ineffective" (Gagné, 1980, p. 6).

Examples of Instruction for Acquisition and Performance. The importance of the foregoing core events is that they are to be flexibly implemented. For example, instruction for the concept "circle" may include a variety of circles of different colors or sizes (presenting the simulus). Examples made of string or rope also may be used (Gagné & Briggs, 1974, p. 129). In addition, the children might be asked to join hands and form a circle.

Then the children may be presented with a variety of pictures and other examples that include different geometric figures. They may be asked to look carefully at each picture in the set and to decide which ones represent circles. Hints or prompts concerning the characteristics of circles may be provided by the teacher as each picture is introduced and included in the set (providing learning guidance). After the children have reviewed carefully the set of examples, they may be asked to point to the ones that are circles (eliciting performance). Incorrect identifications are followed by reminders about the characteristics of circles and comparisons with the examples already identified (providing informative feedback).

In contrast, if the capability to be learned is that of discovering a rule, the core instructional events are executed somewhat differently. For example, the learning task may be to discover the rule of prime numbers. The rule is that these numbers are divisible only by one set of factors (the number itself and the number 1). The student first may be asked to recall that any number can be expressed as the product of various factors (e.g., $4 = 2 \times 2; 4 \times 1$) (Gagné & Briggs, 1974).

Then the student may be presented with a succession of numbers from 1 to 25 and asked to write out all the various factors for the set of numbers (presenting distinctive stimulus features). The learner is next asked if the factors for any of the numbers vary in any way (learning guidance). However, this suggestion may not be sufficient for the student to discover that certain numbers are divisible only by themselves and 1. The student may then be asked the differences between the numbers 3, 5, 7 and 4, 8, 10 (Gagné & Briggs, 1974, p. 129). Learning guidance in the form of questions and prompts continues in this way until the learner discovers the prime numbers.

Retrieval and Transfer. The correct identification of one set of examples, or the application of a rule to one set of situations is insufficient to determine the acquisition of a new capability (Gagné & Briggs, 1974). An important characteristic of learned capabilities is that they can be generalized to a variety of situations. Therefore, the student should be presented with an additional set of examples or situations that require performance of the particular skills (assessing performance). This instructional event ascertains that the learning is not limited to the set of situations included in the initial learning.

Finally, instruction should conclude with stimuli specifically designed to enhance retention and transfer. This may take the form of spaced reviews after a reasonable delay of a day or more following the initial learning (Gagné, 1974). For example, if the student has learned to define the term "legislative" with regard to the U.S. Congress, the spaced reviews may include the definition of legislative with regard to state and city lawmaking bodies (Gagné, 1974, p. 116).

Designing Instruction for Complex Skills

Defining each capability to be learned in the form of a performance objective and selecting the appropriate instructional events are important steps in the design of instruction. Also important, however, is providing for the cumulative nature of human learning. Thus Gagné (1977a) describes the methods by which instruction is to be developed for organizations of complex skills. As described earlier, the two types of capabilities organized from simple to complex are procedures and learning hierarchies. Instructional planning for these two different organizations of skills occurs in somewhat different ways.

Instructional Design for Procedures. The first step in developing instruction for complex skills is to determine the set of skills to be taught. For a procedure, each separate step is first identified. For the procedure of changing a tire, the identified sequential skills include removing the wheel cover, placing a block under the other wheel, using the jack to raise the wheel, and so on (Gagné, 1977a, p. 360).

The motor skills in the sequence are then analyzed into part-skills that also may need to be taught. An example is the skill of backing the car, which is an essential step in parallel parking. Stopping the car at the right point so that it is neither too close nor too far away from the curb is a part-skill in backing the car.

For some procedures, choices between alternative steps may be required. For example, one step in reconciling a bank statement with check records is to determine if the checks are numbered. If the answer is yes, the checks are arranged in numerical order. If the answer is no, the checks are arranged by date of issue (Gagné, 1977a, p. 262). Both alternatives must be included in the instruction.

After the skills and part-skills are identified, the type of capability of each skill is identified. Performance objectives are then written for the skills and part-skills, and instruction is planned for the set of objectives.

Instructional Design for Learning Hierarchies. The task of deriving a learning hierarchy is not necessarily an easy one (Gagné & Briggs, 1974, p. 112). Correct identification of subordinate skills requires the identification of component mental operations, not the identification of items of information (Gagné & Briggs, 1974, p. 113).

Essential prerequisites for the intellectual skills are determined by the method referred to as *learning task analysis* (Gagné & Briggs, 1979). This method is essentially a questioning approach that is first applied to the most complex skill to be taught. The question asked is: "What simpler skill is essential to the learning of the present skill?" The key to the identification of the immediate prerequisite is the word "essential." Many simpler skills may be identified that are not integral components of the skill to be learned. The prerequisite skill is the one that must be recalled by the student if the learning is to proceed rapidly and without difficulties.

An example is the skill "subtracting a one-digit number with borrowing" in Figure 7-2. An immediate prerequisite skill is "subtracting when a zero is understood (bringing down)." Learning to subtract zero from a one-digit number is essential to learning to subtract one-digit numbers that do not require borrowing.

The importance of learning task analysis is illustrated by the objective "converting Fahrenheit to Celsius temperature readings" (Gagné & Briggs, 1974, p. 113). One might be tempted to identify a prerequisite as "knowing that C = ⅝ (F − 32)." This statement, however, is an item of information. In contrast, the prerequisite skills include "finding numerical values of an unknown variable by solving equations," and "substituting numerical values of variables in equations to yield a single numerical value for a variable" (Gagné & Briggs, 1974, p. 113).

Each skill identified by the questioning procedure is also subjected to the same question in order to determine the next simpler set of prerequisites. This analysis by questioning is repeated until a logical endpoint is reached for the particular group of learners to be taught. The logical endpoint is the set of prerequisite skills that the students have already learned. These skills are identified as the entry capabilities for the unit or course of instruction.

Each skill to be taught is then categorized as to type of capability and is written in the form of a performance objective. The relevant verbal information and attitudes also are identified and written as performance objectives. Instruction is developed for each objective, using the instructional events described earlier.

EDUCATIONAL APPLICATIONS

The concept of hierarchies of learning and the use of task analysis became an integral part of curricular design for school learning in a variety of school subjects. The elementary program, "Science—A Process Approach," sponsored by the American Association of the Advancement of Science, was developed directly from Gagné's principles.

Various research techniques have been applied in the verification of skills hierarchies (see Airasian & Bart, 1975; White, 1974). These research applications have indicated that properly identified intellectual skills contribute to the learning of more complex skills.

Classroom Issues

Robert Gagné's approach to the analysis of learning is from the perspective of the needs of instruction. As a result, his work addresses several issues of importance in the classroom.

Learner Characteristics. Individual differences, readiness, and motivation are issues for both the systems approach to designing instruction and the classroom teacher. Gagné (1974, 1980) and Gagné and Briggs (1979) discuss these issues both with regard to instructional design and the delivery of instruction.

Individual Differences. The effectiveness of instruction is influenced by several kinds of individual differences among students. Included are differences in cognitive strategies and rate of learning. Particularly important, however, are differences in student entry capabilities (Gagné, 1974) (see "Readiness" below). Entry capabilities are "the raw materials with which instruction must work" (Gagné, 1974, p. 125). They may be assessed at several beginning points within the curriculum, such as the beginning of a school year or the start of a new course or unit.

Methods of compensating for individual differences in the delivery of instruction include small-group instruction, the tutorial mode, independent learning (Gagné, 1974), and individualized instructional systems (Gagné & Briggs, 1979). The advantage of individualized systems is that they are delivery systems for adjusting instruction to the individual students in a group of 25 or more learners (Gagné & Briggs, 1979, p. 261).

Readiness. For Gagné (1968a, 1977a) developmental readiness is viewed as the individual's relevant capabilities. Readiness is not a matter of maturation in which certain growth changes must occur before learning can occur (referred to as the growth-readiness model; Gagné, 1968a). Nor is readiness a matter of the gradual internalization of logical forms of thought as Piaget (1970) suggests. Both of these models Gagné notes, have assigned a secondary role to the influence of learning in human development. However, since learning is cumulative, readiness for new learning refers to the availability of essential prerequisite capabilities. As discussed earlier, readiness includes the lower skills in the hierarchy of intellectual skills and the essential rules, concepts, and part-skills in procedures.

Motivation. Designing effective instruction includes the identification of student motives and the channeling of those motives into productive activities that accomplish educational goals (Gagné, 1977a, p. 287).

Although often treated as a single characteristic, motivation includes both general and specific types. General motivational states include David McClelland's achievement motivation (1965) and R. W. White's competence motivation (1959) (Gagné, 1977a). More specific types include incentive motivation and task motivation, both of which may be developed through the careful use of reinforcement contingencies. That is, reinforcement for the activities of working with other children, relating to school tasks, and for mastery and accuracy can establish incentive motivation (Gagné, 1977a).

Cognitive Processes and Instruction. Gagné's analysis of learning is conducted from the perspective of the factors that make a difference in instruction. Therefore, the issues of transfer of learning, the students' self-management skills, and the teaching of problem solving are integral components of the conditions of learning.

Transfer of Learning. The concept of learning transfer is the heart of Gagné's model of cumulative learning. First, essential prerequisites are described by Gagné for each of the five varieties of learning. Second, the essential prerequisites within intellectual skills provide for transfer in two ways. They contribute to the learning of the next higher-order skill and they also generalize to other situations. Examples include the skills of adding, subtracting, multiplying, and dividing whole numbers and fractions.

Transfer of learning is also provided for in the sequence of nine instructional events. At the conclusion of learning, cues are provided for retrieval of the capability and new situations are introduced to which the student applies the skill.

Learning "How-to-Learn" Skills. These skills are the cognitive strategies identified by Gagné (1972, 1977a). They are the ways that the individual manages his or her learning, remembering, and thinking. Gagné notes that improving students' "how-to-learn" skills is one of the challenging problems for education so that each student is "working up to potential" (Gagné, 1977a, p. 36).

Teaching Problem Solving. The process of problem solving, according to Gagné (1977a, p. 34) is one in which the learner discovers how to combine some previously learned rules to generate a solution to a problem that is new to the learner. Teaching problem solving requires that (1) the necessary rules are already acquired by the learner, and (2) a problem situation is presented to the learner that he or she has not encountered before (Gagné & Briggs, 1979, p. 71). The learner, in inventing the solution, engages in "discovery learning."

Problem solving, although it includes "discovery learning," differs from the solving of novel problems suggested for cognitive strategies. In cognitive strategies, the learner is *originating* a solution that may require the selection of information from a variety of sources and the combining of information in novel ways. In the problem solving included in intellectual skills, the learner is *generating* a solution that requires the recombination of previously learned related rules. The result is a higher-order rule.

The Social Context for Learning. The methods recommended by Gagné (1977a) and Gagné and Briggs (1979) focus on the design of instructional systems rather than on the development of models of teaching. A major difference between the two is that models of teaching place the teacher or other individual in the role of conducting and/or managing instruction for some identified group of learners. Instructional systems, in contrast, often include sets of materials and activities for which the pacing and management of instruction may reside in the learner. As a result, the context for learning with regard to instructional design is discussed in terms of the effects on the management of instruction (Gagné & Briggs, 1979). That is, the differences in the implementation of instructional events among the tutoring situation, small-group instruction, and large-group instruction are described. The implications of different entry capabilities of students for each of these contexts is also described by Gagné and Briggs.

Developing a Classroom Strategy

The theoretical framework developed by Robert Gagné is incorporated into the Gagné and Briggs model for instructional design. The model is an example of the systems approach for designing instruction. Specifically, systems models are characterized by three major features. The first is that instruction is designed for specified goals and objectives. Second, the development of instruction utilizes media and other technology of instruction. Third, pilot tryouts, materials revision, and field testing of the materials are an integral part of the design process. In other words, systems models specify objectives, design the instruction, and try out the materials with students, revising the instruction until the desired achievement is produced. The design, tryout, and revision process is the major characteristic of systems models; the development is a "closed-loop" process. Systems models originated in the military services. The development of weapons systems required a parallel and concurrent development of personnel systems which included training (Gagné & Briggs, 1974, p. 211).

The systems model described by Gagné and Briggs (1979) includes all the stages in the design of curriculum and instruction (see Figure 7-3). It begins with needs assessment and the development of goal statements.

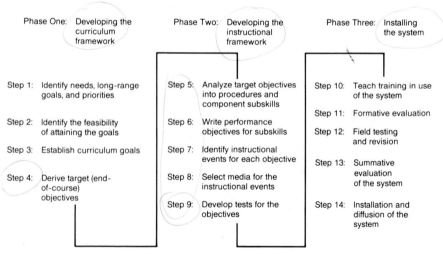

Figure 7-3. Summary of the phases in the Gagné-Briggs systems design model.

The model also includes the derivation of end-of-course objectives, development of specific performance objectives, selection of instructional events, selection of media for instruction, and field testing of the final product.

One important characteristic of the model is that it places lesson development within the total context of curriculum design. In so doing, it extends the concept of cumulative learning beyond instruction to the curriculum level. The relationship between learning at the instructional and course levels is illustrated by the following set of objectives.

Course objective. The student can critically analyze events and situations in a country's judicial, governmental, economic, and political systems, consistent with that country's identified priorities.

Unit objective. The student can demonstrate the relationship between political and economic systems.

Specific subskill. The student can classify systems as "political" or "economic."

In the design model, the term "formative evaluation" (step 11) refers to materials tryout with small groups of students. The purpose is to identify areas in the instruction that are not working effectively and to revise them. After these changes are made, field testing is undertaken with a large group. Minor changes in the materials may be required after the field test. Finally, summative evaluation (step 13) is an evaluation of the materials with a typical population. This evaluation certifies the objectives that are met by the instruction and identifies the population for which the materials are effective.

The complete design model is appropriate primarily for large-scale curriculum-design projects. However, the recommended procedures for lesson design (steps 4 through 9 in the model) may be implemented by classroom teachers at any level of education.

Classroom Example

The lesson in Table 7-8 is an example of instruction designed for the objective of identifying the main idea. The lesson builds on a concept learned previously, that of topic. The lesson illustrates the use of the nine instructional events in specific classroom activities.

Note that in step 4, presenting distinctive stimulus features, the teacher presents core information that illustrates the defining rule of the concept of main idea. This information is applied first by the teacher and then by the students in the identification of concept examples.

During the lesson, instructional events 5, 6, and 7 are repeated to give

Table 7-8. Classroom Example

Capability to be learned: The students can identify statements that represent the main idea for short reading selections (fourth- and fifth-graders).

Instructional Event	Classroom Activity
1. Gaining attention	Teacher asks students to name their favorite TV show or story.
2. Informing learner of the objective	Teacher asks the children if they know how to tell someone what the show (story) is about without retelling the story. Teacher explains that they are going to learn how to find the main idea of story so they can tell a friend what the story is about.
3. Stimulate recall of prior learning	Learners asked to recall the term "topic," (who or what a story is about).
4. Present distinctive stimulus features	Teacher explains that: TOPIC + SOMETHING SPECIAL ABOUT THE TOPIC = MAIN IDEA *Example:* Three Little Pigs *Main idea:* The three pigs (topic) built houses and the wolf blew down all except the brick house.
5. Provide learning guidance	Teacher presents stories and a set of statements about each. In each set, one choice is the main idea; others are specific details. Stories are read, then the choices, and the teacher identifies the correct choice.
6. Elicit performance	Children are given brief situations, each with several choices from which they select the main idea. *Example:* Movie *E.T.* *Choices:* The main idea is: A. E.T. rode on the handlebars of Elliot's bicycle. B. E.T. was left on Earth and wanted to go home, although he had friends on Earth. C. E.T. hid in a closet full of toys in Elliot's house and was hard to tell apart from the toys.

the children experience with two types of statements often confused with the main idea. The two types are general statements that do not describe the topic and specific details. Each type is contrasted separately with examples of the main idea so that the differences may be clearly understood by the children.

Table 7-8, *Continued*

Instructional Event	Classroom Activity
7. Provide feedback	Children are informed as to the correctness of each answer.

Instructional events 5, 6, and 7 are then repeated, with the difference that the other statements about the story are not details; they are general statements. However, they do not describe "something special" about the topic.

> *Example:* A short selection describes edible grasses, and includes wheat, rice, hay, and their uses as food.
>
> *Choices:* The story is about:
> A. How to eat grass
> B. How grass grows
> C. The uses of grass

Instructional events 5, 6, and 7 are then repeated, using a wide selection of statements that may represent the main idea.

> *Example:* A short selection describes tree rings (topic), how they are formed, and what they tell us about a tree's growth.
>
> *Choices:* The story as a whole is about:
> A. Tree rings that are close together.
> B. How rain makes trees grow.
> C. How tree rings tell about trees.

8. Assess performance	Children are given several short reading selections with choices for main ideas (general and specific) and they select the sentence that tells what the whole story is about.
9. Provide retention and transfer	Children talk about the stories and the TV shows mentioned in instructional event 1. The teacher introduces several choices for the main idea of each and the children as a group make a decision about the main idea during a class discussion.

Source: Adapted from an instructional plan by Cheryl Caruso, University of South Carolina.

Retention and transfer is provided a few days after the initial instruction using a discussion of the children's favorite television programs. Additional cues for later recall are acquired by the children at this time.

This lesson illustrates an important characteristic of effective instruction. Too often, too much information is presented to the learner too quickly. Confusion and mislearning often result. In this lesson, one new feature of the concept is presented at a time, with practice by the learner at each stage.

Also demonstrated in the lesson are the major requirements for intellectual skills. Specifically, they are the integration with prior information and the learner's interaction with symbols.

Review of the Theory

Prior learning theorists developed explanations of the learning process in the laboratory and extended the findings to the human situation. Robert Gagné, in contrast, began with the complexity and variety that characterizes human learning and developed a system to account for that variety.

Gagné's analysis yielded five categories or varieties of learning that are distinguished by different performances and different requirements for learning. The five varieties are verbal information, intellectual skills, cognitive strategies, attitudes, and motor skills. In addition, intellectual skills include four discrete skills that form a hierarchy from discrimination learning to higher-order rule learning (problem solving). Unlike other designations, such as "rote learning" or "conceptual learning," the five varieties cut across school subjects, ages of learners, and grade levels.

Each learning variety requires a different set of internal and external conditions for acquisition of the particular capability. Internal conditions include (1) the necessary prerequisite skills, and (2) the nine phases of cognitive processing required for learning. External conditions are the events of instruction that support the learner's cognitive processes.

A major goal of Gagné's theory is the planning of effective classroom instruction. The skills to be learned are written in the form of performance objectives and the variety of learning is identified. Task analysis is then used to identify prerequisite skills and instructional events are selected for each objective to be taught.

Disadvantages. The theory was developed to account for the range of psychological processes observed in prior research on learning and to specify precisely the sequence of instructional events for the identified processes. Thus the theory is easier for a curriculum design team to implement than for the classroom teacher to use (see Table 7-9).

Contributions to Classroom Practice. The best known contribution of the theory is that it operationalizes the concept of cumulative learning and provides a mechanism for designing instruction from simple to complex. The concept of hierarchies of learning has become a standard curriculum component in a variety of subject areas.

Table 7-9. Summary of Gagné's Conditions of Learning

Basic Elements	Definition
Assumptions	Within the parameters established by growth, development is the result of the cumulative effects of learning Learning is characterized by more than a single process, and these processes cannot be reduced or collapsed into one
Learning	The phases of information processing supported by stimulation from the environment executed for the different kinds of learning
Learning outcome	An internal capability manifested in a particular performance for each of the kinds of learning
Components of learning	*Five varieties of learning:* verbal information, intellectual skills, cognitive strategies, attitudes, and motor skills *Internal conditions of learning:* prerequisite skills and the nine phases of information processing *External conditions of learning:* the events of instruction
Designing instruction for complex skills	Provide instructional events for the sequences of skills in procedures and learning hierarchies
Major issues in designing instruction	Identification of capabilities to be learned; task analysis of objectives; selection of appropriate instructional events

Analysis of the Theory	
Disadvantage	Difficult for the classroom teacher to implement without special training
Contributions to classroom practice	Provides a mechanism for designing instruction from simple to complex; identifies the psychological processes in cumulative human learning Accounts for the diversity of human learning Links instructional events to specific phases in information processing

In addition, the theory provides a cohesive framework for the range of findings about the nature of human learning. More recently, the theory provides a mechanism for implementing the concepts identified by information-processing theory.

DISCUSSION QUESTIONS

1. How does Gagné's conception of learning differ from Skinner's view?
2. How does Gagné address the issue of sequencing learning?
3. A classroom teacher is developing a unit on solving for the areas of plane geometric figures. She presents two formulas, $A = lw$ and $A = w \times \frac{1}{2}l$. She then uses the formulas to solve for the area of two rectangles and two triangles. The students are then given several problems to complete for homework. According to Gagné's theory, what are some of the things that the teacher has done wrong?

GLOSSARY

attitudes   The internal capabilities that govern the individual's disposition toward or away from events, objects, and individuals.

capabilities   The changes in states of memory that make possible the prediction of many instances of performances by the learner; the outcomes of learning.

cognitive strategies   The capabilities that govern the learner's thinking and remembering; the executive control processes that must be activated in order for learning to occur.

events of instruction   The set of stimuli in the environment that support the internal processes of learning; each learning event has a parallel stimulus situation. The set of instructional events comprises the external conditions of learning.

intellectual skills   The organized set of human capabilities that involves the use of symbols in interacting with the environment; includes discriminations, concepts (concrete and defined), rules, and higher-order rules (problem solving).

learning   The set of cognitive processes that transforms a state of the individual's memory from one state to another, resulting in one or more capabilities.

learning analysis   The process by which the true (i.e., essential) prerequisites of an intellectual skill are determined.

learning hierarchy   An organized set of intellectual skills from simple to complex that indicates the set of prerequisites for each capability to be learned.

motor skills The capabilities that govern the individual's execution and performance of particular physical acts.

phases of learning The nine internal phases of information processing that transform stimulation from the environment into a new capability; the set of events constitutes the internal conditions of learning and is executed in different ways for different capabilities.

procedures The organization of discrete motor skills into complex activities; usually requires the learning of related concepts and rules. Examples include administering an injection and dissecting a frog.

varieties of learning The five categories of human learning that (1) are differentiated by at least one unique requirement for learning, (2) result in different classes of performance, and (3) are generalizable across subject areas, grade levels, and learners. The five varieties of learning are verbal information, intellectual skills, cognitive strategies, motor skills, and attitudes.

REFERENCES

Airasian, P. W., & Bart, W. M. (1975). Validating a priori instructional hierarchies. *Journal of Educational Measurement, 12*, 163–173.

Bandura, A. (1977). *Social learning theory*. Englewood Cliffs, NJ: Prentice-Hall.

Gagné, R. M. (1962a). Military training and principles of learning. *American Psychologist, 17*, 83–91.

Gagné, R. M. (1962b). The acquisition of knowledge. *Psychological Review, 69*(4), 355–365.

Gagné, R. M. (1965a). The analysis of objectives. In R. Glaser (Ed.), *Teaching machines and programmed learning: II. Data and directions*. Washington, DC: National Education Association, 21–65.

Gagné, R. M. (1965b). *The conditions of learning* (1st ed.). New York: Holt, Rinehart and Winston.

Gagné, R. M. (1968a). Contributions of learning to human development. *Psychological Review, 75*(3), 177–191.

Gagné, R. M. (1968b). Learning hierarchies. *Educational Psychologist, 6*, 1–9.

Gagné, R. M. (1970). Some new views of learning and instruction. *Phi Delta Kappan, 51*, 468–472.

Gagné, R. M. (1972). Domains of learning. *Interchange, 3*(1), 1–8.

Gagné, R. M. (1974). *Essentials of learning for instruction*. Hinsdale, IL: Dryden Press.

Gagné, R. M. (1977a). *The conditions of learning* (3rd ed.). New York: Holt, Rinehart and Winston.

Gagné, R. M. (1977b). Instructional programs. In M. H. Marx & M. E. Bunch (Eds.), *Fundamentals and applications of learning*. New York: Macmillan.

Gagné, R. M. (1980). Preparing the learner for new learning. *Theory into Practice, 19*(1), 6–9.

Gagné, R. M., & Briggs, L. J. (1974). *Principles of instructional design* (1st ed.). New York: Holt, Rinehart and Winston.

Gagné, R. M., & Briggs, L. J. (1979). *Principles of instructional design* (2nd ed.). New York: Holt, Rinehart and Winston.

Gagné, R. M., Wager, W., & Rojas, A. (1981). Planning and authoring computer-assisted instruction lessons. *Educational Technology, 21,* 17–26.

Gagné, R. M., & White, R. T. (1978). Memory structures and learning outcomes. *Review of Educational Research, 48*(2), 187–222.

McClelland, D. C. (1965). Toward a theory of motive acquisition. *American Psychologist, 20,* 321–323.

Melton, A. W. (Ed.). (1964). *Categories of human learning.* New York: Academic Press.

Piaget, J. (1970). Piaget's theory. in P. H. Mussen (Ed.), *Carmichael's manual of psychology* (pp. 703–722). New York: Wiley.

Rothkopf, E. Z. (1970). The concept of mathemagenic activities. *Review of Educational Research, 40,* 325–336.

Skinner, B. F. (1968). *The technology of teaching.* New York: Appleton-Century-Crofts.

White, R. T. (1974) A model for validation of learning hierarchies. *Journal of Research in Science Teaching, 11,* 1–3.

White, R. W. (1959). Motivation reconsidered. The concept of competence. *Psychological Review, 66,* 297–333.

CHAPTER 8

Information-Processing Theories

The brain is not a passive consumer of information. [Rather] it actively selects, attends to, organizes, perceives, encodes, stores, and retrieves information. Sometimes it generates a whole picture from one-half of a chimerical stimulus. Other times, it analyzes complex spatial patterns into simpler imbedded ones. . . . A multiplicity of operations, interpretations and inferences characterizes the complex reality constructed by the brain.
Wittrock, 1978, pp. 99, 101

Research into the ways that the human brain processes information gained impetus primarily from the communications research initiated in World War II and the advent of high-speed computers. The modern computer, which has the capabilities of receiving, storing, and retrieving information as well as solving problems, provides an analogy for human mental functions.

Information processing is currently one area of research within the larger domain of cognitive psychology. Anderson (1980) describes cognitive psychology as the efforts to understand the basic mechanisms that govern human thought. Information-processing research focuses on tracing and describing sequences of mental operations and their products (i.e., information in the execution of particular cognitive tasks) (Anderson, 1980, p. 13). Other areas included in cognitive psychology are the subdomains of language, imagery, memory, perception, artificial intelligence, and cognitive development.

The term "information processing" connotes a particular perspective toward the study of individuals. The primary focus of study is the ways in which human beings perceive, organize, and remember vast amounts of information received daily from the surrounding environment. Listening to the morning news, studying the stock market report, deciphering class notes, and diagnosing a car's engine troubles are all daily activities that depend on the processing of data from the environment.

Comparison with "Pure" Learning Theory.   Information-processing theory differs from typical learning theory in three ways. First, it is not characterized by the work of a single theorist or a particular research approach. It includes such developments as computer programs that simulate human intelligence, studies of visual and auditory processing, descriptive models of memory and cognitive functioning, and research into the differences between novice and expert problem solvers.

The second difference between the two types of theory is represented by the current philosophical split within the cognitive realm. One view maintains that the detailed study of specific information-processing tasks will result in the identification of the fundamental operations in mental activity (see Posner & McLeod, 1982). The various laboratory approaches include studies of eye movements, tabulations of recognition and recall, analyses of abilities to attend to simultaneous tasks, and studies of interference in perceiving and remembering.

In contrast, the importance of developing and refining general models of information processing that relate to real-world problems is advocated by others (Neisser, 1976; Simon, 1979). The problem with the narrow laboratory focus according to this model is that such an approach leads to fragmented and contradictory information applicable only in the laboratory setting. This division between laboratory-defined and real-world problems is reminiscent of the structuralist-functionalist division of the early twentieth century in psychology. Structuralism sought to construct human consciousness from the identification of the mind's elements. Functionalism on the other hand, described the important research goal as the investigation of mental activity in real-life situations.

The third major difference between learning theory and information-processing theories is the degree of emphasis on learning. Information-processing theories do not treat learning as a primary research focus. Instead, it is only one of the processes under investigation and the interconnections between learning and the other subdomains of cognitive psychology remain unclear (Anderson, 1980). Nevertheless, information-processing research contributes to our understanding of the learning process.

PRINCIPLES OF LEARNING

Two areas of particular importance to learning are included in the information-processing approach. They are the investigations into the processes by which the individual acquires and remembers information, and the research into the strategies implemented in problem solving.

Basic Assumptions

The assumptions on which the information-processing theories are based describe (1) the nature of the human memory system, and (2) the ways in which knowledge is represented and stored in memory.

The Nature of Human Memory. The early conception of human memory was that it served simply as a repository for retaining information over long periods of time. Thus it served as a collection of isolated or unrelated bits of information. In the 1960s, however, human memory began to be viewed as a complex structure that processes and organizes all our knowledge (see Neisser, 1967). It is not a passive repository; instead, it is a system that is both organized and active. That is, the human memory actively selects the sensory data that are to be processed, transforms the data into meaningful information, and stores much of the information for later use. The development of information-processing theories has been described as the "direct result of an attempt to view memory as a complex system with many interacting stages" (Norman, 1970, p. 1).

The Multistage Concept. The conceptualization of an active memory system was influenced by Broadbent's (1958) initial description of a multistage memory. For the most part, the early models developed in the 1960s proposed three memory structures. They are (1) a sensory register, (2) a short-term store, and (3) a long-term store (see Atkinson and Shiffrin, 1968).

A generalized model of the three-structure memory system is presented in Figure 8-1. Information is processed in sequential stages, and each stage occurs in a particular structure in the memory system. That is, the sensory registers, primarily visual and auditory, receive a vast array of physical signals from the environment. Many of these signals are lost or are not processed further. Some, however, are retained briefly (0.5 to 2.0 seconds) in the sensory registers. However, unless selected for further processing, data are lost from the system.

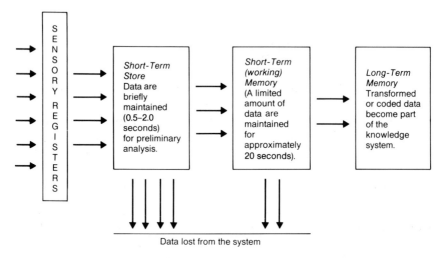

Figure 8-1. Early conceptualization of the human memory as a structural system.

Information that is selected for further processing, however, enters short-term or working memory. Here much of the information is encoded into some meaningful form and transferred to long-term memory for permanent storage. In Gagné's theory, discussed in Chapter 7, the encoding of information and the transfer to long-term memory are the core phases of learning.

Some information in short-term memory, however, is only present for immediate utilization and is not processed further. An example is a little-used telephone number that is looked up and retained only until the call is completed.

The difficulty with the multistore models of memory is that structure has precedence over operations. Once the bins in the flowchart were identified as particular structures, confirming the characteristics of the structures became an important research task. For example, determining the capacity of each structure, nature of the units in it, temporal parameters, and so on, became necessary (Postman, 1975). Research, however, failed to identify specific characteristics associated with the proposed structures.

The "State" Concept. The current view of human memory is that information is in either an inactive or active state. The active state is temporary and is referred to as short-term or working memory (see Figure 8-2).

The conception of short-term memory as the active state of information accounts for such activities as looking up a telephone number and mem-

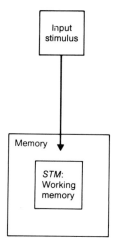

Figure 8-2. Activation of information from long-term memory to short-term memory.

orizing a poem. The digits of the telephone number have already been learned, and looking up and repeating the number establishes new connections among the digits. This information is active until the call is completed, then the sequence is forgotten. The digits, however, remain in long-term memory, while only the particular set of connections between them is lost.

In memorizing a poem, however, new connections are established between many already learned words. This activity is accomplished in working or short-term memory. In contrast to the telephone number, however, the words and their new connections are retained in an inactive state from which they may be later recalled.

The conceptualization of short-term memory as the active state of information also permits the accommodation of qualitatively different processes. Included are the activation of automatic processes of skills learned to a high degree of proficiency as well as the events that require selective attention. Carrying on a conversation with a friend while driving to work is the activation of information in memory that requires selective attention (the conversation) as well as the activation of an automatic process (operating the car).

Two classes of information stored in long-term memory are described by Tulving (1972). One class includes general information that is available in the environment. Examples are the words of a poem, telephone numbers, formulas for chemical compounds, and how to build a house. This type of memory is referred to as *semantic memory*.

In contrast, *episodic memory* includes personal or autobiographical information (i.e., events experienced by the individual). Personal memories are distinguished by the characteristic of vividness and typically include visual scenes.

The Representation of Knowledge. The mechanisms with which the human memory system functions are a major issue in information-processing theories. Another and equally important issue is the nature of the symbolic form in which information is stored in semantic memory. The record of information that is stored is not a literal copy of the stimulus input because (1) the physical signals received by the senses are not perfect representations of the world, and (2) to be remembered, the physical signals must be transformed in some way. The transformation or recoding process increases the probability of later recall of the information at the expense of detail (Lachman, Lachman, & Butterfield, 1979). Therefore, the form of these symbolic codes is an important issue.

Two major views on the form of stored information have been proposed. One is the dual-code model proposed by Paivio (1969, 1970, 1971). The other perspective maintains that information is stored in verbal form only. Although several organizational forms of verbal information have been proposed, the current predominant models are network models (or conceptual-propositional models).

The Dual-Code Model. The essential characteristic of the dual-code model is that information may be stored in long-term memory in either visual or verbal form. The model describes two functionally independent, although interconnected systems for the processing and storing of information. Concrete objects or events, such as dog, house, or a trip to the zoo, are stored in the imagery system. Abstract objects and events such as "soul," "truth," and linguistic structures are stored in the verbal system. Some objects, such as "house," which have both concrete and abstract characteristics, may be coded in both systems; however, one code is likely to be activated more easily than the other. Another characteristic of the model is that the processing of verbal stimuli occurs serially, while the visual processing of concrete stimuli seems to occur all at one time (Paivio, 1969).

Evidence of visual encoding is provided by the "mental rotation" studies (see, e.g., Cooper & Shepard, 1973) and the grid-background tasks (Podgomy & Shepard, 1978). In the former, the reaction times of subjects to images became greater with the degree of rotation of the images. In the latter study, reaction times of subjects asked to imagine a particular stimulus did not differ from the reaction times of subjects originally exposed to the stimulus.

Critics of visual imagery maintain that information storage in picture form would exceed the storage capacity of the brain and would also require a "perceiver" in the brain to "read" the pictures (Pylyshn, 1973). However, the visual encoding theorists maintain that the stored codes are not pictures but rather are analog representations or analog memories. That is, the images are structurally related to the real objects in the same sense that keys and locks are related (Shepard, 1978). Physically, keys and locks are quite different; however, only the correct key will open a particular lock. Similarly, only particular objects will activate the neural processes with which the object is represented.

The Verbal Network Models. The theorists that advocate network models are those that support the concept of a verbal storage system. They do not question the importance of imagery in the processing of information for later recall. However, they maintain that the ultimate representation of information is in verbal form and that images are reconstructed from verbal codes.

Three general types of verbal models have been developed. The current perspective, semantic-network models, has been preceded by two earlier perspectives: clustering models and propositional models. Clustering models illustrate words grouped in memory in particular clusters. For example, eagle, wren, and canary are clustered in terms of their characteristics (e.g., "have feathers").

In contrast, propositional models identify propositions rather than isolated words as the building blocks of memory structure. Introduced in the 1960s and influenced by Noam Chomsky's work in linguistics, these models describe stored information as base strings (Tom is tall) plus related comparative information. The concept was later revised to include visual processing (Clark and Chase, 1972). Propositions are perhaps more easily understood in Kintsch's representation (1972, 1974). He uses a list format to portray the propositions derived from the analysis of sentences and paragraphs. An example is the sentence "the old man smiled," which includes the two propositions of "old, man" and "smiled, man."

The currently accepted network models, like the propositional models, also make use of verbal relationships. However, the word relationships are not restricted to propositions, and they are diagrammed in the form of nodes and their connecting links. The links are labeled lines that indicate the meaningful connections between the nodes.

Semantic Network Models. The first model, developed by Quillian (1969; Collins and Quillian, 1969) used nodes to portray concepts and superordinate concepts in a hierarchical relationship (see Figure 8-3). Deficiencies in Quillian's model in accounting for retrieval times as well as other problems led to the development of other network models. The more recent examples incorporate a variety of relationships among different concepts.

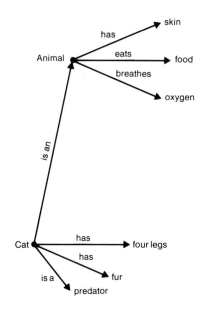

Figure 8-3. Example of an early network model of memory structures.

At the present time, three semantic network models may be identified. They are (1) the propositional network proposed by Anderson (1976, 1980), (2) the "active structural networks" proposed by Norman and Rumelhart (1975), and (3) the "production systems" proposed by Newell and Simon (1972) (see Table 8-1).

All the models describe both declarative knowledge and procedural knowledge. However, Anderson (1980) maintains that procedural knowledge cannot be represented verbally with accuracy. An example is the sailor who is proficient at knot tying and who can recognize poorly tied and expertly tied ropes (Anderson, 1976). Expressing such expertise in verbal form is inaccurate and incomplete.

According to Norman and Rumelhart (1975), the representation of knowledge is no different for propositions and procedures. Therefore, the information that Cathy is a smart girl and the necessary steps in changing the oil in a car are stored in the same form. On the other hand, Newell and Simon state that both declarative and procedural knowledge are stored in the form of condition-action pairs referred to as *productions.* They are stored in long-term memory and are applied to symbols in short-term memory in order to generate actions or behaviors. An example is a physician who identifies symptoms that lead to the recall of appropriate treatments (Simon, 1980).

Table 8-1. Summary of Types of Knowledge in Semantic Network Models

Model	Type of Knowledge Included	Representational Form	Example
Anderson (1980)	Declarative knowledge defined as knowledge that can be expressed verbally	Propositions which are the smallest units that can be judged true or false	Circles are round
Norman and Rumelhart (1975)	Declarative and procedural knowledge	"Active structural networks" which represent both declarative and procedural knowledge	Cathy is smart; to change a tire, first get out the jack, and so on
Newell and Simon (1972)	Declarative and procedural knowledge	Production systems composed of "condition/ action" pairs (if/ then statements)	If a plural subject, then the present tense of the verb "to be" takes the form "are"

Posner (1978, p. 15) suggests that the different representations of information in long-term memory are the result of the study of different phenomena by researchers. That is, different types of data place different demands on the representational system. Therefore, researchers investigating knowledge of stories, faces, procedural steps, class concepts, and so on, identify different modes of memory storage.

Schemas. The dual-code and propositional or semantic network models describe the representation of specific items of knowledge in memory. However, cognitive operations appear to be governed by larger organizations of knowledge. These knowledge structures are referred to as *schemas.*

The term "schema" was first defined by Bartlett (1932, p. 201) as "an active organization of past reactions which must always be supposed to be operating in any well-adapted organic response." Rumelhart and Ortony (1977) describe schemas as data structures that represent the generic concepts underlying objects, events, and actions. Anderson (1980, p. 133) notes that although the definitions of schemas vary, these knowledge structures may be thought of as "equivalent to a set of propositions and images."

The importance of schemas is that they reflect functions for long-term memory other than that of serving as a store of information (Posner, 1978). These functions are: (1) providing a format into which new data must fit in order to be comprehended, (2) serving as a guide for directing attention and for undertaking goal-oriented searches of the environment, and (3) filling in gaps in information received from the environment (Neisser, 1967; Posner, 1978).

The now-classic experiments by Frederic Bartlett (1932) illustrate the influence of schemas in the comprehension of information. In the experiments, the first subject read a folk story from an unfamiliar culture, reproduced the story from memory, and gave this account to the second subject. The second subject read subject one's version, laid it aside, reproduced the events, and handed that accounting to the third subject, and so on. By the time the story reached the tenth subject, it was no longer a folk story about mythical visitors ("The War of the Ghosts"). Instead, it had become a fishing trip. The personal narrative aspect of the story, the ghosts, and the storyteller's reaction to being hit had dropped out of the story and other details were exaggerated.

Bartlett found that the repeated stories had changed in systematic ways: Unfamiliar information was dropped, a few details were retained, and the story became more like the reader's expectations. In other words, information was changed to fit existing schema and to become more coherent to the individual.

Summary of the Basic Assumptions. The basic assumption underlying the information-processing theories is that human memory is an active, complex organizer and processor of information. Within the theoretical framework, two major views about the representation of knowledge in memory exist. They are the dual-code representation, which includes verbal and visual images, and the verbal code perspective. The theorists that advocate the verbal code perspective use circles and lines to represent the linkages between the verbal codes stored in long-term memory. These schematic representations are referred to as network models. Furthermore, cognitive operations are governed by larger organizations of knowledge known as schemas.

The Components of Learning

The research on information processing has included a range of tasks and various descriptions of subjects' activities during the acquisition of information. For the purpose of generating applications to learning and of simplifying an understanding of the findings, the process of learning is described in three stages. They are (1) attending to stimuli, (2) encoding stimuli, and (3) the storage and retrieval of information.

Attending to Stimuli. The processing of information by the human memory system begins when physical signals (visual, accoustical, or tactile) are received by sensory registers in the eyes, ears, and skin. These physical signals are retained briefly, allowing the memory system to begin processing data. The visual·input that is briefly retained is an *icon* and the auditory memory is an *echo* (Neisser, 1967). The third type of signal retention is referred to as *tactile* or *haptic*, though little research has been conducted on the physical stimulus of touch (Neisser, 1976).

The importance of the brief retention of physical signals in the sensory registers is that it permits identification of some of the input. Understanding speech in a newly learned foreign language, for example, is dependent to a great extent on echoic memory (Neisser, 1976).

Some of the vast array of physical signals impinging on the senses is selected for further processing. Two views have been expressed on the nature of the selection process. Some theorists, following Broadbent's model (1958), maintain that initial processing of all stimuli occurs, but that unwanted stimuli are "filtered out" of the system. Neisser (1976), however, maintains that only information for which the system has a schema in long-term memory will be attended to. That is, the system selects only what it will use; it does not receive everything and then filter out some of it. Neisser's analogy is that of apple picking. We pick only the apples we want; we do not pick all the apples and then reject some of them.

Pattern Recognition. An important part of processing information is the identification of selected physical signals. This particular process is referred to as *pattern recognition*. Originally, pattern recognition was believed to occur according to the *template matching theory*. This position describes the comparison of an incoming stimulus to images or "templates" already in the learner's memory. When the appropriate match is made, the stimulus is identified.

The current view, however, maintains that template matching is too cumbersome a process for the rapidity with which identifications are made. Instead, pattern recognition is believed to occur through feature analysis. That is, important characteristics such as horizontal or vertical lines and the important relationships between them are extracted and identified. For example, in the identification of the stimuli "E," " ε ," and " E ," only the critical feature of three spaced horizontal lines connected to a vertical line is required for recognition. According to the template matching theory, however, three different templates would be required.

Processes in Feature Analysis. Pattern recognition is guided by two important processes that may function together or separately. One is *data-driven processing* (Lindsay & Norman, 1972), also referred to as *event-driven* and *bottom-up processing* (Anderson, 1980). An example is the tick of a clock, which is so identified as it is processed. In other words, in data-driven processing, a structure is found within which to place the input (Bobrow & Norman, 1975, p. 140).

The other process is *conceptually driven* or *top-down processing* (Anderson, 1980). This process is guided by motives, goals, and also context. In other words, the input is fitted to expectations. An example is, "For breakfast I had a bowl of c----l," in which expectations and context provide the word "cereal."

Anderson (1980) describes data-driven processing as feature detection and top-down processing as conceptually imposed meanings. In complex skills, such as reading, both types of processes occur.

The Role of Attention. Important in the ways that stimuli are processed is the concept of attention. Some processes, for example, require no attention. They have been practiced so extensively that they are carried out without conscious control. Such processes are referred to as *automatic.* An example is letter identification by good readers.

In contrast, other identification tasks require concentrated effort. They are referred to as *deliberate* processes because they require conscious control. An example is the multiplication of three-digit numbers. In other words, the recognition of familiar patterns is automatic, whereas deliberate processing is required for unfamiliar patterns.

The Encoding of Stimuli. The process of feature detection names the incoming stimuli. For example, in looking up a telephone number, the particular string of digits is identified, such as 895–2010. The stimuli may or may not be processed for later recall. The information may simply remain active only until the call is completed. When it becomes inactive, it is forgotten.

If the number is to be retained in long-term memory in an inactive state, however, further processing is required. This process, referred to as *encoding,* transforms stimuli so that they may be stored and later recalled with ease.

Methods of Encoding. The two major strategies of encoding are maintenance or primary rehearsal and elaborative rehearsal. Reciting a telephone number over and over is an example of *maintenance rehearsal.* In other words, this strategy is simply one of repetition of the information to be remembered (see Woodward, Bjork, and Jongewood, 1973).

In contrast, *elaborative rehearsal* transforms the information in some way. It may be (1) modified so that it relates to information already stored, (2) replaced by another symbol (referred to as substitution by Tulving & Madigan, 1970), or (3) supplemented by additional information to aid in recall. Associating the name of a new acquaintance "Webb" with a spider web is an example of elaborative rehearsal (see Reder, 1980).

The encoding of written material is also influenced by the reader's existing schema, as illustrated by Bartlett. Current research on schema includes the identification of two types used by readers (Anderson, Pickert, & Shirey, 1980). They are textual schema and content schema. Knowledge of particular discourse conventions is a textual schema. Examples include a personal letter schema and a scientific report schema. On the other hand, content schema include the reader's knowledge of the world, both real and imaginary.

Storing and Retrieving Information.   The purpose of the encoding process is to prepare information for storage in long-term memory. Later access and recall depends to a great extent on the form in which information is stored and the relationship of the information to the prior contents of long-term memory. Chess masters and beginners, for example, differ greatly in their ability to recall the board positions of several chess pieces after visual exposure for a few seconds (Chase & Simon, 1973). The master can reconstruct 80%–90% of the board positions, but the beginner can place only a few pieces.

The differences between the two groups are (1) the size of the "chunks" of information stored in long-term memory, and (2) the ways in which new information about board position of the pieces is encoded. The chess master has stored patterns or configurations of pieces, but the beginner has no such stored information. As a result, the master encodes new information in patterns composed of three or four pieces and need only recall the appropriate pattern. The recall of the beginner, however, depends on rote memory for the locations of individual pieces.

The Role of Elaborative Rehearsal.   In contrast to chess skill, many tasks, such as remembering a shopping list, place only moderate demands on long-term memory. For such tasks, both maintenance and elaborative rehearsal can assist in the later recall of information. Of the two processes, elaborative rehearsal is the more effective for later recall. Repetition (maintenance rehearsal) maintains the immediate availability of an item but does little to improve long-term retention. Instead, subsequent recall is enhanced by active processing of the item through elaboration, transformation, and so on (Posner, 1973, p. 201).

Mnemonic Systems.   Included in the mnemonic devices to aid recall are notes, cue cards, teleprompters, and acronyms. For example, a familiar mnemonic device is the use of the word "face" to recall the notes printed in the spaces on a musical staff: "f", "a," "c," and "e."

Another technique, one that began with the early Greek and Roman orators, is known as the *method of loci*. The method supposedly originated with the Greek poet Simonides. A banquet hall, in which Simonides had just delivered a lyric poem praising several Roman aristocrats, collapsed.

All the banquet guests were killed and their bodies so mutilated that identification was impossible. By recalling the location of each guest at the banquet, Simonides identified the bodies.

To use the method of loci, one should select a familiar setting, such as the rooms in a house or the pathway of a customary walk. Then, using mental images, each of the items to be remembered is associated with a particular location. Important in the success of the technique is that the image of the location and the item to be remembered must be an interactive one (see Bower, 1970b). For example, to remember a shopping list using house locations, a large loaf of bread may be visualized in the bathtub.

The success of elaborative rehearsal may be related to the nature of the recall process. Neisser (1976) indicates that the permanent store of information is not some "written tablet" of what is learned. Instead, it is a summary code that comprises information into a label. Thus the process of recall is not the revival of an existing relationship. Instead, it is the construction of a relationship, much as sentences are constructed. In fact, the model implemented by paleontologists to reconstruct animals that once walked the earth describes the model of memory: from a few available bone fragments, a dinosaur evolves (Neisser, 1967, p. 285).

The Nature of Complex Learning

The complex cognitive processes studied by information-processing theorists are those of problem solving. A problem may be defined as "a situation in which an individual is called upon to perform a task not previously encountered and for which externally provided instructions do not specify completely the mode of solution. The particular task, in other words, is new for the individual, although processes or knowledge already available can be called upon for solution" (Resnick & Glaser, 1976, p. 209). This general definition refers to a range of problems, including riddles, puzzles, chess, and subject-matter problems such as algebra and geometry.

Types of Problems. Coupled with the studies of the processes of problem solving are efforts to identify different types of problems. Greeno (1975) has identified four basic types that differ in both the knowledge and the particular skills required for solution. The four types are (1) induction of structure, (2) transformation, (3) arrangement, and (4) hybrid arrangement problems.

Problems of Structure Induction. This type of task is represented by analogy problems and series-completion problems. Examples include "merchant" is to "sell" as "customer" is to "buy" and "1 2 8 3 4 5 6 ?" (Greeno, 1975, p. 242). In this type of problem, a pattern structure is identified from the analysis of the relationship among the given elements (see Table 8-2).

Transformation Problems. The group includes "move" problems and "change" problems. The nature of the task is illustrated by the well-

Table 8-2. Types of Problems and the Associated Requirements for Solution

Type	Examples	Requirements for Solution
Induction of structure	*Analogy:* Driver is to automobile as pilot is to ——. *Series completion:* 3, 6, 9, 8, 4, 7, ?	Ability to identify relationships among problem elements and to integrate them into patterns.
Transformation or logic exercise	*Tower of Hanoi:* Move a stack of different-sized discs from one peg to another without placing a larger disc on top of a smaller one. *Cannibals and Missionaries:* A group of three cannibals and three missionaries must be transported from one side of the river to the other. At no time can the cannibals outnumber the missionaries. *Water-jar problem:* Three jars of different sizes are given (e.g., 8, 5, and 3-quart capacities). The task is to measure a specific amount of water, such as 22 quarts (Luchins, 1942).	Means-ends analysis (analysis of the differences between the problem situation and the problem goal). Skill in selection of operators that reduce the differences between the problem and the goal.
Arrangement problems	Jigsaw puzzles, anagrams, cryptarithmetic problems.	Skill in developing partial solutions and efficient use of constraint information gained in testing partial solutions.
Hybrid arrangement problems	*Transformation of structure:* Katona's matchstick problems.	Perceptual restructuring.
	Induction of structure: "Insight" problems devised by the Gestalt theorists.	Perceptual restructuring.

known move problem referred to as the Tower of Hanoi. The task is to move a set of different-sized discs from one peg to another, one at a time. However, a larger disc may never be placed on top of smaller one. Solution of the problem requires means-ends analysis. Originally identified by Newell and Simon (1972), this process involves representing the given situation (state A), the goal situation (state B), and the situations needed to progress from A to B as the problem solving proceeds.

In the Tower of Hanoi problem, the first subgoal is to free the largest disc so that it can be moved. Accomplishment of this subgoal includes several steps, some of which require returning discs to the original peg at certain points in the problem-resolution process (see Figure 8-4).

Similar problems are the cannibals and missionaries problem and the water jar problem. In each type, some steps are required that further the long-range solution, but which, in the absence of goals, may seem to be

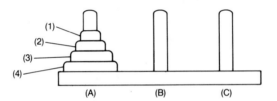

Move disc (1) from peg (A) to peg (B)
Move disc (2) from peg (A) to peg (C)
Move disc (1) from peg (B) to peg (C)
Move disc (3) from peg (A) to peg (B)
Move disc (1) from peg (C) to peg (A)
Move disc (2) from peg (C) to peg (B)
Move disc (1) from peg (A) to peg (B)
Move disc (4) from peg (A) to peg (C)
Move disc (1) from peg (B) to peg (C)
Move disc (2) from peg (B) to peg (A)
Move disc (1) from peg (C) to peg (A)
Move disc (3) from peg (B) to peg (C)
Move disc (1) from peg (A) to peg (B)
Move disc (2) from peg (A) to peg (C)
Move disc (1) from peg (B) to peg (C)

Goal: Move all four discs from peg (A) to peg (C), never placing a larger disc on top of a smaller one.

Figure 8-4. The Tower of Hanoi problem.

counterproductive. To transport the cannibals and missionaries across the river, for example, some moves require the return of some of the group to the original starting point. Such moves are required to meet the constraint of the problem, which is that the cannibals cannot at any time outnumber the missionaries. The task is to devise the sequence of river crossings that do not violate problem constraints.

An example of a change problem is the typical proof-of-theorem problem (Greeno, 1975, p. 245). In such a problem, one or more statements are given and a new statement must be derived according to particular inferential rules.

Arrangement Problems. Jigsaw puzzles, anagrams, and cryptarithmetic are examples of arrangement problems. In each of these tasks, some problem components are provided. The goal is to find a combination of them that fulfills a specified criterion (Greeno, 1975, p. 255). The cryptarithmetic problems are the more complicated examples. In these problems, the task is to substitute numerical values for the letters in a set that form an addition problem. An example is DONALD + GERALD = ROBERT (Bartlett, 1958; Greeno, 1975). Subjects are given the numbers 0 to 9 and the clue that D = 5. The analysis of this type of problem indicates that two factors contribute to success (Newell & Simon, 1972). They are (1) skill in generating partial solutions, and (2) efficient use of the constraint information gained in testing partial solutions.

In the example above, since D = 5, D + D yields T = 0, with a carryover of 1. Therefore, R must be an odd number, because L + L is even (R = L + L + 1). Then analysis of the far-left column (D + G = R) reveals that R must be either 7 or 9 (it is odd, and must be greater than 5 since G ≠ 0; T = 0); and so on.

Hybrid Arrangement Problems. The foregoing arrangement problems provide clues about the overall structure, and the task is to reorder the elements to fit that structure. Hybrid arrangement problems, in contrast, are of two types. One type requires a transformation from one structure to another. Greeno (1975) includes in this category the matchstick problems investigated by Katona (1940). In one such problem, the task is to change an arrangement of seven squares to only five squares by moving no more than three matches (see Figure 8-5).

The other problem type is represented by the situations investigated by the Gestalt psychologists, such as the parallelogram problem described in Chapter 2. Solution of this type requires the learner's induction of structure.

Two other examples are the candle problem and the string problem. The givens in the candle problem are a candle, a box of tacks, and some matches. The task is to mount the candle on a vertical screen or wall.

Problem: Solution:

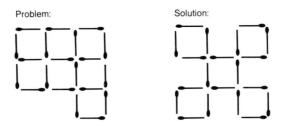

Move three matchsticks to make five squares

Figure 8-5. Matchstick problem used by G. Katona (1940). (© 1940 by Columbia University Press. By Permission.)

Solution depends on the subject's perception of the box as a support rather than as a container.

The task in the string problem is to tie together the ends of two strings that are suspended from the ceiling. A chair and a pair of pliers are given, but the subject cannot tie the ends together by standing on the chair. Instead, the pliers must be tied to one string so that the pliers function as a weight. The string then acts as a pendulum and can be used to catch the other string.

Resnick and Glaser (1976) refer to these situations as invention problems. They are the tasks that require "the invention or construction of a new strategy or material object. Materials or processes are combined to make available something that has not existed before." The pliers are com-combined with the string to form a weighted pendulum and the container for the thumbtacks is mounted on the wall to become a candle holder.

Also included in the hybrid arrangement or invention problems are practical problems in engineering designs, inventions, composition in the arts (music, sculpture, painting), and theory development (Greeno, 1975). Each of these activities requires imposing a new structure in the rearrangement of basic elements.

Problem-Solving Processes.   The problems researched most extensively in the classical literature are the invention problems, such as the pendulum and the candle problems (Resnick & Glaser, 1976). These examples and others were researched in the investigations of "functional fixedness" (Duncker, 1945) discussed in Chapter 4.

Two major areas of contemporary research are computer simulations of problem-solving processes and specific subject-matter investigations using students. Computer programs have been developed that solve logic problems and algebra word problems, play chess, diagnose medical problems, and so on.

The landmark effort that initiated computer simulations of problem solving is the General Problem Solver (GPS) developed by Newell and Simon (1972). The steps, briefly summarized, are (1) represent the problem, the givens, and legal operators; (2) establish goals and subgoals and begin solving for the subgoals; and (3) use means-ends analysis to assess progress, redefining subgoals if necessary.

A somewhat different model of problem solving has been developed by Resnick and Glaser (1976). It applies to the invention or hybrid arrangement problems described earlier. The three general steps in the model are (1) problem detection, (2) feature scanning, and (3) goal analysis (see Table 8-3). Of importance in this model is that the individual often moves back and forth between problem detection (step 1) and feature selection (step 2) in the identification and testing of partial or complete solutions.

The major difference between the two models is in step 2. The Glaser and Resnick model is specifically designed for invention problems, in which the learner must reconstruct the situation to effect a solution. An important component in the model is the early use of means-ends analysis instead of subgoal identification. Specifically, means-ends analysis includes (1) an assessment of the differences between a present state and a desired state, (2) a search for an appropriate operator to reduce the differences, and (3) an evaluation of the results (Simon, 1980, p. 90). In the Resnick and Glaser model, the learner typically moves back and forth between the definition of the problem and scanning the environment for additional clues. In contrast, the Newell and Simon model applies to problems that can be solved in stages; hence the use of subgoals is included.

Table 8-3. Brief Summary of Two General Problem-Solving Strategies

General Problem Solver[a]	**Invention-Problem Strategy**[b]
1. Represent the problem, the givens, and legal operators	1. Construct a representation of the problem in working memory and search long-term memory for a partial or complete solution (problem detection)
2. Establish goals and subgoals and begin solving for the subgoals	2. If solution is not found, scan the task environment for additional information (feature scanning)
3. Use means-ends analysis to assess progress; redefine subgoals, if necessary	3. If step 2 is unsuccessful, redefine the immediate goal (goal analysis)

[a] From Newell and Simon (1972).
[b] From Resnick and Glaser (1976).

PRINCIPLES OF INSTRUCTION

At least two major difficulties exist in the derivation of instructional principles from information-processing research. One, discussed earlier, is that learning is only one of many processes under investigation. The second, ironically, follows from the current dominance of cognitive psychology. The quantity of research conducted on the learner's cognitive activities includes a variety of learner tasks, curriculum areas, organizational models, and age groups. Included, for example, is the learner's cognitive activity in learning from text as well as typical strategies utilized in learning subtraction and reasoning processes in science (see Resnick, 1981). As a result, the division between the information-processing research for the classroom and the larger body of cognitive research has become blurred.

Nevertheless, at least three developments of importance to education have emerged from the emphasis on information processing. One is the increased focus on the processing strategies used by students during learning. The research conducted by Resnick (1981) and others (see Larkin, 1980; Larkin and Reif, 1976) and Robert Gagné's model discussed in Chapter 7 are examples.

A second development is the awareness of a need to teach directly the cognitive processing skills, such as ways to organize one's own knowledge and methods for correcting errors in understanding. The use of process-oriented objectives for instruction to supplement product-oriented objectives is advocated by Greeno (1976).

A third application is in the area of curriculum development. Posner (1978) describes the use of semantic networks to assist in both curriculum organization and content analysis. The semantic networks for two topics, for example, may be compared for common concepts and ways of integrating the two in the curriculum. In content analysis, semantic networks may be used to describe classroom activities and to compare instructional materials with the knowledge structure of the field.

Basic Assumptions

The basic assumptions that underlie information-processing theories describe the nature of the human memory system and the representation of knowledge in memory. Classroom applications of information-processing theories are also derived from the assumption that human memory is an active system that selects, organizes, and encodes for storage the new information or skills to be learned. Thus the primary assumption on which cognitive theorists agree is that successful learning depends on the learner's actions rather than on events in the environment.

The Representation of Knowledge. In general, information-processing theorists are attempting to identify the precise elements that represent the storage of information in long-term memory. Cognitive psychologists, however, often refer to the learner's store of information as *cognitive structure.* Terms used to describe cognitive structure often reflect qualitative characteristics of the acquired knowledge.

Some of the types of cognitive structures are listed in Table 8-4. The terms "rote" (Ausubel, 1968) and "algorithmic" (Greeno, 1973) refer to knowledge that is not anchored to relevant ideas in the learner's cognitive structure. Examples include mechanical rules or formulas. Such cognitive structures may be described as having internal connections only (Mayer & Greeno, 1972).

In contrast, meaningful learning (Ausubel, 1968) or propositional knowledge (Greeno, 1973) includes both concepts and relationships to the student's prior knowledge, also referred to as external connections (Mayer & Greeno, 1972). Both the retention and generalizability of meaningful learning (external connections) are greater than that of rote learning (internal connections).

The Components of Instruction

The essential processes in the acquisition of new information are (1) attending to stimuli, (2) encoding the stimulus, and (3) storage and retrieval of the summary code. The parallel essentials of instruction are (1) guiding the reception of new stimuli, (2) facilitating encoding, and (3) facilitating storage and retrieval.

Guiding the Learner's Reception of New Stimuli. The human memory system selects the environmental stimuli to which it will attend. Thus the reception process requires both (1) attending to the selected stimuli and (2) preliminary identification of the stimulus by some code.

Table 8-4. Summary of Types of Cognitive Structures

Limited Application	Extended (Generalizable) Application
Rote learning	Meaningful learning
Algorithmic knowledge	Propositional knowledge
Internal connections in cognitive structure	External connections in cognitive structure

Instruction for the reception phase of learning, therefore, should first direct the learner's attention to the relevant information (stimulus) to be learned. The importance of providing focus is to facilitate the reception of accurate and complete information. In other words, the important question for instruction to answer initially is: Has the information been received in the learner's working memory?

Two well-known instructional techniques that may be used are behavioral objectives and advance organizers. Objectives describe the skill to be acquired by the student and the context to which it relates. Objectives can assist the student to identify and to attend to the important aspects of new material. However, if narrowly written, they can lead the student to concentrate on the recall of minor details to the exclusion of important concepts.

Advance Organizers. At least three purposes may be accomplished by advance organizers (Ausubel, 1968). First, they provide a conceptual framework for the learning that is to follow. Second, they are carefully selected so that they serve as a link between the student's present store of information and the new learning. Third, because they provide a bridge between the old and yet-to-be acquired cognitive structure, they also facilitate the student's encoding processes.

Advance organizers, however, are not overviews of the material to be learned. Instead, an advance organizer is a brief presentation of visual or verbal information that contains no specific content from the new material to be learned (Mayer, 1979a). Advance organizers represent major concepts that are "umbrellas" for the new material. Ausubel (1968, p. 148) suggests that, to be effective, organizers should be "presented at a higher level of abstraction, generality, and inclusiveness" than the subsequent material. They therefore function as "ideational scaffolding" into which more detailed information will be incorporated. However, subsequent research has indicated that a variety of concrete organizers also are successful (Mayer, 1984). Good organizers have included concrete models, analogies, and examples, as well as sets of broad higher-order rules and discussions of principal themes in familiar terms. The design of advance organizers depends to a certain extent on the nature of the materials, learner characteristics, and delivery mode of the instruction (Mayer, 1979b, p. 162).

Types of Advance Organizers. The two types identified by Mayer (1979b) are expository and comparative. *Expository organizers* provide the mechanism for generating logical relationships in the new materials. In contrast, *comparative organizers* provide the mechanism for relating new and unfamiliar information to existing knowledge (Mayer, 1979a).

The extensive research on advance organizers in the past 20 years has resulted in conflicting claims for their effectiveness. A detailed analysis of 44 studies conducted by Mayer (1979b) supports the effectiveness of organizers. Furthermore, they result in broader learning in situations in which the learner (1) perceives the material to be unorganized or unfamiliar, (2) lacks a rich set of related information or skills, (3) receives a higher-level context for learning, and (4) is tested on the ability to transfer the new learning to other tasks.

Facilitating the Processes of Encoding. The function of encoding during learning is to prepare the new information for storage in long-term memory. This process requires the transformation of the information into a summary code to facilitate later recall.

To be effective, instruction for encoding must consider two important issues. They are the availability of anchoring knowledge in long-term memory and the transfer of these anchors to short-term memory for integration with new knowledge (Mayer, 1979a).

If anchoring knowledge is available for integrating new information, the new knowledge is referred to as "meaningful." The importance of integrating new learning into the student's existing cognitive framework, therefore, is an important factor in the development of "meaningful" learning.

Two different approaches can facilitate encoding. One approach is to provide the cues, elaborations, and mnemonic devices to aid encoding. This approach is referred to here as instruction-based aids. The other approach is to provide opportunities for student-generated elaborations. This approach is described here as learner-based aids.

Instruction-Based Aids. Cues and elaborations provided by instructional materials include advance organizers, high-frequency synonyms for difficult words, adjunct questions placed in text material, chapter summaries and review questions, and acronyms for the learning of arbitrary associations. An example of the latter is providing anatomy students with the rhyme, "On old Olympia's towering top, a Finn and German vault and hop" (Solso, 1979, p. 274). The initial letters of the first line represent the cranial nerves (i.e., olfactory, optic, oculomator, trochlear, trigeminal, etc.).

A less well known technique that facilitates encoding from text is signaling. This technique refers to the strategic placement of noncontent words that emphasize the organization or conceptual structure of the material (Mayer, 1984, p. 37). Signals include preview sentences, paragraph headings, and connectives such as "the problem is. . . ." Also included are "pointer words," such as "unfortunately" and "more importantly." The use of signals can assist the reader in determining the structure of the material.

Learner-Based Aids. Both visual and verbal learner-generated cues can assist in the acquisition of arbitrary associations, such as lists. The method of loci described earlier may be implemented with the following considerations: (1) the cues must be memory images of familiar places that are arranged sequentially; (2) associations between each list item and the location are made in one-to-one pairings; and (3) associations are effected through unusual images (Bower, 1970a).

A specific application of learner-generated cues, referred to as the *keyword method*, has been developed for foreign language learning (Anderson, 1975). The method divides vocabulary learning into two major steps. The first step is for the learner to select an English word that sounds like some part of the foreign language word. This step is the acoustical link (Anderson, 1975, p. 821). The second step is to form a mental image of the keyword interacting with the English equivalent of the foreign language word, referred to as an imagery link. For example, the Spanish word for duck sounds like "pot-o" (acoustical link). An interactive image is that of a duck hiding under an overturned flower pot. Another example (Jones & Hall, 1982) is the use of the keyword "wave" for the Spanish word "huevo" (wave-o), which means "egg." The visual image is that of a giant egg riding the crest of a wave.

Although designed for foreign language learning, the keyword method is also applicable to other learning tasks. Jones and Hall (1982) report its use in learning medical definitions and linking explorers with discoveries. The technique also functioned successfully as a study strategy for eighth graders. Caution is suggested, however, in the use of the method with students of high verbal ability. Initial research tentatively indicated that the method is more effective for students who are of average or of low verbal ability (McDaniel & Pressley, 1984).

The keyword method is useful for information that lacks inherent organization or associations. However, elaboration by students can also facilitate encoding for material in which some organization is present. Underlining and taking notes are two familiar methods used by students. Other recommendations to enhance encoding are training children (1) to illustrate prose passages with stick-figure cartoons (Lesgold, McCormick, & Golinkoff, 1975), and (2) to generate summary sentences for paragraphs (Doctorow, Wittrock, & Marks, 1978).

A more detailed learner-based strategy for reading material described by Mayer (1984) is "structure training." The purpose of the training is to teach students to recognize different kinds of structures used in expository materials. Students trained to recognize three types of phrase structures in science prose (generalization, enumeration, and sequence) demonstrated an increase in high-level information and problem solving, but not in retention of facts (Cook, 1983; Mayer, 1984).

Facilitating Storage and Retrieval. The importance of encoding strategies is that they enhance both the breadth of the initial learning and the later recall. The importance of rhymes, acronyms, verses, key words, and interactive visual images is that they provide retrieval cues for the learner. At the time the information is needed, the student is instructed to recall the information by first thinking of the particular cue. In the method of loci, for example, the student "revisits" the rooms of the house that served as cues for learning the shopping-list items. In the keyword system, the student recalls the visual image that serves as a cue to both sound and meaning of the word to be remembered.

The foregoing strategies are appropriate for lists of information or for paired-associate learning. Much of school learning, however, is related to concepts, definitions, or propositions that have been learned previously. Both instruction-based and learner-based elaborations can establish links with prior learning that also enhance recall.

Designing Instruction for Complex Skills

Given the diversity of research on problem solving, what general statements may be made about designing instruction for these skills? First, a knowledge component is essential in solving problems. Greeno (1980) notes that formerly a sharp distinction was made between performance based on knowledge and performance that represented "solving problems." "Real" problems were those about which the learner had little knowledge. The solution depended on luck or revelation instead of knowledge or skills that might be acquired through instruction. However, "the belief that problem solving occurs only when a person lacks critical knowledge about the problem has put us in a position like that of a man who is digging a hole and never gets it deep enough because, no matter how far he digs, he is still standing on the bottom" (Greeno, 1980, p. 12).

Second, the respective roles of general skills and special knowledge in achieving high-level performance are yet to be determined (Simon, 1980). However, training in problem solving cannot compensate for ignorance in the subject area. "No one, no matter how intelligent, skilled in problem solving or talented, becomes a chess grandmaster without ten years of intense exposure to the task environment of chess" (Simon, 1980, p. 82). Further, research conducted on the development of solutions to open-ended social science problems indicates that declarative knowledge in the subject area is an important factor in the construction of adequate solutions (Voss, Greene, Post, & Penner, 1983).

Third, the strategies used by expert and novice problem solvers differ in several ways. Larkin (1980), researching problem solving in physics, found that the expert tends to identify a problem as a particular type. This identification generates the needed principles for solution. Novices, on the other hand, undertake painstaking step-by-step procedures which often involve the use of subgoals. Differences between novices and experts in solving open-ended social science problems include the novice's (1) lack of an integrated knowledge base, (2) failure to conduct an in-depth analysis of the problem, and (3) failure to provide logical support for and implications of problem solutions (Voss et al., 1983).

Fourth, although the specifics may vary across subject areas, some generic skills are important for instruction. Suchman (1966) suggests teaching a general inquiry mode. The steps in his model are (1) problem identification, (2) development of a tentative explanatory hypothesis, (3) data gathering relative to the hypothesis, (4) hypothesis revision, and (5) repetition of steps 3 and 4 until data are explained.

The importance of Suchman's model is that it provides practice in the search, retrieval, and analysis of information related to a goal. His model provides the classroom steps for means-ends analysis. That is, in means-ends analysis, a memory search is undertaken to find an operator that reduces the present situation to the desired situation. In Suchman's model, the desired situation is an explanation of the data. Application of the model can improve a student's search for the "operator." The model, however, is most appropriate for one-stage problems in which the student is not required to reconceptualize or to redefine the problem.

Problem Formulation. This skill is a vital step in the learning of problem-solving strategies. One instructional approach provided training on eight insight (invention) problems (Wicker, Weinstein, Yelich, and Brooks, 1978). After attempting to solve each problem, each student received the solution, the inappropriate assumption that had to be overcome, and suggestions on ways to formulate reconstruction of the problem. Performance on posttest insight problems was superior to "no training" and "visually imagining the problem."

An approach to be implemented prior to the student's efforts on problems is suggested by Resnick and Glaser (1976). They describe the research conducted by Pellegrino and Schadler (1974), in which children were required to look ahead prior to solving the problem. Children were asked to verbalize their problem goals, a plan of action, and the ways in which the plan would accomplish the goals. No feedback was given as to the correctness of the proposed plans. However, 14 of the 16 children in the experimental group generated correct solutions compared to only 6 of 16 children in the control group.

In summary, teaching general problem-solving strategies may involve as many as four major stages: (1) assisting students to reformulate the problem; (2) identifying relevant subgoals or subproblems; (3) collecting relevant data or initiating steps in a systematic manner to solve subproblems; and (4) evaluating the result, redirecting, if necessary.

EDUCATIONAL APPLICATIONS

Unlike many of the learning theories, information-processing theory as a body of knowledge has not been translated directly into curriculum implementations. Instead, classroom applications tend to make use of a particular construct, principle, or rule in a certain subject area. For example, the schema concepts and the use of elaborations have been used in the teaching of reading (Resnick, 1981), while the results of problem-solving research have been applied in science and mathematics (see Resnick, 1981; Simon, 1980).

Classroom Issues

Classroom issues addressed by information-processing theory are those that are directly related to cognitive processes.

Learner Characteristics. The student characteristics that are important in the management of classroom learning are individual differences, readiness for learning, and motivation. Of these three, the concept of individual differences is addressed directly in relation to problem solving. Specifically, expert and novice problem solvers differ in two ways. The first is the knowledge base that each brings to the problem situation (Greeno, 1980). Experts bring a vast store of knowledge that makes possible the second difference between the two groups. This difference is that of problem representation. Experts represent the problem as an example of a familiar type or model and then proceed to execute the solution. Novices, on the other hand, proceed slowly using both subgoals and trial and error. Differences between expert and novice chess players also include both the amount and the ways in which information about chess patterns is stored in memory.

Cognitive Processes and Instruction. Information-processing theory brings a new perspective to the management of instruction for effective learning. Although the theories do not directly address the issues of transfer of learning and learning ''how-to-learn'' skills, several important steps in the acquisition of knowledge that influence retention and therefore transfer are identified.

Teaching Problem Solving. Researchers continue to search for general models of problem solving that may be applicable to broad areas. However, strategies have been suggested for the problem types referred to as arrangement, logic, transformation, hybrid problems, and open-ended hybrid or ill-structured problems. In learning to solve hybrid problems, one of the most difficult tasks is problem reformulation (i.e., comprehending the problem with its goals and restrictions). Research into artificial intelligence may reveal more specific strategies that can be undertaken to improve the effectiveness and efficiency of human problem-solving strategies.

The Social Context for Learning. Information-processing theories focus on the cognitive mechanisms involved in the comprehension and retention of sensory data from the environment as well as the application of learned information to solving problems. Although much of this learning occurs in a social environment, the theories have yet to address the influence of that environment on cognitive processing.

Developing a Classroom Strategy

The importance of designing instruction for information processing is that logical meaning of the knowledge is transformed into psychological meaning. Logical meaning is the relationship between the symbols, concepts, and rules of the subject area. Psychological meaning is the relationship between the symbols, concepts, and rules to the student's cognitive structure (Ausubel, 1968). Developing psychological meaning in the comprehension of knowledge and in solving problems depends on student interaction with the subject matter.

Comprehension

STEP 1. Develop cues to guide the reception of the new learning.

1.1 What informal questions will access the learner's existing cognitive structure?

1.2 Does the lesson include broadly written objectives or a statement of purpose that can direct the learner's attention?

1.3 How will the new knowledge or skills enhance or build on the learner's existing knowledge?

STEP 2. Select or develop conceptual supports that facilitate the encoding of information.

2.1 What information should be included in advance organizers so that they bridge the student's knowledge and new learning?

2.2 What concepts, episodes, and images already acquired by the student may be used to illustrate the new terms, definitions, or concepts?

2.3 Are there adjunct questions in the text or major points in the text that can be used as a basis for secondary rehearsal by the students?

2.4 What are the logical points in the instruction for students to engage in secondary rehearsal (i.e., visual and/or verbal elaboration)? What are some examples of associative images and verbal codes that can be provided to students?

STEP 3. Develop cues that aid in the retrieval of learned information.

3.1 What are some comparisons with related concepts, terms, or ideas that may be made? For example, if the concept is "morpheme," it may be contrasted with "phoneme" and compared to the term "word."

3.2 What inference questions may be used to conclude the lesson?

Problem Solving. Teaching problem solving includes teaching the general skills of problem formulation, identification of constraints and givens, and the capability of evaluating and revising problem-approach strategies. The following steps are suggested in planning instruction for problem-solving skills.

STEP 1. Analyze the nature of the problem.

1.1 What processes does the problem require (arrangement, transformation, induction, historical analyses, etc.)?

1.2 What are the givens in the problem and the constraints on problem resolution?

1.3 In developing an optimum problem-resolution strategy, what are the steps to be included?

STEP 2. Analyze the behavior of the novice problem solver.

2.1 What problem elements do novice problem solvers typically focus on? How do they differ from problem elements addressed by experts?

2.2 What important problem elements do novices typically ignore or misinterpret?

2.3 What general strategies do novices typically undertake in this type of problem that are nonproductive?

STEP 3.   Present the problem to students and implement appropriate steps to assist the students through the process of solving the problem.

3.1 Assist the students in the identification of the actual problem stated, the minimum number of givens, and the constraints implied by the problem.

3.2 Assist students in formulating subgoals, developing an historical analysis, or other strategies appropriate to the problem (see step 2 for needed information).

3.3 Encourage students to verbalize the problem goals and their strategies for solution before they initiate any steps. If the problem is a physical one, encourage students to visualize the problem and to reexamine their assumptions about the physical reality posed by the problem.

3.4 Provide redirection if necessary. At the conclusion of the exercise, review the strategies and givens identified by the students. Evaluate the strategies attempted for effectiveness and efficiency to improve students' subsequent efforts.

Classroom Example

The following instructional strategy is derived from the in-depth analyses conducted by Voss et al. (1983) of the strategies used in an open-ended social science problem. Such problems, unlike those in science and mathematics, often lack predetermined solutions that are generally accepted. Therefore, the instructional process is not one of assisting students to discover preconceived solutions. Instead, the purpose is to develop student skills in the analysis of complex abstract problems. Toward this end, the students' thinking is monitored for inclusion of the five general activities undertaken by the experts observed by Voss et al. The five activities (observed in two or more of the experts' strategies) are (1) conduct a historical analysis of the problem; (2) identify the constraints operating in the problem context; (3) convert the stated problem into subproblems; (4) develop a solution that addresses each of the subproblems; and (5) evaluate the solution, providing logical support for the solution and stating the implications.

The example presented on the following pages describes the problem presented to the experts in the research conducted by Voss et al. The strategy utilizes questions to encourage students to think in the directions undertaken by the expert problem solvers. The answers included in the strategy are somewhat unrealistic in that they are "ideal" answers that would be reached by the student groups only after much discussion and weighing of alternatives. In addition, the teacher is a key component in the process in redirecting students' attention to the conceptualization of broad issues from specific details. In other words, novice problem solvers tend to view the agricultural problem as one that requires specifics, such as more tractors or more fertilizer. Progress in problem solving is achieved when the students are able to move beyond those details to the more general issue, which is lack of modernization of agriculture.

Problem to be solved: Assume that you are members of a committee convened to advise the Minister of Agriculture in the Soviet Union. The problem is that crop productivity for the past several years has been low and crop production must be increased (Voss et al., 1983, p. 174).

Target population: Advanced high school students in social science who have completed a study of the Soviet Union.

Nature of the problem: Open-ended, with no preestablished solution; may be classified as the most abstract of the hybrid arrangement or invention problems.

Components of an acceptable solution:

1. A historical analysis of the problem is conducted.
2. Existing constraints on the problem are identified.
3. The problem is analyzed into subproblems inherent in the main problem.
4. A solution is proposed that addresses the main problem and the subproblems.
5. Logical arguments that support the solution and implications of the solution are included.

Characteristics of beginning and novice problem solvers: Inadequate knowledge base for dealing with the problem in a comprehensive way; tendency to address specific details rather than the broad scope of the problem; and failure to develop logical support for proposed solutions.

Classroom strategy: Divide the class into groups of six to eight students to develop solutions to the problem. Provide each group member with the description of the problem and the following set of questions. Each group is directed to develop the answers to the questions as a means of developing a solution to the problem. During the exercise the teacher moves among the groups, redirecting the students' thinking when it becomes too specific or when students encounter difficulty with the questions.

At the conclusion of the exercise, each group's solution is shared with the class and critiqued by other class members. Questions raised about aspects of the solution that relate to the students' knowledge of the Soviet Union may be used as a basis for library research on the issues raised.

Purpose of the strategy: To develop students' skills in dealing with multifaceted problems for which a right answer is not readily available. In the following set of questions, the identification of subproblems (question 3) is critical to the development of a solution with breadth and scope.

Questions to be answered by each group about the problem and examples of the experts' answers:

1. What are the historical antecedents of the problem?

Included are the conditions of life under the aristocracy which never introduced modern methods of land management. More recently are the forced collectivization by Stalin and the failure of Khrushchev's Virgin Lands program. In summary, the government has a history of mismanagement of people and resources.

2. What are the existing constraints on the problem?

Several different types of constraints are likely to be identified by different groups. It is unlikely that any one group will think of all the constraints. Thus the class discussion after the group work is important, so that students become aware of other directions. In other words, students tend to develop solutions that are related to the constraints identified by them.

Summary of Constraints

a. Ideological: Party doctrine forbids a free-enterprise system.
b. Political: The power of the Minister of Agriculture is limited.
c. Social/cultural: The peasants are suspicious of outsiders and reluctant to change.
d. Political: Some way must be found to make the farmers work harder on the collective plot than on their private plots.
e. Economic: Existing financial priorities favor the military-industrial complex rather than the farmer.
f. Agricultural: The amount of arable land is limited.

3. What subproblems are inherent in the general problem? Can some of the constraints be restated as subproblems? What is the relationship of identified subproblems to the historical analysis?

Details typically identified by students	*Related subproblems*
Poor management of crop rotation; lack of fertilizer; lack of equipment and repair parts.	Inadequate technological modernization.
Income from private plots outweighs benefits of working the collective; incentives provided by the government for farmers are inadequate; also, inadequate transport facilities for crops.	Financial priorities established by the government needed to be reordered (addresses constraint e).
Peasants do not reinvest money earned from private plots in land or equipment because they fear that the government will take it away; production low for the same reason.	Need for education of farmers and altered policies to ease their insecurity (addresses constraints c and d).
Limited amount of arable land.	Need to improve farm methods and increase acreage under cultivation (constraint f).

Relationship of subproblems to historical analysis: The principles of communism prevent the development of a free-enterprise system. Also, the country has no history of successful agricultural development; therefore, strong arguments will need to be developed for any proposed reforms.

Reanalysis of the main problem: The primary problem is political. That is, in the Soviet Union, economic problems are political problems. Therefore, each subproblem is solvable by technical means provided that the Minister of Agriculture can successfully lobby the Politburo for needed changes. A strong rationale is therefore essential for proposed reforms.

4. What is a possible solution and supporting arguments that address both the subproblems identified and the primary problem?

Suggested Solutions:

1. Each of the identified subproblems may be solved if government priorities are redirected. The Minister must lobby for an increase in capital investment in agriculture. The government must be convinced that agriculture is at least as important as industry. That is, the Soviet Union cannot be dependent on the Western countries for agricultural products; it is an embarrassment and endangers national security.

2. The Minister must lobby for the development of a coherent and consistent set of government policies and educational reforms that will improve agricultural production. These policies must be strong enough so that they can withstand the weight of bureaucratic management, which often dilutes policies and reforms. However, self-sufficiency of the country is the goal; it must not be dependent on potential adversaries. Included in the needed reforms are development of an adequate transportation system, incentives for farmers, and coherent modernization of agriculture.

Review of the Theory

The communications research of World War II and computer simulations of human intellectual capabilities introduced a new paradigm to the study of mental operations. This paradigm is reflected in the information-processing descriptions of mental operations. According to this paradigm, the human memory is an active organized system that selects the information to be processed and then transforms that information into meaningful codes for later use. (See Table 8-5.)

The core of the theory comprises the processes by which individuals perceive, encode, and then store information in long-term memory for later use. The theorists agree that codes are stored internally in some type of cognitive structure. The prevalent view is that this structure takes the form of semantic networks, in which verbal elements are linked to each other.

Research into the coding of information for long-term storage has indicated the importance of both related cognitive structures and elaborative rehearsal for encoding. Similarly, problem-solving research has indicated the importance of problem formulation, means-ends analysis, and the use of subgoals in the development of problem-resolution strategies.

Applications to education include specific recommendations for the use of advance organizers, the development of instruction-based aids, and the use of learner-generated cues for encoding and recall. Included are the use of images and combinations of images and words.

Disadvantages.   Information-processing theory is, in fact, a collection of various approaches to the study of cognitive functions. Furthermore, learning is not the primary process under investigation. As a result, classroom applications of the theoretical perspective are not always clear. Further, the computer analogy to the representation of mental functions may not be valid. Only further research and investigation can answer this question.

Contributions to Classroom Practice. Information-processing theory has described in detail the processes that structuralism and the Gestalt theorists were attempting to identify. For classroom learning, the processes identified in encoding and storage as well as important problem-solving processes indicate the importance of carefully structuring lessons to support these processes. In addition, the teaching of strategies for encoding, recall, and problem formulation and analysis are of equal importance to learning. Table 8-5 summarizes information-processing theory.

Table 8-5. Summary of Information-Processing Theory

Basic Element	Definition
Assumptions	Human memory is a complex and active organizer of information; the memory system transforms information for storage (and later retrieval) in long-term memory
Learning	The processes by which information from the environment are transformed into cognitive structures
Learning outcome	Some form of cognitive structure; the prevalent view is that of semantic networks
Components of learning	The processes of perception, encoding, and storage in long-term memory
Designing instruction for complex skills	Teach students strategies for solving problems (e.g., problem formulation, means-ends analysis, use of subgoals)
Major issues in designing instruction	Relating new learning to existing cognitive structure; providing processing aids in both receptive learning and problem solving
Analysis of the Theory	
Disadvantages	Learning is not the primary process under investigation; therefore, related classroom applications must be inferred indirectly. Computer model of cognitive processes may or may not be valid
Contribution to classroom practice	Identification of the importance of designing instruction for the processes involved in transferring information from input signals to meaningful codes

DISCUSSION QUESTIONS

1. According to information-processing theories, what is the role of the environment in learning?

2. Information-processing theories identify some important considerations in facilitating encoding. Given the importance of learner-generated cues for encoding, what should we spend some time teaching?

3. What is the relationship between the suggested steps in facilitating students' problem solving and Gagné's conditions of learning?

GLOSSARY

advance organizer   An "umbrella" statement that provides a conceptual link between the learner's existing knowledge and the new learning.

attention   The processes of dealing with incoming stimuli; may be automatic, such as attending to usual household sounds, or deliberate, such as attending to unusual noises, a question, a problem, a television program, and others.

dual-code theory   The position that maintains that the information stored in long-term memory may be in either visual or verbal form.

elaboration   One of the mechanisms by which stimuli are transformed for storage in long-term memory and later retrieval. Includes stimulus substitution, association, and other stimulus modifications (also referred to as secondary or constructive rehearsal).

encoding   The process of transforming stimuli so that the information may be stored in long-term memory and retrieved for later use.

feature detection   The process of naming or identifying sensory input (e.g., recognizing the letter A, identifying a friend's voice on the telephone, and others).

keyword method   A mnemonic method for learning new vocabulary, particularly foreign languages. The word to be learned is encoded in a visual image that combines its meaning and its pronunciation (or some other distinguishing feature).

memory, episodic   Personal or autobiographical information, characterized by the vividness of the memories.

memory, long-term   Information in an inactive state that, unless forgotten, may be recalled for future use.

memory, semantic   General information that is part of the common store of knowledge (e.g., historical facts technical information, addresses, phone numbers, and other bodies of knowledge).

memory, short-term Sometimes referred to as working memory; refers to information that is in the active state.

method of loci An associative mechanism for aiding the encoding and storage of stimuli in memory. It involves the construction of bizarre visual images that link the stimuli with familiar, related locations, such as rooms in a house or landmarks on a familiar walk.

propositional network theories The position that information is stored in long-term memory only in verbal form. This perspective describes networks of verbal information composed of nodes and the pathways that link the nodes.

rehearsal, primary Also referred to as maintenance rehearsal; the process of repetition in order to preserve information in memory.

rehearsal, secondary Also referred to as constructive rehearsal or elaboration; the process of modifying stimuli for storage and later retrieval.

schema A knowledge structure that is larger than a specific item. It may be considered to be equivalent to a set of propositions.

symbolic codes The representations of information in long-term memory. Theorists disagree as to their forms [i.e., verbal only or visual and verbal (see propositional networks and dual-code theory)].

REFERENCES

Anderson, J. R. (1976). *Language, memory, and thought*. Hillsdale, NJ: Lawrence Erlbaum.

Anderson, J. R. (1980). *Cognitive psychology and its implications*. San Francisco: W. H. Freeman.

Anderson, R. C. (1975). Mnemotechnics in second-language learning. *American Psychologist, 30*, 821–825.

Anderson, R. C., Pickert, J. W., & Shirey, L. L. (1983). Effects of the reader's schema at different points in time. *Journal of Educational Psychology, 75*, 271–279.

Atkinson, J. R., & Shiffrin, R. M. (1968). Human memory: A proposed system and its control processes. In K. W. Spence and J. T. Spence (Eds.), *The psychology of learning and motivation: Advances in research and theory* (Vol. 2, pp. 89–195). New York: Academic Press.

Ausubel, D. P. (1968). *Educational psychology: A cognitive view*. New York: Holt, Rinehart and Winston.

Bartlett, F. C. (1932). *Remembering*. Cambridge: Cambridge University Press.

Bartlett, F. C. (1958). *Thinking*. New York: Basic Books.

Bobrow, D. G., & Norman, D. A. (1975). Some principles of memory schemata. In D. G. Bobrow & A. Collins (Eds.). *Representation and understanding* (pp. 131–150). New York: Academic Press.

Bower, G. H. (1970a). Analysis of a mnemonic device. *American Scientist, 58,* 495–510.

Bower, G. H. Imagery as a relational organizer in associative learning. *Journal of Verbal Learning and Verbal Behavior, 9,* 529–533.

Broadbent, D. E. (1958). *Perception and communication.* London: Pergamon Press.

Chase, W. G., & Simon, H. A. (1973). The mind's eye in chess. In W. G. Chase & H. A. Simon (Eds.), *Visual information-processing* (pp. 215–281). New York: Academic Press.

Clark, H. H., & Chase, W. G. (1972). On the process of comparing sentences against pictures. *Cognitive Psychology, 3,* 472–517.

Collins, A. M. & Quillian, M. R. (1969). Retrieval time from semantic memory. *Journal of Verbal Learning and Verbal Behavior, 8,* 240–247.

Cook, L. K. (1983). *Effects of reading strategy training on learning from science text.* Unpublished doctoral dissertation. Univ. of Calif., Santa Barbara.

Cooper, L. A., & Shepard, R. N. (1973). The time required to prepare for a rotated stimulus. *Memory and Cognition, 1,* 246–250.

Doctorow, M., Wittrock, M. C., & Marks, C. (1978). Generative processes in reading comprehension. *Journal of Educational Psychology, 70,* 109–118.

Duncker, K. (1945). On problem solving. *Psychological Monographs, 58,* Whole No. 270.

Greeno, J. G. (1975). Nature of problem-solving abilities. In W. K. Estes (Ed.), *Handbook of learning and cognitive processes* (Vol. 5, pp. 239–270). Hillsdale, NJ: Lawrence Erlbaum.

Greeno, J. G. (1976). Indefinite goals in well-structured problems. *Psychological Review, 83,* 479–491.

Greeno, J. G. (1980). Trends in the theory of knowledge for problem-solving. In D. Tuma & F. Reif (Eds.), *Problem-solving and education: Issues in teaching and research* (pp. 9–23). Hillsdale, NJ: Lawrence Erlbaum.

Jones, B. F., & Hall, J. W. (1982). School applications of the mnemonic keyword method as a study strategy for eighth graders. *Journal of Educational Psychology, 74,* 230–237.

Katona, G. (1940). *Organizing and memorizing.* New York: Columbia University Press.

Kintsch, W. (1972). Notes on the structure of semantic memory. In E. Tulving & W. Donaldson (Eds.), *Organization of memory* (pp. 249–305). New York: Academic Press.

Kintsch, W. (1974). *The representation of meaning in memory.* Hillsdale, NJ: Lawrence Erlbaum.

Kosslyn, S. M. (1973). Scanning visual images: Some structural implications. *Perception and Psychophysics, 14,* 90–94.

Lachman, R., Lachman, J. L., & Butterfield, E. C. (1979). *Cognitive psychology and information processing.* Hillsdale, NJ: Lawrence Erlbaum.

Larkin, J. (1980). Teaching problem solving in physics: The psychological laboratory and the practical classroom. In D. Tuma & F. Reif (Eds.), *Problem-solving and education: Issues in teaching and research* (pp. 111–125). Hillsdale, NJ: Lawrence Erlbaum.

Larkin, J., & Reif, F. (1976). Analysis and teaching of a general skill for studying scientific text. *Journal of Educational Psychology, 68*(4), 431–440.

Lesgold, A. M., McCormick, C., & Golinkoff, R. M. (1975). Imagery training and children's prose learning. *Journal of Educational Psychology, 67*(5), 663–667.

⟶ Lindsay, P. H., & Norman, D. A. (1972). *Human information processing: An introduction to psychology*. New York: Academic Press.

Luchins, A. S. (1942). Mechanization in problem-solving. *Psychological Monographs, 54*, No. 248.

Mayer, R. E. (1979a, Spring). Can advance organizers influence meaningful learning? *Review of Educational Research, 49*(2), 271–383.

Mayer, R. E. (1979b). Twenty years of research on advance organizers: Assimilation theory is still the best predictor of results. *Instructional Science, 8*, 133–167.

Mayer, R. E. (1984). Aids to text comprehension. *Educational Psychologist, 19*, 30–42.

Mayer, R. E., & Greeno, J. G. (1972). Structural differences between learning outcomes produced by different instructional methods. *Journal of Educational Psychology, 63*(2), 135–178.

McDaniel, M. A., & Pressley, M. (1984). Putting the keyword method in context. *Journal of Educational Psychology, 76*, 598–609.

Neisser, J. (1967). *Cognitive psychology*. New York: Appleton-Century-Crofts.

⟶ Neisser, U. (1976). *Cognition and reality: Principles and implications of cognitive psychology*. San Francisco: W. H. Freeman.

Newell, A., & Simon, H. A. (1972). *Human problem solving*. Englewood Cliffs, NJ: Prentice-Hall.

Newell, A., Shaw, J. C., & Simon, H. A. (1958). Elements of a theory of problem-solving. *Psychological Review, 65*, 151–166.

Norman, D. A. (1970). I. Introduction: Models of human memory. In D. A. Norman (Ed.), *Models of human memory*. New York: Academic Press, 1–15.

Norman, D. A., & Rumelhart, D. E. (1975). *Explorations in cognition*. San Francisco: W. H. Freeman.

Paivio, A. (1969), Mental imagery in associative learning and memory. *Psychological Review, 76*, 241–263.

Paivio, A. (1970). On the functional significance of imagery. *Psychological Bulletin, 73*, 385–392.

Paivio, A. (1971). *Imagery and verbal processes*. New York: Holt, Rinehart and Winston.

Pellegrino, J. W., & Schadler, M. (1974). Maximizing performance in a problem solving task. Unpublished manuscript, University of Pittsburgh, LRDC Center.

Podgomy, P., & Shepard, R. N. (1978). Functional representations common to visual perception and imagination. *Journal of Experimental Psychology: Human Perception and Performance, 4*, 21–35.

Posner, G. J. (1978, March). Cognitive science: Implications for curricular research and development. Paper presented at the annual meeting of the American Educational Research Association, Toronto.

⟶ Posner, M. I. (1973). Cognition: Natural and artificial. In R. L. Solso (Ed.), *Con-*

temporary issues in contemporary psychology (pp. 167–174). Washington, DC: V. H. Winston.

Posner, M. I., & McLeod, P. (1982). Information-processing models—In search of elementary operations. *Annual Review of Psychology, 33*, 477–514.

Postman, L. (1975). Verbal learning and memory. *Annual Review of Psychology, 26*, 291–335.

Pylyshyn, L. (1973). What the mind's eye tells the mind's brain: A critique of mental imagery. *Psychological Bulletin, 80*, 1–24.

Quillian, M. R. (1968). Semantic memory. In M. Minsky (Ed.), *Semantic information processing*, (pp. 216–270). Cambridge, Mass: MIT Press.

Reder, L. M. (1980). The role of elaboration in the comprehension and retention of prose: A critical review. *Review of Educational Research, 50*(1), 5–53.

Resnick, L. (1981). Instructional psychology. *Annual Review of Psychology, 32*, 660–704.

Resnick, L., & Glaser, R. (1976). Problem solving and intelligence. In L. Resnick & R. Glaser (Eds.), *The Nature of Intelligence*, (pp. 205–230). Hillsdale, NJ: Lawrence Erlbaum.

Rumelhart, D. E., & Ortony, A. (1977). The representation of knowledge in memory. In R. C. Anderson, R. J. Spiro, & W. E. Montague (Eds.), *Schooling and the acquisition of knowledge*. Hillsdale, NJ: Lawrence Erlbaum, 99–136.

Shepard, R. N. (1978). The mental image. *American Psychologist, 33*, 125–137.

Simon, H. A. (1979). Information processing models of cognition. *Annual Review of Psychology, 30*, 363–396.

Simon, H. A. (1980). Problem solving and education. In D. T. Tuma & F. Reif (Eds.), *Problem-solving and education: Issues in teaching and research* (pp. 81–96). Hillsdale, NJ: Lawrence Erlbaum.

Solso, R. L. (1979). *Cognitive psychology*. New York: Harcourt Brace Jovanovich.

Suchman, J. (1966). *Inquiry development program: Developing inquiry*. Chicago: Science Research Associates.

Tulving, E. (1972). Episodic and semantic memory. In E. Tulving & W. Donaldson (Eds.), *Organization of memory* (pp. 382–403). New York: Academic Press.

Tulving, E., & Madigan, S. A. (1970). Memory and verbal learning. *Annual Review of Psychology, 21*, 437–484.

Voss, J. A., Greene, T. R., Post, T. A., & Penner, B. D. (1983). Problem-solving skill in the social sciences. In G. H. Bower (Ed.), *The psychology of learning and motivation* (Vol. 17, pp. 165–214). New York: Academic Press.

Wicker, F. W., Weinstein, C. E., Yelich, C. A., & Brooks, J. D. (1978). Problem-reformulation training and visualization training with insight problems. *Journal of Educational Psychology, 70*, 372–377.

Wittrock, M. C. (1978). Education and the cognitive processes of the brain. In J. S. Chall and A. F. Minsky (Eds.), *The seventy-seventh yearbook of the National Society for the Study of Education, Part II*. Chicago: University of Chicago Press.

Woodward, A. E., Jr., Bjork, R. A., & Jongewood, R. H., Jr. (1973). Recall and recognition as a function of primary rehearsal. *Journal of Verbal Learning and Verbal Behavior, 12*, 608–617.

CHAPTER 9 _____

Jean Piaget's Cognitive-Development Theory

> Knowledge is neither a copy of the object nor taking consciousness of *a priori* forms predetermined in the subject, it's a perceptual construction, made by exchanges between the organism and the environment from the biological point of view and between thought and its object from the cognitive point of view.
> *Piaget, in Bringuier, 1980, p. 110*

Jean Piaget's investigations of human thought processes reintroduced to American psychology the issue of the nature of knowledge. Operant conditioning avoided the issue completely by describing complex achievements as repertoires of behavior. Taking a different approach, the cognitive theorists tacitly accepted knowledge as a given. They then proceeded to describe the ways in which physical signals received by the sensory registers are transformed into knowledge.

The work of Jean Piaget, however, places the issue of the nature of knowledge at the forefront of any consideration of human mental activity. For Piaget, the continuous interaction between the individual and the environment is knowledge. That is, knowledge is a process, not a "thing." An understanding of knowledge therefore requires the identification and description of the various ways that the individual interacts with the environment. "We must not take knowledge with a capital K, as a state in its higher forms, but seek the processes of formation: how one passes from a lesser degree of knowledge to a greater one" (Piaget, in Bringuier, 1980, p. 7).

A conception of knowledge as change and a focus on the qualitative differences in the individual's interaction with the environment are two unique perspectives of the theory. The third unique characteristic is the scope of the subject matter under study. That is, in order to explain qualitative changes in thinking, intellectual functioning at every stage of human life must be analyzed. Thus Piaget's theory is developmental in that it traces intellectual life from the activities of the infant to the reasoning processes of the adult (Piaget, 1975).

The fourth major distinction of Piaget's approach is its interdisciplinary nature. The framework for the theory began with the three disciplines of philosophy, psychology, and biology. From philosophy came the initial questions to be answered. They are: "What is the nature of knowledge?" and "What is the relationship between the knower and reality?" Although these questions traditionally are in the domain of philosophy (i.e., epistemology), Piaget turned to psychology for the method of study. In his view, the questions are factual ones that can be answered only through psychological research (Piaget, 1972b, p. 9). Specifically, the transition from one level of knowledge to another can be determined only through psychological observation.

The contribution of biology is in the framework that describes the nature of intellectual development. Intelligence, like the biological organism, is a living system that grows and develops. Biological organisms and intelligence are both composed of structures and both have mechanisms for regulating activity (Piaget, in Bringuier, 1980, p. 3). Therefore, the adaptation and growth of organisms provide an explanation of the problems and processes involved in the adaptation of intelligence or "knowledge" (Piaget, 1980).

Jean Piaget's interest in cognitive development began early in his career. In 1918, he had completed a doctorate in biology and all but the dissertation in philosophy. Then while working at the Binet laboratory in Paris, Piaget became intrigued with children's wrong answers to questions that involved reasoning. Using the open-ended interviewing technique of the psychoanalysts, Piaget probed for explanations of the errors. He became particularly interested in the children's difficulties with part-whole relationships and their conceptions of causality.

From that beginning emerged Jean Piaget's genetic (developmental) epistemology, a detailed and evolving analysis of the growth of intelligence. By 1930, he had completed four books: *The Language and Thought of the Child* (1923), *Judgement and Reasoning in the Child* (1924), *The Child's Conceptions of the World* (1926), and *The Child's Conception of Physical Causality* (1927). Although translated into English, these early works had much less influence in the United States than in Europe.

Piaget's work was reintroduced to American education in the curriculum reform of the 1960s. His concepts concerning the stages of cognitive functioning were used as a basis for curricula in mathematics, science, and early childhood. However, in Piaget's research, the stages of cognitive development are not the culminating thrust of his work. Instead, since the 1920s, the theory has continued to grow and develop and Piaget (1970b) once described himself as its chief revisionist.

The broad stages of cognitive development described early in the conception of the theory served as the framework for Piaget's analyses of intellectual processes. That emphasis is reflected in this chapter, which focuses on descriptions of the processes rather than describing in detail the stages of cognitive development.

Piaget's emphasis on process is indicated by his later work, undertaken in the 1970s. That period included a reexamination of the individual's self-regulatory processes that function during learning (referred to as *equilibration*) (Piaget, 1977). Also, further similarities were developed by Piaget (1980) between biological adaptations and cognitive adaptations. The latter analysis resulted in the identification of two types of knowledge (endogenous and exogenous, discussed in the following section).

PRINCIPLES OF COGNITIVE DEVELOPMENT

The focus of Jean Piaget's theory is the development of natural thought from birth to adulthood. Understanding the theory depends on an understanding of both the biological assumptions from which it is derived and the implications of those assumptions for defining knowledge (Piaget, 1970b, p. 703).

Basic Assumptions

The goal of the theory is to explain the mechanisms and processes by which the infant and then the child develops into an individual who can reason and think using hypotheses. The basic assumptions on which these descriptions are based are Piaget's definition of cognitive development and his conception of the nature of intelligence.

A Definition of Cognitive Development. Jean Piaget's conception of cognitive development is derived from his analysis of the biological development of certain organisms. His research on mollusks in particular indicated that certain genetic changes in the organism were neither totally inherited nor the result of chance environmental events. He found that certain mollusks, transported from their calm-water habitat to turbulent wind-driven waters, developed shortened shells. This construction by the organism was essential for the mollusks to maintain a foothold on the rocks and thereby survive in rough water. Furthermore, these biological changes, which were constructed by the organism in response to an environmental change, were inherited by some descendents of the mollusks. For some of the organisms, this change persisted even after they were transported back to calmer waters (Piaget, 1980).

Piaget (1980) concluded from this research that the organism is not a passive agent in genetic development. That is, genetic changes are not chance occurrences that lead to survival by some environmentally controlled selection process. Instead, biological adaptation and therefore survival are interactionist processes between the organism and the environment. The organism, in response to altered environmental conditions, constructs the specific biological structures that it needs.

This brief description of biological development also describes the essence of intellectual development. Intelligence, like other living systems, is the process of adaptation to the environment. Cognitive structures, like biological structures, "are not given in advance, neither in the human mind nor in the external world as we perceive and organize it" (Piaget, in Bringuier, 1980, p. 37). Instead, the individual's intelligence grows and develops through interaction with the environment.

Furthermore, intelligence also constructs the cognitive structures necessary for adapting to the environment. For example, young children often maintain that two rows of objects are unequal in number if one row is longer than the other. Realization of the true nature of the situation (number of objects is independent of spatial arrangement) requires a reconstruction of the child's thinking. The child must give up his or her dependence on perceptual cues, such as length of the row, as an indicator of number equality. The result is the construction by the child of a new internal structure about the numbering of objects.

The Outcomes of Cognitive Development. The most advanced form of thought identified by Piaget is referred to as formal operations. These logical thought processes are characterized by the ability to formulate sets of hypotheses. Then the hypotheses that are compatible with the situation under study (Inhelder & Piaget, 1958, p. 250) are tested. At the formal operational level, the individual reasons from a theoretical framework (hypotheses) to the testing of the theory.

Attainment of the level of formal operational thought is preceded by and dependent on the individual's prior cognitive attainments. Piaget has identified three qualitatively different ways of thinking that are prerequisite to the development of formal operational thought: the action schemes of the infant, the semilogical, preoperational thought of children, and the concrete operations of middle childhood. Each of these ways of interacting with the environment is an essential precondition for the next level of development.

The importance of these different levels of cognitive functioning is in the qualitative differences among them. The intellectual activity of formal operations is no more like the action schemes of the infant than the butterfly is like the larva from which it came. The action schemes of the infant are a practical intelligence that functions at a presymbolic and pre-language level. In contrast, formal operations is the testing of hypotheses and the development of theories about proposed relationships. The function of cognitive growth is to produce these powerful cognitive structures that permit the individual to act on the environment with greater flexibility and in more ways (Gruber & Voneche, 1977).

Influential Factors in Cognitive Development.   Four factors are necessary for the development of cognitive functions: the physical environment, maturation, social influences, and the learner's self-regulatory processes, referred to as *equilibration* (Piaget, 1977). Each one is essential for development, but none is sufficient by itself.

Contact with the physical environment is indispensable since the interaction between the individual and the world is the source of new knowledge. However, contact with the physical world is insufficient for developing knowledge unless the individual's intelligence can make use of the experience. Maturation of the nervous system is therefore important because it permits the child to realize maximum benefit from physical experience. In other words, maturation opens up possibilities for development, whereas the lack of it establishes broad limits on cognitive achievement. The emergence of hand-eye coordination in the infant, for example, is essential for the construction of the infant's action schemes, such as "reaching-grasping-pulling."

Although maturation is an important condition for cognitive development, the particular events are not predetermined. Development proceeds at different rates, depending on the nature of the contact with the environment and the learner's own activity.

The third factor, the social environment, includes the role of language and education. The importance of the social environment is that such experiences, like physical experience, can accelerate or retard the development of cognitive structures (Inhelder, Sinclair, & Bovet, 1974).

The foregoing three factors are the classical factors described by other theorists that influence development. In addition, Piaget describes a fourth factor, equilibration. This factor is the learner's self-regulatory and self-correcting processes that function throughout development. However, equilibration is not an "add-on" to the other three factors. Instead, equilibration regulates the individual's specific interactions with the environment as well as physical experience, social experience, and physical development. Equilibration (described in the following section) permits cognitive development to proceed in a coherent and organized fashion.

The Nature of Intelligence. Theories of learning traditionally have defined "learning" and "intelligence" as two separate, although related, entities. Intelligence is viewed as a broad enduring trait that can be measured quantitatively. Learning is considered to be a specific process that occurs within the broad parameters established by intelligence.

Intelligence as Process. For Piaget, intelligence is not a static trait that can be quantitatively assessed. Instead, intelligence is an ongoing and changing process. It is the mechanism by which the individual interacts with the environment at any given moment and a process that continually constructs itself. Intelligence, like a biological system, takes certain basics from the environment and builds the structures it needs in order to function. Thus intelligence is always active and dynamic, for it seeks explanations and understandings in order both to construct itself and to function effectively.

The perspective that intelligence is a dynamic and developing process has important implications for the definition of the term "knowledge." Piaget rejects the traditional view that learning is a matter of acquiring static objective knowledge about a "real" world that existed prior to and independent of the learner. That traditional view, according to Piaget (1970b) is based on two erroneous assumptions. One is that objective knowledge is some entity "out there" in objects and events that can be identified. The second assumption is that the external environment and the individual can be separated into two entities in any definition of knowledge.

Knowledge as Process. Piaget's unique view of knowledge is that in the creation of knowledge, the individual and the object are fused and cannot be separated. Knowledge also contains many subjective components; therefore, it is a relationship and not some a priori given.

More importantly, the relationship between the learner and the object is not static; it is always undergoing transformation. "The relationship between subject (knower) and objects is in no way determined beforehand, and what is more important, it is not stable" (Piaget, 1970b, p. 704). The infant, for example, begins by attempting to assimilate everything into its sensorimotor intelligence. The infant first learns about the environment by putting all objects into its mouth and later, shaking, dropping, pushing, or pulling them. At the most sophisticated level of intelligence, however, scientists and scholars build theories using abstract symbols that may have no concrete counterparts in the environment. The development of new mathematical systems is one result of this type of inter-action. Thus, at one extreme, the activities of the infant represent max-imum subjectivity with regard to the development of knowledge. At the other extreme, the theoretical mathematician represents maximum ob-jectivity and logic. Between the two lies a continuum of ever-changing development.

Therefore, according to Piaget (1970b), to attempt to describe the ac-quisition of knowledge as though it were a particular type of unchanging event between a subject and the environment is in error. The character-istics of the act of knowing are not constant and the identification of the different ways in which the individual constructs knowledge is of funda-mental importance in understanding cognitive development.

In summary, genetic epistemology "above all sees knowledge as a con-tinuous construction" (Piaget, 1972b, p. 17). Since knowledge is con-tructed through the individual's interactions with the environment and intelligence is also so constructed, the issues in understanding knowledge and intelligence are reduced to the same question. In other words, to answer the question "How does the individual progress from a state of less sufficient to more sufficient knowledge?" is to determine the ways in which intelligence is interacting with the environment.

Piaget's theory, in summary, is supported by three major assumptions. The first is that knowledge is not an objective entity in the environment. Instead, it is the interaction between the individual and the environment, and it includes both subjective and objective components. Since the in-dividual and the object in the environment cannot be separated in terms of defining knowledge, the task for genetic epistemology is to determine the characteristics of this ever-changing interaction.

Second, the growth of intelligence, like biological development, is de-pendent on the construction of new structures from prior structures. New structures are constructed as a part of the adaptation of intelligence to the environment. Third, the factors that influence cognitive development are the physical environment, the social environment, maturation, and the individual's self-regulation processes. All these factors are essential for cognitive growth.

The Components of Cognitive Development

The focal point of the theory is the means by which individuals progress from one level of mental development or knowledge to a higher level. Central to the theory is the belief that knowledge is constructed by the individual in continual and ever-changing interactions with the environment.

In seeking to understand the mechanisms of cognitive development, Piaget has described intellectual functioning from three perspectives. They are: (1) the fundamental processes involved in interactions with the environment (assimilation, accommodation, and equilibration), (2) the ways in which knowledge is constructed (physical and logico-mathematical experience), and (3) the qualitative differences in thinking at different stages of development (the action schemes of the infant, preoperational thought, concrete and formal operations).

The Fundamental Processes. Cognitive development according to Piaget (1977, p. 3) is effected by three basic processes: assimilation, accommodation, and equilibration. Briefly summarized, *assimilation* is the integration of new data with existing cognitive structures, *accommodation* is the adjustment of cognitive structures to the new situation, and *equilibration* is the continuing readjustment between assimilation and accommodation.

Assimilation. This process is primarily a biological concept (Piaget, in Bringuier, 1980, p. 42). It is the integration of external elements into the organism's structures, for example, the digestion of food and the incorporation of chlorophyllian in a plant's growth (Piaget, 1970b, p. 307).

In intellectual life, as in biological life, assimilation involves the integration of new data with already existing internal structures. A child who identifies a three-sided figure as a triangle is assimilating that figure into his or her schema. Assimilation, however, is not the process of passively registering a copy of reality, nor is it an association between some environmental stimulus and a response (S→R). Instead, it is the filtering of the stimulus through an action structure so that the structures are themselves enriched (i.e., S⇄R) (Piaget & Inhelder, 1969, p. 6).

Assimilation on the cognitive level is roughly analogous to a rabbit eating a cabbage (Piaget, in Bringuier, 1980). The rabbit does not become the cabbage; instead, the cabbage becomes part of the rabbit.

An important requirement for the occurrence of assimilation is an internal structure that can make use of the information. Young children, for example, base many of their decisions about the environment on perceptual cues alone. Often they do not integrate new information because they lack an appropriate assimilatory structure. For example, when asked to draw a picture of a half-full bottle that is tipped to one side, young children typically draw the water line inaccurately (see Figure 9–1). They show the water level as parallel to the bottom of the bottle regardless of the bottle's relationship to the table.

When confronted with the physical situation, young children fail to see the discrepancy between their drawings and reality (Piaget, 1977, p. 4). This failure is caused by the lack of assimilatory structures needed in the

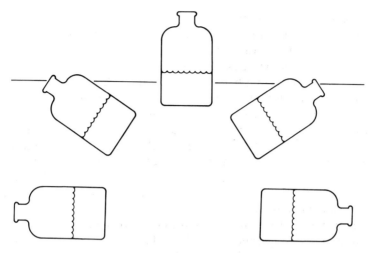

Figure 9-1. Young child's conception of the water line in containers placed at different angles.

situation. The children have not developed a coordinate spatial system that enables them to place the water in a frame of reference outside the bottle.

Accommodation. In the individual's encounters with the environment, accommodation accompanies assimilation. Accommodation is the adjustment of internal structures to the particular characteristics of specific situations. For example, biological structures accommodate to the type and quantity of food at the same time that the food is being assimilated.

Similarly, in cognitive functioning, internal structures adjust to the particular characteristics of new objects and events. The child presented with a green triangle made of felt material assimilates the already familiar characteristics (closed, three-sided figure). At the same time, the internal structure is accommodating to the particular features of the triangle (in this case, color and material).

Assimilation and accommodation function together in encounters with the environment at all levels of cognitive functioning. When the infant has discovered that he or she can grasp everything he or she sees, everything becomes an object to grasp (i.e., assimilation) (Piaget, in Bringuier, 1980, p. 43). For a large object, however, both hands may be needed, and for a small object, the fingers may need to be tightened (accommodation). The same holds for the scientist and the scholar whose theory is an assimilatory scheme that is then adapted to diverse situations (Piaget, in Bringuier, 1980, p. 43).

In cognitive development, accommodation also refers to the modification of the individual's internal cognitive structures. When the learner realizes that his or her ways of thinking are contradicted by events in the environment, the prior ways of thinking are reorganized. This reorganization, which results in a higher level of thinking, is accommodation.

An example is children's experience with shape and size. Typically, young children assert that changing a ball of clay into a sausage shape makes it bigger. Later, they often vacillate between decisions that the ball and the sausage are each bigger. Each decision depends on the particular dimension that the child notices at the moment. Eventually, the child realizes that both decisions cannot be true. This cognitive conflict, referred to as *disequilibrium*, leads to a reorganization of the child's thinking (i.e., accommodation).

Equilibration.   Like assimilation and accommodation, equilibration also has a biological parallel. In biological functioning, the organism must maintain a steady state within itself while at the same time remaining open to the environmental events necessary for growth and survival.

In cognitive development, equilibration is the continuing self-regulation that permits the individual to grow, develop, and change while maintaining stability. Equilibration, however, is not a balance of forces (which would be an immobile state). Instead, it is a dynamic process that continuously regulates behavior (Piaget, in Bringuier, 1980, p. 41).

Equilibration regulates the individual's thinking processes at three different levels of cognitive functioning. They are the relationships between (1) assimilation and accommodation in the individual's daily encounters, (2) emerging subsystems of the individual's knowledge, and (3) parts of the individual's knowledge and total knowledge system.

Regulating Interactions with the Environment.   The role of equilibration in the regulation of assimilation and accommodation is to prevent one from occurring at the expense of the other (Piaget, in Bringuier, 1980). In most situations, assimilation and equilibration are equally balanced. However, for short periods of time, sometimes the dominance of one or the other is necessary. Examples include symbolic play (the dominance of assimilation) and imitation (the dominance of accommodation).

Symbolic play occurs when the young child is developing representational thought and is attempting to subordinate reality to these thought processes. Examples include making playhouses out of boxes and boats out of matchboxes. These activities are "a deforming assimilation of reality to the self" (Piaget, 1967, p. 23). Through symbolic play, the child achieves an affective satisfaction missing in his or her daily efforts to understand a strange and confusing world (see Piaget, 1951).

Imitation, in contrast, is the accommodation of the individual to external models. It is responsible for the child's acquisition of functional social behaviors. Equilibration, however, regulates these two types of childhood activities so that each occurs when appropriate (Piaget & Inhelder, 1969, p. 58).

Regulating Subsystems and Part-Whole Knowledge. Another important role for equilibration is that of establishing a balance between developing subsystems of the individual's knowledge. Since these subsystems develop at different rates, conflicts can arise between them, particularly between numerical and spatial measurement. Two rows of pebbles, for example, may be counted out by the child and determined to be equal. However, the young child will identify an inequality between the two rows if the pebbles in one row are spread out so that the endpoints of one row extend beyond the endpoints of the other. For the young child, no conflict exists. At an elementary level of thinking, the child is able to entertain two opposing judgments without realizing the contradiction. As the child's cognitive development continues, the contradiction between the two judgments becomes apparent to the child. The vacillation between the statements that the numbers are equal and unequal occurs as first number and then length of the row is used as the basis for decisions. The contradiction has led to a disturbance (i.e., disequilibrium) between the two subsystems. The process by which this disturbance is resolved is equilibration.

The disturbance is often resolved by the modification of the individual's internal structure, or accommodation. When accommodation in the child's thinking occurs, a new state of balance or equilibrium has been reached.

On the third level of functioning, equilibration regulates the relationship between the parts of an individual's knowledge and his or her total knowledge. The totality of knowledge, according to Piaget (1977), is constantly being differentiated into parts and integrated back again into the whole. Equilibration regulates this process.

In summary, equilibration is the factor that maintains stability during a process of continuous interactions and continuous change. Without equilibration, cognitive development would lack continuity and cohesiveness, but instead, would become fragmented and disorganized.

The Construction of Knowledge. The fundamental processes operating in the construction of knowledge are assimilation and accommodation regulated by equilibration. In addition, Piaget (1980) has described the construction of knowledge in terms of the types of knowledge experiences in which the learner engages. They are *physical experience* and *logico-mathematical experience.*

Physical Experience. Any direct encounter with the environment in which the individual is abstracting the physical properties of objects is referred to as physical experience. Examples include the infant's taking note of the sound of a rattle and a child's noticing the softness of velvet. In physical experience, a particular property such as color or shape is assimilated into the learner's existing mental structure. At the same time, however, accommodation is occurring. The individual's mental structure may be adjusting to the intensity of the color (bright or dull), the particular shade (light or dark), and so on. Thus physical experience involves both the processes of assimilation and accommodation.

The source of the learner's new knowledge in physical experience is some object external to the learner. The process is one of abstracting the object's physical characteristics by the learner. Therefore, this type of knowledge experience is also referred to by Piaget (1980) as *exogenous knowledge* (external to the learner) or the process of *empirical abstraction*. The defining characteristic of this type of knowledge experience is that it includes only the abstraction of the physical properties inherent in the particular object, such as the greenness of grass or the blue of the sky.

Logico-mathematical Experience. The physical properties of objects are abstracted and integrated into the child's mental framework through physical experience. It is characterized by direct encounters with the environment in which the source of knowledge is some object external to the learner. In contrast, the source of knowledge in logico-mathematical experience is the learner's own thought processes. Any activity in which the individual's thought processes are reorganized on a higher level is an example. This accomplishment has already been referred to as accommodation. However, it is so essential to the learner's cognitive development that it is further described under the particular name *logico-mathematical experience*.

When the infant, for example, reorganizes and coordinates separate acts into an action scheme for obtaining distant objects, intelligence is functioning at a new level. In middle childhood, the learner resolves some of his or her contradictory actions concerning numerical and spatial relations through the construction of number invariance (i.e., logico-mathematical knowledge). Other examples include the constructs "heavier than" and "smaller than," and the capabilities involved in concrete and formal operational thinking.

In logico-mathematical experience, the activity is one of reflecting on current actions and reorganizing them on a more logical level. This activity is therefore referred to as *reflective abstraction* because it involves thought processes "reflecting on themselves."[1]

---

[1] This process has sometimes been referred to as "reflexive abstraction," although reflective appears to be the more common term.

Unlike physical experience, the source of knowledge is internal to the learner (i.e., the learner's own activity). Therefore, the knowledge is referred to as *endogenous*. It differs from exogenous knowledge (the process of empirical abstraction), which derives from objects in the environment. That is, endogenous knowledge (the process of reflective abstraction) is developed from the coordinations of the individual's actions into a new organization (see Table 9-1).

A second difference between the processes of empirical and reflective abstraction is that the latter can exist in a totally pure form. At the level of formal operations, the thought processes are independent of any reference to physical manipulation (unlike concrete operations). This pure form of abstraction is referred to as *reflected abstraction* (Piaget, 1980).

The terms *physical experience* (empirical abstraction) and *logico-mathematical experience* (reflective abstraction) signify different ways of developing new knowledge. However, in the child's interactions with the environment, they are inseparable (DeVries, 1978, p. 84). A child who is looking at six blue blocks and two yellow ones may be thinking about the specific properties; however, a whole network of relationships is also activated by the experience (DeVries, 1978).

The Stages of Cognitive Development. The descriptions of empirical and reflective abstraction indicate different ways by which the individual develops knowledge. During the early years of the child's life the processes of empirical and reflective abstraction in the child's actions are largely undifferentiated. However, the process of empirical abstraction (i.e., physical experience) dominates the child's thinking (DeVries, 1978). During the later childhood years, the logico-mathematical aspect of thinking becomes more fully capable of making logical decisions. Finally, the attainment of "true" logical thinking is characterized by the dominance of the process of reflective abstraction (i.e., logico-mathematical experience).

Table 9-1. Knowledge Experiences and Processes

Individual's Action	Type of Knowledge Experience
Empirical abstraction: the process of abstracting the physical characteristics of some object in the environment through assimilation and accommodation	Exogenous knowledge, physical experience
Reflective abstraction: the process of reorganizing actions into more logical patterns of activity through modification of cognitive structures	Endogenous knowledge, logico-mathematical experience

The early research conducted by Piaget (1967, 1970a) established the framework for the foregoing analysis of thinking processes. Specifically, four broad periods or stages of cognitive development were identified in Piaget's early investigations of children's thinking. They are the sensorimotor, preoperational, concrete operational, and formal operational stages. Each one "extends the preceding period, reconstructs it on a new level and later surpasses it to an even greater degree" (Piaget & Inhelder, 1969, p. 152).

For example, the infant's attainment of the notion of object permanence sets the stage for the preoperational development of qualitative identities. Specifically, $a = a$; that is, the water poured from a tall container is the same water. Similarly, the development of both part-whole relationships (classification) and of seriation in the concrete operational period is essential for the later development of formal operational thinking.

These four stages of development are summarized briefly in Table 9–2. Although individuals move from one stage to another at different ages, the stages occur in a sequential order. Like the embryological stages in the biological organism, each stage in cognitive development is necessary for the following one to occur. The stages have sometimes been taken as the goal of Piaget's work. They are, however, the taxonomy that forms the backdrop for the gradual qualitative changes in cognitive structures. In other words, the changes in cognitive structures from action schemes to prelogical, concrete operational, and formal operational thought are reflected in the broad stages.

The Nature of Complex Thought

A contribution of Piaget's analyses is the identification of the qualitative differences in modes of reasoning from infancy to adulthood. The infant's action schemes gradually give way to the semilogical thought of the young child. This, in turn, develops into the logical thought structures referred to as concrete operations, and later, formal operations.

The term *operations* refers to the cognitive structures that govern logical reasoning in the broad sense (Piaget, 1970a, 1970b). Like other cognitive structures, operations can be carried out both physically and mentally.

Operations differ from other actions in at least two important ways. These differences are summarized in Table 9–3. An operation includes both a transformation and a constant that does not change. Operations are also reversible; they may be returned to the starting point. The act of smoking a pipe is not an operation. When completed, it cannot be reversed (Piaget, 1970a, p. 21).

Table 9-2. Summary of the Four Broad Stages of Development

Stage	Overview
Sensorimotor period (birth to 1½–2 years)	Presymbolic and preverbal. Intelligence involves the development of action schemes. An example is "reaching-grasping-pulling" enacted to reach distant objects. Second year: child differentiates self from the environment. Child develops the identity of his or her body and others in time and space and the concept of the permanence of objects.
Preoperational period (2–3 to 7–8 years)	Partially logical thought begins. Notion of object permanence leads to qualitative identities. Water poured into another container is the same water; $a = a$. Thought processes are based on perceptual cues and child is unaware of contradictory statements. An example is that soap floats because it is small and a piece of iron sinks because it is thin. Language development begins and increases rapidly; child's spontaneous speech is dominated by monologues.
Concrete operational period (7–8 to 12–14 years)	Impulsive behavior replaced by at least rudimentary reflection; child can see another's point of view. Group play includes agreement on rules and cooperation with rules. Logical ways of thinking linked to concrete objects are developed (concrete operations). Thought is independent of perceptual cues; "longer" is not synonymous with "farther."
Formal operational period (older than 14)	Thinking about life plans and adult roles begins. The capability of dealing logically with multifactor situations begins (formal operations). Individuals can reason from the hypothetical situation to the concrete.

The child's construction of operational structure is that of developing an understanding of both the transformation and the constant characteristic in a particular process. The constant or invariant is known also as *conservation* and it is the psychological criterion for the child's completion of an operational structure (Piaget, 1975; Piaget & Inhelder, 1969).

Concrete Operational Structures. Concrete operations include class inclusion operations, seriation, and the conservation constructs of number, length, matter, weight, and volume. The child's construction of these

Table 9-3. Summary of the Characteristics of Operations

Characteristic	Description	Examples
Reversibility	The action can be returned to the starting point	Addition, $9 + 7 = 16$, which can be reversed through subtraction: $16 - 9 = 7$; $16 - 7 = 9$
Conservation	The operation includes a constant or invariant that does not change	Lengthening a row of objects (transformation) does not change the number in the set (constant)
Transformation	The characteristic that does change in the operation	Changing the shape of a ball of clay into a sausage (transformation) does not alter the amount

cognitive structures is a gradual process that first includes cognitive conflict, then vacillation among possible choices, and finally, logical resolution of the conflict. The preoperational child focuses on perceptual cues and static states. The concrete operational child focuses on the transformations and can identify the constant characteristic (that which is conserved).

Conservation of volume, for example, is represented by the typical experiment, in which water is poured from a short, wide glass into a tall, thin one. Extensive research shows that concrete operational children support their correct judgments by three types of arguments (Inhelder, Sinclair, & Bovet, 1974, p. 31). One is reversibility by inversion; that is, if the water is poured back into the first glass, the amount is the same. The others are reversibility by compensation of reciprocal relationships (the water is higher, but the glass is thinner, so it is the same) and additive identity (nothing has been added or taken away).

Class Inclusion Operations. An understanding of part-whole relationships is the essential characteristic of class inclusion operations. An example is roses + tulips = flowers. Preoperational children, when asked if there are more birds or sparrows in the woods, typically reply that they do not know without counting. Class inclusion also includes double classifications. An example is classifying the flowers into red roses, red tulips, white roses and white tulips (see Table 9–4).

The reversibility of class inclusion operations is accomplished by *inverse* or *negation*, which is separating the whole into subclasses. For example, flowers minus the roses leaves the tulips. In double classification, an example of reversibility is the separation of red roses from the

Table 9-4. Multiplication of Classes on the Basis of Two Characteristics

	Color	
Type of Flower	Red	White
Tulips	Red tulips	White tulips
Roses	Red roses	White roses

other three subgroups. Preoperational children focus on one characteristic at a time and are unable to separate color (red or white) from type of flower (tulips or roses). That is, when asked to identify the red roses, they will choose either all the roses or all the red flowers.

Seriation. In contrast to classification, seriation is characterized by transitivity, or the "transfer" of relations. That is, if $A = B$ and $B = C$, then $A = C$. This relationship expresses equality across elements, and it is also symmetric. Other relationships which express "greater than" ($>$) and "less than" ($<$), are asymmetric. For example, $A > B > C > D$. Preoperational children when asked to order a series of sticks from longest to shortest can accomplish the task only by working with the sticks two at a time, and with many errors. In contrast, concrete operational children understand that some element B is both longer than and shorter than some other elements. Therefore, they proceed systematically: first to find the shortest (or longest) stick, then to select the next one in length, and so on.

The reversibility of a series is referred to as *reciprocity*. That is, the reverse of $A = B = C$ is $C = B = A$ and the reverse of $A > B > C$ is $C < B < A$. The importance of classification and seriation is that both are essential for an understanding of numbers.

Formal Operational Structures. The reflected abstractions referred to as *formal operations* differ from concrete operations in several ways. The major difference is that formal operational thinkers can develop and test hypotheses about complex multifactor situations. Concrete operational thinking is restricted to two-factor situations. One reason for the difference is that the concrete operational thinker, given four characteristics, such as red and white and circles and squares, is only able to generate the four subclasses (red circles, red squares, white circles, and white squares). In contrast, the formal operational thinker can also generate the 16 possible combinations of these characteristics. For example, among the possibilities are white squares + red circles, red squares + red circles, and red squares + white circles. Piaget (1970a) refers to this capability as *combinatorial operations*. It is essential for formal operational thinking because it makes possible the analysis of relationships in multifactor situations (Inhelder & Piaget, 1958, p. 313).

However, the individual, when faced with a complex situation, does not actually construct the table of combinations. Instead, he or she begins by conceptualizing some of the possible combinations and systematically testing hypotheses in order to isolate the correct explanation. The important characteristic that distinguishes formal operations from concrete operations is that the subject begins with a theoretical synthesis that implies certain relationships and then proceeds to test the hypothesized relationships (Karmiloff-Smith & Inhelder (1975)). In contrast, concrete operational thought reasons from the empirical data in developing an explanation (Inhelder & Piaget, 1958, p. 251).

The method of concrete operations (i.e., pairing characteristics two by two) does not take into account the situations in which variables are mixed. That is, one effect may be caused by several factors or a single causal factor may be accompanied or masked by several varying factors that are not causes (Inhelder & Piaget, 1958, p. 282).

An example is the colorless liquids experiment (Inhelder & Piaget, 1958). The experimenter adds a substance *g* to each of two beakers of colorless liquid(s). In one case, the new substance produces no change; however, in the other, the color yellow appears. The task for the student is to identify which of four colorless liquids, singly or in combination, produces the yellow color (see Figure 9–2).

Formal operational thinkers will figure out the possible combinations, often jotting them down, and then proceed to test them. Individuals who are at the concrete level of thinking will proceed to test combinations, two by two. However, this approach results in omissions and errors.

In other words, the formal operational thinker surveys a complex situation and first develops a theoretical framework that includes the possible explanations. Then these hypotheses are tested systematically to determine the actual situation. In addition, the formal operational thinker is able to generate the potential set of explanations appropriate for multifactor situations.

Piaget (1972a, p. 10) noted that his research into formal operations had utilized situations likely to be understood by children in an academic setting. However, the applicability of such situations to professional environments is questionable. In other words, carpenters, locksmiths, or mechanics may well reason hypothetically in their speciality. Their unfamiliarity with structured school subjects, however, would hinder them from reasoning in a formal way with the experimental situations used in the research.

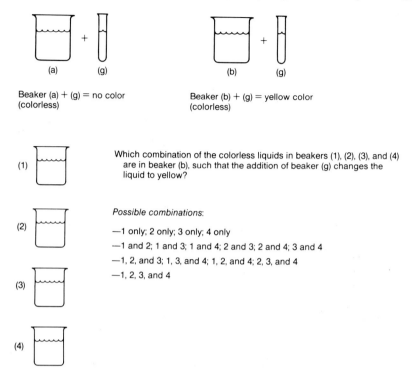

Figure 9-2. The colorless liquids experiment.

Summary

The growth of logical reasoning is a lengthy process that begins in infancy and can continue into adulthood. The development of intelligence may be noted by the qualitative differences in the child's interactions which begin at a preverbal level. Coordinated sequences of activities with which to interact with the environment, referred to as *action schemes*, are constructed by the infant. This milestone is followed by a lengthy period during which language, early relationships with peers, and knowledge about the world develops. As the exploring child begins to develop knowledge about the environment, he or she is constantly making assertions about the causes or reasons for events. Often inaccurate and rudimentary (and therefore referred to as transductive or prelogical thought), this process is essential to later development of operational thinking. Finally, concrete and then formal operations are constructed by the child.

The longitudinal development of logical thinking is effected by three

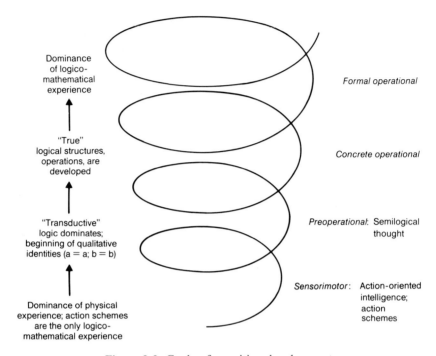

Dominance
of logico-
mathematical
experience

Formal operational

↑

"True"
logical structures,
operations, are
developed

Concrete operational

↑

"Transductive"
logic dominates;
beginning of qualitative
identities (a = a; b = b)

Preoperational: Semilogical
thought

↑

Dominance of physical
experience; action schemes
are the only logico-
mathematical experience

Sensorimotor: Action-oriented
intelligence;
action
schemes

Figure 9-3. Cycle of cognitive development.

fundamental processes: assimilation, accommodation, and equilibration. These processes, which involve the integration of information from the environment with existing cognitive structures and the reorganization of structures on higher levels, are the essence of intellectual growth.

These processes combine in different ways to produce knowledge. Physical experience is the process of abstracting characteristics of particular objects (i.e., empirical abstraction). Logico-mathematical experience, in contrast, is the process of reflecting on existing thought patterns and reconstructing one's cognitive framework on a higher level (i.e., reflective abstraction). The result is that at each stage of development more and more powerful cognitive structures are constructed (see Figure 9–3).

PRINCIPLES OF INSTRUCTION

The derivation of instructional principles from Piaget's developmental epistemology requires careful and thoughtful analysis and interpretation. The primary reason is that the theory describes the qualitative changes in thought processes that lead to logical thinking. Piaget considers that learning in the strict sense, such as learning the capital of Switzerland, is a subset of learning in the broad sense (i.e., cognitive development). Because the focus of the theory is on the development of intelligence, few specific guidelines for organizing instructional content may be developed from the theory. For example, in mathematics, one-to-one correspondence is described, but the details of problem solving in algebra are outside the realm of the theory (Ginsburg, 1981, p. 327).

The derivation of instructional principles is complicated further by the fact that conventional educational psychology is, for the most part, a rational and operationalist philosophy (Easley, 1978, p. 141). It is characterized by objectives, instructional methods, and goal-based evaluation. As a result, early efforts to fit Piaget's genetic epistemology to this quite different framework resulted in misinterpretations of the theory for educational practice (discussed in the section entitled "Educational Applications").

Basic Assumptions

Jean Piaget's perspective on cognitive development establishes requirements for the educational system that differ from those of traditional learning theories. His basic assumptions about the nature of education are derived from his conception of the nature of the child's thought and the ways in which knowledge is constructed.

The Nature of Education. Jean Piaget's study of children's activities as they interact with the world revealed that their thought processes differ qualitatively from adult thinking. Childhood logic is transductive; it does not follow the rules of deductive or inductive thinking. Furthermore, the child's progress to adult thought is a lengthy one during which the child's intelligence must construct over a period of time the needed cognitive structures.

The Child and the School. The perspective of the nature of the child's thinking has important implications for education (Piaget, 1970c). If childhood is believed to be simply a period that the child goes through in order to become an adult, then the relationship between the educational system and the child will be unilateral. The child will receive already finished products of adult knowledge and morality. Educational experiences will be organized and directed by the teacher and transmitted to the child. In such an educational climate, even individual tasks such as writing an essay will be directed toward obedience rather than autonomy (Piaget, 1970c).

However, if childhood is accepted as a necessary and important phase in the development of logical thinking, education will be viewed differently. If the child's mentality is of fundamental importance, then it is not a period in which the child accumulates the information needed to be an adult. Instead, the child's thought patterns are undergoing qualitative changes essential to the development of logical abstract thought. Therefore, the relationship between the educational system and the child must be a reciprocal one (Piaget, 1970c).

Support for the Child's Research.   Instead of the verbal transmission of knowledge, education should be characterized by the use of methods that support the spontaneous research of the child or adolescent (Piaget, 1973). Such an approach is particularly important in the teaching of mathematics and science. The problem with mathematical and physical ideas is that these subjects are taught as though they were a set of truths that can be understood only through an abstract language. Mathematics, however, is composed of actions and operations, and therefore, understanding mathematics should begin with action (Piaget, 1973). Such instruction should begin in nursery school with concrete exercises related to lengths, surfaces, numbers, and so on, progressing to physical and mechanical experiments in secondary school (Piaget, 1973, p. 104).

The basic need for education, according to Piaget (1973), is "to introduce both liberal arts and science students to experimental procedures and the free activity such training implies" (Piaget, 1973, p. 35). The solution he recommends is to provide mixed curricula. Science classes that focus on self-directed experimentation should be included as well as the introduction of individual experimentation whenever possible in other courses. Some psychology classes, for example, could be devoted to individual experimentation in psycholinguistics.

Of course, subjects such as history or Latin cannot be "reinvented" by the students. That is, individuals cannot verify explanatory hypotheses with regard to Greek civilization (Piaget, 1973, p. 47). However, when research reveals some understanding of the ways in which students acquire spontaneous operational thought in historical understanding, methods may change.

The Use of Active Methods.   Piaget (1973) recommends the use of active methods that require the student to rediscover or reconstruct the truths to be learned. However, students are not to be left simply to their own devices. Instead, the teacher's role is that of organizing and creating situations that present useful problems. The teacher also must provide counterexamples to the students that lead to reflection of their often hasty solutions (Piaget, 1973).

Piaget (1970c) noted, however, that only slight progress has been made in changing educational practice from receptive instruction to active instruction. The slow transition, however, is easily understood. Active methods are difficult to implement, require more work and concentrated effort, and require teachers with advanced training. In addition, transmitting instruction is less tiring for the teacher and conforms to the adult's natural tendency to be the "expert" (Piaget, 1970c).

A more subtle problem for the design of an activity-based curriculum is that intuitive methods of teaching often are mistaken for activities. Audiovisual aids are an example. Although an improvement over verbal methods of instruction, they are not spontaneous activities. Therefore, audiovisual aids can serve only as accessories or aids in the student's personal investigations of truth (Piaget, 1970c).

Another requirement that must accompany experimentation is that of collaboration and interchange among the students themselves (Piaget, 1973, p. 108). The traditional school often excludes this interchange, recognizing only the social exchange between teacher and student. However, both independent and collaborative student activity should be included. Using one's intelligence, according to Piaget (1973), assumes the exercise of a critical spirit. Such objectivity, however, can be developed only in the group situation in which "give and take" with one's peers occurs.

In summary, spontaneous activity, with small groups of students brought together by means of their mutual interest in a particular activity, should be a major feature of classroom learning. The classroom should be "a center of real (and experimental) activities carried out in common, so that logical intelligence may be elaborated through action and social change" (Piaget, 1973, p. 47).

The Components of Instruction

The application of Piaget's concepts to instruction depends on sensitivity to a few important issues. First, children naturally try to make sense out of the world. This process often seems lengthy and time consuming to the adult. However, the students must be permitted to make their own mistakes and to correct these errors themselves. Therefore, classroom instruction must be planned to facilitate the processes of construction, assimilation, and accommodation, through which physical/empirical abstraction and reflective abstraction can occur.

Second, the process of experimentation by students at all ages is important. Only through experimentation can the learner acquire the skills that are necessary for formal operational thought. More importantly, experimentation often gives birth to new ideas. For young children, their first new ideas may not seem so original to adults. But such a practice in which children are encouraged to develop new ideas can lead to original discoveries. "The more we can help children to have their own wonderful ideas and feel good about themselves for having them, the more likely it is that they will someday happen upon wonderful ideas that no one else happened upon before" (Duckworth, 1978, p. 231).

In other words, the cognitive activity that is generated by experimentation is essential. "However, being cognitively active does not mean that the child merely manipulates a given type of material; he can be mentally active without physical manipulation, just as he can be mentally passive while actually manipulating objects" (Inhelder et al., 1974, p. 25).

The third and most important issue in the implementation of Piaget's theory is that knowledge is always a construction by the learner. Knowledge is not the same thing as making a figurative copy of reality. Instead, it always involves operative processes that lead to a transformation of reality, either in actions or in thought (Piaget, 1970c). The extensive experiments undertaken by Inhelder, Sinclair, and Bovet (1974) indicate the importance of repeated exposure to intellectually stimulating situations that provide opportunities to act on objects. Children who are intermediate between nonconservation and conservation do attain conservation.

The situations most likely to facilitate progress are those in which the students can compare various modes of reasoning that are individually available to them. Activities or exercises that isolate and present one form of reasoning are to be avoided. They lack the element essential for progress, which is the dynamics of the conflict among modes of thinking (Inhelder et al., 1974, p. 265).

The activities to be used in the classroom setting are discussed here in three sections: "Facilitating the Young Child's Construction of Knowledge," "Facilitating Operational Thinking," and "Facilitating Formal Operational Thinking."

Facilitating the Young Child's Construction of Knowledge.   Organizing education around the child's spontaneous research implies an educational goal to develop the child's intelligence as an organized whole (Kamii, 1975). In other words, the educational goal of teaching fragmented "cognitive skills" in the form of discrete behavioral objectives leads to a fragmented curriculum and an overemphasis on the manipulation of verbal symbols.

Problems with "Direct Teaching."   The verbal transmission of abstract ideas or principles is not recommended (Kamii & DeVries, 1978). First, the logical rule contradicts the child's spontaneous beliefs and therefore confuses the child. The preoperational child can think about only one object at a time. Therefore, the child does not notice the contradictions in his or her own explanations. One child, for example, stated that a wooden blade floats because it is thick and copper wire sinks because it is long (Kamii & DeVries, 1978, p. 32). The fact that the wooden blade also was long was irrelevant to the child. Therefore, since the child is unaware of the contradictions, a logical rule to fit all contingencies at this point is only a verbalization that introduces confusion.

The second problem is that direct teaching of ideas contradictory to the child's beliefs leads to two other undesirable developments (Kamii & DeVries, 1978, p. 36). First, children's initiative in the construction of knowledge is stifled. Second, children may lose confidence in their ability to figure things out and focus instead on picking up cues from the teacher that indicate the desired right answer.

Direct teaching of social rules through verbal means is also inappropriate. For the preoperational child, stressing the importance of sharing and/or attempting to promote an understanding of another's feelings can, at best, only introduce elaborative language (Macomber, 1977). However, models of sharing that can be imitated by the child are important. Of utmost importance, however, is peer interaction in the construction of moral values (Piaget, 1965). Rules of sharing, honesty, and fair play that reflect moral development cannot successfully be imposed by external agents. Instead, such development depends on "many opportunities to relate to peers and to negotiate agreement in conflict situations" (Kamii, 1981, p. 242).

Use of Activities.   Many activities customarily included in preschool curricula can provide opportunities for cognitive development (Kamii & DeVries, 1978). Block painting, fingerpainting, musical games, cooking, dramatic play, and others are easily adaptable to a Piagetian curriculum. The key is to first evaluate the activities during preplanning for their potential to engage the children in empirical and logico-mathematical abstraction. That is, the activities should include problems that cannot be solved on the basis of perceptual cues only. Any activity, of course, can be inappropriate if used in the wrong way. Cuisinaire rods, for example, are inappropriate if the teacher demonstrates their uses and the outcomes that may be achieved (Piaget, 1973).

Some early curriculum developments advocated the diagnosis of the child's level of cognitive functioning and the provision of particular activities appropriate for the different levels in the classroom. In any one class of 30 children, however, various levels of development and breadth of understanding will be represented. Tailoring narrow exercises for individual children, however, is both impractical and unnecessary (Duckworth, 1979). First, the time required to test the children's level of cognitive development for different subsystems (number, space, length, etc.) is prohibitive. Second, logistical problems are generated by efforts to provide continuously a variety of activities and experiences for several different levels.

More importantly, however, is the fact that children construct their own knowledge; therefore, the classroom should provide situations in which children at different cognitive levels can learn about the world in new ways (Duckworth, 1979, p. 311). Stated another way, classroom activities should maximize the child's opportunities to construct and coordinate many relationships that he or she is capable of exercising (DeVries, 1978, p. 85).

Planning activities for classroom use should include consideration of two important factors: (1) the nature of the sensorimotor activities, and (2) the use of teacher questions (i.e., the teacher's role).

Sensorimotor Activities.   For preschool children, Kamii and DeVries (1978, p. 49) identify four criteria for physical activities. Objects should be included that can be acted on directly by the child, and for which different actions by the child will produce different effects. In addition, the effects of the child's actions on the object should be both immediate and observable.

Activities that meet the criteria above can provide opportunities for the enrichment and clarification of the child's awareness of object characteristics, actions, and reactions (i.e., assimilation). Many such activities can also facilitate the process of accommodation that occurs when a cognitive structure adjusts to particular object characteristics. At the preschool level, physical-manipulable and logico-mathematical aspects of the child's actions remain largely undifferentiated (DeVries, 1978). That is, the child is more interested in the observable effects of his or her actions than in relating the result to an organized cognitive structure.

Table 9–5 summarizes an activity for 4- and 5-year-olds that is appropriate for different developmental levels. The nature of the activity is such that it provides numerous opportunities for both empirical and reflective abstraction. The diversity of objects provides maximal oppor-

Table 9-5. Summary of Classroom Activity for Young Children

Activity	Blowing objects with a straw across the water surface in a water table
Objects	A drinking straw for each child; assorted objects, including Ping-Pong balls, cotton balls, crayons, Ivory soap, paper cups, styrofoam bits, a round Tinker Toy, and others
Follow-up activity	Suggest a race with some objects or a hockey game with the Ping-Pong balls
Potential logico-mathematical knowledge	"Lighter than," "heavier than," "faster than"; relationship between angle of straw, blowing effort, and speed
Sample follow-up question	"What happened when you used two straws?" and "What would you like to try next time?" (Kamii & DeVries, 1978, p. 60)

Source: Summarized from Kamii and DeVries (1978).

tunity for children to determine the physical properties of objects in the water. The interaction between blowing and speed of the objects lends itself to an understanding of both physical characteristics and other relationships.

Another type of classroom activity is that of testing predictions. After opportunities to explore physically the relationships between water and different kinds of containers, the teacher introduced a guessing game (Copple, Sigel, & Saunders, 1979, p. 37). In the game, pictures were presented, one at a time, of water flowing through different containers, but the containers were covered. Examples included water flowing through a funnel, eyedropper, and so on. After each decision by the children as to type of container, the answer was tested by pouring water through the identified container and comparing the results with the picture.

The Teacher's Role. Piaget (1973) indicated that no more difficult task exists for the teacher than that of becoming attuned to the spontaneous mental activity of the child or adolescent. Yet intellectual development depends on that constructive activity with all its errors and all the extra time that it seems to consume (Piaget, 1973, p. 107).

According to Piaget (1973), the teacher plays an important role in the classroom by first creating and organizing classroom experiences. Second, the teacher's responsibility is to provide examples that cause students to rethink hastily developed ideas.

Furthermore, children's "errors" that result from their experimentation must not be eliminated by coercion. The information that children use in reaching their conclusions may be inadequate for a correct solution of a specific problem. However, the choice is representative of a certain developmental stage which cannot be bypassed (Inhelder et al., 1974, p. 25). Therefore, games and activities should be reevaluated after implementation since children often take unexpected directions in pursuing their own questions.

In the implementation of activities, teacher questions can play an important role, but they must be carefully planned. Any questions that are used should be simply stated and should be real questions designed to provoke thinking; they should not be rhetorical statements in question form (Copple et al., 1979, p. 213). Children's ideas, however, may be elicited through indirect questions, such as "Tell me about this," or "What else (feels, tastes, looks) like this?" (Copple et al., 1974, pp. 231–232).

Prediction questions, such as "What would happen if . . ." also may be used (Kamii & DeVries, 1978). These types of questions facilitate assimilation and accommodation and encourage children to go beyond physical reality in the construction of new knowledge. Questions such as

"How did you know that the pudding was hot?" focus the child's attention on his or her strategy for reaching a conclusion.

However, with regard to direct actions on physical objects, young children are often unaware of how they obtained a particular effect. For example, 4-year-olds can twirl an object on a string and time its release to land it in a box several feet away. Until the age of 9 or 10, their descriptions of the ways to accomplish this goal differ from their actions (Piaget, 1976). Thus explanations of such effects by 4- and 5-year-olds, and their accompanying understanding of such causes, will be inaccurate.

In summary, rich opportunities to act on objects and to observe the resulting reactions develop both physical knowledge and logico-mathematical knowledge. The major requirements for the curriculum therefore are opportunities for children to interact with the physical world in a variety of ways, to make their own mistakes, and to develop answers for their questions in interaction with their peers.

Facilitating Operational Thinking. True logical thought begins with the child's construction of concrete operational structures, referred to as *concrete operations.* Unlike other internalized actions, concrete operations are both reversible and independent of perceptual cues.

Concrete Operations. These structures include class inclusion and seriation as well as the subsystems of length, number, space, and others. The learner has constructed a particular operational structure when the positive characteristics (affirmations) of a situation are balanced by the child's construction of negations. When a ball of clay is changed into a sausage shape, the young child usually notices only that it is thinner (positive characteristic or affirmation). However, the child who notes that the sausage is also thinner has constructed the accompanying negation that indicates logical thinking with regard to matter.

Recognition of Conflict. Development of concrete operational thought is a long process that includes many transitions. First, the child must recognize the contradiction that exists in his or her judgments. In one example, the child is confronted with two paths made of matchsticks. One path is zigzag and composed of six matches while the straight path contains only four (Inhelder et al., 1974). The preoperational child typically maintains that the first row is longer because it contains six matches. However, when the child's judgment shifts to the endpoints of the two rows, he or she is likely to state that they are the same length. Until the child recognizes that both statements cannot be true, thinking will not be reorganized.

Recognition of a conflict, however, is insufficient to lead to reorganization of thinking. Often, the first reaction is to attempt to cancel the contradiction. Some children, for example, broke one matchstick into two in order to make the second row "agree" with the first. Others placed the last matchstick perpendicular to the others in order to use all the matches and maintain parallel endpoints for the rows (Inhelder et al., 1974).

Finally, the child sees the need for "double compensation," that is, between number and length of the matches, and between the endpoints and shape of the paths. This need for the double compensation leads to the child's construction of conservation of length.

Classroom Activities. Direct teaching of the conservation concepts is to be avoided for several reasons. First, verbal acceptance of a rule does not indicate reconstruction of thinking. Second, even if successful, direct efforts to teach the elements of the Piagetian research tasks are like attempting to fertilize a field by enriching a few soil samples (Sinclair, 1971). Third, and more importantly, progress in the construction of logical thought is the result of the resolution of conflicts between subsystems (e.g., numerical and spatial). Therefore, training procedures that isolate one type of responding are not particularly useful. They have eliminated the element primarily responsible for progress, the conflict between schemes (Inhelder et al., 1974).

The implications for educational practice are important. First, a variety of activities, games, and experiences should be provided so that the learner can exercise his or her developing subsystems. One suggestion is to use individualized mathematics laboratories that utilize a variety of materials for measurement and experimentation. Examples include blocks, dried peas, match boxes, milk straws, pipe cleaners, and so on.

Piaget (1973) noted that teachers sometimes fear that reference to the physical properties of objects will be harmful to the development of deduction and rational thinking. The reverse, however, is true. Operations are internalized actions derived from the reorganization of experience and once internalized, are conducted without the need for physical manipulation.

Second, games and activities that can provide experience with classification and seriation are also needed. Classification games can be developed using blocks or pieces of plastic or felt that vary in two properties, such as color and shape. Circles, squares, and triangles in red, blue, yellow, and green, for example, may be used in a variety of ways. Card games in which the shapes and/or colors are to be matched is one example.

Facilitating Formal Operational Thinking. The experimentation that characterizes concrete operations is that of enumeration, sorting, and establishing relations among objects. This type of thinking, furthermore, proceeds from one element to the next (Piaget, 1972a, p. 3). In contrast, at the formal operational level, the real is subordinated to the realm of the possible. It involves "the linking of all possibilities to one another by necessary implications that encompass the real, but at the same time go beyond it" (Piaget, 1972a, p. 4).

When faced with an experimental problem, the concrete operational child proceeds by trial and error, trying to classify or order events on the basis of covariations. The formal operational thinker, however, may begin by experimenting with the materials, but soon realizes the complexity of the factors involved. Hypotheses are then identified and tested systematically. Factors in the problem are dissociated by testing each one with "all other things being equal" (Piaget, 1972a, p. 40).

Classroom Activities.   Obviously, formal operational thought cannot be taught with "prepackaged experiments." Any experiment that is not carried out by the individual with complete freedom is not an experiment; it is simply drill with no educational worth (Piaget, 1973, p. 20).

For older students, for whom verbal transmission of knowledge often is the dominant instructional mode, some experimentation is essential. Perhaps one class period a week could be devoted entirely to experimentation with a variety of materials. Since the students may lack practice in directing their exploratory activities, they may initially experience difficulty in conducting meaningful exploration. Therefore, materials that pose a problem, such as pendulum problems, weight problems using balances, and similar activities, should be used. However, only the general problem is posed, such as how to make the pendulum go faster or slower. Strategy development should be left to the students.

Few research studies have been conducted on the mechanisms involved in the transitions from concrete to formal operational thinking. However, one study (Kuhn, 1979) investigated the strategies used by individuals in variations of the colorless liquids problem described earlier. Experimental sessions were held once or twice a week for several months and the subjects were observed in the strategies used. No direct teaching was involved.

In the problems posed, the individuals were to determine which of several substances (B, C, or D) caused a reaction in A. The most common error made was that of false inclusion. That is, the subjects tested all three substances in combination and wrongly concluded that all three were responsible (when, in fact, only one was responsible). After several weeks, subjects did exhibit improvement in their strategies; however, progress was slow and uneven and included regressions. The most common difficulty seemed to be not the mastery of new strategies, but the inability to relinguish inadequate strategies.

The foregoing research study and others (Kuhn & Brannock, 1977) substantiate the view that exposure to rich opportunities for experimentation and exploration, without direct teaching, does lead to improvement in the reasoning strategies adopted by students.

EDUCATIONAL APPLICATIONS

During the early twentieth century, John Dewey was advocating the importance of children's inquiry and activity in school learning. During the 1920s, the heyday of the "activity curriculum," Jean Piaget was just beginning his research into the attributes and mechanisms of children's thought. Piaget's theory and the implications for educational practices speak to many of the concerns and issues earlier articulated by Dewey.

Although Piaget's work originally received little attention in the United States, it was reintroduced in this country in the 1960s. The participation of Piaget's chief collaborator, Barbel Inhelder, in the 1959 Woods Hole Conference chaired by Jerome Bruner, precipitated the early interest. Discussions of the work of Bruner (1960) and Flavell (1963) and replications of the early Genevan experiments by Elkind (1961a, 1961b) attracted the attention of educators and psychologists.

In the curriculum reform of the 1960s, Piaget's early work was applied to mathematics, science, and early childhood curricula. The popularization of Piaget's concept of developmental stages also led to a variety of research studies. Some of the studies indicated that conservation concepts could be taught in a few sessions. Conclusions were based on the children's verbal acquiescence to a "right answer," which is insufficient evidence of a change in reasoning processes.

The difficulties that Americans have experienced in the implementation of Piaget's theory in the school setting are evidenced by the early classroom applications. The initial focus was directed toward teaching the research tasks used in the experiments conducted by Inhelder and her associates. However, the research tasks were devised for the purpose of determining children's development and are not designed to function as teaching strategies.

DeVries (1978) has identified several shortcomings of efforts to teach the tasks. First, the theory is reduced to the content of the tasks and to isolated operations. Although the content of a particular task may be taught and a child can learn to carry out a particular operation, such activity does not change the child's basic reasoning structure (DeVries, 1978, p. 78). Further, teaching the tasks reduces the broad stages described by the theory to stages of progress on the particular tasks. That is, operational quantification (broad stage) is not dependent on the child's going through a stage in which he or she believes that more girls than children are in a class (task) (DeVries, 1978, p. 78).

Some of the curriculum misapplications resulted from the failure to coordinate a developmental curriculum with the academic curriculum. Kamii (1981) suggests three general objectives compatible with the school curriculum. Briefly summarized, they are (1) the development of children's autonomy through interactive situations, (2) the decentering and coordination of various points of view by children, and (3) the development of alertness, curiosity, initiative, and confidence in learning (Kamii, 1981, p. 24). These objectives may be integrated into the school curriculum without displacing it.

Classroom Issues

Piaget's theory is neither a theory of academic learning nor a teaching theory. Nevertheless, it does address several educational issues.

Learner Characteristics.   Jean Piaget's theory addresses the broad issues involved in cognitive development. Individual differences, readiness, and motivation are therefore viewed in terms of their relationship to long-term cognitive development.

Individual Differences.   The theory has been criticized by some educators for omitting specific references to individual differences. However, such a concern is simply outside the realm of the theory; the goal was to identify and to study the universal laws of cognitive development.

Nevertheless, cultural differences in the rate of attainment of cognitive structures have been observed. Children in some rural settings are slower than urban children in the attainment of concrete operations. Furthermore, formal operations are not attained by all individuals, nor are they acquired in all areas of expertise (e.g., physics, law, engineering) (Piaget, 1972a).

Readiness.   This term has two meanings in the interpretation of Piaget's theory. One is that of the individual's capacity to assimilate new information; a requirement is a logico-mathematical framework that can make use of the new information.

The second way in which readiness is manifested is in relation to the construction of logical cognitive structures, or operations. Specifically, logical constructions do not result until the subject experiences cognitive conflict and seeks to resolve it on a higher plane. Readiness therefore is the acknowledgment of conflicting statements coupled with the felt need to resolve two subsystems, for example, number and space.

Piaget has mistakenly been viewed at times as a maturationist because he identified four sequential stages of development. However, only the ordering of the stages is invariant; attainment requires learner experience with the environment, learner activity, and interaction with the social environment.

Motivation.   Two sources of motivation are identified by Piaget (1973). One is a general motivating factor that functions at all levels of development—that of need. As in other theories, needs may be physiological, affective, or intellectual. Since intelligence seeks both to understand and to explain, an intellectual need often appears in the form of a question or a problem (Piaget, 1967, p. 5). In Piaget's view, all action, whether movement, thought, or emotion, is in response to a need. In the theory, need is described as a manifestation of disequilibirum (Piaget, 1967). When the need is satisfied, equilibrium is restored.

Disequilibrium represents the general factor of need at all levels of development. However, Piaget cautions that it does not identify the specifics of need at any particular age or period of development. These specifics, the "content" of a particular need, depend on the system of ideas that a child has developed plus his or her affective inclinations. For example, a young child may engage in behavior to gain the approval of a parent, whereas a teenager is more likely to seek the approval of peers.

Cognitive Processes and Instruction. Three important classroom issues are developing "how-to-learn" skills, providing transfer of learning, and teaching problem solving. In the context of Piaget's theory, these issues take on a different meaning.

Developing "How-to-Learn" Skills. The individual's ability to organize his or her own behavior efficiently in order to extract meaning from a situation or to initiate steps to solve some predetermined problem are typically defined as "how-to-learn" skills. In the context of genetic epistemology, however, manipulating and experiencing concrete objects in the environment is the foundation for knowledge construction. Children learn how to learn by generating problems, investigating questions, and examining their answers.

Transfer of Learning. The facilitation of new learning that results from similarities to prior learning is an important classroom issue. Transfer of learning implies some sequencing of learning tasks in order to take advantage of their common properties.

Cognitive development, however, differs from specific learning. The attainment of particular cognitive structures do not "transfer" to the development of the next stage in the sense of isomorphic elements. The cognitive structures attained in any period of development do, however, prepare the learner to undertake the next stage.

Teaching Problem Solving. According to Piaget (1973), the skill of problem solving cannot be directly taught. Instead, the rules of experimentation and therefore, the rules for problem solution must be discovered or reinvented by each student. This experimentation and reinvention is essential to the development of problem-solving skills. In addition, Piaget maintains that the rules or theories that operate in any particular subject area must be reinvented by the individual; they cannot be conveyed verbally.

The Social Context for Learning. Unlike educational approaches that focus on teacher-student interaction, Piaget (1973) emphasizes the importance of peer interactions. Only through this type of interaction does the student acquire the capability of viewing issues from other perspectives. Furthermore, in exchanges with others, students examine their own thinking, explore other alternatives, and reorganize their views and conclusions.

Developing a Classroom Strategy

The implementation of Piaget's concepts at any level of the curriculum can be accomplished using the following four general steps and the subquestions for each step.

STEP 1. Determine which topics in a course or curriculum typically taught by verbal means may be replaced by student-directed research.

1.1 Which aspects of the curriculum are conducive to experimentation?

1.2 Which topics are conducive to problem-solving activity in a group situation?

1.3 Which topics (or concepts) can be introduced at a manipulable level using physical objects prior to verbal treatment?

STEP 2. Select or develop classroom activities for the identified topics. Evaluate the selected activities using the following list of questions.

2.1 Does the activity provide opportunities for a variety of methods of experimentation?

2.2 Can the activity lead to a variety of questions by the students?

2.3 Can the student compare various modes of reasoning in working through the activity?

2.4 Is the problem one that *cannot* be solved on the basis of perceptual cues alone?

2.5 Is the activity one that generates both physical activity and opportunities for cognitive activity? (Inappropriate activities include constructing a picture or diagram or building objects prespecified by the teacher.)

2.6 Can the activity enrich an already learned construct?

STEP 3. Identify opportunities for teacher questions that support the problem-solving process.

3.1 What probing follow-up questions may be used? (Prediction, "what-if" questions.)

3.2 What potential comparisons can be identified within the material that are conducive to spontaneous questions?

STEP 4. Evaluate the implementation of each activity, noting successes and needed revisions.

4.1 What aspect of the activity generated the most intense interest and involvement? Are there ways that this may be capitalized on in the future?

4.2 What aspect of the activity, if any, "fell flat?" Did the activity fail to engage the efforts of one or more learners? What are some alternatives to try next time?

4.3 Did the activity provide opportunities to develop new strategies of investigation or to enhance already learned strategies?

In summary, maximize the opportunities for students to construct knowledge for themselves. Discussions about topics in which answers can be developed through group interaction and that require consideration of a number of variables will enhance the student's construction of knowledge. One social studies class, for example, was divided into small groups, and each group was the local school board. They were given the school's budget for the preceding year and the dollars to be cut from the current year. Each group had to make the cuts and to develop a rationale for their budget reductions. Discussion included investigations into the costs of particular programs as well as developing the awareness that different value systems operate in such decisions.

Finally, whenever possible, provide direct student experience with constructs, rules, and theories prior to any verbalization. Otherwise, the information remains figurative and does not become knowledge.

Classroom Example

The following problem situation meets the criteria identified by Jean Piaget for students at the secondary school level. That is, the teacher may pose a problem to be solved. The direction from that point, however, is determined by the students in a group situation. Also the problems should be of the type for which the solution is not immediately apparent, but which can be solved through experimentation. Such a problem type lends itself to a variety of hypotheses that then may be tested by the students.

Such problems also lend themselves to group interaction in the development of solutions. The problems themselves are inherently intriguing, and the students' curiosity is aroused. Also, such problems do not provide any particular student with an advantage in the development of a solution. Group interaction and discussion of possible alternatives does not need to be forced by the teacher but grows naturally out of the nature of the problem.

The following problem can be posed by a teacher to secondary school students of physics or physical sciences.[2] A man is in a rowboat in a small pond. He has a very heavy safe in the boat. He throws the safe overboard. Does the water level at the sides of pond rise, drop, or remain the same?

The teacher asks the students to predict the result. Typically, all three possible solutions are suggested by one or more students. The teacher also asks each student to state why he or she believes that the selected solution is correct.

The teacher then asks, "What can we do to find out the correct answer?" Various materials are available in the room. Included are containers of various sizes, some objects of high and low density, and water.

The students typically begin to set up the materials to test their answers. One student may fill a large plastic bowl with water to approximately 2 inches from the top. Another may select a small plastic container to represent the rowboat. Others may select a wooden cube for the man and a heavy lead weight for the safe. These objects are placed in the small container floating in the water.

After some discussion, a method is usually devised for marking the side of the bowl at the waterline. A red pencil or some other type of marker may be used. Much discussion and several suggestions usually occur during these events. Then comes the moment of truth. The lead weight is dropped in the water. The water level is marked on the side with a line of some color. Everyone observes the marks that represent the two levels of water.

The teacher then asks students to offer explanations for the results. During this discussion, relationships between volume, weight, density, displacement, and others typically emerge.

---

[2] Example provided by Frances S. O'Tuel, University of South Carolina, and Ruth K. Rawl, Charleston County Schools.

Chracteristics Illustrated by the Problem
Predictions: generated hypotheses.
Experimentation: systematic control of variables; verification of a hypothesis.
Explanation: includes reflection, evaluation, social interaction, and resolution of conflict.

Review of the Theory

Jean Piaget's theory of cognitive development redefines intelligence, knowledge, and the relationship of the learner to the environment. Intelligence, like a biological system, is a continuing process that creates the structures it needs in continuing interactions with the environment. Similarly, knowledge is an interactive process between the learner and the environment. Like the structures created by intelligence, knowledge is highly subjective in infancy and early childhood and becomes more objective in early adulthood.

The development of the individual's different ways of thinking from infancy to adulthood include the action schemes of the infant, preoperations (transductive logic), concrete operations, and formal operations. The processes by which each of these more complex structures is constructed are assimilation and accommodation, regulated by equilibration.

Piaget also describes the process of knowledge construction from another perspective. He describes physical experience or exogenous knowledge, which is the abstraction of the physical characteristics of objects. In contrast, logico-mathematical experience or endogenous knowledge is developed through the reorganization of the learner's thought processes. The action structures referred to as action schemes, as well as concrete and formal operations, are constructed through logico-mathematical experience. (See Table 9-6.)

The role of education in Piaget's view is to support the spontaneous research of the child. Experimentation with real objects and interaction with peers, supported by the teacher's insightful questions, permits the child to construct both physical and logico-mathematical knowledge. The major requirements for the curriculum are rich opportunities for children to interact with the physical world in a variety of ways, to make their own mistakes, and to develop answers through interaction with their peers.

Disadvantages. A major problem in the implementation of Piaget's ideas arises from the different perspective he casts on intelligence, knowledge, and learning. Considerable effort is required to alter one's per-

Table 9-6. Summary of Jean Piaget's Cognitive-Development Theory

Basic Element	Definition
Assumptions	Intelligence, like a biological system, constructs the structures it needs to function. Knowledge is the interaction between the individual and the environment. The growth of intelligence is influenced by four factors (physical and social environment, maturation, and equilibration)
Cognitive development	The growth of logical thinking from infancy to adulthood
Outcomes of cognitive development	The construction of new structures from prior structures (i.e., action schemes, concrete and formal operations)
Components of cognitive development	Assimilation and accommodation, regulated by equilibration Physical experience and logico-mathematical experience
Facilitating logical thinking	Provide rich opportunities for experimentation with physical objects supported by peer interaction and teacher questions
Major issues in designing instruction	Maintenance of reciprocal relationship between child and education; avoidance of direct teaching and correction of children's "errors"

Analysis of the Theory	
Disadvantages	Understanding of basic terms and definitions is difficult Piagetian curriculum is difficult to implement and maintain Perspective excludes the relationship between logical thinking and basic learning, such as reading
Applications to classroom practice	Provides a rich description of the world through the child's eye Identifies problems in current curricula, particularly the teaching of mathematics and science as "socialized knowledge" Operationalizes the often-cited concept, "discovery learning"

spective from intelligence and knowledge as products to treating these concepts totally as process.

The development of curriculum according to Piagetian concepts requires, as Piaget himself indicated, considerable work and effort. Implementation of a Piagetian curriculum is also complicated by the fact that his theory excludes the relationships between logical thinking and curriculum basics, such as reading and writing.

Contributions to Educational Practice. A major contribution of Piaget's work is that he has identified the shortcomings of currently implemented curricula. He clearly delineates the problems and effects of teaching mathematics and science, for example, as "socialized knowledge." In addition to providing us a rich description of the world from the child's eye, he has operationalized the often-cited concept, "discovery learning." Table 9-6 summarizes Piaget's cognitive-development theory.

DISCUSSION QUESTIONS

1. How does Piaget's conception of knowledge differ from that of most other learning theorists?
2. A classroom teacher conducts several classroom exercises in which identification of the differences between the shapes and colors of several objects is the goal of the lesson. According to Piaget, what should the approach be instead?
3. Not all individuals attain the level of formal operational thought. According to Piaget, what might be some of the reasons for this situation?

GLOSSARY

accommodation One of a pair of processes that occurs when an individual takes cognizance of or relates to an object; that is, the individual's internal structures are adjusting to the special characteristics of the object. Also, an alteration or modification of an individual's existing internal structure that occurs as a result of cognitive conflict.

action schemes The cognitive structures that govern the infant's interactions with the world.

affirmations The positive characteristics of objects that may be identified perceptually. When water is poured from a short, wide container into a tall, thin one, the water height is the positive characteristic.

assimilation   The process by which information from the environment is integrated with the subject's internal structure; not a matter of passive registration of characteristics, however.

class inclusion   The ability to deal simultaneously with a general class defined by a general property (e.g., flowers) and with subclasses of the general class that are defined by a restrictive property (e.g., roses). Includes combining classes ($A + A' = B$) and the reverse operation ($B - A' = A$).

cognitive behavior   An outward sign of the assimilatory and accommodatory capacities of a living organism.

cognitive structures   Internal structures that govern the individual's interactions with the environment; internalized actions.

concrete-operational period   The first period in which "true" logical thought begins (approximately age 7 or 8 and continuing until 11 or 12). Referred to as "concrete" because the child's thought patterns are linked to the manipulation of objects and do not encompass hypothetical, multifactor situations.

developmental (genetic) epistemology   The study of the growth of logical thinking from infancy to mature thought.

disequilibrium   A state of nonbalance in the individual's cognitive development that leads to equilibrium on a higher level, for example, the child's recognition that his or her judgments about a situation are in conflict.

equilibrium   A temporary level of understanding to be surpassed by later constructions; for example, concrete operational thought is the equilibrium toward which preoperational thinking is striving.

equilibration   A process that is the coordinating factor of cognitive development in the individual's search for "true" equilibrium. The process includes self-regulations that coordinate (1) the individual's activities of accommodation and assimilation; (2) the development of different subsystems, such as number and space; and (3) the parts and totality of the individual's knowledge.

formal-operational period   The stage in which mature hypothetical reasoning begins. It may begin as early as 11 or 12 and extends into adulthood; characterized by the ability to develop hypotheses about complex, multifactor situations and to test them systematically.

intelligence   The individual's adaptation to the physical and social environment; a growing, developing, changing process that is represented moment by moment in the ways that the individual deals with the world.

knowledge   The constructive interaction between the individual and the object; knowledge is neither some predefined entity in the environment nor is it a preformed innate cognitive structure. Instead, knowledge is constructed by the individual.

empirical abstraction   The process of constructing internally the physical characteristics of objects; also referred to as *exogenous knowledge* and *physical experience.*

reflective abstraction The process of reorganizing or coordinating one's actions on a higher level; also referred to as *endogenous knowledge* and *logico-mathematical experience*.

negation A form of reversibility; for example, in class inclusion, negation is expressed by $B - A' = A$. The action negates the combining of classes. Also, the characteristic of an object that must be constructed by the child, for example, the positive characteristic of lengthening a ball of clay is accompanied by increasing thinness (negation). The construction of operational structures depends on the child's development of both affirmations (positive characteristics) and negations.

preoperational period The lengthy period (approximately from age 2 to 7 or 8) during which the child develops representational thought, social relations with peers, and an imperfect, although necessary "logic" about the world.

reciprocity The reversibility of an ordered series; for example, if $A > B > C$, then $C < B < A$.

reversibility An essential characteristic of operational structures; the capability of returning an operation to its starting point; for example, addition is reversed through subtraction.

seriation (serial ordering) The operational structure by which individuals are able to place objects in a linear sequence from shortest to longest, smallest to largest, and so on. Included is the ordering of both a series $A < B < C$ and its reciprocal $C > B > A$.

transitivity The property that represents the relationships among objects in a series; that is, if $A > B > C$, then $A > C$. Similarly, if $A = B$ and $B = C$, then $A = C$.

REFERENCES

Bringuier, J. C. (1980). *Conversations with Jean Piaget* (B. M. Gulati, Trans.). Chicago: University of Chicago Press.
Bruner, J. (1960). *The process of education.* Cambridge, MA: Harvard University Press.
Copple, C., Sigel, E., & Saunders, R. (1979). *Educating the young thinker: Classroom strategies for cognitive growth.* New York: D. Van Nostrand.
DeVries, R. (1978). Early education and Piagetian theory. In J. M. Gallagher & J. A. Easley, Jr. (Eds.), *Knowledge and development: Vol. 2. Piaget and Education* (pp. 75–91). New York: Plenum Press.
Duckworth, E., (1978). The having of wonderful ideas. *Harvard Educational Review, 42,* 217–231.
Duckworth, E. (1979). Either we're too early and they can't learn it or we're too late and they know it already: The dilemma of "applying Piaget." *Harvard Educational Review, 49,* 297–312.

Easley, J. A. (1978). Symbol manipulation re-examined: An approach to bridging a chasm. In B. Z. Presserien, D. Goldstein, & M. H. Appel (Eds.), *Topics in cognitive development: Vol. 2. Language and operational thought* (pp. 99–111). New York: Plenum Press.

Elkind, D. (1961a). Children's discovery of the conservation of mass, weight, and volume: Piaget replication study II. *Journal of Genetic Psychology, 98,* 219–227.

Elkind, D. (1961b). The development of quantitative thinking: A systematic replication of Piaget's studies. *Journal of Genetic Psychology, 98,* 37–46.

Flavell, J. (1963). *The developmental psychology of Jean Piaget.* Princeton, NJ: D. Van Nostrand.

Ginsburg, H. P. (1981) Piaget and education. The contributions and limits of genetic epistemology. In I. E. Sigel, D. M. Brodzinsky, & R. M. Golinkoff (Eds.), *New directions in Piagetian theory and practice* (pp. 315–330). Hillsdale, NJ: Lawrence Erlbaum.

Gruber, H. E., & Voneche, J. J. (Eds.). (1977). *The essential Piaget.* London: Routledge & Kegan Paul.

Inhelder, B., & Piaget J. (1958). *The growth of logical thinking from childhood to adolescence* (A. Parsons & S. Milgram, Trans.). New York: Basic Books.

Inhelder, B., Sinclair, H., & Bovet, M. (1974). *Learning and the process of cognition.* Cambridge, MA: Harvard University Press.

Kamii, C. (1975). One intelligence indivisible. *Young Children,* 228–238.

Kamii, C. (1981). Application of Piaget's theory to education: The preoperational level. In I. Sigel, D. A. Brodzinsky, & R. M. Golinkoff (Eds.), *New directions in Piagetian theory and practice* (pp. 231–265). Hillsdale, NJ: Lawrence Erlbaum.

Kamii, C., & DeVries, R. (1978). *Physical knowledge in preschool education.* Englewood Cliffs, NJ: Prentice-Hall.

Karmiloff-Smith, A. & Inhelder, B. (1975). If you want to get ahead, get a theory. *Cognition, 3,* 195–212.

Kuhn, D. (1979). The application of Piaget's theory of cognitive development to education. *Harvard Educational Review, 49,* 340–360.

Kuhn, D., & Brannock, J. (1977). Development of the isolation of variables scheme in experimental and "natural experiment" contexts. *Developmental Psychology, 13,* 9–14.

Macomber, L. (1977). Some implications of Jean Piaget's theory for the education of young children. In M. Appel & S. Goldberg (Eds.), *Topics in cognitive development: Vol. I. Equilibration: theory, research, and application.* (pp. 151–163). New York: Plenum Press.

Piaget, J. (1951). *Play, dreams and imitation in children.* New York: W. W. Norton.

Piaget, J. (1965). *The moral judgment of the child.* New York: Free Press.

Piaget, J. (1967). *Six psychological studies* (A. Tenzer, Trans.). New York: Random House.

Piaget, J. (1970a). *Genetic epistemology* (E. Duckworth, Trans.). New York: Columbia University Press.

Piaget, J. (1970b). Piaget's theory. In P. H. Mussen (Ed.), *Carmichael's Manual of Psychology* (chap. 9, pp. 703–732). New York: Wiley.

Piaget, J. (1970c). *Science of education and the psychology of the child.*

Piaget, J. (1972a) Intellectual evolution from adolescence to adulthood. *Human Development, 15*, 1–12.

Piaget, J. (1972b). *The principles of genetic epistemology* (W. Mays, Trans.). New York: Basic Books.

Piaget, J. (1973). *To understand is to invent: The future of education.* New York: Grossman.

Piaget, J. (1975). Comments on mathematical education. *Contemporary Education, 47*(1), 5–10.

Piaget, J. (1976). *The grasp of consciousness: Action and concept in the young child.* Cambridge, MA: Harvard University Press.

Piaget, J. (1977). Problems in equilibration. In M. Appel and S. Goldberg (Eds.), *Topics in cognitive development: Vol. I. Equilibration: Theory, research, and application* (pp. 3–13). New York: Plenum Press.

Piaget, J. (1980) *Adaptation and intelligence: Organic selection and phenocopy* (S. Eames, Trans.). Chicago: University of Chicago Press.

Piaget, J., & Inhelder, B. (1969). *The psychology of the child* (H. Weaver, Trans.). New York: Basic Books.

Sinclair, H. (1971). Piaget's theory of development: The main stages. In M. Roskoff, L. P. Steffe, & S. Taback (Eds.), *Piagetian cognitive-development research and mathematical education* (pp. 1–11). Washington, DC: National Council of Teachers of Mathematics.

_____

CHAPTER 10

Albert Bandura's Social Learning Theory

> In the social learning view, people are nei-
> ther driven by inner forces nor buffeted by
> environmental stimuli. Rather, psycholog-
> ical functioning is explained in terms of a
> continuous reciprocal interaction of per-
> sonal and environmental determinants.
> *Bandura, 1977b, p. 11*

Early in the twentieth century, functionalism advocated the study of mental functioning and human experience in terms of the organism's adaptation to the environment. From the functionalist perspective, the total organism in all its complexity should be the focus of study.

As described earlier, functionalism was absorbed into behaviorism. Thus, the major views of the school were not translated into testable principles of learning. However, the functionalist emphasis on the individual's adjustment to the environment and the importance of mental processes is particularly reflected in social learning theory.

Originally referred to as observational learning (Bandura & Walters, 1963), social learning theory began with the belief that important psychological processes and issues had either been overlooked or only partially studied by other theories. Neglected issues included the capacity of human learners to engage in symbolic thought, the tendency of human beings to undertake self-direction in their learning, and the range of social factors that can influence imitative actions. Of major importance, according to social learning theory, is the ability of individuals to abstract information from the behaviors of others, make decisions about which behaviors to adopt, and later, to enact the selected behaviors. Thus, to exclude the premise that thought can regulate action is to limit a theory's ability to explain complex human behavior (Bandura, 1977b).

Early works identified the role of behavioral models in the learning of both prosocial and antisocial behaviors (Bandura, 1969, 1971a; Bandura & Walters, 1963) and the role of models in the modification of behavior (Bandura, 1965a, 1971a). Bandura (1971b, 1977b) then identified the processes and conditions under which individuals learn complex behaviors from observations of the actions of others (Bandura, 1971b, 1977b). In the late 1970s the theory was extended to include the ways in which the individual's self-regulatory system develops (Bandura, 1974, 1978, in press) and the role of the individual's sense of efficacy in learning (Bandura, 1977a, 1982, in press).

PRINCIPLES OF LEARNING

Albert Bandura's social learning theory seeks to explain learning in the naturalistic setting. Unlike the laboratory setting, the social milieu provides numerous opportunities for individuals to acquire complex skills and abilities through the observation of modeled behaviors and their behavioral consequences.

Basic Assumptions

The assumptions on which social learning theory is based describe (1) the nature of the learning process in the naturalistic setting, (2) the relationship of the learner to the environment, and (3) a definition of what is learned.

The Nature of the Learning Process. Social learning theory began with an analysis of imitative learning as it was described by prior theories. Included in this analysis are (1) the behavioristic theories developed in the laboratory setting, and (2) theories that address the socialization of the child.

The Behavioristic Perspective. In general, the behaviorists treat imitative learning as an association between a particular type of stimulus and a particular type of response (see Table 10-1). Three limitations of these approaches have been identified by Bandura (1972). First, the research has led to an exploration of a narrow learning situation that does not adequately represent learning in the naturalistic setting. Specifically, only the learner's imitation of a specific set of responses (mimicry) has been researched, excluding the range of social variables that operate in most situations (Bandura & Walters, 1963, p. 43).

Table 10-1. Brief Overview of Some Behavioristic Approaches to Imitative Learning

Theoretical Perspective	Description of Learning
N. E. Miller and J. Dollard, *Social learning and imitation* (1941)	Motivated subject copies a modeled behavior and is reinforced for matching behavior
	Learning proceeds by trial and error until the learner is capable of becoming his or her own critic
O. H. Mowrer, *Learning theory and symbolic processes* (1960)	The model may make a response and reward the observer at the same time, or the model may both perform the response and receive the reward
	The observer either experiences the reward directly or the sensory consequences of the model's behavior
Operant conditioning paradigm	Modeled behavior $= (S^D)$
	Matching behavior by the learner $=$ response
	Reinforcement for imitative learning $= (S^{Reinf.})$

Second, and partly as a result of the experimental approach, these theories are unable to account for the acquisition of novel responses. In the natural setting, observers do more than mimic an observed behavior. They often imitate a variety of behaviors and abstract a behavioral repertoire from the activities of several models. For example, children exposed to multiple models who demonstrated diverse aggressive behaviors performed novel responses that were new combinations of observed elements (Bandura, Ross, & Ross, 1963b).

The third limitation of the behaviorist position is that it includes only the phenomenon referred to by Bandura (1971b) as direct learning. That is, the learner performs a response and experiences the consequences. This type of imitation is "instantaneous matching" (Bandura, 1971b) (see Table 10-2).

The behaviorist theories do not explain the situation in which matching behaviors are acquired through exposure to a model and the behaviors are not performed until days or weeks later. Neither performance of the observed behavior nor direct reinforcement to the observer are a requirement for this kind of learning.

Bandura (1971b) describes this event as "delayed matching." For example, a child's classmate may receive praise from the teacher for sharing

Table 10-2. Comparison of Direct and Indirect Learning

Type of Learning	Description
Instantaneous matching (direct learning)	Learner personally performs the response and is reinforced; learner experiences the consequences directly: S^D(model) —— response by learner —— $S^{Reinf.}$
Delayed matching (indirect learning)	Learner observes reinforced behavior and later enacts the same behavior: Model + $S^{Reinf.}$ —— observed by learner S^D(similar situation) —— performance by learner of observed behaviors (response)

behavior. A few days later while playing with the other children, the observer spontaneously shares his or her crayons. At one point in time the stimulus has occurred (modeled behavior), followed by reinforcement to the model (teacher praise). The observer later performs the observed behavior (learner response).

Other Theoretical Perspectives. The explanations offered by the behaviorist theories were restricted by the S-R paradigm. In contrast, other theories maintained that an interpersonal relationship between the child and an adult was responsible for the child's acquisition of social behaviors (Bandura, 1969; Bandura & Walters, 1963). Complex sets of reference events were proposed to account for the child's patterning of the adult's thoughts and actions, referred to as "identification with the model" (Bandura, 1969).

Several mechanisms have been proposed to account for imitative learning. Included are identification with the same-sex parent, nurturance, power, envy, and others (see Table 10-3). The learning of sex-role behaviors, for example, includes more than simply the identification with

Table 10-3. Some Social-Context Explanations of Imitative Learning

Reference Event	Influence
Nurturance withdrawal	Child's imitation of nurturant parent
Presence of adult rival	Male child imitates father because they are rivals for the mother's attention Child envies and then imitates the adult who is a competitor for social and material rewards (affection, food, care, and others)
Fear of attack	Imitation of an aggressor in order to reduce anxiety and fear
Frustration	Aggressive drive is generated which motivates aggressive reaction

the same-sex parent. Role training often begins with the pink or blue treatment given the nursery and continues with the selection of sex-role clothing and toys, coupled with parental reinforcement for sex-appropriate activities. In other words, parents take an active role in sex-role training (Bandura, 1969, p. 215). Research also indicates that imitation is not restricted primarily to one parent (Bandura, 1969). Children in one study that included both male and female models imitated the model who controlled the material resources (Bandura, Ross, & Ross, 1963a).

Early studies of observational learning also indicated that a nurturant relationship is not a prerequisite for imitation. Furthermore, fear of an aggressor is not a sufficient condition for imitation of aggressive behaviors. Instead, in the naturalistic setting, the aggressor demonstrates that dominance through physical and verbal force leads to (1) possession of material resources, (2) changing roles to suit one's own wishes, and (3) gaining control over others (Bandura, 1969, p. 232).

The variety of mechanisms proposed to account for the child's acquisition of prosocial behaviors is paralleled by diverse explanations of the learning of antisocial behaviors. One commonly held belief is the frustration-aggression explanation. According to the belief, frustration activates a frustration drive that then produces aggression. However, the term "frustration" is a category that includes a variety of aversive conditions. Included are physical assault, insult, deprivation, harassment, goal blocking, defeat, and other aversive experiences (Bandura, 1979, p. 329).

More importantly, the aversive stimulation from these conditions produces a state of emotional arousal that leads to not one, but a variety of responses. Examples include withdrawal and resignation, achievement, self-anesthetization with drugs and alcohol, aggression, and other responses.

The variety of responses results in part from the cognitive processing undertaken by the individual (Bandura, 1979). For some individuals, goal blocking may lead to intensified effort. Further, millions of people live in a state of deprivation. Yet comparatively few of those deprived engage in civil disturbances. The important question for social scientists, therefore, is not why aggression occurs in such conditions. The important question is to determine why a majority of the ghetto population is resigned to dismal living conditions in the midst of affluence (Bandura, 1979, p. 333).

In summary, the prior theories have proposed a variety of mechanisms to account for imitative learning. Fear, loss of love, envy, frustration, and direct reinforcement have been suggested. In addition, different mechanisms to account for prosocial and antisocial behaviors have been named. Excluded, however, are the propositions that (1) observers can abstract a range of information from the behavior of others, and (2) observers make decisions about which behaviors to adopt and enact. The process of learning in the naturalistic setting, however, includes both of these factors.

The Relationship Between the Learner and the Environment. According to Bandura (1974), the phenomenon of delayed matching and the range of prosocial and antisocial behaviors acquired by human beings cannot be explained by a unidirectional relationship between the individual and the environment. Both the behaviorists and the humanists propose different unidirectional relationships and both are inadequate. The behaviorists assign primary control to the environment, expressed in the formula $B = f(E)$. In contrast, the humanists assign primary control to human thought and action, expressed in the formula $E = f(B)$ (Bandura, 1974).

In the social learning perspective, both behavior and the environment are modifiable, and neither is the primary determinant of behavioral change. "Books do not influence people unless someone writes them and others select and read them. Rewards and punishments remain in abeyance until prompted by appropriate performances" (Bandura, 1974, p. 866).

The acquisition of complex behaviors, however, is not explained by a simple bidirectional relationship between the environment and the individual. Instead, most environmental influences on behavior are mediated by a variety of internal personal factors. These personal factors, such as the selection of events to be observed and the ways in which events are perceived and judged, intervene between environmental influences and behavior.

Bandura (1978) therefore proposes a three-way interlocking relationship between behavior (B), the environment (E), and the internal events that influence perceptions and actions (P) (see Figure 10-1). For example, after assertiveness training, an individual's behavior activates new environmental reactions (Bandura, 1977b). These reactions, in turn, generate self-confidence in the individual which then mediates future behavior.

The relationships between the environment, internal events, and behaviors are often complex and subtle. Certain personal attributes, such as sex or race, often activate differential social treatment. The individual's self-conception, in turn, is influenced by the treatment such that biases are either altered or maintained.

The relationship between the three factors is referred to as *reciprocal determinism* (Bandura, 1974, 1977b, 1978). The use of the term "determinism," however, does not imply a fatalistic view in which the individual is at the mercy of preestablished "causes." Rather, it is used to mean that effects are produced by events rather than by a prior set of causal external factors (Bandura, 1978).

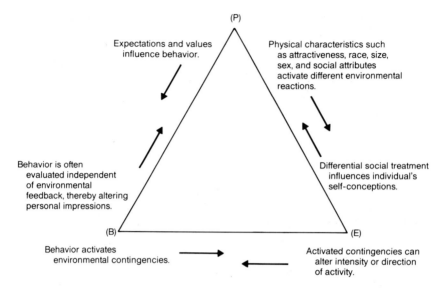

(P)

Expectations and values
influence behavior.

Physical characteristics such
as attractiveness, race, size,
sex, and social attributes
activate different environmental
reactions.

Behavior is often
evaluated independent
of environmental
feedback, thereby altering
personal impressions.

Differential social treatment
influences individual's
self-conceptions.

(B)

(E)

Behavior activates
environmental contingencies.

Activated contingencies can
alter intensity or direction
of activity.

Figure 10-1. Three-way relationship between the environment, personal factors, and behavior. (Summarized from Bandura, 1978.)

The Outcomes of Learning.   The three-way relationship between the environment, internal factors, and behavior specifies that cognitive processes and other personal factors influence behavior. Consistent with this view, learning and performance are differentiated in social learning theory. Individuals acquire symbolic representations of behavior that may or may not be later performed. Observational learning without performance has been documented in situations in which performance by the observers was not the criterion for learning (Bandura, 1965a, 1971a). That is, after observation of models that enacted novel behaviors, observers who did not enact the particular behaviors were able to describe them. Furthermore, accurate performance by the observers was forthcoming through the use of appropriate inducements (Bandura, 1965a, 1971a).

Symbolic representations that are learned are retained in the form of memory codes; their function is to serve as guidelines for future performance. An example is a child who sees an older boy in a fight with the class bully. Admiration from classmates may lead the observer to conclude that fighting in certain circumstances is both acceptable and rewarding. The younger child has acquired both a set of behaviors and a tendency to enact the behaviors at a later point in time.

The memory codes of observed behaviors are symbolic codes referred to as representational systems (Bandura, 1971b, p. 13). The two types of systems are visual and verbal. The visual system includes vivid images of absent physical stimuli (Bandura, 1971). Included are activities, places, and objects. Examples are tennis, New Orleans, and the Eiffel Tower. As a result of repeated exposure to these types of stimuli, they are produced eventually as retrievable visual images (Bandura, 1977b).

Some events, however, are coded in verbal form. Details of a particular procedure, such as checking the oil level in one's car, may be remembered more easily through conversion to a verbal code.

Language symbols are the most used verbal codes in everyday life. However, the system also includes numbers, musical notation, Morse code, and others (Bandura, 1971b). The importance of symbolic codes, both visual and verbal, is that they include a great deal of information in easily stored form (Bandura, 1977b, p. 26).

In summary, three assumptions support social learning theory. They are as follows. First, the learning process requires both the cognitive processing and decision-making skills of the learner. Second, learning is a three-way interlocking relationship between the environment, personal factors, and behavior. Third, learning results in the acquisition of verbal and visual codes of behavior that may or may not later be performed.

The Components of Learning

In the naturalistic setting, individuals learn new behaviors through the observation of models and through the effects of their own actions. The learner's cognitive processes abstract information from a large variety of observed behaviors that are enacted in numerous settings. This information is stored in memory and may later be performed by the learner.

The elements that are present in every act of learning are the behaviors enacted by models, the environmental factors that contribute to the learning of the observed behaviors, and the individual's internal processes. The components of learning are therefore (1) the behavioral model, (2) the consequences of the modeled behavior, and (3) the learner's internal processes.

Behavior, however, is demonstrated and observed in a variety of settings and under different conditions. Every behavior does not result in learning. For learning to occur, the modeled behavior, the reinforcement, and the learner's cognitive processing must meet certain requirements.

The Behavioral Model. The primary role of the modeled behavior is to transmit information to the observer. This role is exemplified in three ways. One is that modeled behavior serves as a social prompt to initiate similar behavior in others. For example, Americans attending the theater in Great Britain are prompted to rise to their feet along with the rest of the audience if the orchestra plays a particular pre-curtain number. Although to Americans, the selection is "My Country 'Tis of Thee," it is, to Britishers, "God Save the Queen." The imitative behavior of respectful attention is prompted by the behavioral models.

The second effect of modeling is to strengthen or weaken the learner's existing restraints against the performance of particular behaviors. Inhibitory effects occur when individuals are restrained from engaging in modeled behavior as a result of observing negative consequences for the activity. Punishment dispensed to the model in general may accomplish this function (this is discussed in detail later in this section).

Disinhibitory effects, on the other hand, weaken the learner's restraints toward the performance of particular behaviors. The modeling of defensible violence adds legitimacy to the use of violence as a solution to problems (Bandura, 1973, p. 33). Verbal and physical abuse by authority figures to restrain rioters is an example. Repeated exposure to such models results in a weakening of the individual's restraints on the use of aggressive solutions.

The third influence of modeling is to transmit new patterns of behavior. A vast range of human behavior, from the baby's first goodbye wave to complex cognitive, motor, and affective repertoires, may be acquired from models.

Types of Modeling Stimuli. Defined functionally, "a model is any stimulus array so organized that an observer can extract and act on the main information conveyed by environmental events without needing to first perform overtly" (Rosenthal & Bandura, 1978, p. 622). Individuals encounter three different types of modeling stimuli in their daily lives. They are described by Bandura (1971b) as the live model, the symbolic model, and verbal descriptions or instructions. Verbal descriptions are nonperformance models; an example is a set of instructions for assembling equipment.

Live models, on the other hand, include family members, friends, work associates, and others with whom the individual has direct contact. These models provide information about the immediate social and work setting within which the individual functions on a day-to-day basis.

The third type, the symbolic model, is a pictorial representation of behavior. In today's society, the mass media are a prolific source of behavioral models. Of the three types, the greatest range of exposure to models in American society is through mass media. Individuals acquire information about the broad social setting beyond their daily environment from television (Bandura, 1977a, p. 16). Television, however, is not real life. The large number of unscrupulous individuals and villains portrayed for the sake of a plot present a distorted picture of human interactions.

Characteristics of Models. An important factor in the learning process is the degree to which the model is attended to by the learner. Some models are more effective than others in attracting the learner's attention. Regular associates and peers are examples. Also, personally engaging and prestigious models are likely to be noticed.

The models who have an impact on observers reflect one or more of the following characteristics. They may appear to deserve trust, portray consensus in a group, offer believable standards to guide observers' aspirations, or provide realistic reference figures for observer comparison (Rosenthal & Bandura, 1978, p. 636). In other words, relevance and credibility for observers are important model characteristics in any learning situation.

A model's characteristics are most influential when the consequences of the behavior are unknown (Bandura, 1971b). In such a situation, the observer is likely to attend to the behavior of a prestigious model. When behavioral outcomes are doubtful, emulating a prestigious model involves minor risk taking for the observer because such models are likely to be successful.

In general, models that have high status, competence, and power are more effective than low-status models in prompting imitative behavior. Their behavior is more likely to be successful than that of models low in vocational, social, or intellectual competence (Bandura, 1977b, p. 88).

High-status models are influential in attracting the learner's attention initially. However, should the modeled behavior prove unsuccessful for the observer or should the model lose status, thereby reducing "success prediction," the model will not continue to be emulated. Baseball players, for example, are emulated often because they maintain impressive batting averages and therefore receive public adulation. Should public favor be withdrawn, however, the players no longer serve as models (Bandura, 1969).

Another stimulus characteristic that influences learning is the degree of intrinsic reward already present in the situation. Watching television is an example. The activity itself is satisfying to the observer (Bandura, 1971c).

The Consequences of Behavior. Like operant conditioning, behavioral consequences are important elements in social learning theory. Two major differences exist between the two theories, however. In operant conditioning, reinforcement is a necessary condition for learning. In social learning theory, reinforcement is only one of the factors that influence learning, and it is a facilitating condition.

Second, operant conditioning includes only consequences that impinge directly on the performer of the response. Social learning theory, in contrast, includes three types of reinforcement. One is the reinforcement described above, referred to by Bandura (1971b) as *direct reinforcement.*

The other two types are *vicarious reinforcement* and *self-reinforcement* (Bandura, 1971b). Vicarious consequences are associated with the observed behaviors of others, and self-produced consequences are related to personal performance standards.

Vicarious Reinforcement. For vicarious reinforcement to occur, (1) a model is reinforced for the execution of a particular behavior, and (2) the observer's performance of the behavior increases in frequency. An example is the situation described earlier in which a child observes a classmate reinforced for sharing and imitates the behavior.

The effects of vicarious reinforcement are summarized in Table 10-4. The informational function indicates the behaviors that earn reinforcement and therefore are considered to be appropriate actions. In the foregoing example, the observer learns that in the classroom setting, sharing is an appropriate action.

The second function, the arousal of emotional responses in the observer, is used extensively by television commercials. Observers tend to identify with the pleasures and other satisfying emotional reactions experienced by models. The athlete in the commercial who gets the pretty girl after using a certain aftershave lotion is an example.

In addition, repeated reinforcement of modeled behavior ordinarily results in incentive-motivational effects in observers. When outcomes are viewed as personally attainable, seeing others reinforced for successful behaviors arouses expectations of similar results in observers. The same reinforcement consequences are anticipated for enactment of the same or similar behaviors. When this phenomenon occurs, the modeled behaviors have acquired functional value (Bandura, 1971b). That is, they predict successful outcomes for the observer.

Vicarious Punishment. Like vicarious reinforcement, punishment received by a model tends to convey three primary effects. First, information is conveyed about behaviors that are likely to be punished and

Table 10-4. Primary Effects of Vicarious Consequences

Vicarious Reinforcement	Vicarious Punishment
Conveys information about which behaviors are appropriate in which settings	Conveys information about which behaviors are inappropriate in which settings
Arousal of the emotional responses of pleasure and satisfaction in the observer	Tends to exert restraining influence on imitation of modeled behavior (inhibitory effect)
After repeated reinforcements, incentive-motivational effects are generated; behavior acquires functional value	Tends to devalue the model's status since a functional behavior was not transmitted

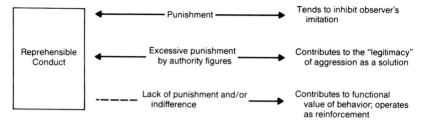

Figure 10-2. Some effects of consequences for reprehensible conduct.

are therefore inappropriate. Second, a restraining influence on imitative aggressive actions is also likely to occur (inhibitory effect).

Finally, because the behavior transmitted to the observers was unsuccessful, the model's status is likely to be devalued. If the model enacts a behavior highly prized by a peer group, such as challenging unfair treatment, punishment may enhance the model's status.[1] Usually, however, the model's status is devalued.

Other outcomes may occur as the result of the presence or absence of punishment. One outcome is that of altering the observer's valuation of reinforcing agents (Bandura, 1977b, p. 51). The misuse of power generates resentment in observers and undermines the legitimacy of the agent's power. The observation of inequitable punishment may release angry observers from self-censure of their own behavior. The result is increased transgression rather than compliance. An example is that of excessive police reaction to crimes committed in certain urban neighborhoods or by members of particular subgroups in society. Outbreaks of vandalism and riots by other members of the subgroup often follow (see Figure 10-2).

The Absence of Punishment. The anticipation of punishment usually restrains the imitation of forbidden actions. However, when individuals are not punished for transgressions, the information conveyed is that of implicit acceptance. An example is a classroom in which the teacher is careless about monitoring examinations and cheating occurs. If the cheating goes unpunished, others are more inclined to cheat on the next examination. The behavior has acquired functional value through the omission of punishment.

Similarly, when aggressive actions go unpunished or when people respond approvingly or indifferently, aggression is viewed as both acceptable and expected in similar circumstances (Bandura, 1973, p. 129). Aggression acquires functional value for the observer.

---

[1]Status is most likely to be enhanced by punishment for principled conduct. Personal communication from Albert Bandura, July 27, 1983.

In some situations, the absence of adverse consequences to the model fulfills a useful purpose. Such a situation exists in the management of the treatment of phobic patients. The vicarious extinction of fears and behavioral inhibitions in phobic patients is facilitated through the observation of models who are unpunished for engaging in fear-inducing behaviors (Bandura, 1971b, 1977a). Snake-phobic patients, for example, experienced reduced fear and anxiety after observing models handle snakes without incurring adverse consequences to themselves.

The influence on observers exerted by vicarious consequences, however, is relative rather than absolute. The extent of the influence varies with the observer's valuation of the type of outcome and the type of behavior (Bandura, 1977b, p. 119). In addition, observed consequences are of minimal influence if observers believe that the model's contingencies do not apply to them. For example, the physical aggression of a soldier is unlikely to enhance imitative aggression in the average citizen (Bandura, 1971b). Moreover, both vicarious and direct reinforcement are operating together in most situations. Therefore, the separate effects of either type are difficult to determine.

Self-reinforcement.   Direct and vicarious reinforcement both involve consequences delivered by the environment. Gold stars awarded for attendance, prizes won on television quiz shows, and minimal prison terms imposed for heinous crimes are dispensed to individuals by some member or agent of society, and they may influence the behavior of others. Self-reinforcement, on the other hand, is independent of the consequences delivered by society. Furthermore, it must be consciously cultivated by the individual. Young children respond to immediate physical consequences (food and physical contact) and other material rewards. Then symbolic consequences, including social reactions of approval and disapproval, become reinforcing or punishing. Next are social contracting arrangements, and finally, individuals become capable of establishing self-evaluative and self-produced consequences (Bandura, 1978, p. 103).

Self-reinforcement involves three subsidiary elements. They are a self-prescribed standard of behavior, reinforcing events under the control of the individual, and the individual as his or her own reinforcing agent. (The development of the individual's self-reinforcement or self-regulatory system is discussed later in the chapter.)

In general, individuals establish performance standards for themselves and tend to respond to their behavior in self-rewarding ways if their performance matches or exceeds the standard. Similarly, they respond in self-criticizing ways if their performance fails to meet the standard. Thus, although human beings, like rats and chimpanzees, respond to reinforcement, the human capacity for thought and self-direction sets the human species apart. Unlike human beings, "rats and chimpanzees are disinclined to pat themselves on the back for commendable performances, or to berate themselves for getting lost in the cul-de-sacs" (Bandura, 1971b, p. 249).

Interactions with External Consequences. An important characteristic of self-imposed consequences is that they often operate together with external consequences (Bandura, 1974). These two sources of reinforcement either supplement each other or they may be in conflict. When external rewards are outweighed by self-condemnation, external rewards are relatively ineffective. An example is the student who seeks to earn an A grade in every course. Earning a B in a particular course in which others earn Cs and Ds does not meet the individual's standards. Earning the highest grade is small consolation.

A second type of conflict that can occur is that of external punishment delivered by the environment for behaviors that the individual values highly (and therefore believes is worthy of reward). Nonconformists, dissenters, and at the extreme, martyrs are in this category. For the latter group, their sense of self-worth is so strongly linked to particular beliefs that they suffer pain and even death rather than relinquish their values.

The Learner's Cognitive Processes. In social learning theory, cognitive processes play a central role. The learner's ability to code and store transitory experiences in symbolic form and to represent future consequences in thought are essential to the acquisition and modification of human behavior.

The cognitive processing of events and potential consequences bridges the gap between the behavior and the outcomes of that behavior (Bandura, 1977b). For example, homeowners do not wait until their houses are burning to buy insurance. Instead, knowledge of the potential loss that can be the consequences of no insurance is the stimulus that prompts individuals to invest in homeowner's protection (Bandura, 1971b). The important point is that the learner's behavior is guided by cognitive processes rather than formed or shaped by reinforced practice (Bandura, 1971a).

Four component processes are responsible for learning and performance. They are attention, retention, motor production, and motivational processes (Bandura, 1971a, 1977b). The mechanisms of attention and retention govern the individual's acquisition of observed actions. The later performance of these actions by the observer is governed by motivation and the motor production mechanisms. The relationships between the behavioral model, the learner's cognitive processes, and learning and performance are illustrated in Figure 10-3.

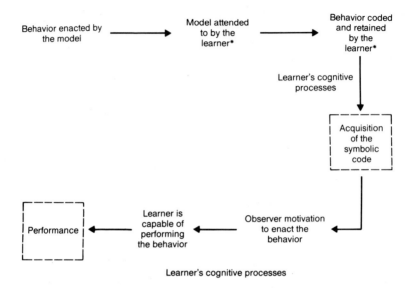

Figure 10-3. Sequence of steps in observational learning according to social learning theory.

Attentional Processes. The importance of the learner's attention is that new behaviors cannot be acquired unless they are attended to and accurately perceived (Bandura, 1977b). The learner's attentional processes, however, are influenced by a variety of factors. Included are the model's characteristics (discussed earlier), characteristics and functional value of the behavior, and observer characteristics. Functional value of an observed behavior is established through reinforcement to the model. Behavior that is successful for the model tends to be attended to and coded by the observer.

Characteristics of the behavior that influence attention include complexity and relevance. For example, long verbal sequences are too complex for young children to process. However, they are able to process visually presented models that are accompanied by a high degree of verbal repetition. The animal characters and the dialogue in "Sesame Street" are an example.

Relevance, in general, refers to the importance of the behavior to the observer. Learning to drive a car, for example, is relevant for a teenager, but not for a 2-year-old child.

Among the observer characteristics that influence attentional processes are perceptual set, observational skills, arousal level, past performance, and sensory capacities (Bandura, 1977b, p. 23). The learner's arousal level and perceptual set influence the selection of activities to be observed, whereas observational skills influence the accuracy of processing.

Retention Processes. These processes are responsible for the symbolic coding of the behavior into visual or verbal codes and the storage of the codes in memory. The importance of these processes is that the learner cannot benefit from the observed behaviors in the model's absence unless the behaviors are coded and retained for later use (Bandura, 1977b). "Transitory experiences leave lasting effects by being coded and stored in symbolic form for memory representation. Internal representations of behavior, constructed from observed examples and from informative response consequences, serve as guides to overt actions on later occasions" (Bandura, 1977b, p. 179).

An important retention process is rehearsal. Both mental rehearsal, in which individuals imagine themselves enacting the behavior, and motor rehearsal (overt action) serve as important memory aids. Mental rehearsal requires that the learner internally represent the absent events. These representations can then guide the motor rehearsal.

Retention processes are, of course, influenced by the learner's development. The ability to represent behaviors in the form of labels and to generate verbal and visual cues enhance retention.

Motor Reproduction Processes. After the observer has acquired a symbolic code, performance of the acquired behaviors depends on the learner's motor reproduction and motivational processes. Motor reproduction includes the selection and organization of responses at the cognitive level, followed by their execution (Bandura, 1977b). Like the processes of retention, motor reproduction is influenced by the developmental level of the individual.

Motivational Processes. The three processes that function as motivators are direct (external) reinforcement, vicarious reinforcement, and self-reinforcement. Anticipation of reinforcement for a particular behavior motivates the observer's performance.

The complexity of the processes involved in observational learning indicate that merely the provision of models, however prominent, will not automatically lead to the same behavior in observers (Bandura, 1977b, p. 29). Careful consideration must be given to the four processes in the analysis of any learning situation. Also, since many of the subprocesses involved in observational learning change as a result of maturation and/or experience, developmental level is a major factor in learning. The learner's skills in selective observation, memory encoding, coordination of sensorimotor and ideomotor systems, as well as the capability to identify probable consequences for imitative behavior are all important factors (Bandura, 1977b, p. 29).

The Nature of Complex Learning

The acquisition of complex skills and abilities depends on more than the processes of attention, retention, motor reproduction, and motivation. Accomplished performance, according to Bandura (1982), requires two other components. They are the learner's sense of self-efficacy and the learner's self-regulatory system.

Perceived Self-Efficacy. A sense of efficacy is the conviction that one can successfully execute the behavior required to produce a particular outcome (Bandura, 1977b). Efficacy, therefore, involves a sense of mastery. For example, a student with a strong sense of efficacy believes that she can earn a sufficiently high score on the Scholastic Aptitude Test to be admitted to the school of her choice.

Perceived self-efficacy influences behavior in at least three ways. It influences (1) the choice of activities to be engaged in, (2) the quality of an individual's performance, and (3) persistence in difficult tasks. It also helps a person withstand failure. Individuals who do not possess a sense of efficacy typically dwell on personal deficiencies and believe that potential obstacles are formidable (Bandura, 1982, p. 123).

Perceived self-efficacy involves self-appraisal; it is "not a fixed act or simply a matter of knowing what to do" (Bandura, 1982, p. 122). For example, men consider themselves efficacious for occupations traditionally held by both men and women. In contrast, women typically consider themselves efficacious only for occupations traditionally held by women (Bandura, 1982). However, in the groups tested, the men and women college students did not differ in their verbal and quantitative abilities on standardized tests (Betz & Hackett, 1981). Further, level of perceived self-efficacy was associated with the careers considered by the students as well as the extent of their interest.

Quality of performance and persistence in difficult tasks are also influenced by efficacy beliefs. Research into the development and maintenance of various coping behaviors indicates perceived self-efficacy to be an important factor in long-term behavioral change (Bandura, 1982). For smokers, perceived self-efficacy in resisting smoking in stressful situations was related to relapses and the reinstitution of self-control after a relapse. That is, the highly self-efficacious individuals reinstated control after a relapse, whereas the less self-efficacious relapsed completely (Bandura, 1982, p. 131). Perceived self-efficacy is also related to persistence in subtraction problems for children with serious deficits in subtraction (Bandura & Schunk, 1981) and for division problems (Schunk, 1981). The importance of the efficacy-persistence relationship is that persistence was also related to the children's success.

Efficacy expectations should not be confused with response-outcome expectations. A response-outcome expectancy is the belief that a particular behavior will lead to certain outcomes, and an efficacy expectation is the belief in one's capability to execute the required behavior successfully (Bandura, 1977b, p. 193). Thus the former is a belief about environmental contingencies, whereas the latter is a self-judgment of one's capabilities.

The Self-Regulatory System. Perceived self-efficacy, when fully developed, exercises considerable influence over behavior. However, this self-regulatory influence is not some psychic agent that exercises behavioral control, nor does it occur simply by an act of will (Bandura, 1978, 1982). Instead, the self system refers to (1) the cognitive structures that provide referents for behavior and its outcomes, and (2) the cognitive subprocesses that perceive, evaluate, and regulate behavior (Bandura, 1978, p. 348). That is, the self system includes standards for one's behavior, and the capabilities of self-observation, self-judgment, and self-response. The response may be either a reward for behavior judged acceptable or negative reactions for behavior that does not meet the individual's standards.

The development of these self-evaluative functions opens up a range of possibilities for the individual (Bandura, 1974, p. 861). Specifically, these processes make self-direction possible. Individuals can pursue activities that promote satisfaction and self-worth, while avoiding activities that lead to self-punishment.

Self-established standards of performance are not based on absolute measures of adequate performance (Bandura, 1977b, 1978). A score on an achievement test or the time required to run a race provides insufficient information. Instead, the evaluative standard is derived from the performance of other individuals, the performance of identified reference groups, or more interestingly, one's own past performance record. Often, comparisons with one's own past performance lead to the setting of higher standards. After a particular level of performance is reached, the challenge is gone and new self-satisfaction is sought through additional improvement (Bandura, 1977b, 1978).

Goal Setting and Self-Evaluation. The critical elements essential for superior accomplishment in any area of endeavor are goal setting and self-evaluation. Familiar examples include concert pianists and other artists. After evaluative standards are established, large amounts of time are expended to improve performance to the point of self-satisfaction (Bandura, 1974, p. 868).

The process of goal setting and self-evaluation is particularly important in the development of innovations, whether artistic or in some other field. Self-generated standards and reinforcements sustain developments that often are resisted initially by society. In the absence of public recognition, self-reinforcement for meeting one's own standards maintains the artist's creative effort.

The Development of the Self-regulatory System.   Examples of self-evaluative reactions provided by models are an important factor in the development of an individual's self-regulatory system. Observers abstract generic standards from the behaviors of various models as well as from the same models in diverse settings (Bandura, 1978, p. 353) (see Figure 10-4). Parents, teachers, work associates, and peers function as sources of information for the self-management of behavior.

Also important are the external reinforcements provided by the environment that support evaluation and the self-reinforcements selected by the individual. Included in external reinforcements are rewards for excellence and negative sanctions for individuals who provide themselves with undeserved self-reward (Bandura, 1977b, 1978; Bandura, Mahoney & Dirks, 1976). Examples include scholarships and other awards for outstanding academic achievements. Prizes, public acclaim, and monetary rewards reinforce winners of arduous sports events (e.g., the Indianapolis 500, the Wimbledon tennis tournament, and the world olympics). Negative sanctions include public dishonor for cheating performances, such as the marathon runner who faked a winning performance.

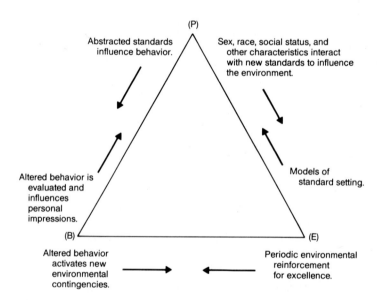

Figure 10-4. Reciprocal determinism in the development of self-regulatory systems.

The behavioral standards used by the individual and the delivery of self-reinforcement depend on the relationship between the particular task and the individual's expertise. A mathematician, for example, would not consider that solving elementary arithmetic problems is deserving of self-reward. On the other hand, a humanities scholar would not devalue his or her poor performance on a test of engineering skills (Bandura, 1971b). Particularly important are the self-reinforcements for engaging in difficult tasks or aversive activities, such as completing homework or speaking up in social situations. Arranged self-reward bridges the gap between initiation of the new behavior and the environmental contingencies that will be activated by competent performance.

Development of Reprehensible Conduct. Reciprocal determinism, given different sets of circumstances, can also lead to the disengagement of self-evaluative capabilities. The result is the development and maintenance of reprehensible conduct and inhumane activities (Bandura, 1977a, 1979). Prior theories have proposed different internal "watchdogs" that are responsible for moral behavior, such as a conscience, superego, or an internalized moral code. Such theories, however, encounter difficulties when they attempt to explain inhuman conduct by otherwise humane moral persons (Bandura, 1982, p. 351).

In the social learning analysis, such acts are performed through processes that disengage the behavior from a self-evaluative reaction. Four sets of dissociative practices have been identified that are responsible for this disengagement (Bandura, 1977a, 1979). One is the practice of rendering the behavior as honorable conduct, referred to as cognitive restructuring. This practice can be accomplished through (1) moral justification, (2) comparison with more heinous crimes, and (3) labeling the act with less emotion-laden terms (euphemistic labeling). Religious persecution is an example of moral justification; describing the extermination of millions of people as "the final solution" is an example of euphemistic labeling.

The other three dissociative practices are (1) the diffusion and displacement of responsibility ("I had no choice; I was only following orders"), (2) minimizing the consequences of the act, and (3) dehumanizing and attaching blame to the victim (Bandura, 1977a, 1977b). These four practices, of course, do not quickly transform a gentle, law-abiding individual into an aggressor (Bandura, 1982). Rather, the process is gradual, beginning with the performance of acts that do not lead to excessive self-censure. Then the individual's discomfort and self-reproach are gradually diminished through repeated performances until brutal acts are committed with little distress (Bandura, 1982, p. 354).

The importance of these analyses is twofold. First, the self system is a critical factor in the development of accomplished skills and capabilities in any field of endeavor. Second, neither the development of self-evaluative reactions nor their disengagement is an automatic process. Rather, a series of particular types of reciprocal interactions between the individual and the environment is required.

PRINCIPLES OF INSTRUCTION

A theory of instruction has yet to be derived from social learning theory. However, the principles of the theory have major implications for the classroom, both for educational practice and for understanding the diminished role of the educational system to transmit information.

In the early twentieth century, the parent, the church, and the school fulfilled the role of transmitting information about the culture, society, and the society's expectations for the next generation. Today, however, the mass media to a great extent have taken over that role (Gerbner, 1974). In today's complex society, the mass media manufacture the common symbolic environment shared by all members. The culture in the mass media is illustrated in terms of power relationships within society, with particular racial and sex-role identities. In addition, family problems are resolved in less than an hour, the criminal either always confesses, is caught, or is killed, and the criminal's victims experience little pain or suffering. These "facts of life" are the hidden curriculum that no one teaches, but which everyone learns (Gerbner, 1974).

In addition, the media portray the home, the school, and other societal institutions in ways that conform to needed plot development for entertainment programs and for human interest in news programs. Thus the media "create and cultivate large heterogeneous publics, define the agenda of public discourse, and represent all other institutions in the vivid imagery of fact and fiction designed for mass publics. Teachers and schools no longer enjoy much autonomy, let alone their former monopoly, as the public dispensers of knowledge" (Gerbner, 1974, p. 471).

Basic Assumptions

The three major assumptions that support the principles of social learning theory are also applicable to classroom instruction. They are: (1) the learner's cognitive processes and decision making are important factors in learning; (2) the three-way interaction between the environment, personal factors, and behavior are responsible for learning; and (3) the outcomes of learning are visual and verbal codes of behavior.

The application of social learning theory is most often associated with affective, motor, or self-regulatory skills (Bandura, 1969, 1971b). However, the theory has also been successfully implemented in the acquisition of cognitive skills: specifically, linguistic rules, concept formation, and problem solving (see Rosenthal & Zimmerman, 1973, 1976, 1978). Research also indicates that learners acquire symbolic codes that are not merely isomorphic images. Rather, they are transformed codes, in which a great deal of response information is reduced and summarized (Bandura & Jeffrey, 1973).

The Components of Instruction

In social learning theory, the essential components of learning are a behavioral model, reinforcement to the model, and the learner's cognitive processing of the modeled behaviors. The components of instruction, therefore, are (1) identifying appropriate models in the classroom, (2) establishing the functional value of behaviors, and (3) engaging the learner's cognitive processes.

Identification of Appropriate Models. In the classroom, both teachers and students can serve as live models for a variety of social and academic behaviors. For adolescents, the influence of peer models often is stressed. However, the teacher is responsible for the classroom and is important as a model of responsibility, integrity, sincerity, and concern for both the individual and collective welfare of the students (Brophy & Putnam, 1979, p. 196). At any level of education, the teacher or faculty member should model emotional maturity, rationality, "common sense," and consistent follow-through on commitments (Brophy & Putnam, 1979).

Other live models that can also demonstrate the foregoing characteristics are community members invited to spend some time in the classroom. Firefighters, police, doctors, nurses, and other members of the work force are of interest to young children. To be maximally effective, however, a planned program of community involvement is needed. Visits or talks that appear to fill up time or give everyone a break on Friday will be ineffective. They may also convey the message that being a responsible adult is not important and does not contribute to self-worth.

Symbolic models also are effective influences in the development of prosocial behaviors. Research on "Sesame Street" and "Mister Rogers' Neighborhood," for example, indicates that the modeled prosocial behaviors enhance children's cooperativeness and friendliness (see Leifer, 1976).

Both live and symbolic models can successfully teach abstract cognitive rules, problem-solving strategies, and sequences of integrated motor behaviors (see Carroll & Bandura, 1982; Rosenthal & Bandura, 1978; Rosenthal & Zimmerman, 1978). The former, referred to as abstract modeling, is the transmission of generic rules, strategies, and judgmental standards by a model.

Teaching problem-solution strategies requires a model who (1) demonstrates the appropriate strategy, and (2) verbalizes aloud the steps to be taken. However, a successful demonstration of behavior for the purposes of instruction differs from skilled performance. In a skilled execution, the decision processes or critical points in the performance cannot be detected. In contrast, a successful demonstration should include both the choices and nonchoices to be made (Olson & Bruner, 1974). In addition, care should be taken so that the presentation of stimuli is not too fast or includes too many clues simultaneously (Rosenthal & Bandura, 1978). Observers may be unable to identify the critical aspects of the demonstration.

The selection of a live or symbolic model often depends on practical considerations. For cognitive and motor skills, the advantages of the live model are (1) the physical demonstration of the behavior in front of the students, and (2) the opportunities for student questions. The chemistry class in which the use of laboratory equipment often is demonstrated by the teacher is an example.

The major advantage of symbolic modeling is that the models may be viewed more than once by students. In a project supervised by this author, videotapes of classroom teachers with their classes were made available to undergraduates in education about to undertake their own student teaching. The undergraduates returned to the tapes time after time, reporting that they found something informative and interesting on each viewing.

This example also illustrates that the selection of the behaviors to be modeled is an important decision in the design of instruction. The behaviors must be of interest to the observer and portrayed at a level of complexity to be understood by the learner.

In addition to the type of stimulus and nature of the behavior, the type and status of the model are also influential in classroom learning. Some research indicates that children are more likely to remember the actions of a friendly, powerful person than those of a colder, more neutral person (Baldwin, 1973).

Nurturance of the model, however, must be implemented with care in powerful models. Since the young child seeks feedback from nurturant authority figures, expressive features can detract the child's attention away from modeled behaviors. This potential problem can be counteracted by the use of verbal directives focused on the relevant behavior as well as the display of minimal expressive reactions during modeling.

Establishing the Functional Value of the Behavior. According to observational learning, individuals pay attention to events in the environment that predict reinforcement (Bandura, 1977b, p. 85). They tend to ignore events that do not include reinforcement predictions. Therefore, the expectancy of positive consequences is an important aspect of instruction. It increases task attention and, more importantly, leads the student to expect positive consequences for future task completion.

Events that predict reinforcement have acquired functional value for the student and will be attended to. In the classroom, the functional value of the modeled behaviors is established in one of two ways: (1) direct reinforcement to the model for performing the behavior, or (2) a cognitive context that predicts reinforcement. Of course, after the observer implements the behavior, reinforcement must be forthcoming from the environment; otherwise, the behavior will not be continued by the learner.

For conceptual learning, the presentation of the modeled behavior serves as a predictor of reinforcement for the observer (Zimmerman & Rosenthal, 1974). In demonstrating the behavior, the teacher is modeling behavior that is sanctioned by society. A perceptual set is established that includes the importance of the task to be learned.

In addition to conceptual learning, establishing the functional value of social behaviors is important in the classroom. Reinforcement to peer models for working quietly, proceeding in an orderly manner to recess, and so on, can influence the adoption of those behaviors by classmates.

Two cautions, however, must be observed with regard to reinforcement. First, vicarious reinforcement differs from implicit reinforcement. Exemplary behavior that is praised in one individual and disregarded in others may to the teacher imply reinforcement to all the students who behaved well. To the slighted individuals, the direct consequences of their behavior, no reinforcement, may be perceived as punishment.

The second caution is that reinforcement, like beauty, is in the eye of the beholder. The same compliment, when given to two different individuals, can have different effects. Individuals develop personal reference standards from the repeated observations of consequences received by others. These reference standards determine how an externally administered reinforcer in effect will serve as a reward or as a punishment. "Thus, for example, the same compliment is likely to be punishing for persons who have seen similar performances by others highly acclaimed, but positively reinforcing when others have been less generously praised" (Bandura, 1971b, p. 229).

Similarly, the omission of expected punishment conveys the impression of permissiveness. Behavioral restraints are reduced and the formerly forbidden behaviors are performed with greater freedom (Bandura, 1971a). Therefore, clearly stated rules in the classroom must be maintained when transgressions occur. Otherwise, students will infer that the formerly prohibited conduct is now permissable. Often, the teacher's look is sufficient admonishment for misconduct that is being initiated. The teacher's reaction conveys information that punishment is forthcoming should the misconduct continue. The teacher's stern look applied to the peer model "signals" punishment.

Guiding the Learner's Cognitive and Motor Reproduction Processes. The recommended instructional activities vary somewhat, depending on the type of skill to be learned. Different emphases are required for cognitive skills and motor skills. However, instruction for both types of skills share two common features. Opportunities must be provided for (1) coding the observed behavior into visual images or word symbols, and (2) mentally rehearsing the modeled behaviors. Unless imitative performances are symbolized in memory codes and then stabilized through rehearsal, neither the memory codes nor the behaviors can later be retrieved (Bandura & Jeffrey, 1973).

Motor Skills. Successful performance of complex motor skills such as golf, skiing, and tennis, depends on the individual's internal monitoring of kinesthetic feedback. This monitoring is both unobservable and difficult to imitate. A recommended strategy is as follows: (1) the presentation of a videotaped model, followed by (2) the opportunity to develop a conceptual representation, and finally, (3) practice with concurrent visual feedback via a monitor (Carroll & Bandura, 1982). These steps can be successful in teaching the acquisition of a novel action pattern normally outside the learner's visual field, such as executing the backstroke. This strategy permits the review of both performance and contextual cues.

Of particular importance in teaching motor skills is that mental rehearsal of the observed skills by the learner should precede physical execution of the skill. According to Jeffrey's research (1976), mental rehearsal results in superior initial performance and superior retention. The important point is that (1) symbolic rehearsal fulfills an organizational function for the performance, and (2) too early an emphasis on motor performance can jeopardize retention at the time when memory codes are unstable.

Thus the relationship between coding and rehearsal is an important one for instruction. For motor skills, the physical rehearsal in the absence of coding does not facilitate retention of the performance. On the other hand, symbolic rehearsal alone of motor skills can lead to blurring or distortion of the motor sequence.

Delayed self-observation following modeling is also very useful for social and communication skills. Students in speech and debate, for example, can acquire important information about needed changes in posture, voice level, gestures, and presentation and response styles.

Conceptual Behavior. Linguistic rules and concepts may be taught by either of two methods. One method is for the model (1) to instruct the student to find the consistencies across situations, and (2) to demonstrate the rule in several situations. Nonrelevant task characteristics are varied while holding the rule constant (Zimmerman & Rosenthal, 1974). Complex sentence structures, verb tenses, and concept examples may be taught in this way.

An alternative method is to provide the learner with a classification code. The code that symbolizes the behavior may be verbal, imaginal, reductive, or elaborative. For example, pictures can serve as codes for two-category linguistic rules such as present/past tense and singular/plural (Kossuth, 1972). The selected code, however, must be meaningful to the student and it must enable the student to summarize and classify information (Zimmerman & Rosenthal, 1974). In one study, memory codes that met both these criteria resulted in a threefold increase in retention compared to codes that met only one criterion (Bandura, Jeffrey & Bachicha, 1974).

Verbalization during modeling should be carefully selected, however. If verbalization conveys little or no information, it may actually hinder observational learning. In addition, irrelevant, attention-getting statements will not only interfere with learning, they may be learned instead. Finally, overt responding by the learner should not be required. Organizing and producing verbal responses appears to interfere with the observation of the behavioral sequence (Zimmerman & Rosenthal, 1974).

Designing Instruction for Complex Skills

Learning theories typically describe the combinations of specific behaviors and skills that represent complex achievement. In contrast, social learning theory includes two general factors that are essential to the acquisition of complex skills. They are the individual's perceived self-efficacy and self-direction. Therefore, classroom instruction should emphasize the learner's development of these skills in addition to the acquisition of content-related skills. The lack of a sense of personal efficacy is followed by less effort and decreased persistence on difficult tasks. Eventually, avoidance of such tasks occurs, accompanied by defensive behavior and negative emotions. Repeated failures lower expectations of mastery, contributing to the development of dysfunctional and maladaptive behaviors.

Three important considerations are suggested by Bandura (1977a) in the design of successful programs to develop efficacy and self-direction. First, efforts to develop a sense of mastery is, by itself, insufficient for the development of complex skills. "Expectation alone will not produce the desired performance if component skills are lacking" (Bandura, 1977a, p. 194). Therefore, effort also must be devoted to the acquisition of prerequisite skills.

Second, new behaviors will be discontinued if they are not reinforced. Students may cease trying because they believe that their skill and performance will not affect the environment (Bandura, 1977a). A student labeled poor or below average, for example, may give up if his or her new skills are not acknowledged. A follow-up study of autistic children indicated that speech gains were maintained in the home settings with supportive parents, but were lost by the children in the institutional settings (Bandura, 1976; Lovaas, Roegel, Simmons, & Stevens, 1973).

Third, personal efficacy operates in conjunction with situational factors (Bandura, 1977a, p. 303). Some situations require greater skill and carry a higher risk of negative consequences than other situations; therefore, efficacy expectations are likely to be less in such contexts. A cumulative final examination, for example, requires mastery of a broader range of content than a weekly quiz. Also, such an examination typically weighs heavily in the final grade and thus carries a higher risk of negative consequences than other tests in the course.

Classroom Environment.   The student spends at least six hours a day for most of each year in the classroom. It can either be a facilitating or debilitating environment for the development of efficacy expectations and self-regulation of learning. For academic tasks, emphasis on learner progress rather than getting the right answer is obviously an important factor in the development and maintenance of task persistence.

A classroom atmosphere that recognizes self-improvement is important. Further, valued patterns of behavior and the standards for self-evaluation must be modeled by the teacher. If the goal is a cooperative atmosphere for learning with the emphasis on improvement, the teacher must be open to student suggestions. Classroom control cannot depend on authoritarian behavior.

Further, the teacher in today's classroom often is interacting with a diverse population of students, some of whom hold values and expectations that differ from the school's expectations. Social learning theory indicates that students are unlikely to participate cooperatively in activities unless they associate them with positive outcomes for themselves.

Programs for Self-efficacy.   Four elements are important in the development of programs to enhance self-efficacy and self-direction. They are (1) the use of subgoals, (2) modeling of persistence and other skills important for mastery (vicarious experiences), (3) enactive experiences in which mastery is achieved, and (4) positive incentives that enhance or authenticate personal effectiveness (Bandura, 1982).

In one study that involved children identified by their teachers as very poor in arithmetic and disinterested in arithmetic activities, the use of subgoals and reinforcement were implemented (Bandura & Schunk, 1981). The children in the subgoal condition were asked to think about completing six pages per session. This group achieved higher arithmetic achievement and demonstrated increased persistence on difficult problems than did either the group with no goals or the group given distant goals.

In another program, the objective was to develop assertiveness. Participants initially were hesitant to engage in the behaviors because they were concerned about errors in performance (Bandura, 1973). However, the program utilized optimistic, forward-looking goals in which improvement with practice was sought rather than instant proficiency (Bandura, 1973, p. 259). The program emphasized that all initial efforts are awkward in any skill learning, and significant changes were achieved by the end of the program.

Positive incentives, as in the foregoing example, are essential in the early stages of learning. Careful planning of contingencies that build positive interaction with the environment is essential. Individuals process and synthesize feedback from events over long intervals about the situations and actions that are required to produce outcomes (Bandura, 1977b). Therefore, environmental support in the early stages of learning for on-task behaviors and improvement is extremely important. Reading is an example in which support must be provided until the behavior itself produces sustaining consequences (Bandura, 1977b).

EDUCATIONAL APPLICATIONS

The importance of social learning theory for education includes two major implications. First, research on the theory has demonstrated that modeling is not governed by a generalized disposition to emulate a model with particular qualities. Rather, individuals tend to select particular behaviors to emulate rather than particular models.

The second important contribution is that the theory extends the learning process beyond direct contact with live models. It also includes situations in which children acquire information from sources other than the family and the school. The rapid increase of the mass media has projected into the living room a variety of modeled behaviors and contexts. Each of these models carries a particular message of the characteristics of social reality.

Research conducted in a variety of settings has demonstrated the effectiveness of modeling and its consequences in observational learning. Included are studies of the effectiveness of model punishment on playing with forbidden toys (Walters & Parke, 1964; Zimmerman & Kinsler, 1979), the effects of models on the transmission of personal standards (Bandura, 1971c), and the importance of modeling task persistence (Zimmerman & Blotner, 1979).

Modeling has also been applied to conceptual learning. Zimmerman and Rosenthal (1974) reviewed a variety of studies in which students abstracted relevant aspects of rule-governed behavior and later applied the rule. Belcher (1975) reports divergent productive responses of verbal behavior following a videotape that illustrated original uses of a common household object. Studies of problem solving have demonstrated increased problem-solving behavior following the use of strategy modeling (Schunk, 1981).

Classroom Issues

Social learning theory addresses some of the issues of concern in the classroom setting. Some learner characteristics and aspects of the social setting for learning are addressed in the theory.

Learner Characteristics.   Individual differences, readiness, and motivation for learning are the student characteristics that interact with instruction. Both individual differences and readiness are discussed in social learning theory in terms of their relationship to learning through observation.

Individual Differences.   Learners differ in their ability to abstract, code, remember, and enact the behaviors that they see. They also differ in their receptivity to models. Behaviors watched intently by nature lovers, for example, will be considered dull and boring by others. Receptivity to a particular model varies along the dimensions of (1) the valuation of the behavior for the observer, and (2) the degree of similarity between the observed model/context of the behavior and the observer's status and situation.

In the classroom, after the early school years, students also will differ on the functional value of the learning outcomes established by the school or the teacher. Some students will enthusiastically engage in learning activities, many will be more or less passively compliant, and others who perceive no social value in the outcomes may engage in antisocial behavior.

Readiness.   The developmental level of the learner and receptivity to particular models are the two major factors that determine the individual's capability for observational learning. The learner's perceptual set and the degree of anticipated reinforcement influence the decision to attend to or to ignore the model. The ability to abstract the important features of the modeled behaviors and to recall them later without error also influence the extent and accuracy of the learning. Young children, for example, cannot process complex sequences of behaviors. Instead, they require short explicit visual sequences with repetition.

Motivation. Although some activities are initiated for direct reinforcement (e.g., activities prompted by thirst, hunger, pain, and others), the primary source of motivation is cognitively based (Bandura, 1977b, p. 161). Two types of cognitive motivators are included. One is the cognitive representation of future consequences for particular behaviors. "Past experiences create expectations that certain actions will bring valued benefits, that others will have no appreciable effects, and that still others will avert future trouble" (Bandura, 1977b, p. 18).

The second type of cognitively based motivation may be referred to as self-motivation because it involves the standard setting and self-evaluative mechanisms of the learner. This type of motivation develops as part of the individual's self-regulatory system, discussed earlier.

Cognitive Processes and Instruction. Transfer of learning, developing the individual's "learning-how-to-learn" skills, and teaching problem solving are cognitive issues of importance to education. Of the three, social learning theory discusses the first issue.

Transfer of Learning. The concept of transfer has been researched in the social learning context in two ways. One is the investigation of different treatments for phobic patients. Self-directed mastery experiences were found to be more effective in providing transfer to generalized threat situations than participant modeling alone (Bandura, 1976; Bandura, Adams, & Beyer, 1977).

Modeling of cognitive behaviors has provided both immediate and delayed transfer to similar tasks. Concept attainment, linguistic rule learning, and problem solution strategies were generalized to similar situations (Zimmerman & Rosenthal, 1974; Schunk, 1981).

The Social Context for Learning. Social learning theory addresses the issue of learning in the naturalistic setting. Thus it describes specifically the mechanisms by which individuals learn from each other as they go about their daily lives. The observation of a variety of models (family models, films, television) and the reinforcements delivered to peers and others are all important influences on learning. In particular, social learning theory reminds the educational system that learning in a media-oriented society extends beyond the classroom in subtle and pervasive ways.

Developing a Classroom Strategy

The design of instruction for observational learning includes a careful analysis of the behaviors to be modeled and the processing requirements for learning.

STEP 1. Analyze the behaviors to be modeled.

   1.1 What is the nature of the behavior? Is it primarily conceptual, motor, or affective?

   1.2 What are the sequential steps in the behavior?

   1.3 What are the critical points in the sequence, such as the steps that may be difficult to observe and those for which alternative incorrect actions are likely?

STEP 2. Establish the functional value of the behavior and select the behavioral model.

   2.1 Does the behavior carry a "success prediction," such as learning to operate equipment essential for a job promotion?

   2.2 If the behavior is a weak success predictor, which potential model is most likely to predict success? Examples include peers, the teacher, and status models that appeal to the target group.

   2.3 Should the model be live or symbolic? Consider cost, the need to repeat the experience for more than one group, and the opportunity for portraying the functional value of the behavior.

   2.4 What reinforcement(s) is the model to receive for the behavior?

STEP 3. Develop the instructional sequence.

   3.1 For motor skills, what are the "do this" but "not this" verbal codes to be used?

   3.2 Which steps in the sequence are to be presented slowly? What are the verbal codes that supplement but do not supplant these steps?

STEP 4. Implement the instruction to guide the learner's cognitive and motor reproduction processes.

Motor skills:
4.1 Present the model.

4.2 Provide students the opportunity for symbolic rehearsal.

4.3 Provide student practice with concurrent visual feedback.

Conceptual behavior:
4.1 Present the model with either (a) supporting verbal codes or (b) directions to find the consistencies across examples.

4.2 Provide students with opportunities to summarize the modeled behaviors.

4.3 If the learning is a problem-solving or strategy application, provide opportunities for participant modeling.

4.4 Provide opportunities for students to generalize to other situations.

Classroom Example

The behaviors modeled in the following example are note-taking skills. The identified population is middle school students (ages 10–14, grades 6–8).[2]

The teacher first models the strategy of note taking from written text. Of importance in this exercise is that the teacher model the process in which a particular recall cue is chosen over another. The teacher should "talk aloud" the cues that come to mind and the reasons for rejection of poor cues. After the teacher's demonstration, the students suggest the notes be taken in the next two exercises. This activity provides for corrective feedback early in the learning. The students then complete a note-taking exercise on their own. This activity provides the symbolic coding and mental rehearsal necessary for conceptual behavior.

The follow-up exercise that demonstrates note taking from audiotaped material should be initiated only after the students have applied their skills for written materials in a variety of situations. Taking notes from an ongoing oral presentation is a difficult skill to learn. It is dependent on good listening skills and practice in the use of temporary auditory memory. In teaching this skill, exercises in listening and recall of oral material may be required prior to the note-taking exercise.

The teacher explains the importance of note taking in helping the stu-

[2] Example designed by Sharon Cohn, University of South Carolina.

dents to remember material that they have heard or read and that good note-taking strategies should improve their grades. The teacher distributes a four-paragraph reading selection and asks the students to read the first paragraph silently while the teacher reads it aloud.

A transparency that illustrates the note-taking format is placed on the overhead projector. It is divided into two columns, headed "recall cues" and "notes."[3] The teacher talks through the first paragraph in terms of its important points. Then under the "notes" column, two summary sentences for the paragraph and associated cues in the "recall cues" column are entered. The teacher verbalizes the ways in which these sentences and the recall words will help students to remember the paragraph.

The teacher then carries out the same procedure with the other two paragraphs. After reading each one aloud, the teacher talks through several alternatives for notes, selects one or two, and enters them in the appropriate column with associated cues. The importance of the exercise is that the students observe the ways in which the teacher analyzes the paragraph and selects summary sentences.

The students and the teacher then work through two or three exercises together, with the students suggesting the study notes. This activity is followed by independent note taking by the students on short passages that they have selected from other sources.

Reading Passage for Note-Taking Exercise.[4]   A land grant of 10 million acres was given to George Calvert, a prominent nobleman from England known as Lord Baltimore. The land given by the king, Charles I, was located near Chesapeake Bay, and this gift enabled George Calvert to exert tremendous power. He was capable of establishing manors that resembled those of the feudal era, and the inhabitants could be treated as serfs. He could also function as a prosecutor and a judge of inhabitants charged with law breaking. George Calvert was called a proprietor, an owner of landholdings, and his colony was known as a proprietary colony.

Prior to the king's seal being affixed to the charter describing the land grant, George Calvert died and his son served as the first proprietor. The colony was known as Maryland, named after the wife of Charles I, Queen Henrietta Maria. Since the Calvert family was Catholic, they intended to establish a Catholic colony in Maryland.

In 1634 the first settlers arrived and established the town of St. Mary's. The settlers could obtain food and other provisions from the adjacent and prosperous colony of Virginia. They did not have to wait for ships from

---

[3] Suggested by W. Pauk, *How to study in college* (New York: Houghton Mifflin, 1962).

[4] Paraphrased from J. A. Garraty et al., *American history* (New York: Harcourt, 1982).

England. They did not waste time looking for gold; instead, they began to grow tobacco immediately.

Recall Cues	Notes
Calvert	George Calvert, Lord Baltimore, was the proprietor of a large land area near the Chesapeake Bay.
Proprietary colony	He had a great deal of power, and his land was a proprietary colony.
Maryland	Calvert's son was the first proprietor of the colony called Maryland. Because Calvert's family was Catholic, they wanted Maryland to be a Catholic colony.
Tobacco	Early settlers in Maryland began to grow tobacco.

Note-Taking Example II. In this exercise, the teacher has previously recorded a script on audiotape. The speech is recorded with short pauses, much as one might give a talk to a group. In the modeling, the teacher plays each paragraph of the recorded tape and demonstrates how to take notes while the tape is playing. She writes recall cues and sentence fragments on the transparency during the brief pauses in the tape. The tape is stopped at the end of each paragraph and the teacher completes the sentence fragments.

After the demonstration, the students and the teacher complete several short paragraphs together. This exercise is usually quite difficult for students because it involves listening and jotting down notes at the same time. Therefore, only very short paragraphs should be used until the students' skills are acquired; this may require several exercises over a period of time.

Taped Paragraph.[5] In the seventeenth century a cluster of religious reformers resided in England. These reformers were critical of the Church of England. However, they did not want to separate from the church. They wished to reform and to purify the church from the inside. These reformers were called Puritans.

Recall Cues	Sentence Fragments	Completed Sentence
Reform	the Church of England	The Puritans wanted to reform and purify the Church of England.
Purify		

[5] Paraphrased from J. A. Garraty et al., *American history* (New York: Harcourt, 1982).

Review of the Theory

Albert Bandura's social learning theory began with his analyses of prior approaches to the learning of imitative behavior. The behaviorist paradigm, in his view, accounted for only the mimicry of specific responses performed by a model. Other theories, in contrast, proposed a variety of mechanisms to account for the adoption of prosocial and antisocial behaviors. Included were nurturance, power, envy, frustration, and others.

In contrast, Bandura proposes a single paradigm to account for the acquisition of both prosocial and antisocial behaviors. The components are (1) the modeled behaviors, (2) the consequences to the model, and (3) the learner's cognitive processes. (See Table 10-5). The consequences received by the model that contribute to the observer's learning the be-

Table 10-5. Summary of Bandura's Social Learning Theory

Basic Elements	Definition
Assumptions	Learning is a three-way interaction between the environment, personal factors, and behavior that also involves the learner's cognitive processes
Components of learning	Modeled behaviors, consequences to the model, and the learner's cognitive processes
Learning outcomes	Verbal and visual codes that may or may not later be performed
Designing instruction for complex skills	In addition to component skills, develop the learner's sense of efficacy and self regulation
Major issues in designing instruction	Provide for mental rehearsal prior to practice; avoid omission of reinforcement or punishment when needed; avoid excessive use of punishment
Analysis of the Theory	
Disadvantages	Difficult to implement the requirements for self-efficacy and self-regulation along with other classroom priorities. Theory excludes some modes of learning typically used in the classroom (e.g., learning from text)
Contributions	Description of the variety of attitudes and behaviors acquired from the mass media. Provides a detailed understanding of the mechanisms of reinforcement and punishment in the group setting

havior include vicarious reinforcement, vicarious punishment, and the absence of anticipated punishment. These consequences signal behaviors that have functional value and therefore may be useful to the observer. Later successful performance by the observer depends in part on the learner's cognitive processes (attention, retention, motor reproduction, and motivation).

Learning, according to Bandura, is represented by a three-way interaction between the environment, the individual's internal events, and the individual's behavior (reciprocal determinism). Also included in the theory is the development of the self-regulatory system, a necessary component in the development of outstanding performance in any area. Included in the system are goal setting, self-evaluation, and self-directed rewards or punishments.

Disadvantages. Bandura identifies reciprocal determinism as the mechanism by which learning occurs. An extension of this concept is the importance of the learner's self-direction and sense of efficacy in interacting with the environment. However, in the limited classroom setting, developing the learner's self-regulatory system and sense of efficacy is a difficult task.

Contributions to Educational Practice. An important contribution is the detailed descriptions of reinforcement and punishment provided by the theory. That is, punishment or lack of it delivered to others as well as vicarious reinforcement are both operating in the classroom setting.

Perhaps the most important contribution of the theory, however, is the identification of the range of behaviors and attitudes that are learned from the mass media. Increased violence and aggression in society at large are explained, in part, by the observational learning described in social learning theory.

DISCUSSION QUESTIONS

1. In what ways does Bandura's analysis of reinforcement differ from Skinner's perspective?
2. How does Bandura summarize the phases of information processing identified by Gagné?
3. What are the implications of social learning theory with regard to the portrayal of violence on television?

GLOSSARY

autonomy   The capability of existing independently; a process or activity carried on without outside control.

cognitive mediation   The learner's internal processes which influence learning. They include the learner's ability to code observed behavior, retain the information in memory, and translate the code into personal performance.

delayed matching   The adoption of a new behavior by the learner days or weeks after it is observed.

encoding   The process of transforming observed experience into memory codes.

environment   The situation in which behavior occurs. It includes both *potential environment* and *actual environment*. The potential environment includes the range of possible consequences that can occur following an individual's response. Actual environment includes all the changes in the situation that occur as a result of the actions of the individual. The learner's behavior transforms the potential environment into the actual environment.

functional value   The utility of a particular behavior. The utility of a behavior is established when the observed behavior leads to positive consequences.

implicit reinforcement   Behavior that is praised in one individual and disregarded in others may be regarded by the teacher as implicit reinforcement. However, it may be perceived by the students as punishment.

indirect learning   The learner does not personally perform the behavior nor experience the consequences of a particular behavior. Instead, the learner observes a model perform the action and receive the consequences.

instantaneous matching   Imitative learning in which the learner copies the behavior immediately after the presentation.

modeling   A demonstrated behavior is the stimulus for learning. The primary function of the model is to transmit information.

perceived self-efficacy   The belief that one can perform successfully the behaviors that lead to positive outcomes.

personal determinant   The influence exerted by the individual on the environment. As the individual's goals and behaviors change, they change the environment.

representational systems   The symbolic codes that are stored in the learner's memory. *Visual codes* are vivid images. *Verbal codes* include language symbols, numbers, and musical notation.

reciprocal determinism   The mutual influence of the individual and the environment on each other.

symbolic model   A visual image of the live model, such as a film or televised presentation.

social behavior   The tendency for an individual to match the behaviors, attitudes, or emotional reactions that are observed in actual or symbolic models.

self-reinforcement   Anticipated and evaluative consequences that are generated by the individual for his or her behavior.

vicarious reinforcement   Observation of positive consequences received by the model which leads to matching behavior by the learner.

REFERENCES

Baldwin, A. L. (1973). Social learning. In F. Kerlinger (Ed.), *Review of research in education* (Vol. I, pp. 34–57). Itasca, IL: Peacock.

Bandura, A. (1965a). Behavioral modification through modeling practices. In L. Krasner & L. Ullman (Eds.), *Research in behavior modification* (pp. 310–340). New York: Holt, Rinehart and Winston.

Bandura, A. (1969). Social-learning theory of identificatory processes. In D. A. Goslin (Ed.), *Handbook of socialization theory and research* (pp. 213–262). Chicago: Rand McNally.

Bandura, A. (1971a). *Psychological modeling: Conflicting theories.* Chicago: Aldine-Atherton.

Bandura, A. (1971b). *Social learning theory.* Englewood Cliffs, NJ: Prentice-Hall.

Bandura, A. (1971c). Vicarious and self-reinforcement processes. In R. Glaser (Ed.), *The nature of reinforcement* (pp. 228–278). New York: Academic Press.

Bandura, A. (1972). Modeling theory: Some traditions, trends, and disputes. In R. D. Parke (Ed.), *Recent trends in social learning theory* (pp. 35–61). New York: Academic Press.

Bandura, A. (1973). *Aggression: A social learning analysis.* Englewood Cliffs, NJ: Prentice-Hall.

Bandura, A. (1974). Behavior theory and the models of man. *American Psychologist, 29,* 859–869.

Bandura, A. (1976). Social learning perspective on behavior change. In A. Burton (Ed.), *What makes behavior change possible?* (pp. 34–57). New York: Brunner/Mazel.

Bandura, A. (1977a). Self-efficacy: Toward a unifying theory of behavioral change. *Psychological Review, 84*(2), 191–215.

Bandura, A. (1977b). *Social learning theory.* Englewood-Cliffs, NJ: Prentice-Hall.

Bandura, A. (1978). The self-system in reciprocal determinism. *American Psychologist, 33,* 344–358.

Bandura, A. (1979). Psychological mechanisms of aggression. In M. von Cranach, K. Foppa, W. Lepenies, & D. Ploog (Eds.), *Human ethology: Claims and limits of a new disciple* (pp. 316–379). Cambridge: Cambridge University Press.

Bandura, A. (1982). Self-efficacy mechanism in human agency. *American Psychologist, 37*, 122–147.

Bandura, A. (1982). The self and mechanisms of agency. In J. Suls (Ed.), *Psychological perspectives on the self* (Vol. 1). Hillsdale, NJ: Lawrence Erlbaum.

Bandura, A., Adams, N., & Beyer, J. (1977). Cognitive processes mediating behavioral change. *Journal of Personality and Social Psychology, 35*, 125–138.

Bandura, A., & Jeffrey, R. W. (1973). Role of symbolic coding and rehearsal processes in observational learning. *Journal of Personality and Social Psychology, 26*, 122–130.

Bandura, A., Jeffrey, R. W., & Bachicha, D. L. (1974). Analysis of memory codes and cumulative rehearsal in observational learning. *Journal of Research in Personality, 7*, 295–305.

Bandura, A., Mahoney, M. J., & Dirks, S. J. (1976). Discriminative activities and maintenance of contingent self-reinforcement. *Behavior Research and Therapy, 14*, 1–6.

Bandura, A., Ross, D., & Ross, S. A. (1963a). A comparative test of status envy, social power, and the secondary reinforcement theories of identification learning. *Journal of Abnormal Social Psychology, 66*, 527–534.

Bandura A., Ross, D., & Ross, S. A. (1963b). Imitation of film-mediated aggression models. *Journal of Abnormal Social Psychology, 66*, 3–11.

Bandura, A., & Schunk, D. H. (1981). Cultivating competence, self-efficacy, and intrinsic interest through proximal self-motivation. *Journal of Personality and Social Psychology, 41*, 586–598.

Bandura, A., & Walters, R. H. (1963). *Social learning theory and personality development*. New York: Holt Rinehart and Winston.

Belcher, T. L. (1975). Modeling divergent responses: An initial investigation. *Journal of Educational Psychology, 67*, 351–358.

Betz, N. E., & Hackett, G. (1981). The relationships of career-related self-efficacy expectations to perceived career options in college men and women. *Journal of Counseling Psychology, 28*, 399–410.

Brophy, J., & Putnam, J. (1979). Classroom management in the elementary grades. In *Classroom management. The eightieth yearbook of the National Society for the Study of education*, (pp. 182–216). Chicago: University of Chicago Press.

Carroll, W., & Bandura, A. (1982). The role of visual monitoring in observational learning of action patterns: Making the unobservable observable. *Journal of Motor Behavior, 14*, 153–167.

Gerbner, G. (1974). Teacher image in mass culture: Symbolic functions of the "hidden curriculum." In D. R. Olson (Ed.), *The form of expression, communication and education. The seventy-third yearbook of the National Society for the Study of Education* (pp. 470–497). Chicago: University of Chicago Press.

Jeffrey, R. S. (1976). The influence of symbolic and motor rehearsal in observational learning. *Journal of Research in Personality, 10*, 117–126.

Kossuth, G. L. (1972). Observational learning of a novel language construction. Unpublished doctoral dissertation, University of Arizona.

Leifer, A. D. (1976). Teaching with television and film. In N. L. Gage (Ed.), *The seventy-fifth yearbook of the National Society for the Study of Education* (pp. 302–334). Chicago: University of Chicago Press.

Lovaas, O. I., Roegel, R., Simmons, J. O., & Stevens, J. (1973). Some generalization and follow-up measures on autistic children in behavior therapy. *Journal of Applied Behavioral Analysis*, *6*, 131–166.

Miller, N. E., & Dollard, J. (1941). *Social learning and imitation*. New Haven, CT: Yale University Press.

Mowrer, O. H. (1960). *Learning theory and the symbolic processes*. New York: Wiley.

Olson, D. R., & Bruner, J. S. (1974). Learning through experience and learning through media. In D. Olson (Ed.), *Media and symbols. The seventy-third yearbook of the National Society for the Study of Education* (pp. 125–250). Chicago, University of Chicago Press.

Rosenthal, T. L., & Bandura, A. (1978). Psychological modeling: Theory and practice. In S. L. Garfield & A. E. Begia (Eds.), *Handbook of psychotherapy and behavior change: An empirical analysis* (2nd ed., pp. 621–658). New York: Wiley.

Rosenthal, T. L., & Zimmerman, B. J. (1973). Organization, observation and guided practice in concept attainment and generalization. *Child Development*, *44* 606–613 (LB 1101.C4).

Rosenthal, T. L., & Zimmerman, B. J. (1976). Organization and stability of transfer in vicarious concept attainment. *Child Development*, *47*, 110–117.

Rosenthal, T. L., & Zimmerman, B. J. (1978). *Social learning theory and cognition*. New York: Academic Press.

Schunk, D. H. (1981). Modeling and attributional effects on children's achievement: A self-efficacy analysis. *Journal of Educational Psychology*, *73*, 93–105.

Walters, R. H., & Parke, R. D. (1964). Influence of response consequences to a social model on resistance to deviation. *Journal of Experimental Child Psychology*, *1*, 269–280.

Zimmerman, B. J., & Blotner, R. (1979). Effects of model persistence and success on children's problem solving. *Journal of Educational Psychology*, *71*(4), 508–513.

Zimmerman, B. J., & Kinsler, K. (1979). Effects of exposure to a punished model and verbal prohibitions on children's toy play. *Journal of Educational Psychology*, *71*(3), 388–395.

Zimmerman, B. J., & Rosenthal, T. L. (1974). Observational learning of rule-governed behavior by children. *Psychological Bulletin*, *81*, 29–42.

CHAPTER 11

Bernard Weiner's Attribution Theory

A central assumption of attribution theory
. . . is that the search for understanding is
a basic "spring of action."
Weiner, 1979, p. 3

The theory developed by Bernard Weiner (1972, 1980b) links two major areas of interest in psychological theory: motivation and attribution research. Early theories of motivation, like theories of learning, were developed primarily from the stimulus-response perspective that was dominant from the mid-1930s to the mid-1950s. The major motivational construct during that period was the concept of drive, an important factor in Clark Hull's theory. However, the drive construct, although interpreted a variety of ways, proved inadequate to account for the complexities of human motivation.

The shift from a stimulus-response perspective to a cognitive perspective began after World War II. Among other developments discussed in prior chapters of this text, this shift ushered in the perspective referred to as attribution theory. The acknowledged founder is Fritz Heider, who identified the basic framework in his 1958 text *The Psychology of Interpersonal Relations.*

The term *attribution* refers to an individual's perceived causes of an event or an outcome. The research focus is the ways in which individuals arrive at causal explanations and the implications of those explanations. In other words, the theories focus on the ways in which people answer the question "Why?" (Kelley, 1973).

Within this general focus, three research directions may be identified. They are (1) the classification of the perceived causes of behavior, (2) the

274

general laws that relate antecedent information and the individual's cognitive structures, and (3) the development of linkages between causal inferences and the subsequent overt behavior (Weiner, 1977).

The theory developed by Bernard Weiner (1972, 1980b) began with the variables identified in John W. Atkinson's theory of achievement motivation (1958, 1964). According to Atkinson, motivation is a function of task variables and the individual's disposition to strive for success or to avoid failure. Weiner (1972), however, maintains that internal events mediate the relationship between the task stimulus and the individual's subsequent behavior. Individuals high in achievement motivation, for example, perceive themselves as more able than those low in achievement motivation, and they also expend more effort on achievement tasks (Weiner & Kukla, 1970). In addition, Weiner and Kukla found that the effects of task variables are not uniform. That is, success on a difficult task generates more pride than success on an easy task.

The early development of Weiner's attribution theory began with the identification of four major causes that individuals typically select for success and failure outcomes and the conceptual links between those outcomes and subsequent behavior (Weiner, 1972, 1979). The four major causes are ability, effort, task difficulty, and luck. The properties or dimensions of the major causes that influence behavior were next identified, as well as the role of affective reactions as motivators of behavior (Weiner, 1980d, 1982). Recent work describes the role of the affective reactions of others on an individual's attributions for success or failure (Weiner, 1980b, 1980c) and the role of helping behavior (Weiner, 1980a; Weiner, Graham, Taylor, & Meyer, in press).

PRINCIPLES OF MOTIVATION

The prior chapters in this text discuss theories of learning that describe the factors necessary for the achievement of particular skills and capabilities. These theories describe either the environmental stimuli that are responsible for the acquisition of particular responses or the cognitive events that lead to changes in cognitive structure and, therefore, new response capabilities.

Attribution theory, in contrast, views human beings from the perspective of their search to understand the world and to achieve personal fulfillment and self-actualization. The primary focus of this chapter, therefore, is on the relationships between achievement-related outcomes, causal beliefs, and subsequent emotions and activities.

Basic Assumptions

The basic assumptions of the theory relate to two general concepts. They are the nature of causal inferences (attributions) and the relationship of those inferences to behavior.

The Nature of Causal Inferences. An important characteristic of causal inferences is that they occur in a broad range of human activities. Attributions are developed for achievement outcomes, such as why a test was failed or why a poor grade was received on a term paper. In addition, attributions are developed in the affiliative and power domains. Examples are: "Why was I rejected for a date?" and "Why did I lose the election?" (Weiner, 1982, p. 186).

One-Dimensional Perspectives. Much of the prior attributional research was based on the assumption that the perceived causes of behavior vary on a single dimension. Events are attributed either to the individual (the self) or to a characteristic of the environment. A well-known example is the locus of control construct developed by Julian Rotter (1966). In his view, the perceived causes of behavior lie on a continuum between the two extremes of internal and external locus of control. Individuals who believe that reinforcements (positive consequences) are contingent on their own behavior also believe that they control their own destiny. They are, therefore, inner-directed (see Table 11-1). Such individuals believe that positive events typically are the result of hard work, careful planning, and so on. They also take responsibility for events in their lives. Arriving late to class is likely to be acknowledged as leaving home too late to find a parking place, rather than some vague external condition.

In contrast, individuals who are outer-directed perceive no relationship between their behavior and reinforcements. Instead, luck, fate, or powerful others are in control. Therefore, the student may believe that a D on a test is the result of lack of ability (internal locus) or the result of teacher bias (external locus).

A variation of this conceptual framework is described in the origin/pawn analysis by deCharms (1968). The terms "intrinsically motivated" and "extrinsically motivated" are another way to describe the origin/pawn conception of causation.

Problems with a One-Dimensional Analysis. The major difficulty with the one-dimensional analysis of attributions is that it does not adequately account for subsequent effects. That is, several outcomes may result from attributions that occur in the same dimension, either internal or external (Weiner, 1972; Weiner et al., 1971). For example, different expectancies for future outcomes follow the attributions of lack of ability and lack of effort, both of which are internal. A poor grade attributed to lack of ability

Table 11-1. Person/Environment Dimension of Attributions

Theoretical Perspective	Personal Control	Environmental Control
Locus of control		
Inner-directed	Reinforcements are contingent on behavior; individuals control their own destiny	
Outer-directed		Luck, fate, or powerful others are in control; no relationship between personal behavior and reinforcements
Origin/pawn analysis		
Origin	An individual who initiates behavior intended to produce a change in the environment	
Pawn		An individual who perceives him- or herself to be pushed around by the environment

will be expected to occur again. However, a poor grade attributed to lack of effort may not be expected in the future since the student's expenditure of effort is subject to change (see Eswara, 1972; McMahan, 1973; Rosenbaum, 1972; Weiner, Neirenberg, & Goldstein, 1976).

In addition, lack of effort is punished more than lack of ability. Both males and females have dispensed the greatest punishment to able hypothetical pupils for failure attributed to lack of effort. The least punishment for failure went to motivated students of little ability (Rest, Neirenberg, Weiner, & Heckhausen, 1973; Weiner & Kukla, 1970). This reward pattern was also observed in reward dispensers who were as young as 16 (Weiner & Peter, 1973).

The differential consequences resulting from attributions in the same locus of causality (internal attributions) led to further analysis. Specifically, the identification of the various dimensions of causal beliefs that predict different outcomes was undertaken. These analyses became the cornerstone of Weiner's theory.

The Relationship of Causal Inferences to Behavior. A primary assumption of attribution theories is that the search for understanding is a major source of human motivation (Weiner, 1979). The pleasure-pain principle is not discounted as a source of human motivation. However, information seeking and verification are undertaken independent of the pleasure-pain principle. That is, as a motivator of action, comprehension ranks along with hedonism as a primary influence on behavior (Weiner, 1979, p. 3).

Some theories have identified relatively stable dispositions to behave in a particular way as the primary sources of motivation. Weiner, however, maintains that the relationship between achievement-related tasks and the individual is a complex one. A "true" cognitive theory must describe the internal events that mediate between the stimulus and the individual's subsequent behavior. The cognitive model is expressed as S-C-R, where C = internal mediating events (Weiner, 1972).

Therefore, another major assumption is that future behavior is influenced by people's belief systems and their cognitive analyses of the causes of positive and negative outcomes. For example, the student who attributes failure to low ability is likely to expect future failures and to believe that he or she has no behavioral response that can alter subsequent events (Weiner, 1979). Therefore, little or no effort will be expended on achievement-related tasks. In contrast, a student who attributes success to ability expects continued success. An occasional failure for such a student is likely to be attributed to a temporary cause, and future effort is not jeopardized.

In summary, three major assumptions support the theory. They are (1) the search for understanding is a primary motivator of action, (2) attributions are complex sources of information about outcomes, that is, they vary on more than a single dimension, and (3) future behavior is determined, in part, by perceived causes of prior outcomes.

The Components of the Attributional Process

The attributional model of motivation includes several components. One important aspect of the model is the relationship between attributions, feelings, and behavior. The logical sequence of psychological linkages, according to Weiner (1972), is that feelings are the outcomes of attributions or cognitions. Feelings do not determine cognitions. For example, to first experience gratitude for a positive outcome and then to decide that help from others is responsible for the success is an illogical sequence (Weiner, 1982, p. 204). Furthermore, feelings can be changed by new information (altered cognitions). Anger toward others can be dissipated, for example, by the information that some other agent is the cause of the problem.

The relationship between beliefs, affective reactions, and subsequent behavior is illustrated in Figure 11-1. The perceived cause of the success or failure leads to expectancies for the future and to particular emotions.

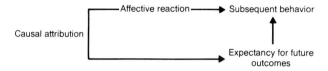

Figure 11-1. Tripartite relationship between causal beliefs, affective reactions and subsequent consequences. (From Weiner, 1980a.)

Subsequent actions are influenced both by the individual's feelings and expected outcomes.

The Attributional Model. The sequence illustrated in Figure 11-2 describes the progression of events from the success or failure outcomes to the subsequent behavior (Weiner, 1979). Individuals first appraise performance and assign it a subjective rating on a continuum from success to failure. Information relevant to this decision includes internal standards, aspiration level, societal standards, and others.

Emotional Reactions. The type of outcome, success or failure, generates emotional reactions that are independent of the perceived cause. Success generates feelings of happiness, pleasure, and satisfaction. Failure, on the other hand, generates displeasure, unhappiness, and sometimes, sadness (Weiner, Russell, & Lerman, 1978, 1979).

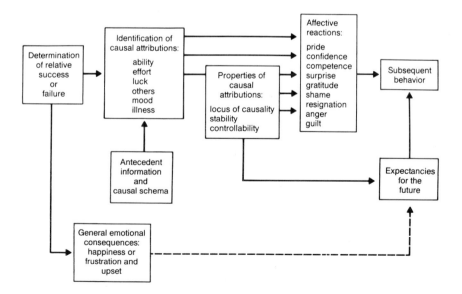

Figure 11-2. Major events in the attributional model of motivation.

After the outcome is identified as success or failure, either a cause is identified or the individual reflectively undertakes a search for the probable cause. The identified "cause" or attribution generates specific emotional reactions. In addition, each of the three major properties of attributions—stability, locus of causality, and controllability—also generate particular emotions.

The importance of the emotional reactions is that they function as the motor for subsequent behavior. Resignation and depression that follow attributions of failure to lack of ability lead to decreased effort. On the other hand, the perceived cause of failure may be the hindrance of others. One's roommate may throw a party the night before an important course examination. Feelings of anger and hostility are generated which may be followed by actions of reprisal.

Typical Attributions. The most likely causes selected for outcomes are ability, effort, task difficulty, and luck. These types of causal inferences were validated by Frieze (1976) using an open-ended format for both academic and nonacademic situations. Other causes of achievement performance also identified include mood, illness, fatigue, help from others, and teacher bias. However, ability, effort, task difficulty, and luck appear to be the most salient in academic settings. Student efforts to account for success or failure are derived most often from estimates of individual ability level, amount of effort, difficulty of the task, and the degree and direction of luck in the situation (Weiner, 1974a).

Applicability of the Model. The model (Figure 11-2) has been researched most extensively with achievement-related situations. Other analyses, however, indicate that the attributional model may generalize to other domains. Loneliness, for example, is viewed in American society as a failure. However attributional analyses of loneliness found that the perceived causes of social success and failure and the dimensions of the causes are similar to those in the achievement model (see Weiner, 1979).

Further, analyses of the causal attributions used by parole boards in their deliberations indicate the importance of the properties of the perceived causes with regard to subsequent decisions (Weiner, 1979). That is, parole will tend to be granted if the cause of the crime is perceived to be the result of external and/or noncontrollable and unstable factors. Included are economic conditions, childhood deprivations, and others (Weiner, 1979, p. 7). On the other hand, a perceived cause that is internal and/or controllable and is also stable does not result in parole. An example is an evil personality.

The attributional model identifies the relationships among outcomes, attributions, and subsequent consequences. Three important components contribute to an understanding of these relationships. They are (1) the kinds of antecedent information used by the individual in the selection of a causal attribution, (2) the properties of causal attributions, and (3) the role of emotional reactions with regard to behavior.

Antecedents of Causal Inferences. The sources of information available to the individual prior to the attribution for an outcome are referred to as antecedents. The three types of antecedents are (1) specific informational cues (such as one's past success history); (2) the individual's internal cognitive structure, referred to as causal schema; and (3) individual predispositions.

Specific Informational Cues. The primary antecedent cues are past success history, social norms, performance patterns, and time spent at the task (Weiner, 1977, p. 181). These cues lead to different causal inferences about success or failure.

The individual's past success history is the primary determinant for the selection of ability or lack of it as an attribution (Weiner, 1974a). A consistent record of prior achievements leads to ability as a selected cause for success. A moderate success record, however, indicates that goal attainment cannot be expected consistently. However, success has occurred fairly often; it is not random. In this case, success is likely to be attributed to effort rather than to either ability (consistent success record) or luck (random success record).

On the other hand, a consistently poor achievement record is associated with lack of ability. Given such a history, the causal inference for current failure is more likely to be lack of ability (stable, internal cause) than luck (unstable, external cause). Similarly, success for the individual with a poor achievement record is likely to be attributed to luck.

Social norms and the performance records of others also provide information about ability. If one succeeds at a task at which others fail, then the individual will likely decide that he or she is able (Weiner, 1974a, p. 53). Similarly, failure on a task at which others succeed is viewed as the result of lack of ability. The percentage of others who succeed or fail at a particular task, however, contributes to the use of task ease or difficulty as a causal belief. The higher the percentage of others who succeed at a task, the greater is the likelihood of ease of task as a causal inference for success. The higher the percentage of task failures, the more likely that the inference for failure will be task difficulty (Weiner, 1974a, p. 53).

Finally, effort is determined primarily by length of time at the task, extent of fatigue, and perceived degree of muscle tension, whereas luck is associated with lack of personal control in the outcome and perceived randomness of the outcome.

Causal Schema. Another source of information for causal ascription is the individual's causal schema (Kelley, 1973; Weiner, 1974a). Causal schemas are the relatively permanent cognitive structures that represent the individual's general beliefs about events and associated causes (Weiner, 1977). Research has identified some fairly common belief systems. One is the belief that success is produced by either ability or effort. Each cause is by itself sufficient to yield success; therefore, this belief is referred to as a sufficient causal schema (Weiner, 1974a, p. 53). This schema often is elicited by a typical success (Kun & Weiner, 1973).

Another causal schema is that success depends on both ability *and* effort. Since neither cause can by itself yield success, this combination of causes is referred to as a necessary causal schema (Weiner, 1977). This combination is often the explanation selected for success on a difficult task. Consistent with these beliefs, failure at a difficult task is ascribed to lack of ability or lack of effort, whereas failure at an easy task is ascribed to both lack of ability and lack of effort (Kun & Weiner, 1973).

Individual Predisposition. In addition to antecedent cues and causal schema, individual characteristics also influence causal attributions. One such characteristic is the need for achievement. Individuals who are high in achievement needs tend to attribute their success outcomes to themselves, that is, to skill or effort. Individuals low in achievement needs, however, tend to identify external factors as responsible for success (Weiner & Kukla, 1970). In addition, persons with high achievement needs tend to attribute initial failure to lack of effort (rather than lack of ability). Their persistence therefore increases, since they believe that increased effort will lead to success. In contrast, persons low in achievement needs often do not attribute the initial failure to lack of effort and therefore they tend to cease trying (Weiner & Kukla, 1970).

Self-concept is also a characteristic that is related to the causal attributions made by children. Research indicates that elementary school children who are high in self-concept credit skill and ability for success. They also engage in more self-reward following success than do low self-concept children (Ames, 1978; Ames, Ames & Felker, 1977).

The Properties of Causal Inferences. The antecedents of causal inferences are sources of information that influence the individual's choice of reasons for particular success or failure outcomes. Once such an inference is made, the next question to be asked about human behavior is: What are the consequences of this choice?

An important contribution of the present model to an understanding of motivation is the identification of attributional characteristics that lead to dissimilar reactions. Weiner (1979, 1982) has identified three such dimensions: locus of causality, stability, and controllability. Locus of causality refers to the internal/external characteristic briefly discussed earlier. Locus of causality refers to the origin of the perceived reason for the outcome (i.e., the environment or the individual). Help from others, for example, is external, whereas ability and effort are internal.

Stability of the perceived cause refers to the endurance of the particular attribution, and controllability refers to the presence or absence of the actor's volitional control (Weiner, 1982). Effort and luck are transient and therefore unstable. However, only effort is controllable; luck is uncontrollable. In contrast, ability and objective task difficulty are enduring and therefore stable. In addition, they are both uncontrollable by the actor.

The three dimensions, locus of causality, stability, and controllability, apply to attributions in the achievement, affiliative, and power domains of motivation. Ability (an achievement attribution), beauty (an attribution for social acceptance), and charisma (an attribution for gaining power) are all perceived to be internal, stable, and uncontrollable. Thus the identification of the dimensions of attributions indicates a functional similarity across seemingly different causal inferences (Weiner, 1982, p. 188). Studies using factor analysis and multidimensional scaling indicate the presence of the three dimensions in each of the foregoing motivational domains (see Meyer & Koelbi, 1982; Michela, Peplau, & Weeks, 1978).

Functions of Causal Dimensions. Two important functions are fulfilled by causal dimensions. One is that they contribute in particular ways to the individual's future goal expectancies. Stability, for example, contributes to unchanged expectations for the future. In other words, failure that is attributed to a stable cause is expected to recur. Included are test failure ascribed to lack of ability, social rejection attributed to physical unattractiveness, and loss of an election attributed to party membership.

The second function is that a particular set of emotional reactions is generated by each attributional dimension. These reactions, in turn, influence subsequent behavior. Internal attributions contribute to the individual's self-image. Further, failure attributed to the internal attributions of lack of ability, lack of effort, and physical unattractiveness contribute to a negative self-image. In contrast, failure attributed to external causes, such as luck or others, does not harm the individual's sense of self-esteem.

The controllability dimension, however, generates a different set of emotional reactions. Typically, for failure, the emotion is either anger or guilt. Anger is generated for failure attributed to the actions of others, whereas failure ascribed to lack of effort typically leads to some guilt.

The often-cited attributions for achievement-related outcomes are ability, effort, task difficulty, luck, mood or illness, and the actions of others. Table 11-2 illustrates the dimensions of each of these attributions. No two of the attributions are exactly alike in their dimensions. The unique combination of dimensions for each attribution generates particular expectancies and particular affective reactions.

Locus of Causality. This dimension refers to the internal/external nature of attributions. Ability, effort, and physical beauty are internal, whereas task difficulty and help (or hindrance) from others are external

Table 11-2. Properties of Major Attributions for Achievement-Related Behavior

	Property					
	Stability		Locus of Causality		Controllability[a]	
Attribution	Stable	Unstable	Internal	External	Con-trollable	Uncon-trollable
Ability	×		×			×
Effort		×	×		×	
Task difficulty	×			×		×
Luck		×		×		×
Mood, illness		×	×			×
Help from others		×		×		×

[a] From the perspective of the individual who experienced the positive or negative outcome.

attributions. This dimension has been associated for the most part with Rotter's concept of locus of control. However, it also has been referred to as the origin/pawn distinction and as intrinsic/extrinsic motivation (Weiner, 1982).

The importance of the internality dimension is the relationship to the individual's sense of self-worth and self-esteem. Positive outcomes attributed to internal causes, such as ability or effort, generate pride and the individual experiences positive self-esteem. However, success attributed to external causes, such as luck or help from others, is not a source of self-esteem (Weiner, 1982). An example is receiving an A grade from a teacher who awards only good grades (external cause); pride is not experienced for the success. In contrast, receiving an A from a teacher who awards few good grades is a source of pride because a personal characteristic (ability or effort) is likely to be cited as the cause (Weiner et al., 1978).

Internal attributions for success also enhance the likelihood of future engagement in achievement-related tasks (Weiner et al., 1976). This consequence occurs whether the cause is controllable, such as effort, or is uncontrollable, such as intelligence (Weiner, 1982, p. 190).

The positive outcome–internal attribution linkage enhances positive self-image. Similarly, the negative outcome–internal attribution situation contributes to negative self-image. Failure outcomes ascribed to lack of ability, lack of effort, or other personal characteristics generate feelings of guilt and shame. These affective reactions are also independent of the controllability property of the attribution. That is, whether the perceived cause of failure is lack of effort or lack of ability, guilt and shame ensue. In both cases, the self is responsible.

Stability. The primary influence of the stability dimension is on the expectancy of future outcomes. If a particular outcome is believed to be the result of stable factors (such as ability), the prior outcome will be predicted. However, attributions to unstable causes (such as luck or effort) raise some doubt about recurrence of the outcome (Weiner, 1979). In other words, test failure ascribed to ability or task difficulty leads to continued expectations for failure. However, a low score attributed to luck does not decrease expectancies for future success. Similarly, success attributed to unstable causes leads to lesser increments in success expectancies than success attributions to stable causes.

The stability dimension influences expectancies independently of the other two dimensions of attributions. Subjects' expectations of future success after prior success experiences indicated that expectancy increments were positively associated only with the stability property (Weiner et al., 1976, p. 64).

The secondary association for the stability characteristic is the influence on the magnitude of emotional reactions. Failure attributed to the two stable causes (ability and task difficulty) contributes to apathy, resignation, and depression. Emotions generated by unstable attributions, however, are unlikely to be extended to future events.

In addition, the feelings generated in others by a particular attribution also tend to be exacerbated when the attribution is stable (Weiner, 1982). Pity toward a blind person is expected to be greater than that extended to someone with a temporary eyesight problem (Weiner, 1982, p. 191).

Controllability. This dimension was first described as intentionality by Rosenbaum (1972). Mood was described as unintentional, and effort was designated as intentional. However, Weiner (1979) redefined the critical difference as that of controllability. That is, failure from lack of effort does not imply an intent to fail. The difference between effort and mood is one of volitional control rather than intent (Weiner, 1979, p. 6).

Summary of Causal Inferences. Each of the three properties of causal inferences—locus of causality, stability, and controllability—has primary and secondary linkages to subsequent events. The locus of causality is linked primarily to the individual's self-esteem. Causes attributed to the self either enhance feelings of self-worth or contribute to a negative self-image (see Figure 11-3).

The primary association for the stability of attributions is the magnitude of expectancy change for success and failure. The secondary association is one of affect; specifically, emotions are maximized for stable attributions.

The controllability property contributes to a variety of emotions. Attributions under personal control lead to feelings of competence or guilt, whereas attributions controlled by others generate personal feelings of gratitude or anger. Controllability is particularly important in interper-

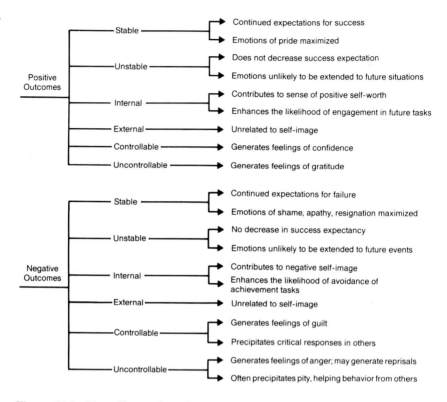

Figure 11-3. The effects of attributional properties in relation to positive and negative outcomes.

sonal situations, in which it influences liking, rewards and punishments, and helping behaviors.

The three attributional properties and their consequences are summarized in Table 11-3 for the inferences of ability, effort, luck, others, and task difficulty. This summary illustrates the importance of each of the three dimensions in determining the effects of attributions for success and failure outcomes.

The controllability dimension influences affective reactions in at least two important ways. First, different emotions are generated for controllable and uncontrollable causes, depending on the nature of the outcomes. Positive outcomes attributed to causes under personal control, such as effort, generate feelings of confidence. Failure outcomes that result from causes under personal control, however, lead to guilt. Further, attributions perceived to be the result of the actions of others typically generate either gratitude or anger. That is, help from others leads to feelings of gratitude, whereas hindrance leads to anger.

Table 11-3. Summary of the Properties of Major Attributions

Attribution	Dimension	Consequences
Ability	Internal	Generates feelings of competence or incompetence and feelings of pride or shame
	Stable	Same outcome expected again; emotions of pride and shame magnified; for failure, resignation and apathy magnified
	Uncontrollable	For failure, magnifies feelings of resignation and apathy
Effort	Internal	Generates feelings of pride for success
	Unstable	Does not decrease success expectancy
	Controllable	Magnifies feelings of pride or guilt
Luck	External	Self-image not altered
	Unstable	No decrease in success expectancy
	Uncontrollable	Generates surprise for both success and failure
Others	External	Self-image not altered
	Unstable	No decrease in success expectancy
	Uncontrollable (by outcome recipient)	Generates gratitude for help and anger for hindrance
Task difficulty	External	No enhancement of self-esteem for success outcome
	Stable	Same outcome expected again
	Uncontrollable	Depression and frustration for failure outcomes

Reactions of Others. The second important aspect of the controllability dimension is the emotional reactions of others. For example, some students were presented with a situation in which an unknown classmate asked to borrow notes for a missed class (Weiner, 1980a). Forty percent of the respondents expressed negative reactions toward the potential borrower who had missed class to go to the beach (controllable cause). However, only 4% expressed negative reactions toward loaning the notes to an unknown classmate with a temporary eye disability (uncontrollable cause).

The importance of the reactions of others is that they are associated with particular behaviors. Pity and helping behavior usually are precipitated by infirmities or conditions that are not under an individual's control. Included are serious illnesses and accidents (Weiner, 1982). On the other hand, negative outcomes that result from conditions perceived to be under the volitional control of the individual typically yield negative reactions and refusals of assistance (Weiner, 1979, 1982). In one study, observer reactions to a person's fall in the subway from either drunkenness or infirmity revealed significant differences in responses (Weiner, 1982). Drunkenness was perceived to be controllable by the subject in contrast to infirmity. Significant differences were reported in negative and positive reactions as well as in the observer's willingness to render assistance (Weiner, 1983b). That is, personal responsibility for falling (drunkenness) elicited negative reactions, disgust, and neglect. The uncontrollable condition, on the other hand, led to the positive reactions of sympathy and judgments of help.

The controllability dimension of causal attributions is particularly important in the relationships between teachers and students. A series of studies has demonstrated that for success on examinations, high effort (controllable cause) is rewarded more often then high ability. For failure, however, punishment is dispensed more frequently for lack of effort (controllable cause) than for lack of ability (uncontrollable cause) (see Rest et al., 1973; Weiner & Kukla, 1970; Weiner & Peter, 1973). The important consideration for educational practice is that the teacher's evaluation is influenced by the perceived controllability or personal responsibility for outcomes (Weiner, 1979, p. 17).

As already described, an important feature of the controllability property is the reactions of others. This property of causal inference may explain in part the difficulty experienced in the solicitation of funds for alcoholism as opposed to fund solicitation for catastrophic illnesses and child abuse (Weiner, 1979).

The Role of Affective Reactions. Three sources of affect are identified in the attributional model (Weiner, 1979, p. 14). One is the result of the type of outcome, success or failure. Another includes the distinct emotions that are associated with particular attributions. Included are gratitude, hostility, surprise, and others. A third source of affect is generated by the properties of the attributions and these affective reactions are associated with self-esteem. Examples include pride, competence, and shame.

An important function of the emotional reactions that are generated is that they serve as motivators of subsequent behavior. "Attributions tell us what to feel, and feelings tell us what to do" (Weiner, 1983b, p. 69). An individual who has experienced apathy, resignation, and feelings of incompetence will cease trying in achievement-related situations. On the other hand, one who feels gratitude and relief is motivated to enact expressions of thankfulness. The individual who experiences feelings of competence, however, will approach achievement-related situations with confidence.

Emotional Cues from Others. A second function of affective reactions is that the reactions of others can serve as cues for people's self-perceptions. Such reactions serve as subtle cues that can convey attributional information following achievement performance (Weiner, Graham, et al., 1982). Specifically, pity and anger are two affective reactions elicited in observers for perceived uncontrollable and controllable causes of achievement.

The hypothesis that the affective reactions of others can serve as the basis for causal inferences has been tested with several age groups (Weiner, Graham et al., 1982). In one experiment, adults were given descriptions of failure situations and the teacher's affective reactions. The subjects accurately perceived the relationships between anger/lack of effort and pity/lack of ability. In a second experiment, the subjects were groups of children of 5, 7, and 9 years of age. Anger/effort associations were made by all age groups, although weakly by 5-year-olds. For 7- and 9-year-olds, the pity/ability linkage was stronger than the pity/effort and anger/ability linkages, indicating some awareness of the relationship between pity and the uncontrollable cause of failure.

In another study, females conveyed sympathy, anger, or no affective reactions to three different groups of sixth-grade children following failure on novel problem-solving tasks (Graham & Weiner, 1983). The children systematically inferred that the angry "teacher" thought they did not try hard enough and that the sympathetic "teacher" believed that they lacked ability. Also, the children's beliefs about the reasons for their failures were influenced by the experimenter's affective reactions. Finally, the children's expectancies for success declined across the four trials for children in the sympathy condition.

The Affective-Linkage Model. The relationship between the adult's affective reactions and those of the children is represented in the five-step model shown in Figure 11-4.

The model illustrates the unintentional attributional cues that are conveyed by the teacher's affective reactions to his or her perceived causes for student failure. Although the sympathy reaction typically is motivated by the goal to protect the student's self-esteem, the results are quite dif-

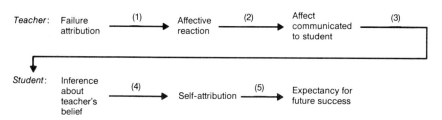

Figure 11-4 Attributional model of teacher affective cues for failure (Weiner, et al., 1983).

ferent (Weiner et al., 1983). Instead, sympathy telegraphs a message of "hopelessness" (i.e., low ability), a trait that is both stable and uncontrollable.

The teacher's affective reaction may also influence his or her subsequent actions, which in themselves convey messages about ability. An example described by Weiner (1983a, p. 173) is the Little League baseball coach who perceives that Johnny is low in playing ability. In deciding who to put in the game, the coach sends in Johnny with the comment that he can play now and that the rules require everyone to play. Johnny also is placed on the field where balls rarely are hit, such as right field.

Recent research with teachers supports the link between teacher attributions and the teacher's subsequent behavior. Rohrkemper and Brophy (1983) asked teachers to evaluate vignettes about student behavior problems in the classroom. Teacher attributions as to locus of causality, controllability, stability, and intentionality of perceived causes were important determinants of teacher affect and the selection of solution strategies.

The Cumulative Effects of Attributions for Success or Failure

The general sequence of events in an individual's analysis of a single positive or negative outcome is as follows: (1) the identification of a perceived cause, (2) affective reactions to the attribution, (3) expectancies for the future, and (4) tendencies to behave in particular ways. The analysis of a particular outcome makes use of several sources of information, including situational cues and past success history. Also important as a source of information, particularly in the classroom, are the affective reactions of others to one's behavior.

Over a period of time, the individual's success or failure history and the accompanying attributions exert a continuing influence on the individual's self-esteem, goal expectancies, and causal attributions in achievement situations. As mentioned earlier, students with a moderate success record have experienced success fairly often—however, not consistently. Therefore, the stable internal attribution, ability, is unlikely to be selected as a cause for success. Nevertheless, success has not been a random outcome for the student. Therefore, luck is unlikely to be the attribution for success. Effort or ease of the task are more probable selections.

In contrast, individuals with a consistent record of success in social and achievement situations have expectations for continued success. In addition, since competence is a major component in self-esteem, such individuals typically are high scorers on measures of self-esteem and self-concept. Conversely, individuals who have experienced a fairly consistent record of failures are low in self-esteem. Research indicates that for these two groups, success and failure outcomes have diffferent meanings. That is, the individual with the consistent success record expects continued success. Therefore, he or she is likely to attribute failure (unexpected outcome) to an unstable and/or external cause, such as illness, mood, or luck (Weiner, 1977, 1979). Such an attribution maintains the expectancy for the recurrence of success which is consistent with past history and also maintains a positive self-image.

Individuals who have a low self-concept of ability, however, tend to ascribe success to unstable factors and to ascribe failure to internal, stable causes. They also have a low expectancy of success in the future. This pattern has been observed in several settings with different age groups. In one study, the researcher (Ames, 1978) found that the fifth-graders who were low in self-concept did not respond favorably to their own successful outcomes.

The Concept of "Learned Helplessness." Of particular concern in the classroom are the individuals who have low self-concept and who have experienced few successes. Such students are likely to see no relationship between their successes and their own actions and to attribute failure to lack of ability. The belief that outcomes are independent of one's actions was researched originally as the construct known as "learned helplessness" (Seligman, 1975). It was described as a particular state that often results when events have been perceived by the individual as uncontrollable. That is, after a series of experiences in which the individual's responses do not alter an outcome, the subject "learns" that behavior and outcomes are independent of each other.

In the initial experimental studies, dogs subjected to inescapable electric shock learned that no response, such as tail wagging, barking, moving, jumping, or others, influenced the shocks. Then when placed in a situation in which knocking down a barrier terminated the shock, the animals first ran around frantically for a few seconds and then lay down, passively submitting to the shock. In other words, after the experience of uncontrollable trauma, the animals lost the motivation to respond and depression and anxiety resulted. Further, even if a response was successful, the animal had difficulty in learning that the response was effective (Seligman, 1975, p. 22). Further studies with human beings have confirmed the phenomenon originally observed in the animal laboratory (see Abramson, Seligman, & Teasdale, 1978).

Learned Helplessness in Children. The construct "personal helplessness" was developed to account for the situation in which outcomes cannot be attained by the individual's actions, although they can be attained by others (Abramson, Seligman, & Teasdale, 1978). An example is the student who studies hard but fails a test that everyone else passes. A characteristic of personal helplessness is that it is accompanied by low self-esteem. This is consistent with the attributional principle that failure attributions to internal factors contribute to a negative self-image.

The phenomenon of learned helplessness in children includes three components: (1) the tendency to give up in the face of failure, (2) avoidance of personal responsibility as the cause of failure, and (3) a tendency, when responsibility is acknowledged, to attribute failure to lack of ability rather than to lack of effort (Dweck, 1975, p. 674). Failure is also followed by a deterioration in performance.

In other words, "helpless" children do not view themselves as instrumental in the determination of outcomes and therefore are less likely to consider adverse circumstances as surmountable. Thus the important factor is not the occurrence of aversive events, but rather, the perceived relationship between the individual's behavior and the event (Dweck, 1975, p. 75).

Analysis of the behavior of mastery-oriented and "helpless" fifth-graders in a discrimination training and testing situation indicated several differences between the two groups (Dweck, 1978). Although both groups had learned the discrimination task equally well, over 50% of the failure-oriented children attributed their failure to lack of ability. Failure explanations, however, given by the mastery-oriented children included bad luck, lack of effort, unfairness of the experimenter, and task difficulty. In contrast, failure-oriented children made comments such as "I am stupid," "I don't have a good memory," and so on. In addition, the performance of the "helpless" children deteriorated over the set of four test problems following initial failure. A progressive decrease in the use of effective problem strategies occurred following failure on task 1 so that by problem 4, over two thirds of the children were making ineffectual responses.

PRINCIPLES OF INSTRUCTION

In the formal educational setting, the young child soon learns that doing well in school is an implicit goal, yet an important one. Throughout the school years, in both formal and informal situations, students are faced with a continuing succession of success/failure assessments of their behavior. The nature of schooling, however, restricts those assessments to a narrow range of human knowledge that to a great extent is dependent on the learner's verbal proficiency.

The child's judgments about his or her successes or failures are relatively unsophisticated at first. However, these judgments gradually become refined and students' reactions to success and failure become an important factor in the further development of their self-esteem. At the end of 12 years of schooling, students have developed beliefs about their skills, abilities, and potential for life success. These beliefs are developed in part from the causal attributions and emotional consequences generated by their achievement-related outcomes in the classroom.

The attributional theory developed by Bernard Weiner is particularly relevant to the educational setting because it (1) addresses the range of effects of successes and failures outcomes, and (2) provides a framework for the analysis of teacher-student interactions in the classroom. Since research in the classroom setting on the applications of the attributional framework is a relatively new venture, specific principles for teaching are yet to be derived. Nevertheless, important guidelines for classroom practice can be identified.

Basic Assumptions

The assumptions on which attribution theory is based also apply to the classroom setting. They are (1) the search for understanding is a source of motivation; and (2) individual behavior is, in part, determined by one's beliefs about the causes of past outcomes. In the classroom setting, an additional assumption is also needed. It is that the beliefs and reactions of others are important contributions to the development of students' causal attributions for success and failure.

The Essentials of Attributional Formation in the Classroom

The classroom setting is one in which hundreds of interactions occur between teachers and students. These interactions are sources of information for both teacher and student beliefs about student abilities and effort on classroom tasks. These beliefs (i.e., attributions) generate affective reactions and serve as motivators for subsequent behavior.

In the interactive classroom setting, the attributional model in Figure 11-2 and the interactive attribution sequence for failure in Figure 11-4 may be combined to illustrate the teacher influence on student attributions for success and failure. This sequence is illustrated in Figure 11-5 and it applies both to formal test situations and to more informal teacher-student exchanges. That is, student performance, whether completion of a test, submission of homework for grading, reading aloud in the reading group, or responding to teacher questions in a class discussion, provides the opportunity for evaluation of the student.

The teacher evaluates the student's behavior and contributes to the student's inferences about his or her ability in three ways. They are (1)

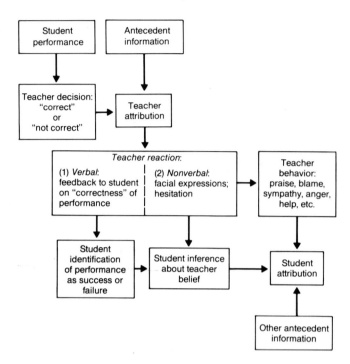

Figure 11-5 Teacher-student interactions in the formulation of attributions for success and failure.

the specific feedback given to the student about the performance, (2) the teacher's nonverbal affective reaction (surprise, sympathy, encouragement, and others), and (3) the teacher's subsequent behavior toward the student (excessive help, additional homework, and so on). The student combines this information, particularly the teacher's affective reaction (Graham & Weiner, 1983; Weiner, 1979, 1980d), with other antecedent information and makes inferences about his or her ability.

An important implication for educational practice is the need to analyze classroom events for the attributional messages that may be conveyed. One of the more important perceptions we make about ourselves and others is that of our ability and its role in producing success or failure outcomes. Because ability typically is viewed as internal, stable, and uncontrollable, it takes on the characteristics (and importance) of the construct of aptitude (Weiner et al., 1983, p. 117). The types of classroom activities, the types of interactions with students, and the evaluative feedback given to students provide both direct and implicit information to the student about academic performance, and therefore, ability.

Developing classroom environments to enhance students' achievement strivings begins with the analysis of the factors in both student and teacher attributions for student success and failure. Although some of the recent literature discusses the importance of the student's subjective identification of success and failure in the process (see Frieze, 1980; Frieze, Francis, & Hanusa, 1983), that discussion is excluded here. Of course, a B+ grade may be a success for one student, whereas it represents another's failure to meet his or her exceptions. The public school setting, however, includes a host of preestablished messages of success or failure that range from gold stars to scores on standardized tests. Therefore, this discussion will focus on the classroom factors that contribute to students' inferences about their academic performance.

Identifying Classroom Factors.   Extensive research on the factors operating in the classroom that convey particular attributional messages is yet to be conducted. However, some information has been identified on factors that influence students' inferences about ability. Already discussed in the first part of this chapter are the affective reactions of sympathy and anger. Sympathy extended to certain students following failure is one of the cues for low-ability inferences (Graham & Weiner, 1983; Weiner, 1982; Weiner et al., 1982). More importantly, the sympathy may (1) prevent the teacher from providing challenging tasks to the student and/or (2) lead to too much teacher help to the student, thereby removing student responsibility for learning (Weiner, 1980d, p. 10).

Three other factors operating in the classroom have also been identified. They are (1) the different teacher behaviors directed toward students who are believed to be unable to succeed, (2) the differential use of praise and blame in the classroom, and (3) student characteristics.

Teacher Behaviors Toward Low Achievers.   For the most part, teacher behavior has been researched from the perspective of teacher expectancy. That is, teachers who expect certain students to perform poorly will treat those students differently, thereby reducing their opportunity to learn and contributing to poor achievement. Good (1980) lists 11 ways that students designated as low achievers are treated differently in some classrooms. Included are seating low achievers farther from the teacher and/or in a group, demanding less work and effort from them, and paying less attention to them. Less attention includes less eye contact, fewer opportunities to respond to teacher questions, less time to answer questions, less detailed feedback on errors, and so on (Good, 1980, p. 88).

From an attributional perspective, such teachers are identifying the cause of student behaviors in the classroom to be lack of ability. This cause is a stable, internal, and uncontrollable attribution. The teacher reactions described above are consistent with the dimensions of this attribution with regard to expectations for the student's future achievement.

Good (1980) refers to such teachers as reactive because they overreact to students perceived as low achievers.

Another type of teacher, however, is identified by Good (1980) as proactive. Such teachers build classroom structures in which the needs of low achievers can be met without ignoring the needs of other students. From an attributional perspective, such teachers are likely to be identifying lack of effort as the cause for failure. This attribution, because it is unstable and controllable, is amenable to modification and change.

For both types of teachers, beliefs are translated into behaviors that can influence both student perceptions and the nature of the activities used in the classroom. The differential treatment sends different attributional messages to the students as well as providing different opportunities for learning.

Another teacher behavior that sometimes conveys messages of low ability is unsolicited help. Aid that is unsolicited may lead the student to conclude that the teacher perceives his or her ability to be low. That is, unrequested help is most likely to be extended when the other's difficulty is the result of factors beyond his or her control, such as lack of ability (Weiner et al., in press).

The Differential Use of Praise and Blame.   Analyses of the use of praise and blame indicate particular classroom patterns that have implications for student attributions (Brophy, 1981; Good, 1980). Two such patterns implemented with students classified as low achievers are (1) excessive criticism of wrong answers, and (2) excessive praise for marginal and correct answers. Both patterns, which are in excess of the criticism and praise received by others, can signal lack of ability, particularly if accompanied by affective reactions.

Praise and blame can also interact with the level of the task. Praise typically is dispensed for effort that is successful. Excessive praise for success at easy tasks therefore conveys the belief that success is due to high effort. However, high effort is necessary when ability is insufficient. The inference from the easy task/praise combination made by the learner is one of low ability (Weier et al., in press). In a series of studies (Meyer, 1982), students praised for success were rated lower in ability than those who received neutral feedback. Further, subjects predicted different expectations for future success for themselves and a fellow student after receiving either praise or blame from a familiar teacher. The predictions were praise/decreased success and blame/increased success. These predictions indicate different ability estimates for praise and criticism following success on easy tasks.

Student Characteristics.   In addition to the antecedents identified earlier, three characteristics also function in the classroom with regard to the formulations of attributions for success and failure. They are developmental level, student self-esteem, and sex of the student.

Developmental level of the student, in general, indicates the onset of attributions to ability. In the early school years, children's attributions are less ability oriented than in later years. Young children do not relate ability level to a prior record of success or failure (see Frieze et al., 1983; Nicholls, 1978; Ruble & Rhales, 1981). That is, in the first and second grades, children tend to rate themselves as able after failure and to feel that they will do well if they try again. Further, kindergarten-aged children are less interested in seeking and using social comparison information as a basis for making decisions about themselves (see Ruble & Rhales, 1981). However, by the second or third grade, children incorporate information about task difficulty, effort, and ability level in their formulation of attributions for success and failure.

Two other characteristics related to the types of attributions for success and failure are self-concept and sex. Subjects who have high self-concepts tend to attribute success to internal causes and failure to external causes.

Of particular importance in the school setting is that the strategies for dealing with failure differ between mastery-oriented and failure-oriented children. Diener and Dweck (1978) found that mastery-oriented children, when faced with failure, initiated searches for remedies. They also engaged in self-directive and self-monitoring activities. Examples of their reactions to failure were " 'I should slow down and try to figure this out' " and " 'The harder it gets, the harder I need to try' " (Diener & Dweck, 1978, p. 459). In contrast, the failure-oriented children reacted to failure with solution-irrelevant statements, stereotypic responses, and derogatory statements.

Planning Classroom Environments. Planning for classroom instruction typically is concerned with the identification and selection of activities that will facilitate cognitive learning in students. The implications of attributional theory, however, are that planning for classroom environments to enhance students' achievement-related efforts is also an important aspect of effective instruction. Classroom research is only beginning to touch on this issue. However, some implications for educational practice may be identified at this time. Although the linkage between teacher behavior and student achievement has yet to be established, Good (1980) discusses classroom programs in which teacher behaviors toward low achievers were altered and student achievement improved.

An immediate remedy may seem to be simply the alteration of teacher behaviors toward low-achieving students. However, the issue of teacher beliefs for student successes and failures needs to be addressed. Reactive teachers as Good defines them may revert to their former behaviors at the conclusion of an experimental program unless their basic beliefs about the causes of student failure are identified and targeted for change.

Of course, in the busy, fast-paced classroom, in which almost instantaneous interpretations of student behaviors must be made, inadvertent errors easily occur. Therefore, some guidelines for planning classroom environments may assist in the avoidance of differential treatment to students. Also important is the use of classroom management strategies that limit and restrict the opportunities for students to infer irremedial failure (i.e., failure due to lack of ability). Of primary importance in such planning is a classroom emphasis on *learning* rather than an emphasis on achievement. An emphasis on learning, by its very nature, places the classroom focus on student effort and the needed changes in student activities, problem approaches, and strategies that will facilitate learning. It also implies specific feedback to students for correction of errors, with the emphasis on student activity rather than the "right" or "wrong" of the answer.

Classroom Learning Environment. An emphasis on learning rather than achievement is one factor that can contribute to a positive classroom environment. Another important factor is the reduction in competitiveness among individuals for a few good grades. Ames (1978) found that in competitive goal structures, failure was detrimental even for children with high self-concepts. Increased self-criticism and lowered perceptions of their own ability resulted.

The mastery learning concept is one mechanism designed to reduce the competitiveness for a limited number of good grades. Mastery standards of performance are set for each unit of instruction and students who do not achieve mastery after the typical group-based instruction are recycled through the materials.

Another mechanism that can contribute to a positive learning environment is the implementation of some form of cooperative learning that is accomplished in small groups. (See Johnson, 1980). Approaches that have been implemented and researched include small-group teaching; the Jigsaw method; Teams, Games, Tournaments (TGT); and Student Teams and Achievement Divisions (STAD). In small-group teaching, students typically select subtopics within a general area and then organize themselves in groups of two to six to prepare for presentation to the total class (Slavin, 1980).

In contrast, the other three methods are highly structured. In the Jigsaw method, all the groups in the class study the same material. Each team member in the five- to six-member group is given a particular task to learn and to present to the others. Upon receiving the specific assignments (prepared in advance on cards), the original groups temporarily disband. New groups are formed composed of students who are working on the same portion of the material. These students help each other learn and prepare the material for presentation to their original Jigsaw group (Aronson et al., 1978).

In Teams, Games, Tournaments, the teacher first forms groups of four to five team members. The teams represent a cross section of ability levels and racial/ethnic groups. The teams, through tutoring, prepare the members for participation in a weekly learning-game tournament. Three students of comparable ability are then assigned to each tournament table and receive weighted scores at the end of play, based on their relative rank. Team scores are computed by adding together the individual scores earned by each member at his or her tournament table. Thus the more the teams help the members learn, the more likely a higher team score (DeVries & Edwards, 1973).

The Student Teams and Achievement Divisions (STAD) replaces the tournaments with 15-minute quizzes. The quiz scores are translated into team scores using an "achievement division" system. Specifically, the six highest scorers earn weighted scores for their team. The top score earns 8 points, the second-highest score earns 6 points, and so on. Similarly, the next group of six scorers are also assigned weighted scores in the same manner. Thus students are compared within a homogeneous group of six rather than with the entire class. Division assignments change from week to week based on a "bumping" procedure that maintains equality (Slavin, 1980).

The cooperative group structure can reduce some of the pressure to achieve and can provide opportunities in which students can develop positive self-images. However, providing success experiences and removing negative consequences of failure are not sufficient to enhance the self-esteem of low-self-concept children (Ames, 1978). An essential ingredient, according to the linkages established by Weiner (1980d; Graham & Weiner, 1983), is the set of attributional messages conveyed by the teacher.

Designing Programs for Attributional Change

An important implication of attribution theory is that of program development for failure-oriented students. Such students exhibit the phenomenon of learned helplessness discussed in the first part of this chapter. They perceive no relationship between task outcomes and their own behavior. Diener and Dweck (1978) report that even after identifiable success, the performance of failure-oriented children deteriorates in the face of failure. In contrast to mastery-oriented children, they typically see themselves as ineffective at school tasks. They react to failure with solution-irrelevant statements, stereotypic responses, and derogatory statements, such as "I never did have a good memory."

One recommended strategy is to redirect the student's failure attributions from lack of ability to lack of effort. Included in such a strategy is training on the completion of specific school tasks with contingent reinforcement for correct answers (Dweck, 1975). Also important is the presence of an authority figure who provides feedback that failure is the result of lack of effort.

Weiner (1980d) provides an explanation for the use of such a strategy. Since lack of ability (aptitude) is both stable and uncontrollable, this attribution generates expectancies for continued failure. A change from lack of ability to lack of effort alters the expectancy of success and, theoretically, places the control for future success in the student's hands. Therefore, persistence at the task (increased effort) should lead to success.

Furthermore, the reasonable success reported by some attributional change programs may be the result of the altered emotional reactions generated by the belief changes (Weiner, 1979). That is, lack of ability generates feelings of incompetence and despair, which, in turn, leads to apathy toward achievement-related tasks. In contrast, lack of effort (unstable, controllable) generates guilt. However, this emotion may motivate increased effort by the student.

Attributional change programs seek to alter a condition that has become a fairly stable behavior pattern. To effect more than temporary change, the program should include three major steps. First, an analysis should be developed of the attributional cues that currently signal failure in the child's experience. This step is particularly important given the role of teacher cues in the child's selection of causal inferences for success or failure. Altering the child's failure orientation over time depends on a consistent set of messages for the child.

Second, identify and implement alternative behaviors that can serve as attributional cues from teacher to student. Included are legitimate positive comments for both effort and activities completed correctly, even though such activities may represent only partial solution strategies. Suggestions for ways to alter ineffective strategies should also be used.

Third, identify group activities that foster beliefs in the importance of developing alternative strategies to reach a goal and which emphasize realistic goal setting. DeCharms (1972) describes the use of stories about peers who succeeded through effort, the use of games that encourage realistic goal setting, and similar classroom activities.

EDUCATIONAL APPLICATIONS

A major contribution of attribution theory to education is related to the analysis of classroom interactions. In the classroom setting, researchers are beginning to apply the attributional framework to analyze teacher messages to students and the influence on student beliefs and behavior (Brophy, 1981; Brophy & Good, 1974; Good, 1980). In addition, Rohrkemper and Brophy (1983) have applied the dimensional framework developed by Weiner to the analysis of teacher reactions to problem students' behaviors.

On a broader scale, attribution theory has implications for the ways that our culture defines success. Frieze et al. (1983) describe several analyses of the American definition of success. It is viewed as attainable by the individual who outperforms others in competitive situations. Such a societal value, by its very nature, relegates some to failure status. In contrast, other cultures define success in terms of group accomplishment and cooperation. At the very least, attribution theory suggests success definitions that emphasize accomplishment through effort and the exercise of learned skills (Frieze, et al, 20).

Classroom Issues

Since the theory is a theory of motivation, the issues of student characteristics, cognitive processes and instruction, and the social context for learning are viewed from that perspective.

Learner Characteristics. The characteristics of major concern to education include individual differences, readiness for learning, and motivation. They are viewed by attribution theory in terms of their relationship to students' causal beliefs about success and failure.

Individual Differences. The theory developed by Bernard Weiner is one which seeks to identify the factors that influence the selection of particular causes for success or failure and the subsequent effects. The theory describes a general attributional model rather than individual differences in the selection of attributions. However, the developmental level of the student and level of self-esteem have been identified as characteristics that influence attribution selection. Young children tend to believe that effort can correct failure, and high-self-esteem individuals tend to attribute failure to external or unstable (i.e., "correctable") causes.

Readiness for Learning. Although readiness is yet to be researched in the attributional framework, the implications for the classroom are clear. Students who consistently attribute failure to lack of ability experience rapid performance deterioration accompanied by ineffective problem solution strategies following errors. Readiness for new learning in terms of the capability to benefit from instruction for new skills is therefore influenced by the student's prior attributions for success or failure.

Motivation. Theories of learning typically treat motivation as a concept that is an adjunct to the principles for generating learning in the student. For the most part, these theories focus on some environmental manipulation that may lead to student motivation, such as arousing the student's attention, examining the role of incentives, or making the material relevant, meaningful, or interesting (Weiner, 1974b).

In contrast, attribution theory views the student, and particularly the student's causal beliefs about success and failure, as primary sources of motivation. In the classroom, therefore, the important motivating events are not the "add-ons" to the instructional materials. Instead, the classroom events that contribute to motivation are teacher and peer reactions to student behavior in achievement-related activities.

Research indicates that in the early grades, pupils believe that success depends on effort and that by trying harder they can succeed. By the age of 11 or 12, however, students separate ability from effort as a cause and children who have experienced continued failure do not react favorably to their own successes.

Sources of information in the classroom that influence student motivation include (1) informational feedback about success or failure from the teacher, (2) the teacher's affective reaction to the outcome (pity, anger, etc.), and (3) the disposition made regarding the student following the outcome. Included in post-outcome actions are opportunities to respond to questions and class seating arrangements.

Cognitive Processes and Instruction.   The three cognitive issues of importance to education are transfer of learning, teaching problem solving, and students' learning "how-to-learn" skills. Of these three constructs, transfer of learning plays a role in the theory. Specifically, a continued past record of either success or failure interacts with current outcomes to influence the student's attribution. That is, students with a consistent success record will attribute an occasional failure to some unstable factor such as luck, lack of effort, or hindrance from others. Students with moderate success records, however, are more likely to attribute a particular failure to lack of ability since high ability (i.e., a consistent success record) has not been confirmed. Similarly, a consistent failure record contributes to a current success attribution to external, unstable causes, such as luck or help from others.

The student's past record also influences the individual's "problem attack" skills. Research described earlier indicates that failure-oriented students execute stereotypic responses and inappropriate strategies when faced with failure, whereas mastery-oriented students undertake search and correction activities.

The Social Context for Learning.   Attribution theory addresses the types of information used by individuals to construct perceptions of their abilities in a variety of situations. In the classroom setting, the theory has identified the teachér as an important source of information for the students' beliefs about their abilities. Specifically, in failure situations, the affective reaction of sympathy conveys the message of lack of ability, whereas anger signals lack of effort as a cause. In addition, research studies indicate differential rewards and punishments and other subtle differences in treatments are dispensed to students on the basis of perceived causes for failure.

The full range of classroom factors that significantly influence student self-perceptions is yet to be identified. Preliminary studies indicate some positive influence resulting from different types of goal structures and different classroom groupings that facilitate cooperative learning.

Developing a Classroom Strategy

Attribution theory describes the antecedent conditions, processsses, and consequences that occur in the formation of causal inferences for personal events. Although the theory focuses on the individual's beliefs and expectancies, these personal characteristics influence both the general classroom climate and student responsiveness to instruction. That is, students who attribute failure to lack of ability often express feelings of incompetence which are likely to impede achievement strivings (Weiner, 1980d). The apathy and depression that result are negative classroom-climate factors.

The application of attribution theory in the classroom implies a need for proactive strategies rather than a reliance on reactive responses to students' achievement-related activities. It also implies a classroom climate that fosters an emphasis on the process of learning rather than on competitive achievement. Such a classroom climate minimizes the number of success-failure judgments with their accompanying self-worth assessments and expectancy consequences. Instead, classroom goals emphasize improved learning strategies, class time is structured to minimize interpersonal competition for a few good grades, and feedback to students minimizes ability or lack of ability as an attribution for classroom outcomes. In other words, the classroom is structured to reinforce the belief that learning is acquired through constructive effort. The following strategy is suggested for the development of a positive proactive environment.

STEP 1.   Restructure classroom objectives in terms of learning processes or strategies.

    1.1 Which objectives, such as "identify words from a list that rhyme," can be rewritten to emphasize a learning strategy? An example is "sounding out pairs of words and evaluating the results".

1.2 What changes are needed in learning materials to emphasize the learning process? Can existing worksheets, for example, be supplemented and/or preceded by others that evaluate the learner's strategy?

1.3 What is the nature of the testing for objectives? Are formative or diagnostic tests with feedback on needed learning-strategy changes included? Are students given a variety of opportunities to demonstrate how much they have learned?

STEP 2. Identify classroom activities that (a) deemphasize interpersonal competitiveness, and (b) facilitate the development of effective task-approach strategies and effort.

2.1 Is the percentage of time devoted to class activities as compared to small-group and individual seatwork activities too high, such as 80–20?

2.2 Which small-group activities may be used to increase the cooperative nature of learning? (Choices include Jigsaw, STAD, TGT, and small-group teaching).

2.3 What individual or group games are available that can enhance student effort and/or improve learning strategies?

STEP 3. Develop verbal feedback statements that convey appropriate attributional messages.

3.1 Is praise appropriately used? (avoided for success at easy tasks, provided for persistence and appropriate strategies as well as success at difficult tasks)

3.2 What constructive teacher strategies may be used instead of sympathy for unsuccessful performance? Are external factors, such as luck, avoided as explanations for success and failure?

3.3 What strategies may be used to encourage students to take responsibility for their own learning?

Classroom Examples

Two classroom strategies are discussed. The first is an academic learning game known as STRATAGEM (Bell, 1982) and the second is a group learning arrangement.

STRATAGEM. The game was developed to ease the pressure of studying for examinations and to increase student effort in thinking through issues in the subject area. STRATAGEM has been used successfully by the author with high school and college students. Other teachers have reported success with middle school students.

The game is a cooperative learning activity in which teams of two to four students take turns in answering questions typed on 3-by-5 cards placed face down in front of the players. Each game requires a banker and two teams of players. Thus a classroom may have as many five games operating simultaneously in order to accommodate the entire class.

Each team is given $1,000 in artificial money at the beginning of the game. The team decides, before seeing the question to be answered, the amount of money to be staked on the team's ability to answer the unseen question. Amounts from $10 to $50 may be selected. The information used by the team in this decision is the coding information provided about the question. This information is on the reverse side of the question card and thus is face up to the team. Questions are coded as one of three levels: 1 = recall; 2 = application; and 3 = inference. The topic of the question is also listed. An example is the question "Asking children to draw pictures about a story that they have just read is an example of _____ ," which is coded "Level 2—Application; Topic: Information-Processing Theory."

After the wager, one member turns the question card over and reads the question aloud. The team then has 3–4 minutes to discuss possible answers. Typically, the members of the other team in the game are also trying to determine the answer. If the team answers a level 1 question correctly, the bank matches the amount wagered. For a level 2 question, the bank pays double the wager, and it triples the amount for level 3 questions. Thus the team, for a $10 wager, may receive an additional $10, $20, or $30. Similarly, for a $50 wager, the bank would pay $50, $100, or $150, depending on the level of the question.

To emphasize the learning process and to ensure that no team runs out of money, the teams lose only the amount of the wager for incorrect or incomplete answers. That is, the level of the question enters only into the reward for correct answers.

When the team announces the selected answer, it is compared with either a list of answers provided to the banker or it may be supplied by the teacher, who is circulating among the games. In practice, after learning the correct answer, both teams typically discuss the answer for a few minutes before the next team takes a turn on the next question. These brief discussions have been permitted because (1) they do not lessen the enthusiasm for the game and (2) they contribute to the learning.

The teacher's role is to circulate among the games, clarifying questions or keeping the discussions from inhibiting the play. In a 45-minute class period, from 25 to 30 questions can be completed. Of the 50 questions developed for each use of the game, approximately two-thirds are application and inference questions. The nature of the questions precipitates discussions that enhance learning.

The ideal time to implement the game is a week or two before a major examination, that is, before the students have begun their detailed study. This practice equalizes performance on the game questions and emphasizes learning.

Teaching Students to identify the Main Idea Instructional events presented by the teacher are as follows (see Chapter 6):

1. Gain attention.
2. Inform learner of the objective.
3. Stimulate recall.
4. Present distinctive stimulus features (topic + something special about the topic = main idea) plus two or three examples.

Event 5 (providing learning guidance) is carried out with small groups. Each group is given the task of selecting four favorite movies or television programs, identifying the main idea of each, and describing why the statement is the main idea. As each group progresses in the activity, the teacher provides feedback about needed changes in the choices. Differences between story details, sweeping statements, and the main idea are pointed out where needed.

At the conclusion of the activity, each group presents its program choices and main idea identifications to the class.

Events 6 and 7 (elicit performance and provide feedback) are completed in the form of a written diagnostic exercise. Children are given a set of eight story lines with four choices of the main idea for each. Feedback is given in the form of changes needed to realign the child's conception of main idea with the concept characteristics.

Events 7 and 8 (retention and transfer) are provided a few days later in a short written exercise.

Review of the Theory

Bernard Weiner's theory of achievement motivation applies the concepts of attributional theory to achievement-related tasks. Attribution theories seek to identify the ways in which individuals arrive at explanations for events and Weiner maintains that the search for understanding is a primary source of motivation for human behavior. (See Table 11-4.)

Table 11-4. Summary of Weiner's Attribution Theory

Basic Elements	Definition
Assumptions	The search for understanding is a primary motivator of action. Attributions are complex sources of information about outcomes. Future behavior is determined, in part, by perceived causes of prior outcomes.
Motivation	Expectancies, self esteem, and the tendency to engage in achievement-related behaviors are influenced by perceived causes of outcomes.
The attributional process	Outcomes are identified as success or failure and perceived causes are identified. Emotions and expectancies are generated by both the nature of the outcome, the particular attribution, and the dimensions of the selected attribution.
Components of motivation	Major attributions (ability, effort, task difficulty, mood or illness, luck, and others) and the dimensions (locus of causality, stability, and controllability).
Designing instruction for complex skills	In order to alleviate the phenomenon of learned helplessness, develop programs to change failure attributions from lack of ability to lack of effort.
Major issues in designing instruction	Effects of teacher attributions for success and failure; teacher cues that signal attributions; attributions that influence self-esteem and effort

Analysis of the Theory	
Disadvantages	Specific classroom procedures for the implementation of attribution theory in the classroom are yet to be developed.
Contributions to classroom practice	Identifies classroom practices that contribute to failure and the psychological links to children's beliefs and actions
	Identifies problems inherent in the competitive nature of much of classroom learning.
	Provides a framework for the research and analysis of many affective events operating in the classroom.

The major components in the theory are (1) the likely explanations given for success and failure outcomes, (2) the characteristics of these causal inferences, and (3) the role of affective reactions in subsequent behavior. Typical explanations given for success and failure are ability, effort, task difficulty, luck, others, and mood or illness. These causal inferences vary on the dimensions of locus of causality, stability, and controllability. These dimensions generate different expectancies for the future and different emotional reactions.

Internal attributions contribute to the individual's self-image, whether positive or negative, while stable attributions lead to expectancies for recurrence of the experienced outcome. The controllability dimension, in contrast, influences emotional reactions, such as pity and anger, as well as the helping behavior of others.

In the classroom setting, continued attributions of lack of ability for failure lead to the phenomenon referred to as learned helplessness. Children in this category typically undertake random strategies for school tasks and they give up easily. Attribution theory suggests the implementation of change programs to alter failure beliefs from lack of ability to lack of effort.

Disadvantages.   Specific classroom procedures are yet to be developed for the implementation of attribution theory in the classroom. Although some promising directions have been identified by the research, further exploration is needed.

Contributions to Educational Practice.   Weiner's attribution theory has identified a major problem in the American classroom. It is the competitive nature of learning and the effects that such an atmosphere can have on many children. Competitiveness, by its very nature, relegates someone to last place, often in a race that has limited long-term value. The theory provides a framework for the research and analysis of many affective events operating in the classroom.

DISCUSSION QUESTIONS

1. What is the relationship between attributions for success and failure and Bandura's concept of efficacy?
2. How would Skinner view the teacher's expressions of sympathy following a student's academic failure if the failure-oriented behavior continued?

3. A teacher is planning a program to redirect children's failure-oriented behaviors. In implementing Weiner's attribution theory, what are some of the kinds of information that the teacher would ascertain about the children's characteristics and behaviors?

GLOSSARY

affect   The general and specific emotions that result from a particular outcome. General emotions include, happiness and frustration. Specific emotions include gratitude, pride, incompetence, and guilt.

antecedent information   The sources of information available to the individual prior to the causal attribution about success or failure. They include past success history, the individual's beliefs about events and associated causes, and individual predispositions, such as need for achievement.

attribution   An inference made by an individual about the causes of a particular outcome.

causal schema   The individual's general beliefs about events and associated causes. For example, success on a difficult task usually is believed to be the result of both ability and effort.

causality dimensions   The characteristics of attributions that lead to different consequences. The three causality dimensions are *locus* (source of the cause), *stability* (temporary or permanent cause), and *control* (internal to the individual or external). Attributions that are internal and stable, for example, strongly influence the individual's feelings of self-worth in contrast to external or unstable causes.

expectancy   The anticipation that some performance will lead to a particular consequence.

personal helplessness   Identified by Seligman, this state is the perception that outcomes inaccessible to the individual are nonetheless accessible to others.

self-perception   An individual's ability to respond differentially to his or her own behavior.

REFERENCES

Abramson, L. Y., Seligman, M. E. P., & Teasdale, J. D. (1978). Learned helplessness in humans: Critique and reformulation. *Journal of Abnormal Psychology, 87*, 49–74.

Ames, C. (1978). Children's achievement attributions and self-reinforcement: Effects of self-concept and competitive reward structure. *Journal of Educational Psychology, 70*, 345–355.

Ames, C., Ames, R., & Felker, D. W. (1977). Effects of a competitive reward structure and valence of outcome on children's achievement attributions. *Journal of Educational Psychology, 60*, 1–8.

Aronson, E., Stephan, C., Sikes, J., Blaney, N., & Snapp, P. (1978). *The jigsaw classroom*. Beverly Hills, CA: Sage.

Atkinson, J. W. (1958). Towards experimental analysis of human motivation in terms of motives, expectancies, and incentives. In J. W. Atkinson (Ed.), *Motives in fantasy, action, and society* (pp. 288–305). Princeton, NJ: D. Van Nostrand.

Atkinson, J. W. (1964). *An introduction to motivation*. Princeton, NJ: D. Van Nostrand.

Bell, M. E. (1982). STRATAGEM: A problem-solving game for use in revision. *Simulation/Games for Learning, 12*(4), 157–164.

Brophy, J. (1981). Teacher praise: A functional analysis. *Review of Educational Research, 51*, 5–32.

Brophy, J., & Good, T. (1974). *Teacher-student relationships: Causes and consequences*. New York: Holt, Rinehart and Winston.

Cooper, H. M., & Burger, J. M. (1980). How teachers explain students' outcomes. *American Educational Research Journal, 17*, 95–109.

deCharms, R. (1968). *Personal causation*. New York: Academic Press.

deCharms, R. (1972). Personal causation training in the schools. *Journal of Applied Social Psychology, 2*(2), 95–113.

DeVries, D., & Edwards, K. (1973). Learning games and student teams: Their effects on classroom process. *American Educational Research Journal, 10*, 307–318.

Diener, C. I., & Dweck, C. S. (1978). An analysis of learned helplessness: Continuous changes in performance, strategy and achievement cognitions following failure. *Journal of Personality and Social Psychology, 36*, 451–462.

Dweck, C. S. (1975). The role of expectations and attributions in the alleviation of learned helplessness. *Journal of Personality and Social Psychology, 31*, 674–685.

Dweck, C. S., Davidson, W., Nelson, W., & Enna, B. (1978). Sex differences in learned helplessness: II. The contingencies of evaluative feedback in the classroom; III. An experimental analysis. *Developmental Psychology, 14*, 268–276.

Eswara, H. A. (1972). Administration of reward and punishment in relation to ability, effort, and performance. *Journal of Social Psychology, 87*, 139–140.

Folkes, V. S. (1982). Communicating the causes of social rejection. *Journal of Experimental Social Psychology, 18*, 235–252.

Frieze, I. H. (1976). Causal attributions and information seeking to explain success and failure. *Journal of Research in Personality, 10*, 293–305.

Frieze, I. H. (1980). Beliefs about success and failure in the classroom. In J. H. McMillan (Ed.), *The social psychology of school learning* (pp. 39–78). New York: Academic Press.

Frieze, I., Francis, W., & Hanusa, B. (1983). Defining success in classroom learning. In J. Levine & M. Wang (Eds.), *Teacher and student perceptions* (pp. 3–28). Hillsdale, NJ: Lawrence Erlbaum.

Good, T. (1980). Classroom expectations: Teacher-pupil interactions. In J. H. McMillan (Ed.), *The social psychology of school learning* (pp. 79–122). New York: Academic Press.

Graham, S., & Weiner, B. (in press). Some educational implications of sympathy and anger from an attributional perspective. In R. Snow & M. Farr (Eds.), *Cognition, affect, and instruction.* Hillsdale, NJ: Lawrence Erlbaum.

Heider, F. (1958). *The psychology of interpersonal relations.* New York: Wiley.

Johnson, D. W. (1980) Group processes: Influences of student-student interaction on school outcomes. In J. H. McMillan (Ed.), *The social psychology of school learning* (pp. 123–168). New York: Academic Press.

Kelley, H., (1973). The processes of causal attribution. *American Psychologist, 28,* 107–128.

Kun, A., & Weiner, B. (1973). Necessary versus sufficient causal schema for success and failure. *Journal of Research in Personality, 7,* 197–203.

McMahan, I. D. (1973). Relationships among causal attributions and expectancy of success. *Journal of Personality and Social Psychology, 28,* 108–114.

Meyer, J. P., & Koelbi, S. L. (1982). Dimensionality of students' causal attributions for test performance. *Personality and Social Psychology Bulletin, 8,* 31–36.

Meyer, W. U. (1982). Indirect communications about perceived ability estimates. *Journal of Educational Psychology, 74,* 688–697.

Michela, J., Peplau, L. A., & Weeks, D. (1978). *Perceived dimensions and consequences of attributions for loneliness.* Unpublished manuscript, University of California, Los Angeles.

Nicholls, J. G. (1978). The development of the concepts of effort and ability, perception of academic attainment, and the understanding that difficult tasks require more ability. *Child Development, 49,* 800–814.

Rest, S., Neirenberg, R., Weiner, B., & Heckhausen, H. (1973). Further evidence concerning the effects of perceptions of effort and ability on achievement evaluation. *Journal of Personality and Social Psychology, 28,* 187–191.

Rohrkemper, M., & Brophy, J. (1983). Teachers' thinking about problem students. In J. Levine & M. Wang (Eds.), *Teacher and student perceptions* (pp. 75–103). Hillsdale, NJ: Lawrence Erlbaum.

Rosenbaum, R. M. (1972). *A dimensional analysis of the perceived causes of success and failure.* Unpublished doctoral dissertation, University of California, Los Angeles.

Rotter, J. B. (1966). Generalized expectancies for internal versus external control of reinforcement. *Psychological Monographs,* 80(1, Whole No. 609).

Ruble, D. N., & Rhales, W. S. (1981). The development of children's perceptions and attributions about their social world. In J. Harvey, W. Ickes, & R. Kidd (Eds.), *New directions in attribution research* (Vol. 3, pp. 3–26). Hillsdale, NJ: Lawrence Erlbaum.

Seligman, M. E. P. (1975). *Helplessness.* San Francisco: W. H. Freeman.

Slavin, R. E. (1980). Cooperative learning. *Review of Educational Research, 50*(2), 315–342.

Weiner, B. (1972). *Theories of motivation from mechanism to cognition.* Chicago: Markham.

Weiner, B. (1974a). An attributional interpretation of expectancy-value theory. In B. Weiner (Ed.), *Cognitive views of human motivation* (pp. 51–69). New York: Academic Press.

Weiner, B. (1974b). Motivational psychology and educational research. *Educational Psychologist, 11,* 96–101.

Weiner, B. (1977). An attributional approach for educational psychology. In L. Shulman (Ed.), *Review of Research in Education* (Vol. 4, pp. 179–209). Itasca, IL: Peacock.

Weiner, B. (1979). A theory of motivation for some classroom experiences. *Journal of Educational Psychology, 71,* 3–25.

Weiner, B. (1980a). A Cognitive (attribution)-emotion-action model of motivated behavior: An analysis of judgments of help-giving. *Journal of Personality and Social Psychology, 39,* 186–200.

Weiner, B. (1980b). *Human motivation.* New York: Holt, Rinehart and Winston.

Weiner, B. (1980c). "May I borrow your class notes?" An attributional analysis of judgments of help-giving in an achievement-related context. *Journal of Educational Psychology, 72,* 676–681.

Weiner, B. (1980d). The role of affect in rational (attributional) approaches to human motivation. *Educational Research, 9,* 4–11.

Weiner, B. (1982). The emotional consequences of causal ascriptions. In M. S. Clark & S. T. Fiske (Eds.), *Affect and cognition: The 17th annual Carnegie symposium on cognition* (pp. 185–208). Hillsdale, NJ: Lawrence Erlbaum.

Weiner, B. (1983b). Speculations regarding the role of affect in achievement-change programs guided by attributional principles. In J. Levine & M. Wang (Eds.), *Teacher and student perceptions* (pp. 57–73). Hillsdale, NJ: Lawrence Erlbaum.

Weiner, B. (1983a). Some thoughts about feelings. In S. G. Paris, G. M. Olson, & H. W. Stevenson (Eds.), *Learning and motivation in the classroom* (pp. 165–178). Hillsdale, NJ: Lawrence Erlbaum.

Weiner, B., & Kukla, A. (1970). An attributional analysis of achievement motivation. *Journal of Personality and Social Psychology, 15,* 1–20.

Weiner, B., & Peter, N. (1973). A cognitive-developmental analysis of achievement and moral judgments. *Developmental Psychology, 9,* 290–309.

Weiner, B., Chandler, S., & Graham, C. (1982). Pity, anger, and guilt: An attributional analysis. *Personality and Social Psychology Bulletin, 8,* 226–232.

Weiner, B., Neirenberg, R., & Goldstein, M. (1976). Social learning (locus of control) versus attributional (causal stability) interpretations of expectancy of success. *Journal of Personality, 44,* 52–68.

Weiner, B., Russell, D., & Lerman, D. (1978). Affective consequences of causal ascription. In J. H. Harvey, W. J. Ickes, & R. F. Kidd (Eds.), *New directions in attribution research* (Vol. 2). Hillsdale, NJ: Lawrence Erlbaum.

Weiner, B., Russell, D., & Lerman, D. (1979). The cognition-emotion process in achievement-related contexts. *Journal of Personality and Social Psychology, 37,* 1211–1220.

Weiner, B., Graham, S., Stern, P., & Lawson, M. (1982). Using affective cues to infer causal thoughts. *Developmental Psychology, 18*, 278–286.

Weiner, B., Graham, S., Taylor, S., & Meyer, W. (1983). Social cognition in the classroom. *Educational Psychologist, 18*, 109–124.

Weiner, B., Frieze, I., Kukla, A., Reed, L., Rest, S., & Rosembaum, R. (1971). *Perceiving the causes of success and failure.* New York: General Learning Press.

CHAPTER 12

Summary

The first systematic conceptions of learning identified either the mind's thought processes or sensory experience as the major factor in human learning. The beginning of psychology, which introduced the experimental method to the study of the mind, led to three research-based theories of learning: Pavlov's classical conditioning, Thorndike's instrumental conditioning, and the Gestalt perspective. Unlike the philosophical perspectives, each theory identified specific variables that contributed to learning. The variables identified were (1) the association of a response to a new stimulus through stimulus pairing; (2) the linking of stimuli and responses through response substitution; and (3) the perceptual reorganization of problem elements to effect a solution.

Two quite different research directions emerged from the early studies: stimulus-response (S-R) and perceptual-cognitive. During the next several years, refinements in S-R theory included Hull's concept of drive and intervening variables and Guthrie's method of breaking habits. The Gestalt theorists identified two factors that influenced problem solving: functional fixedness and problem set. Tolman introduced the new concept of cognitive structure and also demonstrated the phenomenon referred to as latent learning. Motivation was also a new construct and received theoretical treatment in the field theory of Kurt Lewin.

As attention turned from the laboratory to the classroom, six fully developed theories of learning emerged. Each developed a set of learning principles based on a set of assumptions about the learning process. Further, each theory has been applied to learning in the classroom setting, either through the development of explicit instructional principles or by classroom research on the theoretical constructs. Each theory has provided insight about different issues in the design of instruction, and each has made a major contribution to an understanding of human learning (see Table 12-1).

If we accept Ernest Hilgard's view (described in Chapter 5) that each theory describes a part of psychological reality, how are we to make the best use of these theories in the classroom? Table 12-2 lists some general questions about classroom instruction generated from the theories that may be used in either the planning or evaluation of instruction. Note that each theory, in addition to the specific classroom examples provided in the preceding chapters, has an important contribution to make to the total classroom process.

One problem in group-based instruction is accommodating individual differences. A first step in solving this problem is to evaluate the student's readiness for learning. Readiness is conceptualized as prerequisite skills by two of the theorists, Skinner and Gagné. They both caution against the use of age or developmental level as a means of identifying the learner's entry skills. In addition, Gagné identifies specific prerequisites for intellectual skills, which are the lower skills in the hierarchy.

In learning from models, readiness includes the observer's receptivity to the model, anticipation of reinforcement, and capability to abstract important features of the modeled behavior and later recall them. For Piaget, however, readiness refers to the learner's capacity to assimilate new information. That is, readiness is the presence of a logico-mathematical framework that can make use of new information. Further, in the development of concrete operations, readiness is the learner's recognition of cognitive conflict between two or more perceptual judgments and the felt need to resolve two subsystems, such as number and space.

In addition to readiness, several other individual differences have been identified by contemporary learning theorists. Included are learning rate (Skinner and Gagné); cognitive strategies (Gagné); problem-solving abilities, specifically of experts and novices (information-processing theories); levels of attainment in logical thinking (Piaget); abilities to abstract, code, recall, and enact modeled behaviors (Bandura); and success expectancies and willingness to engage in academic-related tasks (Weiner).

Opportunities to solve problems in small groups with a focus on improving strategies can address some of the foregoing characteristics. Further, small-group student work provides the teacher with an opportunity to observe the students and to assess the foregoing skills.

Table 12-1. Brief Summary of Six Contemporary Theories

Theory	Summary of Assumptions	Basic Components	Major Issues in Designing Instruction	Major Contributions
B. F. Skinner's operant conditioning	Learning is behavior; behavioral change, represented by response frequency, is a function of environmental events and conditions	(S^D)–(Response)–$(S^{reinf.})$	Transfer of stimulus control, timing of reinforcement, avoidance of punishment	Analysis of states, such as readiness; analysis of aversive classroom practices; individualized learning materials
Robert Gagné's conditions of learning	Human learning in all its variety is the focus of study. Learning is more than a single process, and these distinct processes cannot be reduced one to the other.	The five varieties of learning, each with its own set of internal and external conditions	Identification of capabilities to be learned; selection of appropriate instructional events; task analysis for cumulative learning	Identification of the psychological processes in cumulative learning; accounts for the diversity of human learning; linked instruction to phases in information processing
Information processing theory	Human memory is a complex and active processor and organizer of information that transforms learning into new cognitive structures	The processes of perception, encoding and storage in long-term memory, and problem solving	Linking new learning to cognitive structures; providing processing aids in comprehension and problem solving	Identification of the active processes in the learning of new information and development of models of problem solving

Theory			
Jean Piaget's cognitive-development theory	Intelligence constructs the structures that it needs to function. Knowledge is an interactive process between the learner and the environment	Assimilation and accommodation, regulated by equilibration; physical experience and logico-mathematical experience	Provide rich opportunities for experimentation with physical objects with peer interaction and support from teacher questions	A rich description of the world through the child's eyes; identifies current curriculum problems; operationalizes discovery learning
Albert Bandura's social learning theory	Learning is a three-way interaction among the environment, personal factors, and behavior	Modeled behaviors, direct, vicarious, and self-reinforcement, and the learner's cognitive processes	Provide models, reinforcement, and rehearsal; develop efficacy and learner's self-regulation	Description of learning from models in the social setting and influence of mass media; detailed analyses of prosocial and antisocial behaviors
Bernard Weiner's attribution theory	The search for understanding is a primary motivator. Attributions are complex sources of information about outcomes, and future action is derived in part from perceived causes of prior outcomes	Expectancies and self-esteem are influenced by six major attributions and their three dimensions	Attributional messages conveyed by the teacher and the classroom; the role of helping behavior	Identification of the psychological linkages between beliefs and action and the linkages between classroom activities and children's beliefs about themselves

Table 12-2. Summary of Major Questions About Classroom Activities

Question	Theory
Who is reinforcing whom for what? (Are positive academic and social behaviors receiving reinforcement, or does the classroom function under aversive control?)	B. F. Skinner's technology of teaching
Are different sets of conditions being used for different kinds of learning? (If not, then "problem solving" may be only rote learning)	Robert Gagné's conditions of learning
Are the stages of information processing considered in planning instruction? Are encoding supports provided or taught to learners? Are problem-solution strategies being taught (instead of rote steps)?	Information-processing theory
Does the learner have an opportunity to experiment with the environment in the exploration of learning? Is peer interaction in the exchange of knowledge provided?	Jean Piaget's cognitive-development theory
What behaviors are modeled and reinforced? (Is the absence of expected punishment serving as reinforcement?) What activities support learner efficacy?	Albert Bandura's social learning theory
What attributional messages are conveyed in the classroom? What activities encourage and support attributions to student effort?	Bernard Weiner's attribution theory

LEARNING THEORIES AND INSTRUCTIONAL NEEDS

Each chapter about a particular theory in this text includes an application of the theory to a specific instructional objective. An important aspect of the application of learning theory, however, is some information about the general types of instructional needs that each theory particularly addresses. For example, only one theory describes the learning experience as learner directed and learner managed. That theory is the cognitive development perspective of Jean Piaget. Education, in his view, should support the spontaneous research of the child.

Regardless of the subject matter, some general instructional needs may be identified and the theories classified in terms of their relationships to those needs. Providing for individual differences, improving students' problem approach and analysis skills, promoting positive self-concepts, enhancing students' comprehension of new ideas, and providing some learner-directed experiences are major instructional needs.

Table 12-3 classifies the theories according to six instructional needs. Theories that provide guidelines for a particular need are identified with an "×." Those theories that do not directly address the particular issue but which provide useful information are identified with a circle "O."

Providing for Individual Differences

Implementing prepackaged instruction in written form (or some combination of written text and media) and implementing microcomputer-directed instruction can accommodate two important learner differences. They are differences in entry skills and differences in learning rate. Both Skinner's principles and Gagné's theory assume teacher-directed or materials-directed instruction. They also both provide guidelines for the design of individualized self-paced instruction. Skinner's programmed instruction addresses the issue of instruction for discrimination skills, such as letters, sounds, words, and others. Gagné's instructional events may be incorporated into either prepackaged instruction in a variety of media or in microcomputer-directed instruction.

In addition, information-processing theory, to the extent that it describes important concerns for encoding and retrieval of learned information provides support for the design of microcomputer instruction, particularly in the use of graphics as encoding supports.

Providing Learner-Directed Experiences

Jean Piaget's theory directly addresses the importance of learner-directed investigations. He speaks to the importance of not teaching subjects as "social knowledge" or as topics that can only be acquired through abstract verbal communication. Also, he notes the difficulty of the teacher's task in providing thought-provoking questions and follow-up activities.

Group interaction, an important component of learner-directed experiences, is a major factor in the development of the learner's skills in critical analysis. The interchange and discussion of ideas among peers is essential in this learning. The group interchange can also contribute to the development of positive self-concepts, given that the group emphasis is on developing problem-resolution strategies.

Recently, the development of the microcomputer language LOGO has been described as providing learner-directed experience with the micro-

Table 12-3. Analysis of Learning Theories and Instructional Needs

Instructional Need	Operant conditioning	Gagné's conditions of learning	Information processing	Piaget's cognitive-development theory	Bandura's social learning theory	Weiner's attribution theory
Provide for individual differences						
Design of prepackaged instruction	X	X	O			
Design of microcomputer-directed instruction	X	X	O			
Design of learner-directed experiences				X		
Design of strategies to improve students' problem approach and analysis skills		O	X	O	O	
Design of strategies to improve students' comprehension of new ideas		X	X	O	O	
Design of classroom management strategies	X				X	
Identification of activities that promote learner self-concept					X	X

computer. The component referred to as "turtle graphics," for example, makes possible the learner's design of computer programs that can create complex geometric designs. However, in the use of learner-directed experiences in the classroom, the outcome may either be that of recreational play or meaningful learning. Peer interaction, careful teacher questioning, and well-planned follow-up activities are needed to ensure meaningful learning.

Improving Students' Problem Approach and Analysis Skills

The, research into problem-solving strategies conducted by some of the information-processing theorists speaks directly to this issue. The research has identified important aspects of problem resolution that may be taught. Specifically, they are (1) problem formulation, identifying only the givens stated in the problem; (2) analysis of the differences between the problem state and the desired state (means-ends analysis); (3) formulation of subgoals; and (4) revision of subgoals if efforts are unsuccesssful.

Improving students' problem approach and analysis skills is one set of capabilities referred to by Gagné as cognitive strategies. These skills are the processes that govern the learner's management of his or her learning, remembering, and thinking. The object of cognitive strategies, in other words, is the learner's own thought processes. They differ from other skills in that they are not critically influenced by minute-by-minute instruction. Because they develop over long periods of time, efforts to teach students efficient problem analysis skills should be planned for more than a few sessions. Such efforts should become an integrated part of the curriculum. The following activities, suggested for building these skills, should therefore be built into the curriculum as ongoing activities.

One method of introducing problem analysis skills to the students is through modeling. Similar to the example provided in Chapter 10, either the teacher or other students can model problem-solving strategies that include the foregoing steps. Different types of general problems may be taken up in different weeks so that the students observe the strategies in a variety of contexts.

During the modeling process, the model verbalizes both the problem situation and the means-ends analysis in an informal way. Verbalization that supports the steps taken by the model in implementing the subgoals is particularly important. In other words, the model demonstrates the steps to be taken to work through a difficult situation, not a rote set of steps to be learned. Also important during the modeling is that the model demonstrate persistence when subgoals require regrouping and revision.

Participant modeling, in which the students work through problems with the model, may then be used. At this point, the students should have acquired some skills that permit them to function in fairly open-ended problem settings. The exploratory learning environment suggested by Piaget, in which a variety of objects are available for experimentation, may be used. Or, the teacher may pose some complex questions to the students, such as the colorless-liquids problem described by Piaget and the example at the end of Chapter 9. The peer interaction provides an opportunity for the students to try out their new skills. At the same time, important rules about the interaction of objects and events are being discovered by the students.

Improving Students' Comprehension of New Ideas

The two theories that focus on the steps involved in comprehension are information-processing theory and Gagné's conditions of learning. Information-processing theory describes the importance of several aids that can assist the student in learning from lectures and text materials. The theory also describes the importance of relating new information to the learner's existing cognitive structure. Included in such processing aids are advance organizers, elaborative rehearsal by the learner, and the development of both instruction-based and learner-generated cues for later retrieval. The importance of using visual images that incorporate much information into a single code is also described.

Gagné, on the other hand, specifically describes the nine phases of information processing undertaken during learning. These learning phases apply to any type of skill to be learned, from definitions to attitudes and motor skills and are executed in different ways for the different skills. Of importance in comprehension, however, is that the nine phases include steps from preparation for the new learning to acquisition and then transfer of the learning.

Each of the nine phases should be considered in selecting instruction for definitions, concepts, and rules. In learning verbal information, for example, the learning phase "semantic encoding" can make use of the elaborative rehearsal suggested by information-processing theory. In learning concepts and rules, however, the student must interact with the subject matter. The instructional events, cueing retrieval and enhancing transfer, may also make use of learner-generated and instruction-based aids.

Designing Classroom Management Strategies

B. F. Skinner's technology of teaching, Albert Bandura's social learning theory, and Bernard Weiner's attribution theory each speak to different issues related to classroom management. Analysis of classroom interactions may therefore be undertaken to determine (1) the discriminative stimuli and reinforcers for behaviors, (2) the behaviors modeled and reinforced (or punished) in the classroom setting, and (3) the attributional messages conveyed by the teacher's emotional reactions and subsequent behaviors for achievement-related outcomes. (For example, are particular attributional messages reinforcing undesirable student behaviors?)

Prosocial behaviors to be emphasized in the classroom may be identified, models selected, and potential reinforcers identified for both the models and other students. If self-efficacy and self-management are to be major classroom goals, then prerequisite behaviors, such as attending to the task and persistence, should be modeled and reinforced.

Using small-group activities to promote cooperative learning should be carefully observed for the effects on students. What behaviors within each group are being modeled and reinforced (or punished)? Are the reinforced behaviors consistent with the classroom goals, or are modifications needed? To what extent is experimentation with the environment contributing to the classroom goals of efficacy and self-management, and so on.

Promoting the Development of Positive Self-Concepts

Learner self-concept in the academic setting is to a great extent influenced by the learner's beliefs about his or her ability and effort. Extreme competitiveness in the classroom for a few good grades can defeat the goal of building positive self-concepts. An emphasis on learning, a reduction in competitiveness for a few "rewards," and the construction of activities that provide rewards for academic-related behaviors, such as expenditure of effort and persistence, may be used.

As in the consideration of classroom management, the modeling and reinforcement of appropriate behaviors are important. Also important is the teaching of strategies that lead to successful performance, such as teaching the problem analysis skills discussed earlier. Providing the appropriate conditions of learning for intellectual skills as they differ from merely the learning of bodies of information is also important. To the extent that students must fill in the gaps between the instructional objectives and the instruction provided in the classroom, the more difficult is the building of essential skills.

CONCLUSION

The philosophical conceptions of learning treated the problem in a global sense. That is, a particular type of activity, whether that of exercising the mind or experiencing aspects of the environment, was believed to be sufficient to facilitate the acquisition of knowledge.

In today's complex society, both learning and education take place on several levels, for different purposes, and in a variety of settings. Education includes informal study groups, preschool experiences, industrial training, and advanced graduate study and research. Each of these educational contexts may foster the learning of a range of different skills, attitudes, and abilities, for which a number of variables that influence learning may be identified. The six theories presented in this text provide a rich and detailed source of information for the analysis of learning and instruction in each of these various contexts.

Index

Ability, in attribution theory, 275,
280, 281, 282, 283, 284, 286,
287, 288, 289, 290, 291, 292,
293, 294, 296, 297, 299, 300
in instructional principles, 293, 294,
295, 296, 297, 299–300
as stable dimension, 285
Abramson, L. Y., 291
Abstract modeling, in social learning
theory, 256
Abstraction, process of, in cognitive
development
empirical, 202, 203
reflective, 202–203
Accommodation, in cognitive
development, 198, 199–200,
210, 228
relationship with assimilation, 199–
200
Achievement, 6, 275
in attribution theory, 68, 275
causal inferences concerning,
276–278, 281
classroom environment affecting,
294–295, 297–299
cumulative effects of attributions
for, 290–292
dimensions of attributions
concerning, 282–287
emotional reactions to, 278–280
individual differences in
achievement needs, 282
in instructional principles, 295–
296, 297–298
by other persons, 281

and teacher behavior toward low
achievers, 295–296, 297–298
and use of praise, 296, 304
in social learning theory, and
perceived self-efficacy, 250–
251, 259–261
Action schemes, in cognitive
development, 194, 195, 205,
209, 227, 228
Active instructional methods, in
cognitive-development theory,
212–213, 215–216, 219, 220
classroom strategy for, 224–225
Adams, N., 263
Advance organizers, 172–173, 179
Affective-linkage model in attribution
theory, 289–290
Affective reactions. *See* Emotional
reactions
Affirmations, in cognitive
development, 218
Aggressive behavior, 236, 238, 245
Airasian, P. W., 139
Algorithmic knowledge, 171
Ames, C., 282, 291, 298, 299
Analogy problems, solving of, 164–
165
Anderson, J. R., 151, 152, 158, 159,
162, 174
Anderson, R. C., 163
Angell, J. R., 28
Anger, in attribution theory, 278, 280,
285, 289, 295